TEACHING INFORMATION LITERACY AND WRITING STUDIES

Volume 1

First-Year Composition Courses

Purdue Information Literacy Handbooks

Clarence Maybee, Series Editor
Sharon Weiner, Founding Series Editor

TEACHING INFORMATION LITERACY AND WRITING STUDIES

Volume 1

First-Year Composition Courses

edited by Grace Veach

Purdue University Press, West Lafayette, Indiana

Printed in the United States of America.

Cataloging-in-Publication Data available from the Library of Congress.
Paper ISBN: 978-1-55753-828-4
ePub ISBN: 978-1-61249-547-7
ePDF ISBN: 978-1-61249-548-4

Cover images
Top: Wavebreakmedia/iStock/Thinkstock
Bottom left: Jacob Ammentorp Lund/iStock/Thinkstock
Bottom center: Wavebreakmedia/iStock/Thinkstock
Bottom right: Dekdoyjaidee/iStock/Thinkstock

CONTENTS

PART II *Collaboration and Conversation*

PART III *Pedagogies and Practices*

FOREWORD

I am pleased to introduce this third volume in the Purdue Information Literacy Handbooks series. This book is highly relevant for all college and university first-year curricula. Many institutions require first-year students to take writing courses. These courses are optimal for preparing students with the foundation for working critically with information for academic purposes. Grace Veach compiled an outstanding array of perspectives and approaches to collaboration on teaching first-year writing courses. The chapter authors depict experts in two academic disciplines—library science and writing studies—who have shared with each other their knowledge of current theories, methods, and models. They reconciled differences in perspective, terminology, models, and disciplinary knowledge to arrive at customized teaching strategies that develop students' understanding of using information in research processes. The authors articulate the richness, depth, and effectiveness of their particular collaborations in a manner that shows how far the integration of information literacy with first-year writing courses has progressed in our field and, specifically, in these schools.

This book is impressive for its insight, depth, and openness to working with different theories and models in both writing studies and information literacy. Faculty and graduate students who teach first-year writing courses and information literacy librarians would benefit greatly from studying it together, discussing it, and applying it in their teaching.

Sharon Weiner, EdD, MLS
Founding Series Editor
Professor of Library Science Emerita and W. Wayne Booker Chair Emerita in Information Literacy, Purdue University Libraries
August 2018

INTRODUCTION

In 2011 when I began my doctoral dissertation on information literacy and writing studies, I discovered two fields—library science and writing studies—that both claimed interest in information literacy and researched and wrote about it. Information literacy (IL) has been the topic of discussion in multiple disciplines, but only in librarianship is information literacy crucial to the life or death of the discipline. I may be exaggerating a bit here, but the situation in librarianship in the early 21st century is such that the existence of libraries is being questioned and librarians have felt a pressing need to prove their worth.

Since the 1980s, information literacy has borne a large portion of the burden of this proof in academic librarianship. With the increasing pressure from accrediting bodies to assess outcomes, librarians, with their traditional emphasis on storage and retrieval of physical items, have been hard pressed to prove their worth through the traditional numbers of items held or books checked out. Even the traditional librarian function of indexing and cataloging data is increasingly centralized; services such as OCLC provide more and more of the cataloging before physical items reach the library, and database providers have already indexed and cataloged their information.[1] The traditional "how to use the databases" function of the librarian is also being eroded by the rapidly growing adoption of discovery services, which pre-index all of a library's database content into one searchable database. The emphasis on learning outcomes, coupled with the growing availability of materials in electronic formats, has made the traditional means of assessing the library (i.e., collection size) nearly irrelevant. Information literacy, then, not only provides student learning outcomes that can be assessed, but it has been an area of the curriculum not already staked out as the possession of another discipline.

Information literacy also plays a key role in the health of Rhetoric and Composition. A perpetual underdog discipline, Rhetoric and Composition has struggled to gain a foothold in English departments where it has been placed. Other academic departments often see it as only a stepping-stone to "real" writing, defined by them as writing in their academic discipline. By forming and strengthening partnerships with library faculty, compositionists will gain valuable allies in the constant fight for institutional capital. Even more important, the coordinated efforts of two disciplines with overlapping masteries in information literacy should have a positive effect on student learning. Students who learn to skillfully incorporate high-quality sources into their academic writing will make both the librarians and the writing instructors valuable colleagues to their peers in the other disciplines.

With a few exceptions, though (Arp, Woodard, Lindstrom, & Shonrock, 2006; Black, Crest, & Volland, 2001; Elmborg, 2005; Farber, 1999; Julien & Given, 2002; Mazziotti & Grettano, 2011), the two disciplines generally stayed in their respective corners. Both disciplines had their own approaches and their own domains (i.e., what they expected to "own" and what they expected the other discipline to cover) (Ackerson & Young, 1994; Bizup, 2008; Britt & Aglinskas, 2002; Leeder, Markey, & Yakel, 2012; Spivey & King, 1989).

With the publication of the *Framework for Success in Postsecondary Writing* (2011) and the ACRL's *Framework for Information Literacy for Higher Education* (Association of College and Research Libraries, 2015), the disciplines, which had been approaching each other in the intervening years, began to have full-fledged conversations. Although they may have been centered on those two frameworks in the early days of the collaborations, they began to branch out and cover nearly every area where they converged, and even to find new convergences.

Into this conversation, then, comes this volume, which examines information literacy as it is taught to and used by first-year college students in first-year writing (FYW) programs. Schools use varied terminology for first-year programs, so some chapters will refer to first-year composition (FYC) or first-year experience (FYE) classes as well as FYW. These chapters offer practical suggestions for successfully incorporating information literacy into first-year writing classes, with theoretical support from key scholars in both librarianship and writing studies. In many cases, these chapters are cowritten by librarians and writing specialists who are collaborating on a local level as they investigate information literacy teaching through different theoretical lenses and pedagogical styles.

The book is divided into five sections. Part I, "Lenses, Thresholds, and Frameworks," examines the disciplines as they negotiate the teaching of information literacy in various higher education settings. It appeared to many of us who were working in the intersection of writing studies and information literacy that in 2014–2015, there occurred a "fortunate convergence of exigencies" as Chapter 1 contributors Anderson, Blalock, Louis, and Wolff Murphy term it, involving the introduction of the ACRL's *Framework for Information Literacy for Higher Education* (Association of College and Research Libraries, 2015), the revised WPA *Outcomes Statement* (WPA, 2014), and the publication of *Naming What We Know* (Adler-Kassner & Wardle, 2015), which each highlighted threshold concepts and desired outcomes in their respective disciplines. In Chapter 1, Anderson and her coauthors describe their institution's reaction to a curriculum revision that was mandated during this time period, and the efforts of librarians and writing faculty to allow the disciplines to collaborate in designing a new freshman-level course that would combine writing and research by allowing the two disciplines to inform each other.

Similarly, Margaret Artman and Erica Frisicaro-Pawlowski compare the ACRL *Framework* with the WPA *Outcomes Statement* (WPA, 2014) from the point of view of writing program administrators redesigning local curriculum. They posit that the WPA document, centered on outcomes, lacks attention to students' processes, but that this gap is supplied by the ACRL *Framework*. By supplementing the *Outcomes* with the *Framework*, they feel more confident about attending to the process of student learning during first-year composition than if they had relied on the *Outcomes Statement* alone.

Brittney Johnson and I. Moriah McCracken describe a model information literacy lesson plan that uses threshold concepts from both the *Framework* and from *Naming What We Know* (Adler-Kassner & Wardle, 2015) (i.e., from information literacy and writing studies) as its foundation. Focusing on Scholarship as Conversation as a particularly accessible frame for first-year writers, they describe the design and teaching of a multiple-session information literacy module within a first-year writing course. Using two students' experiences, they show how first introducing students to the idea of Scholarship as Conversation and later inviting them to enter the conversation can enrich students' research experiences.

Part II, "Collaboration and Conversation," is composed of examples of various approaches to teaching IL to first-year students based on the work of faculty from both the library and writing studies working together. There is not just one model; in fact, this section of the book describes multiple possibilities for faculty and librarian interaction with first-year students all centered around information literacy and writing. Valerie Ross and Dana M. Walker describe the University of Pennsylvania's move away from the research paper in its first-year writing courses to the more authentic literature review. At the University of Alabama in Huntsville, Alanna Frost and her coauthors, working with the university's Honors College, collaborated to design a semester-long group research project focused on giving advice to incoming students in the Honors Program. This project allowed students to become familiar with information they themselves would need to successfully navigate their college experiences, while also introducing them to the knowledge-making function of research and writing.

William FitzGerald and Zara Wilkinson take the opportunity provided to two newcomers to leadership roles to design the First-Year Composition sequence to incorporate information literacy frameworks' threshold concepts from both disciplines in both semesters of instruction, while Katherine Field-Rothschild highlights the Research as Inquiry frame as she problematizes students' research behaviors. Librarians and writing professors think of Google as the "junk food" of research, yet all too many students—and professors—are content with poorly constructed and insufficiently answered research questions. Community college students, often underprepared for college research, are the audience for Melissa Dennihy and Neera Mohess's scaffolded, flipped information literacy curriculum.

In Part III, "Pedagogies and Practices," scholars use different pedagogical lenses to take a fresh look at teaching information literacy. Robert Hallis challenges professors to teach to an appropriate level of satisficing through reflective mentoring and appreciative inquiry, while Emily Standridge and Vandy Dubre collaborated to use commercially marketed information literacy tutorials in conjunction with reflective writing to ensure that students reached higher levels of Bloom's Taxonomy in their thinking about information literacy. Crystal Goldman and Tamara Rhodes describe the use of primary sources as objects for study in first-year writing courses. They find that primary sources generate interest in first-year writers as professors use them to model information-literate behaviors and to deepen critical thinking.

In Part IV, "Classroom-Centered Approaches to Information Literacy," we are treated to a wide range of innovative approaches to teaching information literacy in first-year classrooms. Cassie Hemstrom and Kathy Anders are using a discourse communities project to teach information literacy, weaving in both the ACRL *Framework* and the *Elon Statement on Writing Transfer* ("Elon Statement on Writing Transfer," 2013). A librarian and an English professor discover Joseph Bizup's (2008) BEAM schema independently and use that synchronicity to build a partnered instruction program that also incorporates a metaphor of research based on an umbrella's structure in Amy Lee Locklear and Samantha McNeilly's piece.

Tom Pace finds that having his students incorporate research into personal writing leads them toward some of the ACRL *Framework*'s threshold concepts; the exigency of a personal situation can evoke more curiosity and questioning than the standard research paper assignment, while M. Delores Carlito involves students in researching not only the topics of their research but ways to present that research in a multimodal setting. Dagmar Stuehrk Scharold and Lindsey Simard engage Hispanic students in project-based learning to heighten their awareness of real-world information literacy concerns, and Emily Crist and Libby Miles, also working with second-language students, describe a curriculum that employs social narrative to scaffold information literacy learning throughout the course.

The final section deals with what happens after the class: transfer and assessment. In Part V, "Making a Difference," Nicholas Behm, Margaret Cook, and Tina Kazan write about the use of dynamic criteria mapping (DCM) in assessment. As a local and organic process, DCM allowed librarians and writing instructors to develop shared vocabulary and goals for assessment. Lilian W. Mina, Jeanne Law Bohannon, and Jinrong Li advance an assessment methodology that uses the ACRL *Framework* as a rubric of sorts for measuring students' research activities. By studying multilingual writers in this way, they not only identify a methodology, but they offer specifics of second-language learners' difficulties and coping strategies in researching to write in English.

Brewer, Kruy, McGuckin, and Slaga-Metivier focus on the embedded librarian. How can the effect of an embedded librarian in a composition class be assessed? Is this model an effective and efficient way to teach information literacy? They report on an ongoing attempt to utilize the embedded librarian as a complement to the composition instructor in first-year composition courses.

Jerry Stinnett and Marcia Rapchak examine the traditional instructor of first-year writing, a graduate student in English, often literature, who has no previous experience in teaching writing. A lack of awareness about information literacy as well as about rhetoric can limit these teachers' ability to pass on information literacy skills to their students; Stinnett and Rapchak recommend acquainting the novice teachers with the threshold concepts in both areas to give them the "bigger picture" view of the two disciplines.

A team at Central Connecticut State University reports on the embedded librarian model of information literacy teaching. After scaffolding the research process with several librarian visits, they used the AAC&U's *Information Literacy VALUE Rubric* (2014) combined with an indirect measure to assess information literacy learning in first-year writing students. The volume concludes with a call for deep collaboration among librarians and writing instructors with the goal of fully sharing vocabulary and outcomes in order to maximize student learning.

Conversation and collaboration between librarians and writing professors can only strengthen the two disciplines, as each group brings its own strengths to the table. By demonstrating early in students' careers that librarians and teaching faculty work hand-in-hand and emphasize the same habits of mind, we can give them a solid foundation as they progress into their majors. Of course, this conversation and collaboration doesn't end after students' finish their Composition classes, and the forthcoming Volume 2 of *Teaching Information Literacy and Writing Studies* will address information literacy and writing studies' work with other levels and sectors of the academy.

NOTE

1. Often this process is automated, or at best provided by nonlibrarians who are not as expensive to employ.

REFERENCES

Ackerson, L., & Young, V. (1994). Evaluating the impact of library instruction methods on the quality of student research. *Research Strategies, 12*(3), 132–144.

Adler-Kassner, L., & Wardle, E. (2015). *Naming what we know: Threshold concepts of writing studies.* Logan, UT: Utah State University Press.

Arp, L., Woodard, B. S., Lindstrom, J., & Shonrock, D. D. (2006). Faculty-librarian collaboration to achieve integration of information literacy. *Reference & User Services Quarterly, 46*(1), 18–23.

Association of College and Research Libraries. (2015, February 9). Framework for information literacy for higher education. Retrieved January 27, 2017, from http://www.ala.org/acrl/standards/ilframework

Bizup, J. (2008). BEAM: A rhetorical vocabulary for teaching research-based writing. *Rhetoric Review, 27*(1), 72–86.

Black, C., Crest, S., & Volland, M. (2001). Building a successful information literacy infrastructure on the foundation of librarian–faculty collaboration. *Research Strategies, 18*(3), 215–225. https://doi.org/10.1016/S0734-3310(02)00085-X

Britt, M. A., & Aglinskas, C. (2002). Improving students' ability to identify and use source information. *Cognition and Instruction, 20*(4), 485–522.

Elmborg, J. K. (2005). Libraries and writing centers in collaboration: A basis in theory. In *Centers for Learning: Writing Centers and Libraries in Collaboration* (pp. 1–20). Chicago: Association of College and Research Libraries.

Elon statement on writing transfer. (2013). Retrieved February 28, 2017, from http://www.elon.edu/e-web/academics/teaching/ers/writing_transfer/statement.xhtml

Farber, E. (1999). Faculty-librarian cooperation: A personal retrospective. *Reference Services Review, 27*(3), 229–234.

Framework for success in postsecondary writing. (2011). Retrieved July 12, 2017, from http://wpacouncil.org/framework

Information literacy VALUE rubric. (2014, July 31). Retrieved July 12, 2017, from https://www.aacu.org/value/rubrics/information-literacy

Julien, H., & Given, L. M. (2002). Faculty-librarian relationships in the information literacy context: A content analysis of librarians' expressed attitudes and experiences. *Canadian Journal of Information & Library Sciences, 27*(3), 65–87.

Leeder, C., Markey, K., & Yakel, E. (2012). A faceted taxonomy for rating student bibliographies in an online information literacy game. *College & Research Libraries, 73*(2), 115–133.

Mazziotti, D., & Grettano, T. (2011). "Hanging together": Collaboration between information literacy and writing programs based on the ACRL Standards and the WPA Outcomes (pp. 180–190). Presented at the ACRL, Philadelphia.

Spivey, N. N., & King, J. R. (1989). *Readers as writers composing from sources* (Technical Report No. 18). Berkeley, CA: National Center for the Study of Writing.

WPA. (2014). WPA outcomes statement for first-year composition. Retrieved January 28, 2017, from http://wpacouncil.org/files/WPA%20Outcomes%20Statement%20Adopted%20Revisions%5B1%5D.pdf

PART I

Lenses, Thresholds, and Frameworks

CHAPTER 1

COLLABORATION AS CONVERSATIONS

When Writing Studies and the Library Use the Same Conceptual Lenses

Jennifer Anderson
Glenn Blalock
Lisa Louis
Susan Wolff Murphy

At Texas A&M University–Corpus Christi (TAMU–CC), librarians and faculty teaching in the First-Year Writing Program have a history of collaborating on information literacy efforts. In 2014, a fortunate convergence of exigencies transformed this collaboration into an intentional and sustained conversation about effectively integrating information literacy with our first-year writing course and our First-Year Learning Communities Program. These ongoing conversations among writing faculty and librarians have expanded our views about how we might best enhance student learning in the first year and beyond by providing students with a conceptual framework for thinking about and using writing and developing information literacy.

In this chapter, we argue that librarians and writing faculty need to work together to understand the threshold concepts of our two disciplines, see the overlaps between writing and research processes and forms of knowledge, and help our colleagues reconceive their approach to instruction in both writing and research for the thousands of first-year college students who cross our doorsteps each year. We need to abolish the formulaic writing of the research paper and the mechanical searching for and use of sources in favor of more generative, productive, and transferable practice in exercising the knowledges and skills of research and writing. We recognize the difficulty, however, in crossing the thresholds of each discipline. Many of us, writing faculty, librarians, and students included, have more traditional or commonsense beliefs about both writing and information, and these can cause resistance to change. This chapter chronicles our experiences as we actively worked to bring our two disciplines together in the service of student learning, using the guiding documents of our professions and our own expertise. We uncovered a surprising number of intersections and points of agreement, and the results, we believe, can provide inspiration for similar efforts at other institutions.

EXIGENCIES

In 2014, our university approved a significant change in the Core Curriculum, to take effect in fall 2016: First-year students would be required to complete only one semester of first-year writing, instead of two. Facing the task of reducing two writing courses to one, the writing faculty began a yearlong process to design the new course. The faculty wanted the course to be based on the current disciplinary conversations about outcomes (*Outcomes Statement for First Year Writing* [Council for Writing Program Administrators, 2014]), threshold concepts (*Naming What We Know: Threshold Concepts in Writing Studies* [Adler-Kassner & Wardle, 2015]), teaching/learning for transfer (*Writing across Contexts* [Yancey, Robertson, & Taczak, 2014]), the "Elon Statement on Writing Transfer" (2013), and the *Framework for Success in Postsecondary Writing* (Council for Writing Program Administrators, 2011).

At the same time, the Association of College and Research Libraries (ACRL) was developing the *Framework for Information Literacy for Higher Education.* Librarians at TAMU–CC knew they would need to revisit the design of the library instruction program, which at the time was based on ACRL's earlier guidelines for information literacy, *Information Literacy Competency Standards for Higher Education* (2000). They approached the writing faculty to discuss how they might transform the program, especially now that there was only going to be one first-year writing course.

BEGINNING CONVERSATIONS

Because of these exigent circumstances, four of us, two librarians and two writing studies faculty, began working together to integrate information literacy more effectively into our revised first-year course, and to undertake the larger project of integrating information literacy throughout our writing studies curriculum. We immediately recognized that the ACRL *Framework* was theoretically congruent with the texts that the writing faculty were using to guide the redesign of the first-year writing course. However, we also saw that more communication and collaboration between library faculty and writing faculty would be essential if we were to develop a more effective approach to helping students master information literacy. To begin, we needed to educate one another about what we were currently doing and why.

LIBRARY

Since 1994 (when TAMU–CC enrolled its first class of first-year students), the library's instruction program has supported our First-Year Writing Program and First-Year Learning Communities Program, offering students new to the university an introduction to the resources and services that the library provides for them. Librarians and faculty in the learning communities have worked together to design research assignments and classes to help students learn about research strategies and tools. The library sessions, based on the one-shot model of instruction, were typically very skills-based and focused on using library databases to find credible information sources for writing assignments.

Librarians have been frustrated with this model. A single 50- or 75-minute session can only have a very limited impact on the educational experience of any student, especially when students' mental models of research are almost exclusively defined by the use of Google and Wikipedia. These brief sessions give librarians very little time to discuss foundational concepts that might help students build new mental models and develop a more nuanced understanding of information sources and their uses.

WRITING

Since 1994, our First-Year Writing Program had evolved along with current approaches to thinking about and teaching writing. By 2014, we had framed our classes around the threshold concepts, Beaufort's five kinds of knowledge, habits of mind, and the *Writing about Writing* textbook. Writing courses focused on rhetorical approaches for different discourse communities; recursive processes, including invention, drafting, revising, editing; and academic argument and research. We struggled with the complexities of learning and transfer and continually attempted to use student reflection to assist in metacognitive awareness (Beaufort, 2008; Russell, 1995, 1997; Yancey et al., 2014). The reduction of two classes to one put increasing pressure on the program to refine the course content to what was essential.

THE ELEPHANT IN THE ROOM

Attempts to emphasize a broader vision of information literacy have been stymied in part because our writing courses and librarians were connected primarily through the ubiquitous research paper (or term paper) assignment that is a staple of most first-year writing programs. Unfortunately, the research paper assignment itself can be a barrier to student success. For first-year, first-semester students, the research paper process is a minefield of opportunities for failure. Students can be stalled at any point by the tasks of finding a research question, visiting the library, using the databases, finding sources, reading those sources, and finally attempting to integrate and cite them in that research paper. Often, students have not done tasks like this before, do not understand the reasons for these activities, and are not motivated by an authentic audience, purpose, or genre (Fister, 2013; Head, 2013; Howard, Jamieson, & Serviss, 2011; Larson, 1982; Russell, 1995, 1997).

From the library's perspective, the first-year research paper is somewhat of a straightjacket. In classes built around the typical research paper assignment, librarians were seen as providing a service to the composition classes, helping students find sources related to a chosen topic. In this model, research was almost completely divorced from the process of question-generation and from the discovery process of initial learning about the subject of interest, and instead presented as a tool for identifying results (often with specific characteristics like "peer-reviewed journal articles") that could then be cited in a bibliography to meet assignment requirements. This kind of class never gets to questions about why to use sources in the first place or where sources come from or a host of other important foundational concepts related to information creation, dissemination, and use, nor does a class taught this way inspire students to see research as a good in and of itself, an activity that can lead to learning and inspire genuine curiosity about the world and students' place in it.

Writing faculty assign the research paper and librarians support with good intentions, because we are attempting to introduce students to academic research and writing practices. However, librarians and writing instructors need to reconsider how we might help students engage with research and writing using assignments with more potential for helping them cross conceptual thresholds and redefine these activities for their own purposes. By practicing authentic research and using writing for different situations, students can develop metacognitive awareness and will be more likely to extend their abilities and knowledge in meaningful ways to different contexts, to subsequent courses, and beyond (Ambrose, Bridges, DiPietro, Lovett, & Norman, 2010).

CONVERSATIONS AS COLLABORATION: TROUBLESOME KNOWLEDGE AND TROUBLING PRACTICES

The authors entered the 2015–2016 academic year with a shared conviction that we had, from our *Frameworks* and other guiding documents as well as our conversations to date, sufficient agreement among us to proceed with the transformation of our approach to teaching information literacy in the first-year program, a transformation to occur simultaneously with the first-year writing course redesign. We decided to begin with an examination of threshold concepts in information literacy and writing studies in collaboration with our Center for Faculty Excellence. We reintroduced the new ACRL *Framework* to the first-year program faculty at an August

"Best Practices" session. The writing program faculty then started to meet regularly to discuss their course redesign with librarians invited to participate. The Center for Faculty Excellence purchased copies of *Naming What We Know* (Adler-Kassner & Wardle, 2015), so the group could read and discuss the threshold concepts for writing identified in that book alongside the other guiding documents. In addition to those readings, we read information about transfer of learning and librarian Barbara Fister's 2013 LOEX talk, "Decode Academy."

These early efforts focused on mapping the territory of writing and research, combining the important concepts from our several documents into an overarching matrix. We explored the overlaps and intersections. In those conversations, we recognized common terminology and shared views of how information (as text) is produced, disseminated, and used. Moreover, we recognized that similar theories of learning were informing our shared documents, all of which confirmed for us that our curricular partnership could be more tightly integrated than it had been. We found many points of agreement, supplemental and complementary. We shared similar goals and vision, and similar theoretical lenses to think about student learning.

For example, early in our conversations, we developed a table to show connections between ACRL threshold concepts and those we were using from *Naming What We Know*. (Brittney Johnson and Moriah McCracken [2016] have done similar but more in-depth work in this vein.) We discovered that many of the threshold concepts in *Naming What We Know* were so closely aligned with our aims for information literacy and our experience of the research process that we could frequently substitute the word "research" for "writing" in a section of the text and find that the result was completely appropriate to our purpose. We saw similarly close alignments when we compared the ACRL *Framework* with the *Framework for Success in Postsecondary Writing*.

CONTINUING CONVERSATIONS: FROM TEACHING TO LEARNING

To help us see the bigger picture that would encompass all the documents with which we were working, one of the authors printed all our documents, cut them apart, statement by statement, and reserved a large conference room with ample table space in the library. There, several librarians spent time arranging and rearranging the slips of paper, classifying and reclassifying the various concepts, themes, and statements to attempt to represent visually and materially the overarching matrix that we had been envisioning. As they were assembling this big picture, they discovered natural categories and created new headings, including, for instance, how the information world works, authority, disciplines, habits of mind, privilege, intellectual property, scholarship as a conversation, formats/genre, and the writing/research process.

Librarians and writing faculty gathered one afternoon to see and discuss the results of this work. We circulated among the tables, discussing what might be the best way to organize all this so that faculty, librarians, and students might understand information literacy, research, and writing in new ways. Halfway through this afternoon of conversation we discovered a fundamentally different way to think about and represent the connections between information literacy and writing. We recognized that in our conversations, we were explaining connections in terms related to the ways we want students to approach writing. In other words, we could most effectively see and explain connections and relationships among all the statements on these tables when we envisioned what we want students to experience as writers and researchers, and more specifically when we were able to envision students engaged in the recursive processes of writing or research.

Using the idea of process as our lens and as the organizing principle for all the materials we were attempting to integrate enabled us to make connections among concepts in more concrete ways. We realized that we did not want or need a single overarching matrix representing the connections between these frameworks and outcomes. Instead, connections would be dynamic and situational. Students, librarians, and faculty could and would make sense of the concepts we were introducing in different ways, emphasizing elements of the frameworks and of the outcomes differently, and expanding their learning related to writing and information literacy over time as they experienced new situations in which they would use writing, research, or information literacy. Instead of focusing on *teaching* students *about* the frameworks and outcomes, we realized that we should focus on *enabling* students' *learning* how to learn to use writing, research, and information literacy in varying contexts and situations, for varying purposes. We then turned our attention to conversations about developing learning environments and experiences that enabled and promoted deep, transferable learning.

To help support these efforts we wrote two parallel statements in which we offered (necessarily linear and possibly incomplete) explanations of "What do writers do?" and "What do researchers do?" (see Boxes 1.1 and 1.2). These documents were designed to help writing faculty recognize which elements of our conceptual frameworks they might emphasize and which outcomes they might focus on as they designed activities and assignments for writing classes and/or information literacy instruction. These statements are designed to help writing faculty and librarians make the alignment of these concepts, knowledge practices, and dispositions more explicit to students.

With the fall 2016 semester fast approaching, we rewrote student learning outcomes (see Box 1.3). We were focusing on how to create learning experiences, assignment sequences, and activities that would challenge students to cross thresholds, act from a different set of beliefs about writing and research, and internalize new understandings of writing and information literacy. We knew that we had to find ways for students to do a variety of things differently, and to reflect on the differences.

We developed a new assignment sequence, allowing faculty flexibility. Discovery and inquiry connect to audience, purpose, genre, and context from the beginning of the semester. Students can experience, for example, how "authority is constructed," "scholarship is conversation," and "writing is a social and rhetorical activity" simultaneously during the discovery phase of the course. Concepts related to information literacy and writing will seem less discrete or abstract because students engage with them while they are writing and researching (see Box 1.4).

Students move through a sequence that begins with discovery and exploration of information related to one or more of their areas of interest. They are encouraged to develop and refine research questions to

BOX 1.1
WHAT DO WRITERS DO? (Excerpt from our revised ENGL 1302 course information)

When we see writing as an activity, as social, and as rhetorical, we envision writers as participants in "activity systems," as members of various communities (of discourse, of knowledge, of practice).

- Individuals encounter "situations" that call on them to use writing as a way to achieve a specific purpose.
- Recognizing these situations as "rhetorical" (or as "activity systems") enables writers to understand how aspects of the situation affect the ways their uses of writing can be successful or not (effective or not).
- As a result, writers analyze the "rhetorical situation" (or the "activity system") and they use what they learn from this analysis to help them recognize what choices they have as writers about most effective genres (kinds of writing, forms of writing) to consider.
- Writers recognize that choosing a genre brings further choices about which of the genre conventions are flexible and which are not.
- Writers also use analyses of rhetorical situations (or activity systems) to determine what kinds of information they need to achieve their purposes.
- Through "research as inquiry" and "strategic searching for information," writers locate information that helps them learn more about what they may need to know to achieve their purpose.
- Through [ability to analyze, interpret, evaluate, select and use (integrate) effectively the results of inquiry] writers select information from what they have learned to use in their writing.
- Following conventions appropriate for the rhetorical situation and the genre they are using, writers integrate the information they have selected into their writing.
- Writers know that production of a text is a process, and they choose to use the process that will enable them to produce the most effective text, given the constraints and affordances of the rhetorical situation.
- Depending on their situation, writers often work with diverse others, collaborating during the process of invention, drafting, sharing/responding, revising, and editing.
- As writers gain experience, they learn that writing for new rhetorical situations means that writers may be novices, or have limited experience with writing in these situations, which may mean that their processes may include "failed" drafts, ideas that don't quite work, choices that aren't effective. Writers understand that this is normal, and can contribute significantly to their learning.

broaden and deepen their research. For at least the first half of the semester, teachers encourage students to engage with diverging inquiries instead of emphasizing the typical converging inquiry that leads too soon to closure with a focus and thesis statement. With expectations for using the library resources and librarians throughout the semester, we envision multiple class visits to the library or multiple class periods devoted to research in the classroom. As students identify and locate sources of information, we encourage them to map conversations, consider credibility and value of information, and practice summarizing information and synthesizing multiple sources. We emphasize this part of the sequence as researching a subject or issue *for the sake of learning*, not writing. As they learn more, through research, about the subject, we invite them to begin to consider how they might enter the "conversation" and why. Eventually students reach the point where they propose and create genres for particular audiences and purposes, a variation on the "composition in three genres" assignment from *Writing across Contexts* (Yancey et al.,

BOX 1.2

WHAT DO RESEARCHERS DO? (Excerpt from our revised ENGL 1302 course information)

When we see research and inquiry as an activity, as social, and as rhetorical, we envision researchers as participants in "activity systems," as members of various communities (of discourse, of knowledge, of practice).

- Individuals encounter "situations" that call on them to use research as a way to achieve a specific purpose.
- Recognizing these situations as "rhetorical" (or as "activity systems") enables researchers to understand how aspects of the situation affect the ways their uses of research can be successful or not (effective or not).
- As a result, researchers analyze the "rhetorical situation" (or the "activity system") and they use what they learn from this analysis to help them recognize what choices they have as researchers about which types of information sources, search tools, and strategies to consider.
- Researchers recognize that choosing a specific type of information source, tool, or strategy means starting down a path toward some sources and away from others, and therefore multiple searches may be required to see the full spectrum of relevant information.
- Researchers understand that searching is recursive, not linear.
- Researchers also use analyses of rhetorical situations (or activity systems) to determine what kinds of information they need to achieve their purposes.
- Through "research as inquiry" and "strategic searching for information," researchers locate information that helps them learn more about what they may need to know to achieve their purpose. [Scholarship as conversation]
- Through [ability to analyze, interpret, evaluate, select and use (integrate) effectively the results of inquiry] researchers select information from what they have discovered to use in argument / decision-making / learning. [Authority is constructed and contextual; information has value]
- Following conventions appropriate for the rhetorical situation and the genre they are using, researchers integrate the information they have selected into their understanding of the subject.
- Researchers know that research is a process, and they choose to use the process that will enable them to produce the most thorough understanding possible, given the constraints and affordances of the situation.
- Depending on their situation, researchers may work with others, collaborating during the process of discovery, revision of strategies, sharing/responding, and synthesis.
- As researchers gain experience, they learn that researching in response to new information needs means that researchers may be novices, or have limited experience with research in these situations, which may mean that their processes may include "failed" searches, dead ends, and confusion about vocabulary and concepts. Researchers understand that this is normal, and can contribute significantly to their learning.

2014). They return to what they have learned through research and must determine how much of that research they might use, what further research they need to do, and how they will use the results to help them achieve a particular purpose with a specific audience using a specific genre. Throughout this sequence, students reflect regularly on how information literacy concepts, writing concepts, habits of mind, and key terms relate to their work.

In our assignment sequence, students are focusing less on using tools to find sources on a topic about which they have to write.

BOX 1.3
EXCERPT FROM OUR REVISED ENGL 1302 COURSE INFORMATION

Course Description
English 1302 introduces students to writing studies, rhetoric, and academic research (information literacy). Students will read, apply, and reflect on the current research and scholarship in writing studies, especially threshold concepts, kinds of knowledge about writing, and rhetoric. Students will learn how to transfer, deepen, and extend their ability to use writing in various contexts.

ENGL 1302 Outcomes
Students' portfolios will demonstrate the extent to which they have achieved the following outcomes.

1. Identify how their views of writing have changed as a result of the work they have done in the course
2. Demonstrate their ability to analyze different rhetorical situations (in academic, workplace, or civic contexts)
3. Demonstrate their ability to use their analyses of rhetorical situations to identify options and to make appropriate choices that will enable them to use writing to achieve specific purposes
4. Demonstrate their ability to locate, read, evaluate, select, and use (integrate) effectively information from appropriate sources with their own ideas
5. Demonstrate control of situation-appropriate conventions of writing
6. Explain what they have learned from being a novice in new writing situations, and describe how these experiences, which might include failure, contribute to their willingness to accept new challenges as a writer
7. Demonstrate their ability to collaborate effectively as members of diverse teams/groups of writers
8. Evaluate the ways in which they have become a more reflective (mindful, self-aware, thoughtful) writer

Key Terms
For ENGL 1302, we have identified the following key terms we want to emphasize (throughout the semester). These complement the threshold concepts that will be the focus of our reading and much of our informal and reflective writing.

- Rhetorical Situation: audience, purpose, context, exigency
- Discourse Communities and/or Activity Systems
- Genre and genre conventions
- Research as Learning/Information Literacy
- Composing Processes: planning, researching, drafting, sharing and responding, revising, editing, publishing, reflecting
- Reflection, metacognition, transfer/expansion

Habits of Mind
English 1302 will promote students' development of the eight habits of mind that are essential to students' success in college writing (The Framework for Success in Postsecondary Writing). You will also find these same concepts in the ACRL Information Literacy reading, where they are described as "dispositions" that support and promote the development of students' information literacy.

- *Curiosity:* the desire to know more about the world
- *Openness:* the willingness to consider new ways of being and thinking in the world
- *Engagement:* a sense of investment and involvement in learning
- *Creativity:* the ability to use novel approaches for generating, investigating, and representing ideas
- *Persistence:* the ability to sustain interest in and attention to short- and long-term projects
- *Responsibility:* the ability to take ownership of one's actions and understand the consequences of those actions for oneself and others
- *Flexibility:* the ability to adapt to situations, expectations, or demands
- *Metacognition:* the ability to reflect on one's own thinking as well as on the individual and cultural processes used to structure knowledge

BOX 1.4

EXCERPT FROM OUR REVISED ENGL 1302 COURSE INFORMATION

In our new course, for the first half of the semester, we propose three parallel threads of writing activities: One in which students write About Me; a second thread in which students Write About Writing, about themselves as writers, and about their understanding of the reading in Naming What We Know; and a third thread, Research as Learning, in which students write about themselves as researchers, engage in discovery research, and engage with assigned readings from the ACRL Framework. Below are excerpts from our writing faculty website with an overview of how we explain this to faculty.

ENGL 1302: Assignment/Activity Suggestions

For our first uses of the new text and different approaches to assignments, we could focus on two possible ways we will engage with students differently.

1. Be intentional about using a shared conceptual vocabulary, talking about writing and research by using the language from our Key Terms, from our text, and from the ACRL Framework.
2. Integrate more informal writing that engages students with the readings, concepts, vocabulary. Generate class discussions from this student writing.
    - This is not saying that we won't engage students with writing projects that produce finished documents resulting from revision.

Considering the above, these following sections offer various ways to use writing activities/assignments to engage students with our new textbook, to engage students with "information literacy"/research as learning, and to engage students in ongoing self-assessment and reflection/metacognition.

We all might think about the "shape" or "trajectory" of our assignment sequences in these ways: The first part of the semester, leading to the midterm portfolio, would engage students in three parallel threads of reading, writing, research, and reflection, resulting in numerous less-finished pieces of writing and two "finished" pieces: The extensive Reflective Overview of the portfolio and a proposal for the writing and research they want to do for the second half of the semester.

Thread One Focus

Possible ways to think about this thread:

- About Me (and/or Defining Myself):
- Personal/Writer/Researcher/Learner
- Who Am I: prior knowledge/future plans
- This I Believe: About Writing/Research/Learning
- Self-Assessing/Reflecting

Course materials for reading:

- Suggest students use *Habits of Mind* and *Key Terms* to help respond to some of the these kinds of prompts.

Prompts for this thread of writings could focus on personal characteristics and others that ask students to Self-Assess/Reflect, and Exploring Who am I as a writer, researcher, reader, learner (with examples).

Thread Two Focus

Possible ways to label or think about this thread:

- Learning (More) About Writing
- Crossing Thresholds

Texts/Readings include:

- Key Terms
- What Do Writers Do
- *NWWK:* for example
    - Preface: First two paragraphs, pages ix–x
    - Last paragraph on page 2, beginning with "Threshold concepts are . . ."
    - "Metaconcept," pages 15–16
    - NWWK 1.0
        - Related Key Terms, etc.
    - NWWK 2.0
        - Related Key Terms, etc.
    - NWWK 3.1, 3.2, and 3.3
        - Related Key Terms, etc.
    - NWWK 4.0, 4.2, 4.3, 4.4
        - Related Key Terms, etc.
    - NWWK 5.3, 5.4
        - Related Key Terms, etc.

Continued

BOX 1.4
EXCERPT FROM OUR REVISED ENGL 1302 COURSE INFORMATION—cont'd

Possible description to students:

> One of the primary goals of this course (and any course you take over the years) is to expand what you know about a particular subject and what you know how to do with what you know. In a very broad sense, in this course, we want you to expand/add to/create new knowledge with the kind of quality information you currently have/know about writing (written communication/communication) and expand the ways you can use this information effectively/ more effectively.
>
> When we say "expand," we mean more than just adding more knowledge or skills, more than adding more information. Instead, we mean that what you are learning, the new information, will combine with/interact with/integrate with what you knew and what you now know and this synthesis will transform what you know and know how to do in ways that are difficult (probably impossible) to undo.
>
> Here's a simplistic analogy or example, as a way to understand what we mean by "threshold concepts." Think of a threshold as a boundary, starting point, beginning, dividing line, start of something new/different, the indication of change of state or status. (For example, some common uses of the word: threshold of pain, of consciousness, of manhood, of a new discovery). Consider opposing words or ways of thinking. Instead of a "threshold" we might see only closing, closure, completion, finale, finish, period, stop, termination, end, ending, or barrier. In other words, "threshold" in the sense we want to use means more, other, different, and we want to see it as something we want to pass through or over. We don't want to think of learning as ending. We don't want to think that we have come to the "end" or our learning about writing (or anything else, for that matter). In our courses, we want learners to be curious, open, persistent, positive.

Thread Three Focus

Possible label for this thread:
- Research to Learn
- Discovery as Research

Texts to Use:
- Research as Learning
    - *ACRL Framework for Information Literacy in Higher Education* (edited version)
- Information Literacy Infographics
- What Do Researchers Do
- The "Information Cycle"
    - http://www.library.illinois.edu/ugl/howdoi/informationcycle.html
        - Undergraduate Library at the University of Illinois Urbana-Champaign
    - https://www.youtube.com/watch?v=MwdFqjMUlhY
        - UCF Libraries
    - https://vimeo.com/89231161
        - Josh Vossler http://www.joshuavossler.com/
    - From Topic to Problem to Questions
    - PhraseBank

Pedagogical Focus:
- Consider how we might engage students with research from the very first weeks of class, inviting them to identify relevant "topics" for their research without the pressure of having to use the results.
- Consider an ongoing, semester-long research log, in which students record their ongoing work without having to focus on precise documentation or to annotate fully. Instead, try to help them develop a habit of exploring, discovering, and keeping track of what they do and find, especially early in the semester.

Continued

BOX 1.4
ENGL 1302 ASSIGNMENT/ACTIVITY SUGGESTIONS—cont'd

- If students can begin to see "research" as discovery, we can over the semester introduce more structured practices, more attention to evaluating sources, recording the data that will result in a full citation, summarizing some of their results in ways that will help them use information later. In a sense, we might think of showing students how research as learning can be a habit, and one that can be developed without the dreaded "research paper" as motivation.
- To help students practice identifying and integrating results of research with their own thinking, consider introducing them to PhraseBank. In their informal research log entries they might use different sentence kernels to practice integrating quotes, summaries, paraphrases. Phrasebank might also help them consider different ways they might use a source, based on the options for integrating.
- The explanations of the five concepts we are using from the ACRL Framework also include descriptions of knowledge practices and dispositions for each concept. Asking students to engage with either of those sections could lead to productive informal writing and class conversations—to consider how the recommended knowledge practices align with their own, or to consider how the dispositions align with their own Habits of Mind.

One set of possible prompts for writing would ask about students' experiences with research and with finding information more generally. Another set of possible prompts would invite students to offer their candid self-assessment of their ability to do tasks listed and to offer an example to demonstrate their competence. The list of tasks would come from the "Knowledge Practices" and "Dispositions" included for each Information Literacy concept in the ACRL Framework.

See https://goo.gl/HfZS5T for more complete explanations.

Instead, they are using research as a means of discovery and learning, gathering information without necessarily having to use it in writing, which makes the research process itself significant and useful. Librarians work with students to show them how to use the library's Discovery service to learn about a subject of interest from a variety of perspectives and develop questions that spark curiosity and motivate them to learn more. The research classes with a librarian become sessions about discovering, not finding, and are designed to help students explore broad ideas (and expand their ideas about research itself) and to make better decisions about how to focus their interests as they investigate compelling, authentic reasons to use writing.

WHAT NEXT: WHAT WE ARE LEARNING

As we were writing this chapter in fall 2016, we were offering the new writing course for the first time to approximately 1,250 first-year students, one-half of our entering first-year class. We will be assessing portfolios from a large sampling of those students to determine what we can learn about how students engaged with aspects of the course and how fully teachers implemented the new features of the course. For now, we share these lessons learned as a result of our collaboration.

We discovered that we had more in common than we ever suspected, not just with regard to our guiding documents or our disciplinary approaches to research and writing, but even our roles within the university. We found that both of our programs had a "service" role with respect to other units on campus: the writing program was tasked with teaching students to write; the library was expected to teach students how to do research; and we both labored beneath unrealistic expectations, that a single class session (in the case of information literacy) or a single course or course sequence (in the case of writing studies) could prepare students for their entire college careers. Perhaps this burden of expectations may have encouraged a kinship and mutual understanding to develop, which made our collaboration even more fruitful.

Before this collaboration began, our relationships were affected by what seemed to be the natural dynamic of first-year writing courses being clients of the library, contracting every semester for a specific service, whether a class or an online research guide. We had never discussed our disciplinary identities and fields of expertise in any depth. Our interactions had been the kind one would expect between professionals from different disciplines; based on mutual respect but, perhaps, not a lot of mutual understanding.

Through our conversations, we began interacting as scholars/professionals from different disciplines, with disciplinary knowledge and evidence-based professional practices. We were connecting as members of communities of practice. We became more than short-term partners in a knowledge-economy exchange; we became co-learners exploring the threshold concepts and troublesome knowledge of our two disciplines.

Our initial common ground was commitment to student learning. However, as we began to read and process the frameworks and other documents, we could see how, in fact, we were ourselves learning: encountering and crossing thresholds in both writing and information literacy. We were beginning to experience a benefit suggested in the ACRL *Framework*'s (2015) appendix:

> A vital benefit in using threshold concepts as one of the underpinnings for the *Framework* is the potential for collaboration among disciplinary faculty, librarians, teaching and learning center staff, and others. Creating a community of conversations about this enlarged understanding should engender more collaboration, more innovative course designs, and a more inclusive consideration of learning within and beyond the classroom. (p. 13)

As we should have expected, however, when we went to share our findings with our colleagues, we learned that our shared knowledge was not so easily transferable to other librarians and writing faculty, which leads to another lesson. What made sense to the four of us as we talked about assignments, activities, and resources did not immediately resonate with our colleagues. The solutions to the problems we were identifying were classic examples of troublesome knowledge and practices, associated with threshold concepts we had not considered, and much work remains ahead of us in terms of sharing our discoveries with fellow librarians, writing faculty, and other stakeholders.

Through our conversations, we also discovered the need to examine and either change or reclaim the discourse we use when talking about writing, research, and information literacy. in his "Preface" to *Naming What We Know* (2015), Ray Land offers an insightful observation about a relation between language use and learning.

> In our work in the field of threshold concepts and troublesome knowledge, my colleague Erik Meyer and I noted from the outset how the conceptual transformations and shifts in subjectivity students experienced in the various disciplines we investigated were invariably and inextricably accompanied by changes in their own use of discourse. (p. xi)

To be successful in our future collaborations, we (faculty, librarians, and students) must develop a new, shared terminology to use in our discourse if we expect to achieve the kinds of "conceptual transformations and shifts in subjectivity" we hope to accomplish.

Consider these few examples as terminology that has negative connotations: "research paper," "write a paper," "writing course," "research." Consider what students hear and feel when they hear these words/phrases. Consider their "prior knowledge" and their motivation to engage further in any of the activities associated with these words (Box 1.4). In addition, consider the impact of the phrase "research paper," which yokes research and writing together as if research is done only for a paper or a writing assignment. In our case, we have decided we want to separate the two, helping students recognize them as distinct and equally valuable activities.

How do we help students learn to use different genres? How is a "paper" a different genre? Librarians teach about genres in almost every class: what is a journal article if not an example of genre? However, we don't talk about them that way even though our students are being taught that term and using it would help reinforce their learning. Consider the ways we talk about writing and research: do we focus on nouns and nominalizations or verbs and action or activity? English faculty and librarians should be sensitive to language use, to help us reinforce each other's teaching more effectively.

One other lesson we may have already known but that we understand even better now is that developing "information literacy" is a lifelong process. And information literacy is dynamic, perhaps even organic, and not "content" or "skills" that can be "taught" one way for everyone. Although information literacy as an initiative may have its home in the library (it should), it will not succeed without participation and support from faculty across the campus, at all levels. Why? Because information literacy concepts and practices need to be integrated in courses across and throughout the curriculum. To imagine that even the most robust library staff could implement this kind of initiative alone is unrealistic and not even really desirable. Ideally, librarians should work closely with faculty in the disciplines, helping them with curricular revisions and effective pedagogical practices, and identifying information literacy concepts relevant to faculty members' disciplinary specialties. Faculty need to learn from librarians, not just use them as a service, and then take an active role in teaching information literacy to their students.

A final lesson relates to what we do not know well enough. As professionals responsible for enabling and promoting learning, we must educate ourselves and our colleagues about how people learn. We must ensure that the experiences, activities and assignments we are designing will align authentically with the principles of learning as they are set forth in such texts as Ambrose and colleagues'

> **BOX 1.5**
> PRINCIPLES OF LEARNING
>
> - "Students' prior knowledge can help or hinder learning." (p. 4)
> - "How students organize knowledge influences how they learn and apply what they know." (p. 4)
> - "Students' motivation determines, directs, and sustains what they do to learn." (p. 5)
> - "To develop mastery, students must acquire component skills, practice integrating them, and know when to apply what they have learned." (p. 5)
> - "Goal-directed practice coupled with targeted feedback enhances the quality of students' learning." (p. 5)
> - "Students' current level of development interacts with the social, emotional, and intellectual climate of the course to impact learning." (p. 6)
> - "To become self-directed learners, students must learn to monitor and adjust their approaches to learning." (p. 6)
>
> (From *How Learning Works* [Ambrose et al., 2010, pp. 3–7].)

(2010) *How Learning Works* (see Box 1.5) and a precursor of that work from the National Research Council (2000), *How People Learn*. We need to think beyond the taxonomic tyranny of Bloom and the performance focus of "teaching." We produce learning, not grades or credit hours, or library visits. Barbara Fister (2013) says this well:

> The purpose of a university is rather like the purpose of a library—to promote without prejudice both learning and discovery, to support the creation of new knowledge, and to preserve and pass down what we know. (p. 3)

For the past two years at TAMU–CC, the four of us have collaborated, conversed, and learned together. We intend to continue and to invite more faculty and more librarians to join us. We four agree with Fister (2013) that one of our central goals as professionals is "helping [students] discover within themselves the ability to create new knowledge; to develop the skills that will not only help them recognize authority, but to become, themselves, authors of the world they're stepping into when they graduate" (p. 2).

REFERENCES

Adler-Kassner, L., & Wardle, E. (2015). *Naming what we know: Threshold concepts in writing studies*. Logan, UT: Utah State University Press.

Ambrose, S. A., Bridges, M. W., DiPietro, M., Lovett, M., & Norman, M. K. (2010). *How learning works: Seven research-based principles for smart teaching*. San Francisco, CA: Jossey-Bass.

Association of College and Research Libraries. (2000). *Information literacy competency standards for higher education*. Retrieved from http://www.ala.org/acrl/standards/informationliteracycompetency

Association of College and Research Libraries. (2015). *Framework for information literacy for higher education*. Retrieved from http://www.ala.org/acrl/standards/ilframework

Beaufort, A. (2008). *College writing and beyond*. Logan, UT: Utah State University Press.

Council for Writing Program Administrators. (2014). *WPA outcomes statement for first-year writing 3.0*. Retrieved from http://wpacouncil.org/positions/outcomes.html

Council for Writing Program Administrators, National Council of Teachers of English, and

National Writing Project. (2011). *Framework for success in postsecondary writing.* Retrieved from http://wpacouncil.org/framework

Elon statement on writing transfer. (2013, July 29). Retrieved from http://www.centerforengagedlearning.org/elon-statement-on-writing-transfer/

Fister, B. (2013). Decode academy. *LOEX (Library Orientation Exchange)* national conference. Text of talk retrieved from http://homepages.gac.edu/~fister/loex13.pdf

Head, A. (2013). *Passage Studies Research Report: Learning the ropes: How freshmen conduct course research once they enter college.* Retrieved from http://www.projectinfolit.org/uploads/2/7/5/4/27541717/pil_2013_freshmenstudy_fullreportv2.pdf

Howard, R. M., Jamieson, S., & Serviss, T. C. (2011). *The Citation Project: Preventing plagiarism, teaching writing.* Retrieved from http://site.citationproject.net/

Johnson, B., & McCracken, I. M. (2016). Reading for integration, identifying complementary threshold concepts: The ACRL Framework in conversation with Naming What We Know: Threshold Concepts of Writing Studies. *Communications in Information Literacy, 10*(2), 178–198.

Land, R. (2015). "Preface." In L. Adler Kassner & E. Wardle (Eds.), *Naming what we know: Threshold concepts in writing studies.* Logan, UT: Utah State University Press.

Larson, R. L. (1982). The "research paper" in the first-year writing course: A non-form of writing. *College English, 44*(8), 811–816.

National Research Council. (2000). *How people learn: Brain, mind, experience, and school. Expanded edition.* Washington, D.C.: National Academies Press.

Russell, D. (1995). Activity theory and its implications for writing instruction. In J. Petraglia (Ed.), *Reconceiving writing, rethinking writing instruction* (pp. 15–78). Hillsdale, NJ: Erlbaum.

Russell, D. (1997). Rethinking genre in school and society: An activity theory analysis. *Written Communication, 14,* 504–554.

Yancey, K. B., Robertson, L., & Taczak, K. (2014). *Writing across contexts: Transfer, composition, and sites of writing.* Logan, UT: Utah State University Press.

CHAPTER 2

KNOWLEDGE PROCESSES AND PROGRAM PRACTICES

Using the WPA Outcomes Statement and the ACRL Framework for Information Literacy *for Curricular Renewal*

Margaret Artman
Erica Frisicaro-Pawlowski

INTRODUCTION

As this volume attests, the number of composition and library professionals exploring connections between writing studies and information literacy has expanded significantly in recent years. This proliferation of interest related to writing and research as complex, generative, and intertwined practices has resulted in renewed attention to the guiding principles for first-year writing programs. In particular, the serendipitous publication of the 2014 revision of the Council of Writing Program Administrators' *Outcomes Statement for First-Year Composition* (WPA OS version 3.0) and the ACRL *Framework for Information Literacy for Higher Education* (finalized in 2015) resulted in what Gwendolynne Reid (2014) has called a "kairotic moment" (p. 4) for reconsidering, reconceptualizing, and ultimately renewing goals for first-year composition.

In order to highlight the potential of this moment, this chapter offers insights into how the *Framework* document, in its attention to threshold concepts, provides writing program administrators (WPAs) with a powerful tool for revitalizing goals for first-year composition when viewed in tandem with the WPA OS. Such revitalization is especially important in first-year programs where outcomes-based models have led instructors and students alike to envision composition (and hence writing) as a set of rote skills and services within the general education curriculum—or in which one fixed model of the rhetorical situation, the writing process, or the research paper holds sway. Estrem (2015) noted that threshold models (like those offered within the *Framework* document) can be used to counter the dominance of outcomes-based conceptions of first-year composition (like those in the WPA OS) because they offer "a differently meaningful framework for intervening in commonplace understandings about writing," enabling "faculty to articulate the content of their courses, identify student learning throughout the course experience, and create shared values for writing in a way that a focus on end products—on outcomes—cannot" (p. 90). Differences across the documents—in language, in emphasis, and, we argue, in their underlying conceptualization of composing processes—therefore offer a fertile ground for curricular negotiation with program renewal in mind.

Within this chapter, we address how writing program administrators can navigate important distinctions inherent in the WPA OS and the *Framework* document in order to revitalize notions of process in first-year writing curricula. In particular, the chapter calls attention to curriculum development and outreach strategies that both foster program-specific decision-making called for in the WPA OS and answer key questions posed to faculty by the *Framework*: specifically, how do we, as writing administrators, design curricula to "help students view themselves as information producers" (ACRL, 2016, p. 13)?

WHY PROCESS?

The ACRL's question regarding student development prompts us to consider student participation in general education; as such, it is clearly related to fundamental questions posed by writing program administrators about how our programs position students as information consumers and producers. Indeed, in describing the revision of the WPA OS in 2014, the Council of Writing Program Administrators' Outcomes Statement Revision Task Force indicated how such questions guided key changes to the document: specifically, participants at a 2012 workshop session preceding the revisions "were concerned that students were becoming consumers and producers of digital media without having much opportunity to reflect critically and capitalize on 'affordances' that digital media provide" (Dryer et al., 2014, p. 132).

In their 2014 revision, the Task Force sought to emphasize an expansive vision of purposes and processes for writing, as well as the importance of first-year composition in helping students to "'integrate their ideas with those of others' (version 2.0)" (as cited in Dryer et al., 2014, p. 136). The 2014 updates were, at least in part, driven by composition scholarship highlighting the shortcomings of stage-process models for writing (e.g., Breuch, 2002; DeJoy, 2004; Kent, 1999). These models, dominant in the 1970s and 1980s, often depicted writing as a three-step process (prewriting, drafting, and revising). In many cases, instructors translated such models as a series of discrete, linear steps, ignoring the recursive and dynamic nature of writing processes. In keeping with the Task Force's observation that, at the time of the revision, "stage-process models had continued their retreat" (Dryer et al., 2014, p. 136), the WPA OS version 3.0 changed the language of the document to invite consideration of multiple, varied composing processes and to eliminate some of the references to stage-process models, as indicated in the excerpts in Box 2.1.

While the revised language places a greater emphasis on student involvement in the composing process (using terms like *develop, adapt, experience*, and *reflect* instead of *understand, learn,* and *be aware*), the WPA OS still presents writing program administrators with fundamental challenges when used for curricular design. These challenges were anticipated by Beaufort (2012) in her critique of the "Processes" section of the WPA OS (version 2.0): "outcomes in the Processes category seem misplaced . . . or vague ('understand the collaborative and social aspects of writing process'—how will anyone know either what to teach, or how to assess this outcome?)" (pp. 182–183). While the Task Force clearly attempted to address such concerns through revision, version 3.0's "Processes" outcomes remain both somewhat vague and rather daunting, in light of constraints that frame first-year composition courses on many campuses. Beaufort's questions about process outcomes—what to teach and how to measure achievement—therefore loom large for writing program administrators aiming to adapt new approaches and aims for composition.

In revising the nature of our goals for first-year composition, then, it is up to WPAs to deliberately and purposefully reframe process in ways that acknowledge the nature of curricular "uptake" that influences day-to-day practices within our programs. And though composition theory has moved somewhat beyond discussions of process as central to building disciplinary knowledge, questions of writing processes—how they take shape in student writing, how they are facilitated within classrooms and assignments, and, perhaps most importantly, who has ownership over definitions and determinants of such processes—are still of vital importance in the ongoing work of first-year programs.

Yet whether we use the WPA OS to establish process as a distinct set of stages or as a set of flexible, individualized practices writers can adapt, revise, and develop over time, we may not effectively transform the ways in which our programs enact the nature of learning,

BOX 2.1
COMPARISON OF WPA OUTCOMES STATEMENTS FROM 2008 (2.0) AND 2014 (3.0)

WPA OS (2.0): "Processes" Section

By the end of first-year composition, students should

- be aware that it usually takes multiple drafts to create and complete a successful text;
- develop flexible strategies for generating, revising, editing, and proof-reading;
- understand writing as an open process that permits writers to use later invention and re-thinking to revise their work;
- understand the collaborative and social aspects of writing processes;
- learn to critique their own and others' works;
- learn to balance the advantages of relying on others with the responsibility of doing their part;
- use a variety of technologies to address a range of audiences;

Faculty in all programs and departments can build on this preparation by helping students learn to

- build final results in stages;
- review work-in-progress in collaborative peer groups for purposes other than editing;
- save extensive editing for later parts of the writing process;
- apply the technologies commonly used to research and communicate within their fields;

WPA OS (3.0): "Processes" Section

By the end of first-year composition, students should

- develop a writing project through multiple drafts;
- develop flexible strategies for reading, drafting, reviewing, collaborating, revising, rewriting, rereading, and editing;
- use composing processes and tools as a means to discover and reconsider ideas;
- experience the collaborative and social aspects of writing processes;
- learn to give and to act on productive feedback to works in progress;
- adapt composing processes for a variety of technologies and modalities;
- reflect on the development of composing practices and how those practices influence their work.

Faculty in all programs and departments can build on this preparation by helping students learn to

- employ the methods and technologies commonly used for research and communication within their fields;
- develop projects using the characteristic processes of their fields;
- review work-in-progress for the purpose of developing ideas before surface-level editing;
- participate effectively in collaborative processes typical of their field.

participation, or information production we value in first-year composition curricula. Instead, in this chapter we affirm a vision for negotiating curricular renewal shared by DeJoy (2004) in *Process This: Undergraduate Writing in Composition Studies:*

> While many revised process-based approaches claim transformative power, . . . I am more interested in creating a transitional approach, one that acknowledges first-phase process model assumptions as the starting point for many teachers and students, and that attempts to create ways for us to move together toward literacy practices that center participation and contribution as possibilities for all members of the writing classes. (p. 12)

Because it emphasizes knowledge practices and metaliteracies, the *Framework* reminds us that both student learning and professional development are always transitional processes, always grounded in "behavioral, affective, cognitive, and metacognitive engagement with the information ecosystem" (ACRL, 2016, p. 2). Therefore, it offers us ways of reframing the nature, goals, and gaps inherent in the WPA OS's discussion of process. Negotiating distinctions between the WPA OS and *Framework* can help us develop curricula that support students in their transition from consumers to producers. This act of negotiation can also facilitate program renewal in moving both teachers and students away from basic process model assumptions and toward more multidimensional frameworks for engaging composing as a generative and collaborative process.

WHY THRESHOLDS?

Meyer and Land (2006) defined a threshold concept as "a portal, opening up a new and previously inaccessible way of thinking about something. It represents a transformed way of understanding, or interpreting, or viewing something without which the learner cannot progress" (p. 3). Thresholds, then, offer us ways to think about writing, to think about thinking rather than writing as a set of skills. Yet, too often, outcomes models continue to focus on a set of measurable skills. According to Maid and D'Angelo (2016),

> Both ACRL and WPA created their original documents out of the need for assessment and accountability. It appears that the latest revision of the WPA Outcomes Statement is still in that mode. ACRL, on the other hand, has moved to a new framework that stresses threshold concepts—or ways of changing how students think about information. (p. 48)

While outcomes are important to measure student performance, the WPA OS "leaves us entangled in a model that conceives of learning as a straight line . . . when we know learning is much more like scrambling across rocky terrain" (Estrem, 2015, p. 93).

This straight line is embodied in the WPA OS "Critical Thinking, Reading, and Composing" and the ACRL *Framework*'s "Research as Inquiry" as illustrated in Box 2.2.

The WPA outcomes establish what students need to accomplish by the end of first-year composition while the ACRL knowledge practices provide the process to reach these outcomes. For example, the last outcome in the WPA OS indicates the student will use a variety of strategies to compose texts integrating the student's and others' ideas. The ACRL breaks down this outcome in several ways: developing a research question, organizing information, synthesizing ideas, and drawing conclusions. In tandem, these documents assist instructors in designing assignments and courses to focus on composing and critical thinking processes to reach the desired outcome.

While the ACRL's knowledge practices "may on the surface appear to be similar to the standards model: a listing of skills or abilities or practices that can be discretely assessed" (Maid and D'Angelo, 2016, p. 48), the inclusion of dispositions in the *Framework* allows writing program administrators to "articulate the messiness of student learning in a way outcomes alone won't" (Estrem, 2015, p. 103). The dispositions acknowledge the unending education process, which students may begin to recognize in first-year composition: "value intellectual curiosity," "maintain an open

BOX 2.2
COMPARISON OF WPA OUTCOMES AND ACRL "RESEARCH AS INQUIRY" KNOWLEDGE PRACTICES

WPA OS (3.0): "Critical Thinking, Reading, and Composing" Section

By the end of first-year composition, students should

- use composing and reading for inquiry, learning, critical thinking, and communicating in various rhetorical contexts;
- read a diverse range of texts, attending especially to relationships between assertion and evidence, to patterns of organization, to the interplay between verbal and nonverbal elements, and to how these features function for different audiences and situations;
- locate and evaluate (for credibility, sufficiency, accuracy, timeliness, bias and so on) primary and secondary research materials, including journal articles and essays, books, scholarly and professionally established and maintained databases or archives, and informal electronic networks and internet sources;
- use strategies—such as interpretation, synthesis, response, critique, and design/redesign—to compose texts that integrate the writer's ideas with those from appropriate sources.

ACRL *Framework*: "Research as Inquiry" Section

Learners who are developing their information literate abilities

- formulate questions for research based on information gaps or on reexamination of existing, possibly conflicting, information;
- determine an appropriate scope of investigation;
- deal with complex research by breaking complex questions into simple ones, limiting the scope of investigations;
- use various research methods, based on need, circumstance, and type of inquiry;
- monitor gathered information and assess for gaps or weaknesses;
- organize information in meaningful ways;
- synthesize ideas gathered from multiple sources;
- draw reasonable conclusions based on the analysis and interpretation of information.

mind," and "value persistence, adaptability, and flexibility" (ACRL, 2016, p. 7). None of these dispositions can be measured in a final product. Consequently, the *Framework*, in its articulation of key thresholds centered on reading, research, and composing as generative processes, can be used successfully in tandem with the WPA OS for program renewal.

FOSTERING PROGRAM-SPECIFIC DECISION-MAKING

In the following section, we outline two sets of administrative processes in which the negotiation of outcomes and thresholds can be used to animate process in first-year writing programs: in revising curricular aims and objectives, and in expanding or extending curricular conversations about writing.

Revitalizing Curriculum Design: Revising Curricular Aims and Objectives

Recent research has outlined both threshold concepts in writing studies (see, in particular, Adler-Kassner & Wardle, 2015), as well as practical strategies for incorporating information literacy within the design of first-year composition programs (D'Angelo, Jamieson, Maid, & Walker, 2016; Downs & Robertson,

2015; LaFrance, 2016). In this growing body of literature, four prevailing patterns emerge that are most relevant to negotiating the WPA OS and the *Framework* for the purposes of program administration and renewal:

- *Diversifying and valuing students' experiences with research processes in first-year composition:* For too long, first-year composition programs have remained reliant on models of "the research paper" as the culmination of first-year composition course work. Yet scholarship on student research practices (Howard & Jamieson 2013; Blythe & Gonzalez, 2016) demonstrates the insufficiency of using this model to teach processes that transfer and apply to the various communicative contexts students encounter over time.
- *Scaffolding writing curricula to incorporate multiple related assignments:* Well-sequenced writing tasks call upon students to use research and writing as inquiry-driven activities that wed reading, writing, and information literacy beyond the "final research paper." Designing and scaffolding curricula around diverse experiences with research simultaneously engages students in both composing and inquiry as interrelated processes—processes that spur students to consciously revise, reconsider, and adapt their roles as writers and participants in response to variations in the selected information context (see, for example, Holliday & Fagerheim, 2006; Blackwell-Starnes, 2016).
- *Using clear language to articulate program goals and practices*: One of the benefits of employing the WPA OS and the *Framework* in tandem is their tendency to offer terminology that attends to curricular practices (WPA OS), aspirational behaviors (*Framework*), and shared goals for curricula. This terminology can be used consistently across guidelines and assignments program-wide to prominently frame research and writing processes.

  For example, consider the related elements from the WPA OS and the *Framework* document shown in Box 2.3.

  Note that the language of the OS indicates that the process of reflection takes place for "students" at a stable point ("by the end of first-year composition") and, presumably, after written work has been composed and stabilized. The *Framework*, in contrast, casts *both the learner and what is learned* in terms of process, noting the learners are "developing." Additionally, the *Framework* emphasizes a degree of agency that is not inherent to the OS, indicating that the "creation processes" are "their [learners'] own," and that their choices have an impact. As such, the language of the latter document positions students more actively within the curriculum, pointing to the importance of the composer's choices in determining both purpose and effectiveness. This language is necessary if we wish to cast students in the role of information producers within our programs and classrooms.

  Such distinctions point to great potential for revitalizing the language of program outcomes to incorporate active processes and to engage students. Viewed together, the documents point to ways in which process goals can be connected to real, autonomous writers and related to cogent rhetorical situations in which both research and composing play a part.
- *Making metaliteracy visible and attainable*: By revitalizing the description of key processes in our course curricula, we can begin to realign the language of program outcomes to foster metacognitive goals for transfer of learning and to highlight learners' contributions as composers. As noted by Maid and D'Angelo (2016), both the

BOX 2.3
SELECTED COMPARISON OF WPA OUTCOMES AND ACRL "INFORMATION CREATION IS A PROCESS" KNOWLEDGE PRACTICE

WPA OS (3.0): "Processes" Section	ACRL *Framework*: "Information Creation Is a Process" Section
By the end of first-year composition, students should • reflect on the development of composing practices and how those practices influence their work.	*Learners who are developing their information literate abilities* • develop, in their own creation processes, an understanding that their choices impact the purposes for which the information product will be used and the message it conveys.

WPA OS and the *Framework* call attention to the importance of metaliteracy and metacognition in curricular design. As noted previously, the ACRL (2015) integrates key "behavioral, affective, cognitive, and metacognitive" forms of "engagement" within the *Framework*, linking knowledge practices to "dispositions" that define how conscious participation takes shape in research processes (p. 2). The Council of Writing Program Administrators has created a second document, the *Framework for Success in Postsecondary Writing*, to establish central "habits of mind" important to writing development; yet, according to Maid and D'Angelo (2016), the ACRL *Framework* "presents a more integrated whole in terms of contextualizing student learning" (p. 45).

It then falls to local programs—and, in particular, to writing program administrators—to articulate the ways in which curricular goals call upon students to develop, examine, and refine the ways of learning, thinking, and composing that underlie meaningful participation within writing contexts. This articulation cannot take place without affirming the kinds of processes that take place in the classroom, through which the aims of the program are shaped and reinterpreted. Using the *Framework* to inform the language of the WPA OS as adapted within particular programs can help foreground the linkages between program practices and program outcomes in ways that speak to Beaufort's (2012) questions about what to teach, and how to assess it, in first-year composition.

Revitalizing Collaboration: Developing Relationships With Stakeholders

The *Framework*'s (2016) first appendix presents suggestions for librarians, faculty, and administrators on how to use the document (pp. 10–14). Because librarians are the primary audience for the *Framework*, most of the work is placed in their hands. Yet, writing program administrators are in a unique position for incorporating information literacy frameworks within first-year composition, writing across the curriculum, and writing in the discipline programs. By collaborating on curriculum redesign, WPAs and librarians can create relationships with a variety of stakeholders and develop a common language to talk about writing and information literacy, which is central to revitalization and renewal of composition programs.

- *Creating relationships*: Because first-year composition is typically a required course for all students, a variety of people and programs have a stake in its design and implementation: writing instructors, writing centers, student support services, centers for teaching and learning, general education and curriculum committees, and administrators. Reaching out, formally and informally, to these stakeholders can introduce them to the types of goals and knowledge practices students encounter in these courses.
- *Creating a common language*: Too often, WPAs encounter outside stakeholders who claim students can't write even though they can't articulate what makes the writing poor. While the WPA OS may help faculty articulate what desirable qualities are absent in student writing, it can also reinscribe the notion that students *should* have a clear set of skills they develop (and transfer) "by the end of first-year composition" (Council of Writing Program Administrators, 2014). The language of the *Framework*'s thresholds can help to counter these perceptions. Hallway conversations, workshops, and meetings explaining thresholds can introduce stakeholders to a process in which students are learning along a continuum rather than meeting defined outcomes at the end of first-year composition.
- *Creating investment*: In addition, this common language could ease the transition for composition instructors such as adjuncts and graduate teaching assistants who may not be composition specialists, are unaware of information literacy concepts, or are teaching at a variety of institutions with differing curricula and research databases. By working together with librarians and all writing instructors to develop a first-year writing curriculum, participants are more likely to have a vested interest in its implementation.

REVITALIZING PROGRAMS: IMPERATIVES FOR CURRICULUM DESIGN

Using the *Framework for Information Literacy* in combination with the WPA OS in order to renew first-year composition curricula can help us to achieve a number of theoretical, pedagogical, and administrative aims. However, to effectively translate these aims within curricular practice, it is important to recall two additional imperatives for shaping first-year composition programs in light of both writing processes and information literacy:

- The WPA Outcomes Statement (version 3.0) must be adapted to reflect the values, attributes, and institutional aims of individual writing programs. The introduction to the revised statement (2014) notes that the document "intentionally defines only 'outcomes,' or types of results, and not 'standards,' or precise levels of achievement" (p. 144). The *Framework* document, while not intended to provide a list of standards for programs, does offer distinct language and complementary concepts that can aid in adaptation. As noted previously, collaboration with a range of stakeholders allows for greater inclusion and ownership in the process and is therefore essential to program revitalization.

- In developing outcomes and curricular revisions, WPAs must understand that a "transitional approach," to borrow the language of DeJoy (2004), requires building both knowledge and participation among these stakeholders over time. As noted by Dryer et al. (2014), the WPA OS is widely utilized, though "most of those encountering the document are neither the general public nor expert writing teachers" (p. 139). Using the *Framework* to build upon familiarity with stage-process models (likely among students and instructors) can help writing program administrators extend and collaboratively develop those models with writing for information literacy in mind. Doing so can add depth and complexity to discussions of curricular aims, practices, and standards while fostering greater inclusion.

Revitalizing first-year composition curricula to reflect the changing nature of both writing and inquiry is important as programs grapple with new disciplinary knowledge, new models for learning, and new writing processes suitable to diverse rhetorical situations. Knowledgeable negotiation of the WPA OS and the *Frameworks* document offers perhaps the best basis for creating curricular designs that help students navigate dynamic composing processes over time and in various informational contexts.

REFERENCES

Adler-Kassner, L., & Wardle, E. (2015). *Naming what we know: Threshold concepts of writing studies*. Logan, UT: Utah State University Press.

Association of College and Research Libraries. (2016, Jan. 11). *Framework for information literacy for higher education*. Retrieved from http://www.ala.org/acrl/sites/ala.org.acrl/files/content/issues/infolit/Framework_ILHE.pdf

Beaufort, A. (2012). The matters of key knowledge domains and transfer of learning in the outcomes statement. *Writing Program Administration, 36*(1), 180–187.

Blackwell-Starnes, K. (2016). Preliminary paths to information literacy: introducing research in core courses. In B. J. D'Angelo, S. Jamieson, B. Maid, & J. R. Walker (Eds.), *Information literacy: Research and collaboration across disciplines* (pp. 139–161). Fort Collins, CO: WAC Clearinghouse. Retrieved from http://wac.colostate.edu/books/infolit/chapter7.pdf

Blythe, S., & Gonzalez, L. (2016). Coordination and transfer across the metagenre of secondary research. *College Composition and Communication, 67*(4), 607–633.

Breuch, L. M. K. (2002). Post-process "pedagogy": A philosophical exercise. *JAC, 22*(1), 119–150.

Council of Writing Program Administrators. (2008, July). *WPA outcomes statement for first-year composition (2.0)*. Retrieved from https://www.in.gov/che/files/WPA_Outcomes_Statement_for_First-Year_Composition.pdf

Council of Writing Program Administrators. (2011, January). *Framework for success in postsecondary writing*. Retrieved from http://wpacouncil.org/files/framework-for-success-postsecondary-writing.pdf

Council of Writing Program Administrators. (2014, July 17). *WPA outcomes statement for first-year composition (3.0)*. Retrieved from http://wpacouncil.org/files/WPA%20Outcomes%20Statement%20Adopted%20Revisions%5B1%5D_0.pdf

D'Angelo, B. J., Jamieson, S., Maid, B., & Walker, J. R. (Eds.). (2016). *Information literacy:*

Research and collaboration across disciplines. Fort Collins, CO: WAC Clearinghouse. Retrieved from http://wac.colostate.edu/books/infolit/

DeJoy, N. (2004). *Process this: Undergraduate writing in composition studies*. Logan, UT: Utah State University Press.

Downs, D., & Robertson, L. (2015). Threshold concepts in first-year composition. In L. Adler-Kassner & E. Wardle (Eds.), *Naming what we know: Threshold concepts and writing studies* (pp. 105–121). Logan, UT: Utah State University Press.

Dryer, D. B., Bowden, D., Brunk-Chavez, B., Harrington, S., Halbritter, B., & Yancey, K. B. (2014). Revising FYC outcomes for a multimodal, digitally composed world: The WPA outcomes statement for first-year composition (version 3.0). *Writing Program Administration, 38*(1), 129–143.

Estrem, H. (2015). Threshold concepts and student learning outcomes. In L. Adler-Kassner & E. Wardle (Eds.), *Naming what we know: Threshold concepts of writing studies* (pp. 89–104). Logan, UT: Utah State University Press.

Holliday, W., & Fagerheim, B. A. (2006). Integrating information literacy with a sequenced English composition curriculum. *portal: Libraries and the Academy, 6*(2), 169–184.

Howard, R. M., & Jamieson, S. (2013). Researched writing. In G. Tate, A. R. Taggart, K. Schick, & H. B. Hessler (Eds.), *A guide to composition pedagogies* (2nd ed.) (pp. 231–247). New York, NY: Oxford University Press.

Kent, T. (ed.). (1999). *Post-process theory: Beyond the writing-process paradigm*. Carbondale, IL: Southern Illinois University Press.

LaFrance, M. (2016). An institutional ethnography of information literacy instruction: Key terms, local/material contexts, and institutional practice. *Writing Program Administration, 39*(2), 105–123.

Maid, B., & D'Angelo, B. J. (2016). Threshold concepts: Integrating and applying information literacy and writing instruction. In B. J. D'Angelo, S. Jamieson, B. Maid, & J. R. Walker (Eds.), *Information literacy: Research and collaboration across disciplines* (pp. 37–50). Fort Collins, CO: WAC Clearinghouse. Retrieved from http://wac.colostate.edu/books/infolit/chapter2.pdf

Meyer, J. H. F., & Land, R. (2006). Threshold concepts and troublesome knowledge: An introduction. In J. H. F. Meyer & R. Land (Eds.), *Overcoming barriers to student understanding. Threshold concepts and troublesome knowledge* (pp. 3–18). New York, NY: Routledge.

Reid, G. (2014). Updating the FYC-library partnership: Recent work on information literacy and writing classrooms. In R. Haswell & D. Dryer (Eds.), *WPA-CompPile research bibliographies*. Retrieved from http://comppile.org/wpa/bibliographies/Bib25/FYC-Library_Partnership.pdf

CHAPTER 3

WRITING WITH THE LIBRARY

Using Threshold Concepts to Collaboratively Teach Multisession Information Literacy Experiences in First-Year Writing

Brittney Johnson

I. Moriah McCracken

RATIONALE FOR PEDAGOGICAL INTEGRATION

The threshold-concept redesign of the ACRL *Framework* creates an opportunity for information literacy instructional programs to reconceive the work that happens in collaboration with first-year writing classes. Because the redesign focused on incorporating essential understandings and larger concepts of information literacy, not simply skills, it is essential for instructors—in the library and in the writing classroom—to have a shared vocabulary for discussing how students might integrate these two fields for lifelong learning. In "Reading for Integration, Identifying Complementary Threshold Concepts: The *ACRL Framework* in Conversation with *Naming What We Know: Threshold Concepts of Writing Studies*," we argue that the publication of two documents—the ACRL's *Framework* and *Naming What We Know (NWWK)*—has created a "kairotic moment" for information literacy and writing programs "to advocate collectively against one-off, skills-focused writing and research instruction" (2016, p. 178). In reading the documents side by side, we identified a set of complementary threshold concepts of information literacy and writing studies, which form the foundation of the multisession introduction to information literacy (IL) we discuss here. This chapter describes the integrated, multisession approach we use to teach the shared threshold concepts (TCs) of information literacy and writing studies. The pedagogical integration and complementary concepts embedded in these sessions intentionally blur the boundary between the writing program and the IL program because these boundaries must be blurred, if not fully dissolved, if students are going to embrace the necessary habits and practices that will allow them to develop as undergraduate scholars and researchers.

The multisession model described here was first piloted during the spring semester of 2015. Our initial collaboration began because both writing and library instructors felt a dissatisfaction with traditional one-shot information literacy sessions. In particular, instructors knew first-year students were not clear about how to approach answering a research question, nor did students understand why scholars ask research questions; thus, we wanted to help them build a schema for how to think about research, and TCs provided us with a way to develop this conceptual knowledge. As we have argued elsewhere, we see the TCs of writing studies and information literacy as complementary: the TCs of writing studies focus on the production of information, while the TCs of information literacy focus on the consumption of information. Thus, we advocate that through a co-teaching of shared TCs of writing studies and information literacy, students are provided with multiple entry points into developing a deeper understanding of the interconnectedness of research and writing.

Our multisession model relies on Scholarship as Conversation as the driver for teaching the other ACRL frames because this frame, more than any other, resonates with first-year students and the goals of first-year writing courses. Students can quickly recognize the value that the metaphor of a conversation adds to their understanding of research; more importantly, the idea of research occurring as an ongoing conversation between scholars over time disrupts their misconceptions of research as simply the reporting of facts and collating of information. We also begin with Scholarship as

Conversation because the other concepts are more meaningful if students have already begun to make a conceptual shift in their identities as student scholars. If students don't believe themselves to be scholars and researchers contributing to conversations, then the remaining frames are merely skills to be applied and, subsequently, disregarded. However, if students see themselves as undergraduate scholars—as researchers expected to produce and give back to communities of practice—then we can more effectively engage them in conversations about "the reflective discovery of information, the understanding of how information is produced and valued, and the use of information in creating new knowledge and participating ethically in communities of learning" (ACRL, 2015). Figure 3.1 represents the relationship we see between the six frames; we'll use this image to illustrate how Scholarship as Conversation can be a common thread, what we call a driver, for building a foundational experience for a multiyear, multicourse IL program. We do not articulate the shared threshold concepts of our disciplines here (because this discussion can be found in our 2016 article, "Reading for Integration"); however, we will describe how one frame can be integrated into first-year writing courses to reshape how students think about their work as researchers.

CO-TEACHING INTEGRATED, SHARED THRESHOLD CONCEPTS

The multisession, integrated model of information literacy instruction described here uses the information literacy threshold concept of Scholarship as Conversation as the driver around which students learn concepts and strategies for engaging in scholarly conversations through research and writing—the primary outcome for our second-semester, first-year writing course. As Figure 3.1 illustrates, the six frames of information literacy are themselves interconnected and layered. By designing instruction with Scholarship as Conversation as the driver, we are able to build

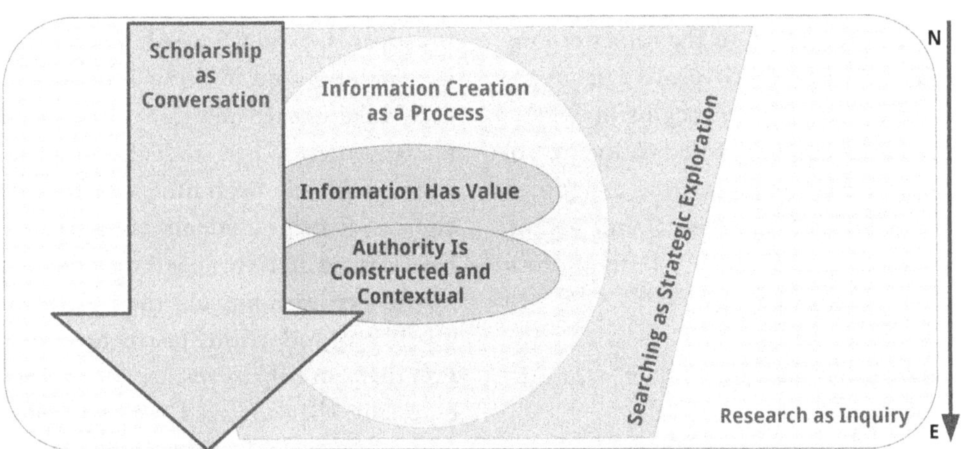

Figure 3.1 Making Scholarship as Conversation the driver for the remaining frames.

a conceptual understanding and approach for research and writing first, and then we interweave other concepts of information literacy as they apply. Here we share our pedagogical design for each session in the multisession model, as well as evidence of growth from two students, Karolyn and Shelby, as they progress through the sessions.

Pedagogical Design Using Multisession Model

The multisession model is effective because it is a pedagogically integrated method of collaborative teaching. Sessions are planned collaboratively with writing instructors and seamlessly integrated into the writing course content; the design is such that activities in both the writing class and the information literacy sessions reinforce the concepts of the other. This pedagogical integration matters because the conceptual nature of our driver—Scholarship as Conversation—is meant to influence how students approach their research-based writing; therefore, our multisession design focuses on helping students write strong research questions and curate useful research sources. Our IL multisession design actually begins before students are introduced to the semester-long, inquiry-based research project sequence. This time frame, which begins in Week 5 of 15, works because most faculty are collecting the first major writing assignment (a rhetorical analysis project) and because all students participate in a fairly uniform research-proposal process:

1. Submission and approval of a research question;
2. Proposal for research design, including preliminary identification of sources and research methodology (primary and secondary data collection); and
3. Submission of an annotated bibliography.

While our multisession design, as seen in Table 3.1, draws heavily from local context and need, the conceptual elements of the four sessions, which we describe below, can be easily adapted to any first-year writing program that asks students to complete a research-based project.

Multisession Objectives: An Overview

Assessing the conceptual content of these multisessions required us to identify students' preexisting writing and research practices; to do this work, students begin the semester by completing a Literacy Strategies Inventory (LSI) (see Figure 3.2). Inspired by a writing strategies inventory designed by Betsy Sargent for the University of Alberta Writing Studies Department, this revised inventory helps students reflect on their attitudes toward their writing, reading, and research processes as well as their understandings of key concepts related to writing studies and information literacy. There are seven sections to the inventory (including Reading Practices; Getting Started, Drafting, and Researching; and Writing Processes), and each Likert-scale question offers 5 possible responses. When students complete the LSI at both the beginning and end of our courses, it helps students assess what they have learned and what goals they might have for further learning, and the LSI responses give library and writing instructors information that can help us track student progress, especially when analyzed alongside reflective writing assessments. Data from one year of multisessions shows a difference in students'

TABLE 3.1 *Multisession Model of Information Literacy Instruction for First-Year Writing*

Week	Session	Objectives	Assessment Collection Activities
1			Literacy Strategies Inventory (LSI)
5	1	→ Students will build a **conceptual** understanding of Scholarship as Conversation. → Students will develop strategies for **eavesdropping** on an ongoing conversation in order to determine its focus and varied perspectives.	IL Session 1 Reflective Writing
6	2	→ Students will develop strategies for **listening** to the overarching conversation. → Students will understand various ways in which **information is communicated** (i.e., types of sources).	IL Session 2 Reflective Writing Searching & Metacognition Video Research Project Reflection
7	3	→ Students will develop strategies for **engaging** in the conversation. → Students will be able to search for relevant perspectives (sources) that pertain to their topic of inquiry (conversation).	Research Project Proposal Report on Research Progress Inquiry-Based Research Project Postproject Reflection
9–13	4	→ Students will understand ways in which they can **contribute** to the conversation.	Postproject Reflection
15			Literacy Strategies Inventory (LSI)

pre- and postmean scores for our information literacy–specific questions.

Session 1: What Is a(n) (Academic) Conversation?

Prior to Session 1, students engage in readings in the writing class selected to prime the discussion of our driver, the concept of Scholarship as Conversation (see Table 3.2). For example, in Week 1, writing instructors assign Karen Rosenberg's "Reading Games: Strategies for Reading Scholarly Sources," a reading that challenges students to "read smarter, not harder" (2011, p. 211), an idea that she explicitly connects to "Joining the Conversation," one of her section headings. Pedagogically, this reading assignment fits into the student learning objectives of the writing class because it offers an architecture for reading scholarly texts. For the multisession design, it plants a seed in the writing classroom and in the students' discussions about how and why sources are used. As Rosenberg argues,

> Even though it may seem like a solitary, isolated activity, when you read a scholarly work, you are participating in a conversation. Academic writers do not make up

Can you identify the conversation occurring within a text?

- ◯ Question doesn't make sense to me.
- ◯ No/Never Tried
- ◯ Rarely/Not Very Well
- ◯ Sometimes/Somewhat
- ◯ Yes/Often/Fairly Well

Can you ask questions about the quality of the research and/or evidence used within a text?

- ◯ Question doesn't make sense to me.
- ◯ No/Never Tried
- ◯ Rarely/Not Very Well
- ◯ Sometimes/Somewhat
- ◯ Yes/Often/Fairly Well

Figure 3.2 Sample Literacy Strategies Inventory questions.

> their arguments off the top of their heads (or solely from creative inspiration). Rather, they look at how others have approached similar issues and problems. Your job—and one for which you'll get plenty of help from your professors and your peers—is to locate the writer and yourself in this larger conversation. (2011, p. 212)

By introducing the idea of conversation to students and connecting it to how they are reading research-based work, the students are exposed to the concepts of Session 1, during which they will explore their connection as student researchers to the idea of Scholarship as Conversation. Furthermore, by asking instructors to complete a series of pedagogically integrated and scaffolded activities, such as these connected readings, we are removing the plug-and-play baggage that comes with the more traditional one-shot sessions. Too many faculty felt that the previous IL

TABLE 3.2 *Session 1 Activities and Assessment Table*

Writing Class Activities	Session 1 Activities	Assessment
Karen Rosenberg's "Reading Games: Strategies for Reading Scholarly Sources"	3 different video clips during which students note topic, terminology, interesting points, questions Whole-class discussion to identify common threads, differences, etc. in videos Discussion question: What does this idea of "Scholarship is a Conversation" mean for you as student researchers?	**Writing Class** LSI Rhetorical Analysis Assignment **IL Session** Reflective Writing 1

sessions were identical, semester after semester and year after year. But, when the writing faculty have an active role in the vertical integration of concepts across a curriculum, they are invested in co-teaching the material because the intellectual payoff for students is more apparent.

During Session 1, students wrestle with the concept that research is ongoing and happens when scholars in a particular discipline engage in **conversation** with one another over an extended period of time (see Figure 3.3). Students engage in an activity in which they are inserted into the middle of a conversation with no context and must develop strategies (such as paying attention to specific cues like terminology or big ideas) for determining the overarching topic of the conversation, as well as understanding how various perspectives shape that conversation. The session ends with a reflective writing assessment in which students must consider how the idea of Scholarship as Conversation changes or shapes their approach to research (see Box 3.1). Because TCs cannot be assessed on skills alone, these reflective writing prompts capture emerging shifts in student thinking and form a baseline for assessing individual growth and understanding.

When asked "How does understanding this idea that scholarship is a conversation set the stage for the research that you are about to undertake?" Karolyn notes that the concept

BOX 3.1
SESSION 1 IL ASSESSMENT: REFLECTIVE WRITING 1 QUESTIONS

1. How does understanding this idea that scholarship is a conversation set the stage for the research that you are about to undertake?
2. How does a conversation (instead of a pro-con debate or for-against positions) change how you think about research and what you will need to do differently?

SESSION 1: Build a Conceptual Understanding

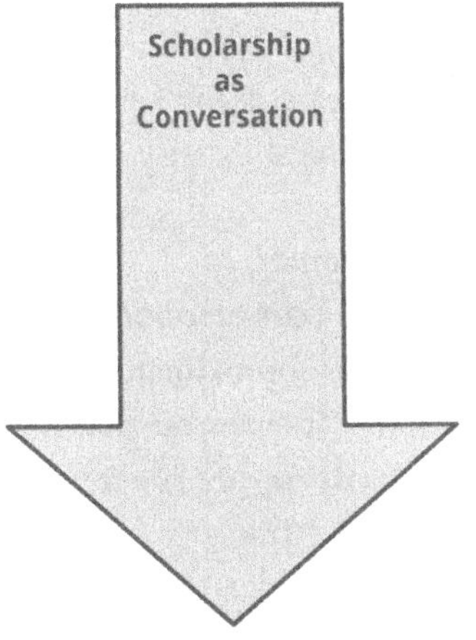

Session 1 | Objectives

→ Students will build a *conceptual* understanding of Scholarship as Conversation.

→ Students will develop strategies for *eavesdropping* on an ongoing conversation in order to determine its focus and varied perspectives.

Figure 3.3 Session 1 overview.

"sets the stage for a more open-ended stance" for her research. She explains that in her high school "scholarly sources and articles were 'kept under glass' and 'served' rather than 'used.'" Here, she quotes an article read in the writing class (Elbow, 1995) and references the IL session, citing both explicitly: "This introductory unit [in the writing class] and the activity today have helped me understand that the research we will be compiling and incorporating in our writing is dynamic and part of an ongoing discussion with multiple perspectives." By linking the content of the session to the content of her writing class and connecting each to her research strategies, Karolyn reveals the power of the complementary threshold concepts and the pedagogical integration of our sessions.

For Shelby, the value of Session 1 comes in understanding how to reshape her thinking about research. Rather than feeling pressured to immediately contribute to a conversation, Shelby notes that she must first "see [herself] as an eavesdropper on the conversation of scholarship for the research project [she is] about to undertake." Before she can make a contribution, she must begin by "listening to and understanding what other people have to say about it." Shelby goes on to describe this eavesdropping as preparation: "In some ways this would be preparing myself to enter the conversation by getting all the other perspectives and ideas that are already out there so that I can eventually contribute something new."

The second reflective question from Session 1 focuses on conversations: "How does a conversation (instead of a pro-con debate or for-against positions) change how you think about research and what you will need to do differently?" When explaining how the concept of a conversation changes how she thinks about her research, Karolyn shifts away from taking sides: "Instead of seeing an issue as having black and white 'sides'—which is often convenient but not fully investigating an issue—a conversation allows for more than one or two perspectives and 'takes' on issues." We also hear emerging changes in her understanding of the purpose of research. Karolyn no longer believes she and her colleagues are supposed to be "writing our point (our argument) and the refutation of the opposition." They are expected to "take into account all sides of a conversation that's more of a round table than a rectangular one with two opposing heads." For her work, Karolyn acknowledges that she will have to "branch out more when doing research, to try to bring multiple perspectives of the issue into [her] writing rather than just present [her] argument and refute the 'opposite' side." This is a sentiment echoed by Shelby, who notes that the driver makes "the project less intimidating to see scholarship as a conversation as opposed to an argument or debate." She, too, will bring a more "open mind because there isn't pressure to 'pick a side' or pressure to prove that one side is right or wrong." Instead, Shelby believes she is supposed "to listen to what's out there." In this reflective writing, we see how students' perceptions about what they should and should not be doing are shifting as they head into Session 2.

Session 2: Listening to an Academic Conversation

Session 2 occurs approximately one week after Session 1 and focuses on moving students beyond **eavesdropping** on conversations by offering specific strategies for **listening** to a conversation in order to develop narrowed, focused research questions that will guide their process of inquiry (see Figure 3.4).

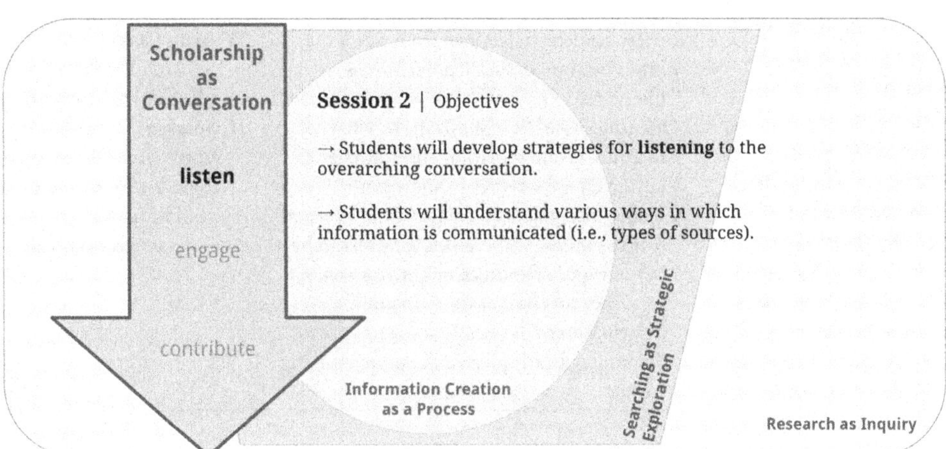

Figure 3.4 Session 2 overview.

Between Sessions 1 and 2, students discuss readings and engage in activities in the writing class that focus on the development of guiding research questions—for example, these activities help students further explore the purpose of a research question and the importance of presearch in helping shape research questions and give them opportunities to collaboratively workshop research questions (see Table 3.3).

During Session 2, students first consider factors that contribute to the creation of different information formats, such as the characteristics of the writing style, the authority of the author, the audience, the purpose, and where the information can be accessed. Students then use this foundational understanding to develop strategies for *presearch*, a term taken from a writing class reading that means selecting sources appropriate for building context for (listening to) a conversation, which they then implement after the session in order to narrow the focus of their research. At the end of Session 2, students again reflect on the content of the IL session and its role in the work they must complete in the writing class. When asked "How do you plan to apply what you learned today to narrow your research topic and further engage in the conversation?" Karolyn has a clear research strategy informed by our conceptual driver. She notes that her "entry-way into the conversation will be through Google and Wikipedia, just like many students." She goes on to note that because the session focused on "displaying all of the possible sources we could use on the board," she will also likely use "magazines, news, blogs, websites, videos, and all sorts of other more 'informal' sources to listen to the conversation and gather background. In order to narrow my research topic, I'll need to have this background to go from."

After Session 2, students may participate in an optional Searching & Metacognition Videos activity. Inspired by the LILAC Project and designed to capture their initial presearch behaviors, this assessment (which also serves as a valuable pedagogical learning

TABLE 3.3 *Session 2 Activities and Assessment Table*

Writing Class Activities	Session 2 Activities	Assessment
Bernice Olivas, "Cupping the Spark in Our Hands: Developing a Better Understanding of the Research Question in Inquiry-Based Research" Randall McClure, "Googlepedia: Turning Information Behaviors into Research Skills"	Review student reflections from Session 1. Build visual model of Scholarship as Conversation. Opening discussion question: In what mediums is information communicated? Outline characteristics of sources. Closing discussion question: What types of sources might you consult for presearch? What types of sources might you consult to gather specific, or more focused, information? Offer strategies for presearch and narrowing a topic.	**Writing Class** Research Project Reflection **IL Session** Word Clouds Reflective Writing 2 Searching & Metacognition Video

tool) requires students to screen-capture the first 15 minutes of their presearch practice and narrate their behaviors and the reasoning behind those behaviors. By combining the reflective writing from Sessions 1 and 2 with a metacognition video, we can compare students' information-seeking behaviors with self-reported data as they participate in the multisessions. We can see what strategies students bring into the class for listening to conversations and which recommendations they adopt for their research projects. As the students describe what they are doing and why, they reveal not only how complicated assessing the Scholarship as Conversation frame is and why teaching for concepts cannot be stripped down to skills-based assessment measures, but also how we can learn more about what students are learning when we watch the videos in light of reflective writing.

Karolyn, for instance, does what she reported in her reflective writing. She starts in Google because she is "not quite sure how [she is] going to word [her] question," and she hopes "maybe [Google] will help." She types in her topic ("creativity in scientific writing"), and then does the "cliché thing" and selects the "first link." Karolyn immediately identifies the type of source she's located, noting that the first link "looks like it's an academic journal." Her next click is on a *Scientific American* article, which she chose "because it seems like a reliable source." She explains, "It is maybe more of an informal magazine or news source." After identifying key words she wants to look up later ("dissertation chapters"), we see Karolyn organize her research, as seen in Box 3.2, creating a research folder and a separate presearch file into which she copies and pastes links to her sources; she also identifies the type of media she has located, something she might not have done without Session 2.

Like Karolyn, Shelby starts her resource search in Google because she wants broad terms to narrow down. She is conscious enough of Google's sponsored links to jump down before opening a source, and just as she explained in her reflective writing after Session 1, she's not looking for definitions or

BOX 3.2
KAROLYN'S SOURCES LOCATED WHILE RECORDING METACOGNITION VIDEO

GOOGLE

http://blogs.scientificamerican.com/urban-scientist/science-writing-academic-creative/

- dissertations = projects we complete? (explore further)
- science blogging = place in academia?
- BLOG/more INFORMAL

MUNDAY LIBRARY

https://login/ezproxy.stedwards.edu/login?url=http://search.ebscohost.com/login/aspx?direct=true&db=edsjsr&AN=edsjsr.40186599&site=eds-live&scope=site

- creativity, spirituality, awe, and wonder

*ACADEMIC JOURNAL

a single answer. Instead, she repeats the conceptual ideas of Session 1, looking for sources "kind of based on" her larger question. This may explain why Shelby quickly moves from search terms to a question, and in skimming through her sources, she, like Karolyn, begins making choices based on media types. One source references a poll, and we learn that she thinks this kind of information could be useful (although we don't know why). She also creates a digital repository, bookmarking pages to a folder as she surfs. Like Karolyn, we hear how she is refining and complicating her question and how she is using methodological information in the sources to assess their relevance and credibility.

Session 3: Engaging in an Academic Conversation

By the time students participate in Session 3, they have engaged with Scholarship as Conversation on a conceptual level and experimented with different strategies for finding sources relevant to their research question. Session 3, then, provides students with more narrow strategies for **engaging** in a conversation through developing an understanding of how to find specific perspectives that pertain to their questions. This is the most conventional IL session because it is the first time students rely on library resources for locating information. Students create a concept map for their questions and consider relevant presearch that is helping their conversation take shape; then, the session focuses on helping students understand concepts articulated in the IL frame of Searching as Strategic Exploration, and the students workshop to dive deeper into their research. For example, we may discuss refining search terms based on date or source type.

For Session 3, there are no information literacy–specific assessments because the success of these sessions can best be seen in the final research projects completed by students (see Figure 3.5). For example, the students completed a final reflective writing assignment for the writing course in which they were expected to explain which strategies and processes from the preceding weeks contributed to their knowledge about writing and research in higher education. To complete

TABLE 3.4 *Session 3 Activities and Assessment Table*

Writing Class Activities	Session 3 Activities	Assessment
	Concept Mapping Activity: Consider the Conversation Students reflect on presearch strategies and results Introduce strategies for refined searching and synthesis of conversations Hands-on workshop with institutional resources	Inquiry-Based Research Project, *including* Research Project Proposal Report on Research Progress Postproject Reflection

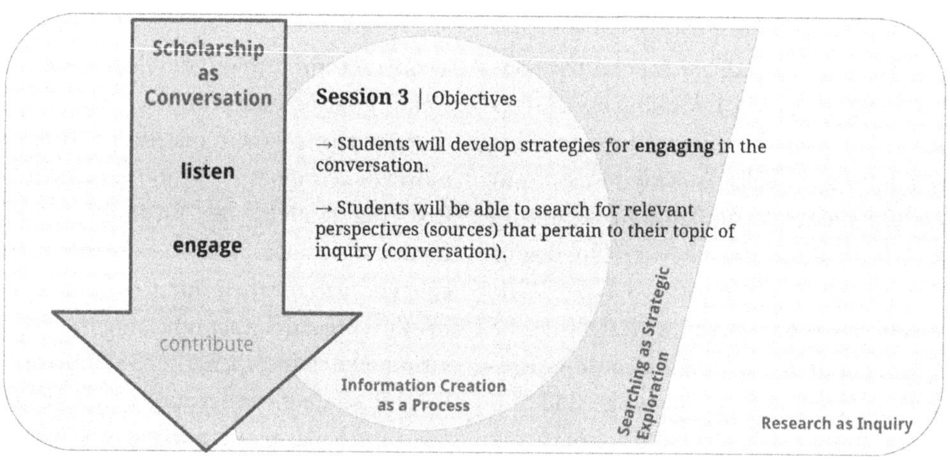

Figure 3.5 Session 3 overview.

this assignment, students were expected to "point to particular strategies [they] used during the researching, drafting, and writing process." In her reflection, Shelby notes that she changed her major during this process, a choice that affected her initial research question; she does list the metacognition video as one of the "exercises [that] got [her] thinking about research questions and methods which was helpful when [she] went back and found new sources for [her research proposal]."

Karolyn also experienced a significant shift in her project during the IL process. She notes in her reflection that she was able to "find a few sources about the role (or lack thereof) of creativity in scientific writing," but she also notes a limitation. "Before [she] even read the sources," she could articulate an answer to her question. Because the IL sessions focused on contributing to conversations, not merely reporting what she already knew, Karolyn knew a change was required: "Because I felt

I already knew the answer, and having read Olivas's (2009) paper on student inquiry-based research, I knew that going forward with my original question would basically be a waste of my time since I wouldn't truly be learning or gaining anything in the process."

Session 4: Contributing to an Academic Conversation

The final session in this multisession model of information literacy instruction prepares students to **contribute** to the scholarly conversation in which they are engaging (see Figure 3.6). Session 4 is flexible in that writing instructors can choose the option that best fits the specific needs of their students, and on our campus, there have been two popular versions for this final session of the semester. Session 4a (see Table 3.5) focuses on helping students understand *what* to contribute to an ongoing conversation, which is why Session 4a occurs as students are preparing the final drafts of their research projects (and beginning to think about their final assignment of the term). The session touches on the frame of Research as Inquiry and includes activities that help students synthesize their research in order to identify gaps; these gaps can then be addressed by either revising the research question and reiterating the process of searching or by using the gap as an entry point into the conversation and "filling" it with a new perspective.

In contrast, Session 4b focuses on helping students understand *how* to contribute to a conversation. This "how" session occurs after students have completed their formal writing project. This version of the session returns to the frame of Information Creation as a Process, as students reconsider ways in which information is created and apply that understanding to create a "remixed" version of their academic paper.

Both Karolyn and Shelby participated in Session 4a, and their writing class included a reflective writing prompt with the final project submission. The reflective prompt included questions about the students'

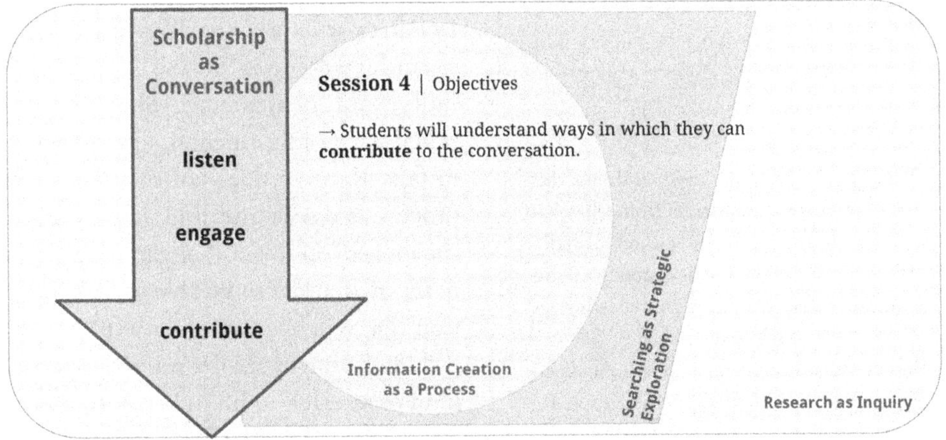

Figure 3.6 Session 4 overview.

TABLE 3.5 *Session 4 Activities and Assessment Table*

Writing Class Activities	Session 4 Activities	Assessment
	Session 4a Analysis of how sources connect to question and to each other with two (2) end goals for further research: 1. students identifying gaps in research → revising question, or 2. students identifying gaps in research → entry point into conversation. **Session 4b** Examine "remix" of a book in three genres *Discussion:* conventions, purpose, audience, selection of content	Postproject Reflection

audience choice, process-based decisions, and, for the purposes of our multisession design, research process questions (see Box 3.3). For Karolyn, the research for this project—a remixing of her research project into three new genres for a nonacademic audience—was more "supplemental," but there is a key practice she picked up from the multisession experience: the "info literacy skill of refining and reframing [her] search questions and terms." She unsuccessfully searched for "statistics about students and scientific writing," but she successfully filled in her own knowledge gap with "some troubleshooting research with the platform for [her] video genre" when she couldn't make the voiceover work properly. She made these adjustments because the sessions focused on concepts, not skills; in fact, Karolyn even "adjust[s] the location of where [she] conducted searches (from library to outside databases to Google Scholar to Google) and what types of search terms [she] was using." She explains, "After accepting that I wasn't going to get any data or statistics, I decided to move into a gap in my research I hadn't previously considered: reasons why scientific writing is 'boring' (e.g. why aren't fluffy words okay to use)." She was not frustrated by the adjustment. Quite the opposite, in fact. Karolyn does not treat her research process as a seek and find activity; instead, she moves "on to another gap or exploration pathway in order to be able to find information that was relevant and useful."

BOX 3.3
WRITING CLASSES' POSTPROJECT REFLECTIVE WRITING QUESTIONS ABOUT RESEARCH PRACTICES

1. What kind of research did you do for this project? How was it different from what you did for [the inquiry-based research paper]?
2. What information literacy practices did you use to help you adapt your existing research to your selected audience?
3. What adjustments did you have to make to your strategies to find appropriate support?

Like Karolyn, Shelby wanted a particular kind of research to fill in her gaps; more specifically, she "tried to find some sources that had statistics about first-year writing practices but unfortunately had no luck." She, too, strayed "from trying to do traditional academic research," and, like Karolyn, she knows this is acceptable "because it just didn't seem to fit into [her] genres." She also completed research related to the genres she was creating in this final assignment. She "was mostly just looking for examples for the types of genres [she] wanted to create," which became "templates" she could consult to identify "what moves" she was supposed to make.

CHANGING PERCEPTIONS OF RESEARCH AND WRITING

Teaching first-year writing students a complementary threshold concept, Scholarship as Conversation, from two disciplinary perspectives through a multisession model of pedagogical integrated information literacy sessions is creating subtle changes in how students on our campus perceive research-based writing in higher education. Our combination of assessments—specifically the pre- and postinventories, reflective writing assignments, and metacognition videos—have captured evidence of students' shifting schemas. For example, in the closing paragraph of her reflection for her major research assignment, Karolyn wrote the following:

> Through this process I also gained insights into the research process: there won't always be secondary sources that directly address your inquiry or exact topic, but you can always use those to help you enter the discussion, gain background knowledge, or they may be related your topic indirectly.

She is a first-semester freshman who left the multisession experience articulating the idea that research is a conversation; this is a conceptual shift for Karolyn, especially if we consider that during Week 1 of the semester she chose "Yes / Often / Fairly Well" when responding to "Can you identify the conversation occurring within a text?" on the LSI. When responding to "Can you ask questions about the quality of the research and/or evidence used within a text?," she opted for "Sometimes / Somewhat," but she was not among the students confused by these questions or perspectives.

The complementary TCs of information literacy and writing studies are complex, and integrating them into two programs requires pedagogical collaboration because the *Framework* cannot be reduced to rote skills or standardized learning outcomes. As our data from teaching the TC of Scholarship as Conversation suggests, students wrestle with this concept in increasingly complex ways as they progress through their research-and-writing projects. Their understanding organically develops as the integrated, scaffolded instruction aims to meet them where they are. Our instructors knew the timing of the traditional one-shot sessions was wrong, as too many students were sitting in sessions before their research projects were even assigned; more importantly, we realized students were not ready to look for sources because they did not understand the larger purpose: research is about joining an ongoing conversation and contributing something back to a community. The multisession experience we have designed for first-year writers starts with this premise; using the idea of a conversation as the driver, we are able to bring students into the research experience rather than positioning them as mere reporters on the sidelines.

REFERENCES

Adler-Kassner, L., & Wardle, E. (Eds.). (2015). *Naming what we know: Threshold concepts of writing studies.* Boulder, CO: Utah State University Press.

Association of College and Research Libraries. (2015). *Framework for information literacy for higher education.* Retrieved from http://www.ala.org/acrl/standards/ilframework

Elbow, P. (1995). Being a writer vs. being an academic: A conflict in goals. *College Composition and Communication, 46*(1), 72–83. https://doi.org/10.2307/358871

Johnson, B., & McCracken, I. M. (2016). Reading for integration, identifying complementary threshold concepts: The ACRL *Framework* in conversation with *Naming what we know: Threshold concepts of writing studies. Communications in Information Literacy, 10*(2), 178–198.

Olivas, B. (2009). Cupping the spark in our hands: Developing a better understanding of the research question in inquiry-based writing. *Young Scholars in Writing, 7,* 6–18. Retrieved from http://arc.lib.montana.edu/ojs/index.php/Young-Scholars-In-Writing/article/view/142/98

Rosenberg, K. (2011). Reading games: Strategies for reading scholarly sources. *Writing Spaces, 2,* 210–220. Retrieved from https://wac.colostate.edu/books/writingspaces2/rosenberg--reading-games.pdf

PART II

Collaboration and Conversation

CHAPTER 4

SUPPLANTING THE RESEARCH PAPER AND ONE-SHOT LIBRARY VISIT

A Collaborative Approach to Writing Instruction and Information Literacy

Valerie Ross

Dana M. Walker

Founded in 2003, the Critical Writing Program of the University of Pennsylvania has built an evidence-based, "lab style" curriculum that is taught by faculty from across the disciplines. All teach a shared curriculum inflected by writing in their own disciplines as well as by their individual course topics and readings. A core mission of the program has been to develop a curriculum that positions students as authentic participants in generative knowledge practices. Our chapter will explore the development of our curriculum and our collaborative approach to teaching information literacy, highlighting productive areas of overlap between writing studies and information science and literacy scholarship, including the ACRL *Framework* (ACRL, 2015; Elmborg, 2003; Norgaard, 2003). It will address some of our challenges and mishaps as well as successes, including the development of an organic, mutually beneficial form of professional development that reinforced curricular development, advancing our shared understanding of generative knowledge practices and how students learn.

BACKGROUND

The Critical Writing Program of the University of Pennsylvania is one of about 60 independent writing in the disciplines programs in the United States. The program rosters the first-year writing course required of all students enrolled in the university's four undergraduate schools: the College of Arts and Sciences, the Wharton School, the School of Nursing, and the School of Engineering. The writing seminar is the only course taken by all Penn undergraduates and as such represents a uniquely shared academic experience. As an ideal vehicle for reaching all students, the course is perpetually at risk of becoming an outlet for promoting organizations and events for all who wish to connect with students.

Our faculty are varied in terms of their disciplinary interests. Nearly all hold PhDs in a diverse range of disciplines from the humanities to the social and natural sciences; a few have terminal degrees in journalism and creative writing; and six doctoral candidates from across the disciplines are recipients of a competitive teaching fellowship designed to mentor them in best practices in writing studies. Our faculty choose their own topics and texts, based on their disciplines and interests, and use a range of approaches to teach a set of shared writing assignments. Penn's program is distinct from most other first-year writing programs in that our writing curriculum functions as a kind of lab in which faculty immerse students in individual disciplines and topics but all students complete the same set of writing assignments, including a literature review and digitally based editorial. With approximately 2,600 students enrolled in our seminars each year, we have sufficient data to share, test, and refine our approaches to writing instruction. As such, our intensively collaborative, outcomes-based curriculum is always a work in progress, built by a multitude of constituencies: faculty across the disciplines, administration, students, employers, librarians, our own writing faculty and administration, as well as other scholars and practitioners in the field of writing studies. Our main objective is to teach students how to adapt to new writing situations based on generative knowledge practices. Our committed interdisciplinary faculty has fostered a productively layered process of inquiry and problem-solving within and across the 100 seminars rostered each semester. Over the past decade, faculty and students have steadily transformed the curriculum into an increasingly more authentic, active learning experience, including in its approach to information literacy (IL).

THE WRITING CURRICULUM—RETHINKING THE RESEARCH PAPER

The first great challenge to creating an authentic writing curriculum was posed by the research paper. By 2003, many in writing studies were rejecting or substantially revamping their approach to research papers (Hood, 2010). In keeping with this trend, many faculty in our program experimented with various alternatives to research papers, including websites, podcasts, maps, recipes, case studies, and posters. The sheer range of alternatives taught us all much about different sorts of literacies, from their remarkably diverse processes of production to the differing demands on faculty and university resources each entailed. This proliferation of new source-based assignments also led us, counterintuitively, to developing a shared curriculum. Depending on which course students enrolled in, they might face profoundly different demands upon their time as well as radically different assessment criteria. How were we to assess the differing skills, knowledge, process, and products of students who might be creating cookbooks in one class and a 30-page research paper in another? Furthermore, what could we confidently conclude about student learning when they faced such a variety of topics, disciplines, approaches, and assignments? This was further complicated by the fact that seminars were capped at 16, a sample size too small to allow for generalizations about learning outcomes.

Our Writing Center, part of the Critical Writing Program, was in these early years also exploring how best to support students who came to the center for help with their writing assignments. To get a stronger sense of the range of assignments our students were encountering, we asked our undergraduate tutors, as part of their training, to interview professors across the disciplines about their own practices as writers as well as the kinds of writing they were asking students to do. Over 40 disciplines and 100 interviews later, the findings were unsurprising: Professors were mostly assigning timed essay questions, short response papers, and conventional research papers. And these assignments had at most an attenuated relationship to the kinds of writing the professors themselves were doing.

The research paper is an assignment as familiar to the library community as it is to the writing studies community. Its aim is to teach students how to find, synthesize, and document sources in a paper that makes and supports a claim about a topic. Students are meant to immerse themselves in library resources, looking up information, narrowing their scope, reading, note-taking, and documenting sources. Sometimes the students are taught to research as they write, concomitantly; sometimes they are given a more scaffolded approach (e.g., annotated bibliographies, note cards, outlines). In many cases, they are given topics, questions, even a set of suggested sources or a particular database. Nearly all the intellectual work is done for them by the teacher or professor, an elaborate scavenger hunt followed by laborious documentation substituting for the purposefulness and excitement of actual academic research, where one seeks solutions to problems that others presumably regard as significant and engaging.

Despite its longstanding popularity among teachers and professors, the "research paper" has been criticized for many years by those in writing studies and is rarely assigned in writing classes, though source-based writing remains a central feature of writing curricula (Brent, 2013; Hood, 2010). As a "mutt genre" (Wardle, 2009), the research paper is "school writing" as distinct from authentic writing. Students perform it to assure a teacher that they are able to go through certain motions: finding and reading sources; quoting, paraphrasing, documenting them; delivering them in a paper that is coherent and unified. While such practices mimic aspects of authentic academic genres, just as sifting and measuring flour mimics aspects of baking a cake, the typical research paper assignment has no social or intellectual purpose, no readership. Equally important, as Larson (1982) observes, the research paper misleads students in terms of how real scholars research and write. Larson notes that the *activity* of research contributes to innumerable academic and popular genres, from literature reviews and lab reports to grant proposals, research articles, and biographies. But the research paper we assign to students has no such motive, no future; it is an end in itself written for a grade rather than a purpose. "If almost any paper is potentially a paper incorporating the fruits of research, the term 'research paper' has virtually no value as an identification of a kind of substance in a paper" (Larson, 1982, p. 813).

As members of our writing faculty from across the disciplines put increasing pressure on the research paper, its artificiality and limitations grew difficult to ignore. In addition to the sorts of critiques being generated by those in the field of writing studies, our interdisciplinary faculty realized that the word "research" itself was nearly nonsensical when we attempted to use it program-wide. Most obviously, "research" is not an activity limited to library search, nor is it broadly understood as the activity of locating secondary sources, except within a handful of text-based fields such as literary studies. What we were calling "research papers" were actually exercises in locating and patching together a set of secondary sources that had little to do with the research practices in any of our fields. As writing studies scholars have pointed out, when a student is asked to write outside a genre's "natural environment" the writing becomes "pseudotransactional" (Petraglia, 1995). Where transactional writing is authentic in both its audience and purpose, the pseudotransactional research paper is written merely to meet a teacher's expectations, rather than to create or transfer knowledge to an interested audience. Stripped of context and purpose, the research paper is a classroom exercise that does not organically lead to more authentic research and writing skills. Instead of learning how to build knowledge, students are asked to practice a set of behaviors that actually muddy students' understanding of why, when, and how scholars seek, write about, and document secondary sources. Recent research suggests that the research paper may even be teaching students how to become increasingly sophisticated if unwitting patchwork plagiarists (Howard, Serviss, & Rodrigue, 2010). Information scientists have recognized this problem when it comes to retrieval. Teaching people to find information in the abstract—devoid of an actual information need—creates fake procedures that get in the way of understanding how to find information when one actually needs it. Writing without a purpose (beyond fulfilling an assignment) has been shown to decrease skill transferability (e.g., Wardle, 2009); the same is true of searching without a purpose: As Purdue (2003) noted, "information literacy cannot exist in a vacuum; it has to be part of a lived response to research."

The research paper also poses a problem from the perspective of teaching situated information literacy practices. Information scientists have long understood that information needs change throughout search (Bates, 1989). Using the analogy of "berrypicking," Bates (1989) argued that in a real search users engage in a "bit-at-a-time" retrieval where the information need and information query changes as new information is gleaned. However, the way a student research paper is often conceived is that it follows a very specific, and sometimes static, sequence of events. These student papers commonly have a minimum number of sources that are required (e.g., "find and cite seven other papers"). Naturally, students who are working to fulfill these basic requirements also tend to use a minimum number of search strategies and venues to find their required sources. Moreover, under this curricular model, information search practices or other library "research" skills are commonly taught in a single class, to students who already believe they are highly proficient in search and online search technologies (Brown, Murphy, & Nanny, 2003). As a result, the larger conception of search, or writing, being iterative is frequently lost.

Also within this student research paper curriculum, being informationally "literate" is a term that is problematized by most information literacy researchers (e.g., ACRL, 2015; Purdue, 2003). Learning how to authentically write requires an understanding of how text is produced, accessed, and distributed (Norgaard, 2003). If the writing and scholarship is to be authentic, it also requires writers to place themselves into that larger academic discussion or what Bruffee (1999) notes as an approach to teaching that helps students "converse with increasing facility in the language of the communities they want to join." Information scientists understand this notion of scholarship as conversation. As the ACRL framework (2015) sets out, scholarship is ongoing. For example, practices such as attribution are not simply an ethical obligation of participation. These forms of attribution are what actually allow "the conversation to move forward" (ACRL, 2015). The goal of information literacy is to allow those who are apprentices to recognize that conversations are ongoing, to seek them out, and to ultimately learn to contribute to those discussions.

Our faculty set out to find a replacement for the research paper—a genre that was authentic, identifiable, that could be found in each of our disciplines, that was purposeful and instructive, that asked and answered questions we could not anticipate for the student; that advanced students' skills as information-seekers and rhetoricians; that sought to transfer and build knowledge; and that had an intended, interested audience beyond the professor as grader. After much discussion and debate, we landed on the literature review in 2015. Faculty from the different disciplines were asked to post examples of literature reviews in their fields, at which time we learned that there was much variation in how each discipline approached the review but in the end the social functions and knowledge practices, as well as the strategies for finding and documenting sources, were reasonably shared enterprises. What we didn't anticipate was how difficult it would be to break students of the bad habits they had developed from years of writing research papers.

THE WRITING CURRICULUM—RETHINKING THE ONE-SHOT LIBRARY VISIT

As with rethinking the research paper, we quickly recognized that we also needed to rethink the one-shot library visit, which had been a feature of our writing courses, as we discovered in the early years of the program that our students tuned out during these "talking head" visits and only began to show concern for finding sources when they were in the midst of trying to do their assignments. A few of our instructors also quizzed students after library visits about what they had learned and, to the instructors' dismay, discovered that the students had very low recall of what had been presented in the hour-plus class time absorbed.

The 80-minute one-shot librarian instruction approach is widely viewed as ineffective (see Artman, Frisicaro-Pawlowski, & Monge, 2010; Jacobs & Jacobs, 2009). As Norgaard (2003) pointed out, information literacy isn't simply an act of being able to find a piece of information online. Rather the social context—or activity system—in which that information is produced must also be understood and evaluated. Moreover, the research process exists in a larger process of writing (Elmborg, 2003). Effective research requires revision, thinking through, and reflection (Jacobs & Jacobs, 2009).

To address this problem, we partnered with the libraries to develop a process that abandoned the talking-head, skills-based workshop in favor of a more authentic process. In 2009 two things happened: (1) a source-based writing assignment appeared that was not yet the literature review but rather an improved "mutt genre" that was based on Kenneth Bruffee's (1993) source synthesis assignment, which had the virtue of being self-directed and of teaching students how to create and transfer knowledge; and (2) the writing program began a formal collaboration with Penn's undergraduate library. The first move was the fall 2009 introduction of a program-wide writing assignment that was designed to allow students to legitimately engage in a disciplinary discourse community. Each writing seminar was to be designed around a different research text—an accessible but well-cited scholarly monograph. In the various seminars, students would read the text and its bibliography. The introduction of the research text to the seminar allowed the undergraduate, primarily freshman, apprentice scholar to quickly engage in a scholarly conversation, as defined within that research text, and also understand the network of citations within that text. Students would then use the research text and one of its citations to begin a project of synthesis. Those first two sources—the research text and one of its sources—were the beginning of their writing assignment. This helped students define their own topic of research. It also gave them a real and credible starting point for the research and writing process. The resultant paper, a complex synthesis, served as a major component of their semester's writing portfolio.

In order to write this explanatory paper, students needed to acquire a series of information literacy skills. At the most basic level, they had to be able to read and locate bibliographic references as well as engage in keyword searching. Those two processes, however, were multilayered in terms of the writing and information skills required. Students had to learn how to read a citation, evaluate source credibility, understand why scholars use certain kinds of sources as evidence (e.g., specialist vs. nonspecialist texts), citation chase, and generate discipline-appropriate keywords. They also had to learn how to cite the source within the appropriate disciplinary context, integrate those sources effectively into their writing, and treat them ethically. At the same time, students needed to learn how to write while researching, since the synthesis of these scholarly sources was an intellectually demanding process.

In the summer of 2009, the second move was made in which the writing program began to partner with Penn's undergraduate library to introduce library research into the writing seminars. Each writing seminar was paired with a related subject librarian. Prior to the semester's start, librarians and faculty were asked to meet to discuss the research text and the kinds of sources the student might need to engage in. Many of the subject librarians read the seminar's research text and became familiar with its bibliography. Like other library–writing program collaborations (e.g., Jacobs & Jacobs, 2009), writing faculty had productive discussions among themselves and with the librarians about what constituted a research source within their fields. Some working in new media, for example, had to deal with issues of recency and outdated controlled vocabulary. Others needed to understand when primary sources were appropriate and when they were not.

As a result of the partnership, the Critical Writing Program and the undergraduate library produced a series of instructional artifacts and sessions to support students and writing faculty. The most successful was having librarians attend all seminars each term in order to provide a hands-on library research workshop. Librarians, in cooperation with the writing program, developed an instructional script. Early in the student's research process, the librarian was invited to the class. Each librarian was asked to spend 15 to 20 minutes providing a targeted review of some of the primary multidisciplinary databases as well as a few subject-specific resources available to students. Many librarians used one of the student's research topics as a way to model a search process. In successful sessions, librarians were often able to show the students the differences between the large-scale Google Scholar searches versus the results list in a PsychInfo search. Students were asked to follow along with the search, getting some hands-on experience with the databases. The next 60 minutes were dedicated to workshop time when students did their own searching and the librarian was available for consultation and brainstorming, as well as for when students got stuck. The librarians also produced customized online library guides for each class. This resource included links to the primary multidisciplinary and subject-specific databases students would be expected to use in the class, tips on how to read a citation, and a walk-through on how to use the library to find known citations. Finally, the class library session and online library guide were meant to create a personal connection between the student and librarian. The online guide provided a photo of the librarian as well as his or her direct contact information. Students were encouraged by the librarian and many of the faculty to follow up with the class librarian throughout the course of their research.

The next curricular move was in the fall of 2015 when the writing program made the switch to teaching authentic writing genres.

Instead of a complex synthesis paper, students are now asked to write small-scale, stand-alone scholarly literature reviews. From a writing studies perspective, this curricular move brought an end to the "student research paper" and invited students to engage in a real-world writing genre. From an information literacy perspective, the literature review posed some similar challenges for students' information skills—search, credibility, documentation. However, the literature review assignment did something that the previous synthesis paper did not. It forced students and faculty (and, perhaps, the librarians) to more authentically grapple with the scholarly conversations that comprise academic discourse communities. The literature review assignment starts in a similar way to the previous complex synthesis assignment: the research text was the basis and from there students were to find sources, define a field of research, and write a review of that field. The challenge for students and faculty has been scaling and understanding what comprises a field of research. Students have to start drawing lines and mapping fields of inquiry by understanding some of the disciplinary connections (and disconnects) within those inquiry fields. This pushes students to think beyond ACRL's scholarly conversations and strategic searching. They can't just search for some keywords. They have to learn about scholarly timelines and understand the contours of a research inquiry over time. They have to make decisions about validity, whether or not scholars in different research fields are really talking about the same thing (and therefore would be contained in the same literature review). They also have to make decisions about scale, how generalizable a statement they can make when they have to operate within a necessarily limited source set.

DISCUSSION

Through our eight-year partnership, we have clarified many of the goals and outcomes in keeping with a commitment to continuous improvement of our curriculum. However, many challenges remain. The curricular structure is the first serious impediment. How do we simulate the messy, recursive practices of source-based writing? Students, whose habits have been formed by "research papers" that they typically binge-write, are (not unlike their instructors and librarians) likely to view the workshop as the day when they find the sources for their projects. Yet experts know that such a lockstep, linear approach, such a belief in tidy stages, are an unattainable fantasy. Our literature review is structured as a five-draft process with students meant to integrate their sources as they go along, but some students do the majority of their research in their first drafts, binge-style, while others have brief, undeveloped drafts until the end of the cycle. Most, however, follow the assignment's suggested path and build in chunks, though some complain that it feels artificial to do so. This is because they are generally not writing bona fide literature reviews. One of our greatest surprises was how difficult it was for all of us—students, instructors, librarians, and writing tutors—to shift from research papers to literature reviews. The negative transfer—which is to say, the problematic application of something one has learned in the past to a current problem—has never been so evident as when we ask students to abandon their well-practiced mutt genre and instead write something that looks suspiciously like that same mutt genre. It typically takes students the entire semester to absorb the difference between a "research paper" and a literature review, which points to why, perhaps, college graduates have such difficulty adapting to writing in the workplace. Meanwhile, instructors and librarians exhibit textbook "tacit knowledge" behavior when they try to explain the differences between a research paper and a literature review. They know when something isn't a literature review but is instead a patchwork of paraphrased and direct quotations hitched together by "transitions," as students are taught to call them, to support a claim. But none of us as yet has developed sufficient language and concepts to help students build a bridge from the research paper to the literature review. Despite a mountain of analogies, examples, and scaffolding, students seem mostly to be experiencing their epiphanies through the old-fashioned means of osmosis, imitation, and trial and error with feedback. However, once they grasp the difference, their understanding of scholarly inquiry blossoms.

Another timing challenge has to do with how (or whether) to keep students involved with their librarians throughout the semester. Anecdotally, freshman usage of the library jumped substantially when our partnership first began; unfortunately we did not think to track it. Our study of knowledge transfer from the writing seminar to other writing situations, now in its fourth year, suggests that students are building upon the topics and research strategies that they learn from their instructors and librarians. In our partner meeting of 2014, some librarians wondered whether we should be concerned that some of our students were continuing to work with the librarians on projects they had commenced in their freshmen seminars, rather than developing interests in new topics. From the point of view of scholarship, the question seemed surprising but points to how common it is to see students as writing a series of papers rather than building knowledge. In the past several years, students have developed sustained scholarly projects that they began during their freshman year writing seminar. After taking a writing seminar on ancient magic, for example, one Penn student went on to develop his research from the class, taking additional coursework, collaborating with faculty in Penn's Classics department, and ultimately helping to curate a new exhibit at the Penn Museum entitled "Magic in the Ancient World." Currently he is working on finding and categorizing magic gems, developing new definitions—all of which he intends to include in his senior thesis.

A third issue concerning timing has to do with when to run the library workshops, and how many to run. Visits set early in the semester proved too abstract for students; those set too late felt to them like busywork. We have been experimenting with how to divide the responsibility of teaching information literacy skills, and this in part depends on the research sophistication and experience of the instructor. Our latest approach is to allow instructors and librarians to work out their own schedules. In general, experienced writing instructors introduce students to known-item searching and citation networks. When questions arise that are beyond the instructor's expertise, they contact their librarian via chat or videocast—thus modeling for students the social activity of research, which is characterized by uncertainty and cooperation—or they invite the librarian to visit the class; sometimes the best solution is for an individual student to meet one-on-one with the librarian. In general, librarians are responsible for teaching students how to generate and strategize about keyword searches and then, together, the librarians and instructors provide students with strategies for evaluating and narrowing down sources. Many of our writing instructors have observed that these sessions have over the years substantially advanced their own library research skills; in turn, librarians remark that what they learn from working with instructors and students in these semester-long relationships illuminates the complexities of teaching source-based writing. Less experienced instructors often invite librarians back for second and third class visits, underscoring the centrality and expertise of librarians in the research enterprise. In many cases, librarians develop customized materials for each of their classes, and together the instructor and librarian for a given class may come up with a range of extracurricular activities, such as trips to special collections. This structure allows instructors to remain the primary educator when it comes to citation, credibility, and plagiarism in their fields, while also introducing students to librarians as expert researchers and problem-solvers to whom they can turn throughout their academic careers.

Without doubt, the greatest challenge for all of us is that old habits die hard. Some instructors and librarians are deeply averse to the risk of not having the answers, even though uncertainty and commitment to finding answers are at the very heart of research and thus contain the richest lessons for novices. Some librarians have been doing "one-shot" library sessions for years; and of course most of our faculty have been audiences as well as arrangers of such workshops. For a few years we asked instructors to write brief transcriptions of the visits so that we could get a sense of the kinds of questions and problem-solving activities that took place during the hands-on sessions. Perusing a mound of these transcripts in an effort to gather data for this article, we were astonished to see how instructor after instructor described in great detail the first 10 or 15 scripted minutes of the workshop—during which librarians uniformly discussed such things as hours, services, features of the library website—and then wrote almost nothing about the 30 minutes of hands-on activities, reducing this to a sentence or two about how "they helped students with their questions for the remainder of the session," a testament to how teaching is still trapped in the "banking concept" of education, in which the key activity of teaching is to insert factoids into the heads of students, rather than actively engage them in authentic learning experiences (Freire, 2000).

Some librarians do not relish the chaos and gregariousness that characterize the active learning workshops; and some instructors do not like handing their classroom and authority over to the librarian. The desire on both sides to formalize the interaction, to (re) turn it to a one-shot visit with a couple of prefabricated exercises and a Q&A, is seductively familiar and predictable. Yet all agree that, when things fall into place, the workshop is an extraordinarily rich learning environment. The instructor and librarian have conferred with each other prior to the workshop; often the librarian has read the texts assigned to students; the students have come to the class ready to commence or advance their research; and as students in the workshop begin to encounter roadblocks, from the simple ("How do I tell if this is an article or a chapter in a book?") to the complex ("How do I know if this is a good source for the literature review?"), it all comes together, not only the process, but the attitude (Edelson, 1998). Everyone is listening, thinking, attempting to help each other out; there is cooperation and competition and commitment, the stuff that makes research pleasurable and engaging. Moreover, the librarian and instructor together see what students face as novice researchers; and students are able to see how experts, their librarian and their instructor, tackle research problems. Sometimes other students chime in who have already begun their research and encountered (and in some cases solved) that very problem. Each such moment is an initiation into the authentic practices and social life of research. While we know that students are actively engaging in sophisticated IL and writing skills, and we know that instructors and librarians are informing each other's approaches to research and writing, we are only beginning to explore how our collaboration may contribute to our combined fields and to the pedagogical complexity of source-based writing. It remains to be seen whether this emphasis on authentic learning experience will prove fruitful. For now, it appears to be pointing us in useful directions.

REFERENCES

Artman, M., Frisicaro-Pawlowski, E., & Monge, R. (2010). Not just one shot: Extending the dialogue about information literacy in composition classes. *Composition Studies, 38*(2), 93–110.

Association of College and Research Libraries. (2015). *Framework for Information Literacy for Higher Education* (Document ID: b910a6c4-6c8a-0d44-7dbc-a5dcbd509e3f). Washington, DC: American Library Association.

Bates, M. J. (1989). The design of browsing and berrypicking techniques for the online search interface. *Online Review, 13*(5), 407–424.

Brent, D. (2013). The research paper and why we should still care. *WPA: Writing Program Administration, 37*(1), 33–53.

Brown, C., Murphy, T. J., & Nanny, M. (2003). Turning techno-savvy into info-savvy: Authentically integrating information literacy into the college curriculum. *Journal of Academic Librarianship, 29*(6), 386–398.

Bruffee, K. A. (1993). *A short course in writing: Composition, collaborative learning, and constructive reading.* New York, NY: HarperCollins College Publishers.

Bruffee, K. A. (1999). *Collaborative learning: Higher education, interdependence, and the authority of knowledge.* Baltimore, MD: Johns Hopkins University Press.

Edelson, D. C. (1998). Realising authentic science learning through the adaptation of scientific practice. In B. J. Fraser & K. G. Tobin (Eds.), *International handbook of science education* (pp. 317–332). Dordrecht, The Netherlands: Kluwer Academic Publishers.

Elmborg, J. K. (2003). Information literacy and writing across the curriculum: Sharing the vision. *Reference Services Review, 31*(1), 68–80.

Freire, P. (2000). *Pedagogy of the Oppressed.* New York: Continuum.

Hood, C. L. (2010). Ways of research: The status of the traditional research paper assignment in first-year writing/composition courses. In *Composition Forum* (Vol. 22). Association of Teachers of Advanced Composition.

Howard, R. M., Serviss, T., & Rodrigue, T. K. (2010). Writing from sources, writing from sentences. *Writing and Pedagogy, 2*(2), 177–192.

Jacobs, H. L. M., & Jacobs, D. (2009). Transforming the one-shot library session into pedagogical collaboration: Information literacy and the English composition class. *Reference & User Services Quarterly, 49*(1), 72–82.

Larson, R. (1982). The "research paper" in the writing course: A non-form of writing. *College English, 44*(8), 811–816.

Norgaard, R. (2003). Writing information literacy: Contributions to a concept. *Reference & User Services Quarterly, 43*(2), 124–130.

Penn Museum. (2016). Penn student delves into magic . . . In the ancient world. [Press release]. Retrieved from https://www.penn.museum/information/press-room/press-releases/1049-penn-student-delves-into-magic-in-the-ancient-world

Petraglia, J. (1995). Spinning like a kite: A closer look at the pseudotransactional function of writing. *JAC: A Journal of Composition Theory, 15*(1), 19–33.

Purdue, J. (2003). Stories, not information: Transforming information literacy. *portal: Libraries and the Academy 3*(4), 653–662.

Wardle, E. (2009). "Mutt genres" and the goal of FYC: Can we help students write the genres of the university? *College Composition and Communication, 60*(4), 765–789.

CHAPTER 5

PRIORITIZING ACADEMIC INQUIRY IN THE FIRST-YEAR EXPERIENCE

Information Literacy and Writing Studies in Collaboration

Alanna Frost
Lacy Marschalk
David Cook
Michael Manasco
with Gaines Hubbell

The argument made transparent in Andrea Baer's (2016) recent book, *Information Literacy and Writing Studies in Conversation*, frames the project we describe in this chapter. We, an instructional reference librarian, the campus coordinator of student research, and two English Department faculty, recently collaborated on a first-year experience (FYE) curriculum that specifically drew from information literacy (IL) and writing studies (WS) work that articulates the dispositions demanded of a curious student to discern contextually appropriate information and credible authority, craft a written argument, and demonstrate adherence to a dynamic academic discourse community. Asked to plan the curriculum for an Honors FYE course, we chose to contribute what we each knew best. Heeding the arguments of Baer (2016) and those scholars who preceded her (Braunstein, Tobery, & Gocsik, 2016; Norgaard, 2003, 2004; Simmons, 2005), we chose to ground our curriculum in academic inquiry and designed a semester-long project that asked students to gather their own primary and diverse secondary information to answer the question "What advice would you give to first-year students?"

We were supported in our collaboration by scholars like Rolf Norgaard (2003) and Michelle H. Simmons (2005), who argue for an interdisciplinary approach to teaching information literacy. Baer (2016) specifically cites connections between the position statements of the Association of College and Research Libraries (ACRL) and the Council of Writing Program Administrators (WPA) as evidence of collaborative exigencies, arguing that they "illustrate that writing and information literacy education must be collaborative efforts that are pursued within university writing programs" (p. 87). We were further supported by IL and WS scholars' resistance to perceptions of library instruction and composition as the "places" where one learns the rules for the search and the writing, respectively. Baer (2016) refers to Norgaard's (2003) oft-cited call to challenge the "one-stop shop" concept in her assertion that the "once and done" model itself perpetuates "a perception of information literacy as being simply about search mechanics" (p. 5) and "writing as a mechanical and simple skill" (p. 8). Importantly, we found support undergirding much current IL and WS research, which works to make transparent the complexity of research and writing and to encourage pedagogies that reflect the complexity of information, discourse, genre, and inquiry. As we report in this chapter, our findings from our preliminary data analysis support our collaborative efforts. Finally, and importantly, we were supported materially, as the FYE course itself is compensated with a stipend. Thus, in this chapter, we describe the exigencies for this collaboration and describe our process and the curriculum we designed; additionally, to offer a model for investigating this partnership, we outline our methods for assessing our curriculum and discuss preliminary findings from a small sample of interview participants. We feel that our experiences and those we anecdotally describe of our students suggest the merits of such an institutional partnership.

THE COLLABORATION

At our public research university, all incoming first-year students are required to take a one-credit FYE course. The year before our collaboration began, each college, including the Honors College, was tasked with individualizing the FYE course to meet the needs of students in their majors. The first iteration of the Honors College FYE had students in split classes with their honors and home college cohorts. So they met in small honors sections for part of the time and in large lecture-style sessions with, for example, the College of Engineering part of the time. Although this sort of dual enrollment had some merits, it made it difficult to build community—one of the most important objectives of FYE—and resulted in some information being repeated between colleges while other information was missed entirely. Thus, after the inaugural semester, the Honors College dean met with FYE faculty to discuss the future of the course, and the decision was made to develop a curriculum specifically geared toward the needs of all honors students. Rather than dividing their time, the students would spend the entire semester with their Honors College peers and Honors FYE instructor. The four of us, all experienced FYE instructors, answered the dean's request for a committee to develop this new curriculum.

We decided to design the course around a semester-long group research project, which would help foster community while also allowing for the teaching and reinforcement of information literacy and academic writing. These skills are particularly important to honors students, who are required to take a first-year English seminar (EH 105) and who must complete a capstone project near the end of their undergraduate studies. Thus, we began by imagining how best to foster student engagement with the complexity that is academic inquiry. Acknowledgment of this complexity, we feel, cements arguments for IL and WS collaborations and counters pedagogical philosophies of one-time inoculations. In her apt summary of IL and WS scholarship, Baer (2016) asserts that this work "reflects how critical inquiry and knowledge creation are at the heart of both composing and information practices" (p. 11). We decided to pay particular attention to the ACRL and WPA framework statements, which work to make transparent the practices and dispositions of researchers' complex practices. Specifically, we heeded Douglas Downs and Elizabeth Wardle (2007), who argue that conducting primary research is particularly important to "clarify for students the nature of scholarly writing" (p. 562). Finally, when planning assignments, we considered scholars such as Jody Shipka (2005), who argue that students should be encouraged to present arguments using the most appropriate media and modes to persuade an audience.

We saw an opportunity to counter the "one and done" measure of library instruction typically found in FYE and composition and to support the research and writing that students produce in EH 105. EH 105, which is taken in the same semester as FYE, was instituted in part because many honors students were placing out of English Composition I and II but were underprepared for the research and writing requirements of their upper-level courses and especially for the capstone project. By having two English department faculty members, who also teach EH 105, on a committee with research and information literacy specialists, we were able to address the needs of both the composition and honors programs and bring them together in this new FYE curriculum. What we felt the FYE course could be, in conjunction with EH 105, was a dual support system for students' first introductory forays into academic inquiry—into becoming meaning-makers.

THE CURRICULUM

In order to be ready for a fall 2016 launch date, we began meeting in February 2016, and we met as often as once a week, even during the summer. From the beginning, our committee wanted to make the entire course a research "experience" rather than just several interconnected classes that happened to talk "about" research. Rather than viewing the tenets of information literacy as afterthought or supplementary content, we took advantage of this opportunity to create an inquiry-driven, exploratory course that would allow our students to become more information literate by engaging in research built around the six core frames for information literacy established by the ACRL. The *Framework*'s (2016) emphasis on information literacy concepts and abilities that empower students "as consumers and creators of information who can participate successfully in collaborative spaces" was especially attractive to our committee, as was the flexibility of the system. The frames are broad enough to capture the general, translatable concepts of research skills that a student of any discipline should hone, but also interconnected and structured enough to maintain a coherent and somewhat directed experience. As we examined the ACRL *Framework*, the fourth frame, Research as Inquiry, became our overall mantra and the thematic center of our design process.

At the same time, because we were designing an FYE course and not an "introduction to information literacy," there were specific topics that needed to be integrated into our curriculum and program objectives unique to our institution that needed to be met. Collaborative learning is strongly encouraged at our university, especially in FYE, so we knew student collaboration and community building had to be at the heart of our curriculum. We also knew the course needed to address certain academic/life skills, such as time management, and to underscore the Honors College's degree requirements, advising process, thesis/capstone project, and undergraduate research opportunities. To meet all of these objectives, we designed a semester-long group project that focused on a research question commonly found in FYE curricula: "What advice would you give to incoming first-year students?" Rather than posing this question at the end of the term, though, we wanted students to reflect on this question from day one, work together to develop an evolving thesis based on personal and experiential data, locate and evaluate sources to support their findings, and creatively present their conclusions at the end of the semester. We found that this approach served the same purpose as Shipka's (2005) "task-based multimodal framework" in that it "offer[ed] students opportunities to engage with course materials that are, at once, personally and socially relevant and intellectually rigorous" (p. 284).

On the first day of class, students were assigned the course project, placed into groups, and given a collaborative folder in Google Drive to serve as their team's information repository and workspace throughout the semester. The folder gave the students a chance to engage with one another in a way that loosely invoked the second ACRL frame, Information Creation as a Process. While this frame was not a primary focal point when designing the course, developing a collaborative, customized library of resources allowed the students to become aware of the value of having different methods of information dissemination for multiple purposes at their disposal, as implied in one of Frame 2's Dispositions. While their group members had permissions to edit and add to this folder, the other groups in class had "viewing" privileges, which encouraged students to look outside their own experiential data in the research process. For example, one of the smaller projects assigned at the beginning of the term asked the groups to adopt one of six time management models for a week. In the second week, the groups modified the model to better suit their needs, and in the third week they presented their findings to the class. The visual artifacts they generated along the way—including scans of planner pages, screenshots of calendar applications, and self-designed spreadsheets and time management tools—were placed in their folders, where this information could be used by other groups interested in advising future first-year students on the importance of time management. The time management module, along with a later assignment about academic advising and degree planning, allowed the students a means of developing and sharing a rudimentary understanding of experiential and primary data early in the semester. While we addressed primary data more thoroughly later in the course, these "data collection" activities were helpful in demonstrating the impact of their own observations in the latter stages of the research process.

These early modules were then followed by six weeks of intensive information literacy training; the "one-and-done" library session from previous years was reconceived and expanded into three instructional sessions, each followed by a praxis week. The research sessions were designed in a way that not only taught basic navigation skills of our library resources but also enabled and empowered the students to seek out, navigate, and evaluate resources on the Web. In the first session, students were brought to the library for a librarian-led introduction to basic information literacy concepts, including differentiating between popular and scholarly content and giving attribution to others' ideas. This session, which included an introduction to library resources and the concept of information "paywalls," also encouraged the students to examine their own information privilege as university affiliates with access to expensive electronic databases. The second IL session, led by the FYE instructor using librarian-designed materials, explored concepts related to the ACRL's first, fifth, and sixth frames: Authority Is Constructed and Contextual, Scholarship as Conversation, and Searching as Strategic Exploration. Our committee found these frames most useful in their emphasis on encouraging students to question traditional notions of information "authority," to view themselves as researchers entering into a scholarly conversation, and to consider thoughtfully matching the correct resource with the appropriate information need. The third IL session, also taught by the FYE instructor and entitled "Thinking Outside the Journal," challenged students to consider sources outside of the curated "library" experience, including the use of think tank reports and raw data sets. This session also afforded the opportunity to further discuss the concept of primary data and to consider how students' own documented experiences fit in thus far in the context of academic conversation.

By the end of this inquiry-focused research project, the groups had been exposed to a blend of peer-supplied experiential data, traditional academic sources, and a variety of public-domain information types. The *Framework*'s flexibility and concept-driven design philosophies provided our committee with enough structure to implement the research-focused course we had envisioned. It was also invaluable in framing the acquisition and refinement of research skills in the context of core, threshold information literacy concepts that our interdisciplinary group of honors students could apply beyond the First-Year Experience.

METHOD

In addition to designing the course, we were interested in measuring its success. To see where students stood in terms of a baseline understanding of information literacy and its applications in conducting research, a pre- and postsemester survey was sent to all eligible first-year composition students. Institutional review board (IRB) approval was applied for and granted by the university's IRB committee. The student populations were both honors and nonhonors students. Honors students participated in the Honors First-Year Experience (FYE) curriculum and were enrolled in English composition for honors students (EH 105). Nonhonors students participated in the FYE curriculum designed by the college in which they majored and were enrolled in English composition 1 or 2 (EH 101S, EH 101, or EH 102). The surveys were made up of both Likert questions to gauge students' feelings about research and multiple-choice questions to assess their understanding of key concepts. The surveys were strictly voluntary, and unfortunately we did not get productive response rates. We were, however, able to use convenience sampling to recruit a small number (N = 14) of interview participants (both honors and nonhonors). The students were sent an e-mail inviting them to participate in the interview, and if they expressed interest in participating, a member of the research team answered any questions they had about participation and arranged the interview. In order to reduce the perception that the students' grades depended upon participation or specific interview responses, each student was interviewed by a researcher who was not their instructor.

For the purposes of this chapter, we offer a discussion of the themes that emerged from our honors students' pre- and postsemester interviews. Our sample size here, too, is small (N = 6), but our purpose was to explore methods of qualifying students' information literacy and to create a dialogue with subjects about how they conduct research and how their research process evolved over the course of the semester. We find, at least anecdotally, that we can offer results in these specific terms.

PRESEMESTER INTERVIEWS: RESEARCH = SEARCHING THE INTERNET AND WRITING

The first interviews took place early in the semester before the FYE information literacy sessions and before the EH 105 research essay was written. We crafted presemester questions that would help us gauge the participants' understanding of the research process at the outset of their university careers. We were curious about their existing knowledge of academic research and what kinds of research projects—if any—they had been assigned in high school. Essentially, we wanted a baseline of participants' conceptual frameworks for approaching an assignment, engaging with scholarship, and reporting their findings. As such, we asked students to explain their research process and then prompted them to discuss that process in terms of a particular project. Finally, we asked how they felt about conducting research. The themes that emerged from our questions indicate that, for these participants, "research" specifically indicated searching for source material and producing a document.

What we feel that the themes from our presemester interviews touch on are the participants' narrow or limited understanding of research. Our initial interviews offered participants limited time to explain their processes, but we were most interested in investigating students' "sense" of their own research concepts. Thus, in terms of our conclusion of the limits of that "sense," participants' explanations of the research process revealed that, for these six students, "research" *is* the search for information, and for five of the participants, "research" *is* the search and the written product. Indeed, the immediate response of five of the six participants to our first question, "Describe your research process," was to explain their information-searching strategies. Four of those participants specifically detailed the search engines they use (e.g., conduct "a basic Google search") or strategies they had been taught (e.g., "look for EDUs"). The one participant who did not directly complete the "process" question with her Internet-search practices responded with the second most common concept that "research is the written product." As she offered, "First I try to formulate where I am going to be coming from. What my thesis will be, roughly, and what the course of the essay will take, so introduction and conclusion and the research that I do will make up the body paragraphs." A second participant offered a similar "outlining" process in her interview; a third followed her discussion of her Internet search with a very specific, "Then of course you would use the MLA citation and all that, and quote your references throughout your paper."

These preliminary presemester themes, the students' sentiment that research equals searching the Internet and writing, cohere directly with the work that both librarian and composition instructors prepare to do with first-year students. They position our understanding of "where students are" in terms of an understanding of research that equates it with information gathering and reporting. That students are immersed in "find-report" research concepts makes some sense. Indeed, as we assert in the introduction to this chapter, much of the scholarship of both IL and WS is framed by the exigency that we remain mired in public and educational views of library-pedagogy and the composition program as the "one-stop shop" for, respectively, "research" and "writing" skills acquisition. We can suspect, then, that the students we have interviewed have experienced library and writing instruction that coheres with the very perceptions IL and WS are engaged in challenging.

But of course, ultimately, we are asking students to construct their own meaning from vastly complex information and by employing complex rhetorical practices. We want first-year students to engage in this complexity of meaning making and not simply complete the find-report process they may imagine. Constructing knowledge, making one's own meaning from one's own and others' data and arguments, frames all the work we reviewed for this chapter. As Baer (2016) asserts, the goal of the researcher's "writing and source-based research" is "ultimately communication about the relationship between one's own ideas and those presented by others" (p. 4). In the introduction to the ACRL *Framework*, its creators offer that "[s]tudents have a greater role and responsibility in creating new knowledge" (ACRL intro), and as Simmons (2005) argues, "facilitating students' understanding that they can be participants in scholarly conversations encourages them to think of research not as a task of collecting information but instead as a task of *constructing meaning* [emphasis added]" (p. 299). In her research on the differing epistemological stances of student and experienced academic writers, Ellen Barton (1993) refers to the work of Carl Bereiter and Marlene Scardamalito (1983), who found that students' writing involves "knowledge-telling" while experienced academic writing involves "knowledge-making" (p. 765). This work has informed our understanding of our participants' reflections on their research process. At least preliminarily, these students' find-report responses support a knowledge-telling view of research.

POSTSEMESTER INTERVIEW: RESEARCH = CRITICAL SEARCH, AND WRITING = KNOWLEDGE MAKING

The second interview took place at the end of the semester, and participants were asked to bring their research essays to the interview and to explain the research processes they used to complete the essays. In our postsemester interviews, we worked to determine how students' research concepts had changed over the course of the semester and as they completed their final honors composition essays. We asked them how they approached the research for this project; how they found, selected, and/or rejected material; and finally, how they felt their understanding of research had changed. The themes that emerged from these second interviews indicate that their research, in terms of the search for information, had become more critical, and they were beginning to understand the complex knowledge-making nature of research.

When the students described the process they engaged to research their final essays, we found that participants described search strategies more critical than their presemester references to an Internet search. Students demonstrated their critical strategies by, in five of six cases, referring to productive library-based and public databases and by making reference to engaging in an iterative process of research. Students expressed confidence in using library-supported tools and resources, such as our university's OneSearch discovery service, as a productive resource for academic articles or JSTOR for literary criticism specifically (mentioned by three of six). Further, four of six students made references to the iterative nature of their research. For these students, their research process seems to have evolved from simply finding materials to support a static argument. One student explained that he now understood that he didn't need to find material that precisely matched his own topic. He explained that his interest in "self and other" in a novel could be explored by exhausting a search on "the self and other in *Ender's Game*" and then by searching for material on "self and other" and "*Ender's Game*" separately and applying the concepts to support his original claims. Another student, working on an ethnographic study of a theater performance, explained the search adjustment she engaged during her process:

> First, I just started searching ethnographic theater, kind of just broad, kind of just before I started doing my actual research. So I was finding articles that were geared towards my studying actors rather than the student community, so I started off with those, and then after I'd done my primary research, I went back and looked for more articles that were more focused on autoethnography and based on student collaboration.

In these cases, students' find-report processes had clearly been complicated by their first-semester's research.

Most interestingly, in five of six cases, the students' understanding of research, in terms of reporting their own findings, seems to have evolved from reporting the information of others into a process of making their own arguments. In terms of the knowledge construction our curriculum was meant to facilitate, five of six students described their processes and what they had learned in terms that indicated their understanding of knowledge-making, as opposed to knowledge-telling. Our final question, about how their research had evolved, elicited interesting responses in this regard. One response hinted about an evolution to a knowledge-making philosophy: "I had to do most of the connections and the research, instead of branching my points off of other people's research," while another more directly indicated this growth: "I think it's more shifted from that view of taking what already exists and summarizing into more of a using what already exists to support a new idea." In at least two cases, engagement with the variety of information-gathering we asked of students in the FYE curriculum, and specifically primary data, seems to have influenced their different research perspectives. One student referred to a survey he and his FYE team distributed to their friends: "it wasn't a huge sample size, but how people with larger sample sizes, the work they have to do to comb through all that data and find what they want, it was definitely interesting to see that side of it, rather than just the . . . [l]ook at a source and pull up some stuff." Finally, another student directly cited her primary research work: "I guess research that I've done in the past, I haven't been able to do primary research. It's all been just taking secondary resources and pulling them together to kind of recite things that have already been said. But then I got to look at secondary resources and then provide my own research as well. So that was cool." These students relate a research process clearly more complex than that which they articulated at the outset of the semester.

CONCLUSION

In their references to the iterative and knowledge-making nature of research, four of six honors students demonstrated that their research concepts were more complex than at the outset of the semester, when they seemed to equate research with a static research-report process. We are excited by these cursory findings. We feel the process we engaged in, of collaboratively planning the FYE curriculum to employ an inquiry frame and of investigating our students' progress, offers evidence that the FYE intervention can only reinforce what the composition programs do and, further, that the collaborative efforts of library and composition faculty offer a particularly salient relationship in terms of students' sustained education in academic inquiry.

REFERENCES

Baer, A. (2016). *Information literacy and writing studies in conversation: Reenvisioning library-writing program connections.* Duluth, MN: Litwin Books.

Barton, E. L. (1993). Evidentials, argumentation, and epistemological stance. *College English, 55*(7), 745–769.

Bereiter, C., & Scardamalito, M. (1983). Does learning to write have to be so difficult? In A. Freedman, I. Pringle, & J. Yalden (Eds.), *Learning to write: First language/second language* (pp. 20–33). New York, NY: Longman.

Braunstein, L., Tobery, C., & Gocsik, K. (2016). Approximating the university: The information literacy practices of novice researchers. *Dartmouth Library Staff Publications and Presentations*, 4. Dartmouth Digital Commons, https://digitalcommons.dartmouth.edu/dlstaffpubs/4

Downs, D., & Wardle, E. (2007). Teaching about writing, righting misconceptions: (Re)envisioning "first-year composition" as "introduction to writing studies." *College Composition & Communication, 58*(4), 552–584.

Framework for information literacy for higher education. (2016). Retrieved from http://www.ala.org/acrl/standards/ilframework

Norgaard, R. (2003). Writing information literacy: Contributions to a concept. *Reference & User Services Quarterly, 43*(2), 124–130.

Norgaard, R. (2004). Writing information literacy in the classroom: Pedagogical enactments and implications. *Reference & User Services Quarterly, 43*(3), 220–226.

Shipka, J. (2005). A multimodal task-based framework for composing. *College Composition and Communication, 57*(2): 277–306.

Simmons, M. H. (2005). Librarians as disciplinary discourse mediators: Using genre theory to move toward critical information literacy. *portal: Libraries and the Academy, 5*(3), 297–311.

CHAPTER 6

PRESSING THE RESET BUTTON ON (INFORMATION) LITERACY IN FYW

Opportunities for Library and Writing Program Collaboration in Research-Based Composition

William T. FitzGerald
Zara T. Wilkinson

Plus ça change, plus c'est la même chose. The more things change, the more they stay the same. It's a sentiment relevant in times of change in relations between university writing programs and libraries. With anything new comes a sense of *déjà vu*. Haven't we been here before? We bear this sentiment in mind as we implement new models of collaboration between the first-year writing program and the library at Rutgers University–Camden. Much as we might wish to begin anew, we feel the tug of inertia. Still, we say, things will be different this time.

In this chapter, we report on efforts to reshape cocurricular cooperation following a change of leadership in our respective programs. This change comes at a time when new approaches to literacy and undergraduate research hold promise to invest writing, especially research-based writing, with renewed possibilities for student agency and success. These include a shift from outcomes and standards (in their focus on ends) to ecological models of development over time and in specific environments, as articulated in paradigm-breaking documents such as the 2015 Association of College and Research Libraries' (ACRL) *Framework for Information Literacy for Higher Education* and the 2011 Council of Writing Program Administrators' (WPA) *Framework for Success in Postsecondary Writing*. In light of local and national developments, we find it an opportune moment to hit the reset button on information literacy in first-year writing.

Like others working at the intersection of academic and information literacy, we come to our task aware of persistent challenges in teaching students "how to use the library," especially in writing papers. We know the critiques, substantial and long-standing, leveled against the traditional research paper (Fister, 2011; Hood, 2010; Larson, 1982) extending back to Larson (1982) as a "non-form of writing" (p. 811) as well as arguments for its redeeming value (Brent, 2013). We identify as "pro" research, even in first-year composition, if not pro "research paper." Indeed, we find arguments for undergraduate research as a high-impact educational practice (Kuh, 2008) compelling and begin our collaboration in the belief that first-year writing is foundational for experiences of research.

But first a bit of background. Librarian Zara Wilkinson and Associate Professor of English Bill FitzGerald came to positions of program leadership only recently. In fall 2015, Bill became the director of the Writing Program, whose home is the Department of English. Bill came to Rutgers–Camden in 2006 as a specialist in rhetoric and composition. Early in his career, Bill helped lead a large upper-level writing program at another university in a position that involved significant collaboration with library instructional staff. In 2016, Zara took over as coordinator of the Robeson Library's instructional outreach to the Writing Program. Zara joined the Paul Robeson Library in 2012 as a reference and instruction librarian. Her liaison responsibilities include several Humanities departments, including English. Before assuming these new responsibilities at Rutgers–Camden, Zara and Bill applied their expertise on different sides of the equation to help students with research-based writing. Undergraduate research and mentoring has played a major role in Bill's teaching for years. More recently, Bill (with Joseph Bizup) revised the classic guide, *The Craft of Research,* 4th ed., a text that makes heuristics of research accessible to novices.

Harnessing the untapped potential of research-based writing was central to Bill's decision to direct the Writing Program for three years or longer. At Rutgers–Camden, first-year writing is a required two-course sequence, English 101 and English 102. Additionally, the preliminary courses of English 098 and English 099 support developing writers. The primary focus of English 101 is writing as argument; the primary focus of English 102 is writing as research. This basic structure did not change when Bill became director. However, the content of each course and the program's relations with the library did.

Prior to fall 2015, both composition courses were largely theme-based, involving a mix of literary and nonliterary texts used as sites for analysis (in 101) or as a springboard for library-based research. In 101, typical assignments were largely skill based, for example, perform a close reading of a text, formulate a thesis-driven interpretation supported by textual evidence. Under this scenario, the library played no role; indeed, students might even be discouraged from relying on "outside" sources in their writing. By contrast, English 102 moved students from modes of argument (e.g., comparison/contrast) in an early assignment to a "research paper" incorporating at least three outside sources. Typically, papers were anchored in assigned course texts. Students would extend a theme in a research project. In this second-semester course, students came to the library for a "one-shot" instructional session after identifying a "topic" for an annotated bibliography, a precursor to a final paper. Under this syllabus, most students first encounter the library and librarians in late spring of the first year. (Large numbers of our students arrive as transfers, after completing composition courses at area community colleges.)

When Zara and Bill met in summer 2015 to discuss relations between the writing program and the library (though we knew each other already), library instruction was overseen by a longtime librarian near to retirement. As Bill walked his library colleagues through a new syllabus soon to be implemented, a basic consideration arose that was not front and center initially: When will students first come to the library and under what premises? It was illuminating for Bill to learn that though he had imagined a more robust approach to research in revamped comp courses, he hadn't thought through the role of library instruction or, more broadly, the place of information literacy in the new curriculum. In the ensuing "pilot" year, Zara and Bill would frequently confer on more intentional collaboration than had previously been the case. If there is one difference between then and now, it is the insight that the writing program *must* work closely with the library to articulate and deliver on meaningful learning outcomes. Here, we sketch ongoing efforts to realize that objective in the near and long term.

Any writing program that defers "writing with sources" until late in a second semester misses opportunities to bring students into university life (Brent, 2013, p. 38) and risks a crucial loss of student engagement. Although correlation certainly does not equal causation, several recent studies have identified positive relationships between students' use of the library and their academic success, particularly in their first year (Haddow & Joseph, 2010; Murray, Ireland, & Hackathorn, 2015; Soria, Fransen, & Nackerud, 2017). As one such study found, "library use—of any kind—was predictive of freshman-to-sophomore and sophomore-to-junior retention, with freshman library users being nine times more likely to be retained than nonusers" (Murray et al., 2015, p. 639). In devising new curricula, broader notions of academic and information literacy drive our decisions on structuring and supporting writing assignments. In our new syllabi, students are introduced to the library in 101. In 102, students engage in research in ways that go beyond the bounds of the traditional research paper. In the next sections, we describe the role of library instruction and information literacy in our composition courses. We trace a change in focus from acquiring skills (e.g., distinguishing scholarly from popular sources, citing sources in a specific documentation style) to a more dynamic, rhetorical understanding of research as a form of engaging sources and readers in a conversation.

TO THE LIBRARY IN ENGLISH 101

A primary objective of college composition, we think, is to introduce students to the resources of academic libraries. But what notions of literacy govern this objective, which admittedly is not universal? Indeed, it's possible to distinguish information literacy from other literacies, as we do to an extent when librarians, experts in information literacy, guide students through an instructional module on "library day." It's also possible to teach students to write *from* sources (rather than *with* sources) by integrating and citing source material, independent of *finding* or *evaluating* sources. We thus recognize possibilities for overlap as well as disjuncture between information literacy and academic literacy. As Bill and Zara discussed strategies for more intentional collaboration between the writing program and the library, this overlap became a site to intuit. In practical terms, it meant agreeing that students should visit the library in the first semester, in 101.

While this move may seem obvious, it was not immediately clear what broad ends it would serve. Students will go (or, depending on one's perspective, come) to the library, but once there what will they do? Zara and Bill concluded that this initial visit would not be tied to a specific research task; rather, it would serve to orient students to the library itself as a hub for information. While there's only so much that can be accomplished in a session lasting, often, just 50 minutes, decoupling a general introduction to the library from a focus on research has its advantages.

On the plus side, this orientation gives library instructional staff a full period to present the library on its own terms, with due attention to its range of resources. That range gets truncated when the goal of instruction is to move students swiftly to investigating a topic. At this point in their career, if they've been to the library at all, students may only be acquainted with computer terminals used for purposes other than research. In English 101, students are exposed to the library and to librarians without the stress of a major research assignment, providing an early opportunity to demonstrate that the library is a helpful, welcoming place. In her groundbreaking discussion of library anxiety, Constance A. Mellon (1986) encouraged librarians to emphasize helpfulness alongside library resources, allowing an instruction session to double as what she called a "warmth seminar" (p. 164). Of course, the flip side to getting students into the library ahead of a research task is that they benefit little from the exposure. It was thus important to stress that this initial visit in 101 was paired with a second visit in 102, when the focus would be on actual research.

The absence, historically, of a class-sponsored visit to the library for students in composition was something we sought to address squarely in a course redesign. We were especially mindful that the composition sequence satisfied general education "foundational" requirements and was specifically dedicated to learning outcomes in information literacy. Beyond the immediate purposes of a writing course, Bill and Zara believed that 101 and 102 were committed to preparing students for information literacy expectations beyond the first year. Soria and colleagues (2017) found that those students who attended library classes "were more likely than their peers to earn a higher grade point average by the end of their fall semester" (p. 20). Similarly, "first-year students who used web-based library services (like electronic journals, databases, and the library website) were more likely than their peers to be engaged in academic activities, develop academic skills, focus on scholarly work, and have higher grade point averages" (p. 20). Whether these results reveal a cause of academic improvement or merely the habits of academically strong students, they suggest that introducing first-year students to the library and its services have benefits that may continue throughout their academic careers. Thus, the earlier that students have a hands-on experience with (and *in*) the library, the better.

In planning for fall 2015 and beyond, Zara and Bill decided that the new library orientation sessions for 101 would occur in weeks 8 through 11, or between late October and Thanksgiving break in fall semesters. This period coincides with the beginning of a series of linked assignments in 101 that anticipate a need for research but do not make research an end in itself. By this point in 101, students have completed three assignments, none requiring sources beyond assigned texts. For the remaining assignments, however, students are required to draw on source materials. The first of these linked assignments ("My Take") is an open letter with a topic and an audience of a student's choosing. To pen this letter, students must keep in mind that this same topic is the basis of the remaining two assignments. In the second of the linked units ("To Think That . . ."), students represent counterarguments to a position they voiced in their open letter. (They don't write in feigned opposition; rather, they identify the grounds, or warrants, by which others may reasonably disagree.) For the final assignment ("Take Two"), students recast that open letter into an "academic" essay with evidence in support of claims and recognition of alternative perspectives. This remediated open letter is as a draft submission to *The Scarlet Review,* Rutgers–Camden's undergraduate journal of first-year writing.

These last two assignments in 101 send students *back* to the library after their orientation session and propel them to consider a range of appropriate sources, scholarly or not. The linked units thus explore the nature of information and credibility. At the same time, students are not asked to produce a conventional research paper with a minimum number of sources or even master the mechanics of citation. Learning to properly cite sources in MLA or APA style is not a focus of the unit. Instead, they engage with sources as a step beyond taking a position in a effort to construct evidence-based arguments. Through examples and instructor-led exercises, students see how their civic arguments in an open letter are further shaped by expectations of academic standards of argument.

Neither Zara nor Bill think 101 is a satisfactory end for our students' engagement with critical information literacy (Elmborg, 2006) and academic research. Fortunately, the first course is an appropriate *entry,* and a base on which to build in a second semester.

INTERLUDE: BETWEEN SEMESTERS

In many ways, 102 echoes the assignment arc of 101. Students begin our second writing course with a turn to personal writing in a unit on literacy narratives. A second unit puts students in the role of researchers to produce a "profile of a discourse community." A third unit, fully half the course, is devoted to a research project with several stages and deliverables. Finally, students complete a digital portfolio to showcase revised work across one or two semesters. The explicit and primary objective is to give every student an authentic experience of research.

To meet that objective, we conclude that there is no "one size fits all" approach to research, lest we devolve into teaching formulaic genres like the "research paper" whose implicit goal is to serve as a platform for demonstrating measurable skills. Like others, we wish to go "beyond mechanics" in the teaching of academic and information literacy (Margolin & Hayden, 2015). As collaborators in teaching research-based writing, Zara and Bill are influenced by pedagogical movements emphasizing the progression of learning in "communities of practice" (Lave & Wenger, 1998) and the cultivation of distinct habits of mind over the acquisition of concrete skills. Such notions provide a common language to describe our goals and a common motive for collaboration.

In the discipline of writing studies (an alternative name for composition), the notion of "threshold concepts" has gained a foothold as a way to summarize the core understanding that separates novices from experts in a field (Meyer and Land, 2005). This notion suggests that in acquiring expert knowledge, whether driving a big rig, practicing law, or mastering an academic field, we pass through transformational stages that can be likened to crossing a threshold. Once learned, threshold concepts can't be unlearned. Yet, while in the liminal space of learning, they are forms of "troublesome knowledge" confounding naive notions typically held by nonexperts (p. 377).

The notion of threshold concepts has energized writing studies in recent year. A recent book, *Naming What We Know: Threshold Concepts of Writing* (Adler-Kassner & Wardle, 2015), gathers a team of writing studies scholars to crowdsource 37 core concepts—the disciplinary knowledge of the field. Under several major headings, these concepts animate the teaching of writing and the administration of writing programs. One macro-concept (1.0) is that "writing is a social and a rhetorical activity"; a related micro-concept (1.1) is that "writing is a knowledge-making activity." Under a second macro-concept (2.0), "Writing speaks to situations through recognizable forms," is a micro-concept (2.6), "Texts get their meaning from other texts." These are working principles that those trained in writing studies bring to their profession. To some extent, those who learn to write successfully in any domain intuit variations on these principles even if they lack a vocabulary to express them. It is not that students in a given writing course *must* be taught these concepts explicitly. However, certain concepts *can* be introduced to demystify or correct notions that limit understanding or impede progress.

Thus, in teaching research-based writing, it helps for instructors to keep in mind that "writing is a knowledge-*making* activity" and not, as students may assume, a knowledge-*reporting* activity. Misunderstanding by students (or instructors) of the nature of research as an act of knowledge creation leads to formulaic efforts like the traditional research paper. Yet once students see writing as contributing to knowledge (if only, early on, to *their* knowledge) they can move beyond insipid forms aimed to show a teacher that they have learned to find and represent information. A focus on information-related skills cannot in itself help students see the larger paradigm of knowledge creation in which such skills are productive tools. At issue in writing pedagogy across the K–16 spectrum is to what extent skills can be learned independently of the spheres in which they are productive.

As Zara and Bill have discovered, similar constructs are shaping their respective fields. In information literacy, the *Framework for Information Literacy for Higher Education*, adopted by the Association of College and Research Libraries (ACRL), likewise recognizes threshold concepts as instrumental for learning. The *Framework* posits six "frames": (1) Authority Is Constructed and Textual, (2) Information Creation as a Process, (3) Information Has Value, (4) Research as Inquiry, (5) Scholarship as Conversation, (6) Searching as Strategic Exploration. For each frame, the document identifies "knowledge practices" and "dispositions" integral to that frame. For example, included under Research as Inquiry are these knowledge practices: the ability to "formulate questions for research based on information gaps or on reexamination of existing, possibly conflicting, information; determine an appropriate scope of investigation [and] deal with complex research by breaking complex questions into simple ones." Equally important are dispositions associated with a given frame. Again under Research as Inquiry, the ACRL text asserts that "learners who are developing their information literate abilities" must "consider research as open-ended exploration and engagement with information; appreciate that a question may appear to be simple but still disruptive and important to research; value intellectual curiosity in developing questions and learning new investigative methods" and six additional habits of mind, such as "persistence" and "intellectual humility," or inclinations, such as "seek appropriate help when needed" or "follow ethical and legal guidelines" (*Framework*).

These dispositions find an analog in a similarly titled document in writing instruction, *Framework for Success in Postsecondary Writing*, produced jointly by the Council of Writing Program Administrators (CWPA), the National Council of Teachers of English (NCTE), and the National Writing Project (NWP). This 2011 text considers notions of college readiness with an emphasis on necessary "habits of mind," including curiosity, persistence, creativity, and flexibility, with such habits to be fostered through "writing, reading, and critical analysis." As in the ARCL's *Framework*, the objective is not to teach specific concepts but to chart how learners move from peripheral participation to more central participation in communities of practice. They do so by naturalizing relevant knowledge practices and normalizing relevant dispositions. This process takes time, but not *just* time. It also takes deliberate scaffolding and some explicit teaching of concepts. Especially, we think, it takes carefully designed learning experiences that bring students into the liminal spaces of the activity systems in which critical threshold concepts like "information has value" and "writing is a knowledge-making activity" are experienced.

BEYOND THE RESEARCH PAPER IN 102

Overall, Bill and Zara endorse the "frameworks" approach to information literacy and writing instruction. In particular, we find the notion of threshold concepts useful in imagining the potential for instruction to spur development in multiple literacies. But a commitment to a model of learning does not lead directly to a curriculum, let alone to collaboration between writing instructors and librarians. Enacting a shared vision of literacy instruction depends on multiple factors, not least on finding ways to "bureaucratize" that vision with forms for collaboration. In most respects, this burden lies with writing programs to (1) fashion a course of study responsive to literacy expectations implicit in constructs of "information" and "research," and (2) reach out to the library as a partner in pedagogy.

At Rutgers–Camden, as we have noted, literacy and research are foregrounded, with specific units in 102 giving students opportunities to engage with their own literacy development and "real" research. There's a risk that such opportunities will be missed, given the challenge of moving learning and instruction from well-trod paths. There are reasons why the traditional research paper and one-shot library session persist, despite recognized limitations, just as there are reasons to worry that changes to these institutional staples will be largely superficial. We recognize the challenge of change.

The most visible change at the level of collaboration is a decision to require *two* instructional visits to the library, the first in 101 and the second in 102. If the goal in 101 is to bring students to the library as part of a broad commitment to information literacy, the goal in 102 is to move students beyond exposure and toward specific research-oriented goals. This goal is a work in progress, but a commitment to dialogue and collaboration is instrumental to meeting it. For maintaining an instructional partnership is just the beginning of a process to discern how best to support the overlapping domains of information literacy, writing, and undergraduate research. Zara and Bill recognize that the mere fact of a second instructional visit to "do research" is no guarantee of advancement. At issue is what broader learning goals are served by aligning writing instruction with information literacy. Bill and Zara agreed it was necessary to go "beyond the research paper" in 102 if larger literacy goals were to be met.

At a distance, our "new" library instruction in 102 looks much like the old. Early in the third unit (dedicated to research), roughly mid-semester, students come to the library to hone search strategies and vetting strategies for information they find. Guided by library staff, they learn to distinguish "degrees" of sources (primary, secondary, tertiary) and scholarly from popular sources. At this time, they are introduced to specialized databases and other reference tools and to the notion of "bread crumbs" in using one source to locate others. Ideally, students come to see research as an iterative process, rather than a linear one, in moving from a topic to a research question to an arguable claim supported by available evidence. By this effort, we hope students go beyond thinking of research as simply providing backup for positions they already hold but lack the authority to claim on their own.

Our approach uses terms and strategies from *The Craft of Research* (Booth, Colomb, Williams, & Bizup, 2016), a text that puts research into the context of contributing to an ongoing, critical conversation, if not necessarily an academic one. Bill (with Joe Bizup) recently updated this classic guide, and it serves as a foundational text in 102. Our intention is to teach not the research *paper*, but research *process*. This process includes writing up the results of research to share with a community of readers, ideally an audience beyond the instructor, as well as practices of inquiry and "engaging sources" (a chapter title in *Craft*).

To be clear, this understanding of the research process doesn't just *happen* after one or more instructional sessions. For it to occur, the model of research that shapes our curriculum must actively push against reductive notions embodied in the "school genre" of the research paper, with a prescribed number of "outside" sources (though *never* Wikipedia) and a slate of predictable topics (Bean, 1996). The research paper, in untold numbers across disciplines, is conceived by both students and instructors as a simulacrum suitable for learning the mechanics of research for use one day, perhaps, in *real* research. So conceived, the fruits of information literacy wither on the vine; "research" becomes a desultory ticking of boxes: scholarly journal, *check;* MLA format, *check*.

Note again our words of caution (to ourselves) that begin this essay. Zara and Bill, like our counterparts elsewhere, cannot simply ordain that meaningful practices of research and information literacy take root. Even the sage advice in *The Craft of Research* cannot easily prevent superficial approaches to "source-based writing" (Howard, Serviss, & Rodrigue, 2010, p. 188). The Citation Project found that students in first-year writing engage secondary sources quite superficially, typically referencing material only from the first few pages of a source and rarely employing summary in favor of quotation, acceptable and unacceptable paraphrase (Jamieson, Howard, & Serviss, 2010).

We make no bold claims of success; we only express a desire to embed notions of literacy in a more expansive, and ecological, framework than our previous models. We do so to promote a rhetorical sensibility in our students, a disposition to perceive oneself as having agency in one's learning and within a broader sphere of social action. Bill and Zara see our task as at once academic *and* civic in import: to introduce students to practices and habits of mind of the university *and* to underscore their own participation (and the university's participation) in a wider ecology, not just as consumers of knowledge but contributors as well.

Make no mistake, we're talking about first-year students; much professionalizing lies ahead. All the more reason to engage a flow of ideas and discourse that is not narrowly focused in academic disciplines but oriented to norms of civic argument. We concur with Wardle (2009), who maintains that the research paper in first-year composition does not help students meet future disciplinary norms. We do not place those hopes in the research-based writing we sponsor in 101 and 102. The broader engagement we imagine involves, as we have noted, a more expansive approach to research than is typically experienced in a first-year writing course in the form of "going to the library." In implementing principles articulated in both "frameworks" texts for our programs, we look to curricular and pedagogical decisions that put research front and center.

At a curricular level, perhaps the most significant intervention is the creation of the unit "Profile of a Discourse Community" as the second major project of 102. In this ethnographic unit, students engage in various types of primary research to investigate a community to which they belong or otherwise have access. They observe, collect materials, interview members, and conduct surveys to better understand how their object of study *is* a discourse community, and hence uses modes and genres of communication (text, talk, and other media) to further its objectives. The assignment puts students into the role of "researcher," applying definitions from Swales (1990), Gee (1989), and others in ways that foreground their agency as contributors to knowledge. To produce this 5–6 page essay, they learn to pose a research question (why is *this* group a discourse community?) and apply methods of data collection and analysis. They learn to recognize expertise and authority and to sort out conflicting accounts in data they collect. Indeed, they learn to transform information (assembled through fieldwork) into evidence that supports their reading of a cultural practice. The assignment underscores the fact that research, understood as a practice of systematic inquiry accountable to communal norms, is something that students *can* do and, indeed, have *already* done before they begin the third unit of 102, focused on research.

This third unit returns students to a more familiar stance of research in dialogue with sources largely obtained through libraries and the Internet. (But other approaches are possible.) By now, however, they have conducted *primary* research in a focused inquiry emphasizing the ACRL frame Information Has Value. The (re)turn to *secondary* research likewise reinforces notions of Scholarship as Conversation (*Framework*) rather than underscores implicit dependence on authoritative sources to make one's argument. Here, we can turn to several optional texts that extend the structure of inquiry articulated in *Craft of Research*. In particular, many instructors continue to use *They Say/I Say* (Graff, Birkenstein, & Durst, 2006) for its advice on how to engage with source material. (This text was required in the previous version of 102.) Some instructors turn to "BEAM: A Rhetorical Vocabulary for Teaching Research-Based Writing" to help students understand what roles the sources they engage can play in their own arguments: B(ackground), E(xhibit), A(rgument), and M(ethod) (Bizup, 2008). Bizup's heuristic, applied to an intermediate assignment of an annotated bibliography summarizing four to eight sources, helps to minimize the "cherry picking" of convenient material from sources in favor of more strategic models of dialogue.

We hope that students find themselves in "threshold" spaces where they begin to see research and inquiry as forms of conversation among agents with differing motives, subjectivities, and degrees of expertise. Ideally, they approach the tasks in this unit and the course as a whole through the construct of apprenticeship. This is an invitation we can't expect students to accept fully at this early stage, however. Most will remain in at best a liminal state, still attached to notions and identities that mark them as outsiders to academic discourse, yet perhaps open to the value of research as a door-opening skill set. Breakthrough moments occur when students see themselves as novices on a path to expertise.

When students return to the library for that second instructional session in 102, after their first visit in 101, they've already engaged in independent research and have read early chapters of *The Craft of Research*. Especially, they've considered the essential progression of research—from topic to question to problem (i.e., a question that others also want answered) to sources—that structures *The Craft of Research*. Our students come to the library soon after they've identified a topic and begun to formulate a research question (Nutefall & Ryder, 2010). We hope that both classroom and library instruction take students beyond "finding information on a topic" to the ACRL frame Searching as Strategic Exploration.

Here, even the best-laid plans go awry, as inexperienced researchers confront the complexities and constraints, or "mess," of research (Rickly, 2007). In truth, there's little time in a semester for students to gain adequate expertise on any topic, make sense of a surfeit of information, and contribute substantially to a conversation. It can take years in many cases. It can be hard to spot bias and reliability in information to mount informed arguments on complex issues. At best, students can agree or disagree with some claims. We have no illusions that students can avoid entirely the many pitfalls on the road to information literacy. Yet we also think well-supported students can succeed, in the main, through heuristics for problem-posing and problem-solving in the context of information literacy and rhetorical approaches to argumentation.

An aid to reaching these goals is stronger collaboration between writing instructors and their library counterparts. Zara and Bill further concluded that a missing element in relations prior to our involvement was dialogue ahead of a class visit. Often, a cleavage exists between the writing class instructor and library instruction. Bill and Zara decided that several weeks before a scheduled visit, instructors will meet with library instructional staff to discuss the design and pace of their course. This meeting determines where students will be in their projects when they arrive for group instruction; what follow-up assignments, including one-on-one consultations with library staff, are anticipated; and what emphases would be ideal. In effect, each composition sequence requires *three* visits to the library, one in 101 and two in 102, including one for the *instructor.*

A year into this effort, we are working to maximize the potential for productive dialogue. There are issues of turnover and training, but it's clear that exploring research and information literacy goals with library staff is a net gain because learning goals are more tightly integrated into the course. Beyond this, a need for tailored instruction follows from increasingly varied approaches to research in 102. Some instructors focus on archival research or quantitative literacy. Others extend the research activities of the second unit, on discourse communities, into the third unit. Still others are thinking through a range of alternative genres in the direction of "multiwriting" (Davis & Shadle, 2007). As a whole, the program is moving beyond the 8–10 page academic essay and toward diverse ways of engaging and representing information. These include opportunities to compose and circulate texts in digital environments. The default deliverable in 102 is still a research report of some kind, but we anticipate other modes of contributing to knowledge through multimodal compositions.

The final unit of 102 is not the researched essay or its variants, however, but a digital portfolio in which the work of 102 (and optionally 101) is re-presented in digital form; we use Wordpress as a platform. In the portfolio, students revise or expand on their work as well as reflect on their growth as writers and researchers. Like the final essay in 101 that might appear online in a journal of undergraduate writing, the portfolio contributes to students' development of digital and media literacies and to their identity as agents writing beyond the audience of a teacher. Students are introduced to the portfolio at the beginning of 102 and encouraged to take advantage of the affordances of digital media, including linking to information sources where possible. In this way, digital literacy reinforces information literacy within a larger framework of civic and academic literacies.

CONCLUSION: PARTNERS IN PEDAGOGY

Bill and Zara embrace (uncommonly, we think) a common vision of pedagogy and partnership of great practical benefit to our students and colleagues. Behind the scenes of instruction in the classroom and the library, we're working not for the cause of efficiency (much as we value it) but for moments of discovery as yet unrealized by students and instructors who must complete the program of study we anticipate for them, coloring inside (or outside) lines we have drawn. We have built up traffic between our programs with increased visits and consultations, ensuring that students receive scaffolded support in what can be a gaping hole in their education. Information literacy falls between the cracks of formal education. Not owned by any discipline, it is an infrastructure for content-based instruction. In this, it forms an essential bond with writing programs, invested as each are in equipping students to participate in the academy and beyond. The more vibrant and substantive the encounter with information, the nearer students come to realizing their potential as agents in the knowledge economy.

Beyond a more vibrant partnership, then, Zara and Bill are creating a model of collaboration between the writing program and the library that's anything but static in engaging students in transformative learning experiences. In the 21st century, this means going beyond the research paper as an academic exercise. It means pushing students into the flow of information through emerging forms of academic and civic participation; it means outfitting students with critical literacy skills to interrogate, even resist, information and to recognize the distributed nature of information in networked ecologies.

Still in the early days of a partnership, Bill and Zara are solidifying collaboration through appropriate assessment of instruction and products of that instruction. Together, Zara and Bill will look for opportunities to build on success and address deficits, in ways as simple as sharing student work with library colleagues. Bill and Zara further recognize that this partnership plays a vital role in the broader mission of the university. Beyond immediate goals of instruction, the library's relationship with the writing program serves as a catalyst for change in a vertical curriculum. We see ourselves accountable to our colleagues for what we do to sustain a model of instruction grounded in notions of threshold concepts, for the "threshold" is very much an elongated portal through which students traverse, at varying rates, in the course of their education.

REFERENCES

ACRL. (2015). *Framework for information literacy for higher education*. Retrieved from http://www.ala.org/acrl/standards/ilframework.

Adler-Kassner, L., & Wardle, E. (2015). *Naming what we know: Threshold concepts of writing.* Boulder: University Press of Colorado.

Bean, J. C. (1996). *Engaging ideas. The professor's guide to integrating writing, critical thinking, and active learning in the classroom.* San Francisco: Jossey-Bass.

Bizup, J. (2008) BEAM: A rhetorical vocabulary for teaching research-based writing. *Rhetoric Review, 27*(1), 72–86. Communication & Mass Media Complete. Web. February 4, 2014.

Booth, W. C., Colomb, G., Williams, J., & Bizup, J. (2016). *The craft of research* (4th ed.). Chicago: University of Chicago Press.

Brent, D. (2013). The research paper, and why we should still care. *Writing Program Administration, 37*(1), 33–53. Retrieved from http://wpacouncil.org/journalarchives

Council of Writing Program Administrators (CWPA). (2011). *Framework for success in postsecondary writing.* Retrieved from http://wpacouncil.org/files/framework-for-success-postsecondary-writing.pdf

Davis, R. L., & Shadle, M. F. (2007). *Teaching multiwriting: Researching and composing with multiple genres, media, disciplines, and cultures.* SIU Press.

Elmborg, J. (2006). Critical information literacy: Implications for instructional practice. *Journal of academic librarianship, 32*(2), 192–199.

Fister, B. (2011, April 12a). Why the 'research paper' isn't working. Library Babel Fish Blog: Inside Higher Ed. Retrieved from https://www.insidehighered.com/blogs/library_ babel_fish/why_the_research_paper_isn_t_working

Gee, J. P. (1989). Literacy, discourse, and linguistics: Introduction. *Journal of Education, 171*(1), 5–176.

Graff, G., Birkenstein, C., & Durst, R. (2006). *They say / I say.* W. W. Norton.

Haddow, G., & Joseph, J. (2010). Loans, logins, and lasting the course: Academic library use and student retention. *Australian Academic & Research Libraries, 41*(4), 233–244.

Hood, C. L. (2010). Ways of research: The status of the traditional research paper assignment in first-year writing/composition courses. *Composition Forum.* Retrieved from http://compositionforum.com/

Howard, R. M., Serviss, T., & Rodrigue, T. K. (2010). Writing from sources, writing from sentences. *Writing and Pedagogy, 2*(2), 177–192.

Jamieson, S., & Howard, R. M. (2013). Sentence-mining: Uncovering the amount of reading and reading comprehension in college writers' researched writing. *The New Digital Scholar: Exploring and Enriching the Research and Writing Practices of Nextgen Students,* 111–133.

Kuh, G. D. (2008). Excerpt from *High-impact educational practices: What they are, who has access to them, and why they matter.* Association of American Colleges and Universities.

Larson, R. L. (1982). The 'research paper' in the writing course: A non-form of writing. *College English, 44*(8), 811–816.

Margolin, S., & Hayden, W. (2015). Beyond mechanics: Reframing the pedagogy and development of information literacy teaching tools. *Journal of Academic Librarianship, 41*(5), 602–612.

Mellon, C. A. (1986). Library anxiety: A grounded theory and its development. *College & Research Libraries, 47*(2), 160–165.

Meyer, J. H., & Land, R. (2005). Threshold concepts and troublesome knowledge (2): Epistemological considerations and a conceptual framework for teaching and learning. *Higher Education, 49*(3), 373–388.

Murray, A., Ireland A., & Hackathorn, J. (2015). The value of academic libraries: Library services as a predictor of student retention. *College & Research Libraries, 77*(5), 631–642.

Nutefall, J. E., & Ryder, P. M. (2010). The timing of the research question: First-year writing faculty and instruction librarians' differing perspectives. *portal: Libraries and the Academy, 10*(4), 437–449.

Rickly, R. (2007). Messy contexts: Research as a rhetorical situation. *Digital Writing Research: Technologies, Methodologies, and Ethical Issues,* 377–397.

Scarlet Review. Retrieved from http://scarletreview.camden.rutgers.edu.

Soria, K. M., Fransen, J., & Nackerud, S. (2017). Beyond books: The extended academic benefits of library use for first-year college students. *College & Research Libraries, 78*(1), 8–22.

Swales, J. M. (1990). *Genre analysis: English in academic and research settings.* Cambridge: Cambridge University Press.

Wardle, E. (2009). 'Mutt genres' and the goal of FYC: Can we help students write the genres of the university? *College Composition and Communication, 60*(4), 765–789.

Wenger, E. (1998). *Communities of practice: Learning, meaning, and identity.* Cambridge: Cambridge University Press.

CHAPTER 7

RESEARCH AS INQUIRY

Teaching Questioning in FYC for Research Skills Transfer

Katherine Field-Rothschild

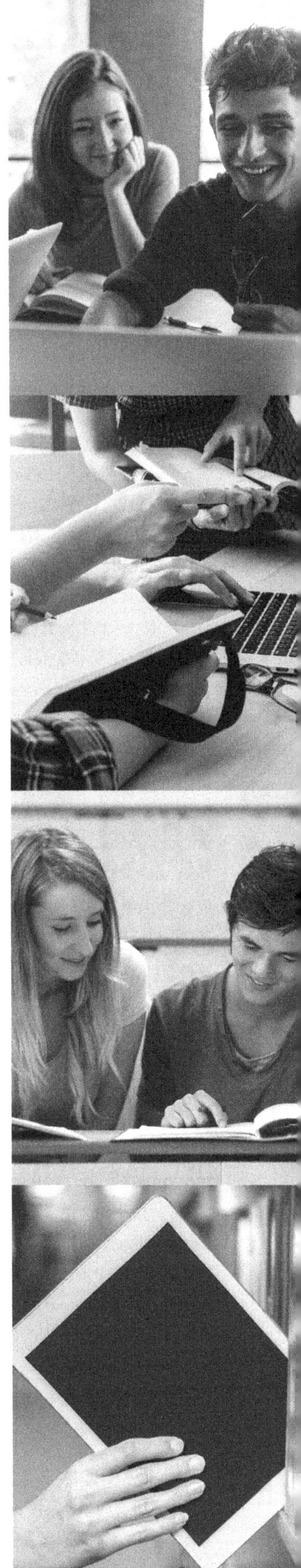

According to the 2016 Project Information Literacy Report, while some information literacy (IL) skills are transferring beyond college, our college graduates are still missing the element of questioning as a foundation for academic inquiry (Head, 2016). The IL challenges facing first-year composition (FYC) instructors are myriad, and include a lack of shared terminology from the common core to college instructors and librarians (Brown & Walker, 2016), a confusion of knowledge of technology skills with knowledge of information literacy skills for both students and high school instructors (Stockham & Collins, 2012), a lack of ability for instructors to collaborate with librarians (Gregory & McCall, 2016; Stec & Varleis, 2014; Wojahn et al., 2016), and professors' hesitancy to engage with librarians during, prior to, and after library sessions (Zoellner, Samson, & Hines, 2008). Space and time in the classroom might be blamed for many of these pushbacks against directly integrating IL instruction into FYC. However, information literacy is a foundation of today's Internet-centered research, and having excellent information literacy skills will be necessary for tomorrow's scholars. The question is: How can we begin to train these scholars in our classrooms? Is it possible to include direct IL instruction in an already overburdened FYC curriculum?

There may be an ongoing argument as to what the role of FYC is (Fulkerson, 2005), but most FYC courses prepare students to be researchers in their disciplines. The first step in becoming a researcher is to develop the curiosity and inquiry skills needed to begin discovery. Although all of the above issues deserve to be addressed, instruction that directly supports the ACRL *Framework* Research as Inquiry frame is highly suited to already existing classroom practices in FYC. Including inquiry as a learning outcome in FYC may have the power to alter students' Google-dependent research methods, to form foundational inquiry behaviors, and to transfer those positive research practices to discipline-specific courses and the workplace. Addressing the need for classroom-ready and classroom-tested methods, this chapter will briefly explore the barriers and challenges to Research as Inquiry before illustrating how inquiry might be a strongly transferable skill, and offering several malleable applications for integrating Research as Inquiry into any FYC.

BARRIERS AND CHALLENGES TO RESEARCH AS INQUIRY

Students with poor research habits were likely common in FYC courses well before writing studies asserted itself as a discipline in the 1970s, yet the advent of Internet research has given students the impression that they already know how to research any information they desire—through Google. As most instructors of FYC may observe, students' confidence in their search skills is often misguided, and when students are faced with search platforms other than Google, they can become easily frustrated (Corbett, 2010). Much research has shown that students depend almost solely on Google for their research (Purcell et al., 2013), that new high school instructors believe that understanding how to Google constitutes information literacy (Purcell et al., 2013; Stockham & Collins, 2016), that dependence on Google as a go-to research tool confuses students' understanding of the Internet itself (Corbett, 2010; Wojahn et al., 2016), and that library databases, which require instruction in order to adequately use them, can be overwhelming and frustrating for students who are mainly Google-literate (Corbett, 2010; Wojahn et al., 2016; Yancey, 2016).

A further argument is that students' reliance on Google has created an expectation of expediency that is problematic given the slow and often circular pattern of research. This expectation of immediacy is paired with standardized testing's creation of students whose dispositions, when influenced by current K–12 testing, are answer-oriented (Wardle, 2012). The linear, answer-oriented behavior of entering a few search terms into Google and the search engine returning "answers" is in conflict with the more circular pattern of research, or as Purcell and colleagues (2013) describe it, the "slow process of intellectual curiosity." This slower process of circular research based on curiosity is necessary to achieve what the ACRL IL *Framework* calls Research as Inquiry. "Research as Inquiry" is defined by the board as such: "Research is iterative and depends upon asking increasingly complex or new questions whose answers in turn develop additional questions or lines of inquiry in any field." This iterative nature depends upon students' ability to refine their search terminology and to revisit their initial research question in a circular pattern of behavior, which is in direct conflict with the linear pattern of searching Google for an answer. This is not to argue that Google has no place in the academic world—most instructors use Google as regularly as students do. However, actively teaching Research as Inquiry can offer students pathways to less frustrating interactions with databases, and can encourage students to modify—or make more circular—all of their research habits.

The first knowledge practice of Research as Inquiry is that students are able to "formulate questions for research based on information gaps or on reexamination of existing, possibly conflicting, information" (ACRL, 2015). It is in this initial formulation of a question that students often become mired. Although it is beyond the scope of this chapter to argue that our society is becoming more pliable and less able to create lines of inquiry due to the mass of information available on the Internet, this may be a factor in students' struggles. The "Google effect," as Corbett (2010, p. 267) calls students' inability to understand that the Internet is not *simply* Google, has created a one-stop shop for answers, and few opportunities for students to create questions in their classrooms or in their lives. In fact, students often expect answers to un-formed questions. This inability to create questions in the face of multiple, conflicting sources will become pervasive throughout students' discipline-specific courses if not addressed at the threshold of their college education—in FYC. Practice with inquiry as a transferable skill can encourage students to bring those modified, potentially more circular, research habits into their discipline-specific courses.

Inquiry as Transferable

As a study, transfer of knowledge is in its infancy. Defined by Dana Driscoll, transfer is "how much knowledge from one context is used or adapted in new contexts" (2011). Knowledge is learned, then carried to a new situation where prior knowledge becomes the basis for further learning. Researchers have offered some initial behaviors needed for a strong possibility of transfer, including reflection (Adler-Kassner, Clark, Robertson, Taczak, & Yancey, 2015), cuing students (Brent, 2011), and increasing metacognitive awareness to enable students to ask "good questions" about writing situations (*Elon*, 2015). The ability to create lines of inquiry into any discipline and any topic should and can be highly transferable into disciplines outside of writing studies.

It's notable, then, that the *Elon Statement on Writing Transfer* acknowledges that "Prior knowledge is a complex construct that can benefit or hinder writing transfer" (2015). Prior knowledge can include attitudes and beliefs that impact students' abilities and dispositions. Yancey in Adler-Kassner and colleagues (2015) asserts, "all writers are influenced by factors of prior knowledge that are . . . very powerful, and often in unhelpful ways" (p. 37). In Information Literacy, prior knowledge almost always includes the use of Google for research. Even when students are taught to use databases during library sessions, as many researchers have shown, students are likely to believe that databases are for school, whereas Google is for life (Corbett, 2010; Purcell et al., 2013; Wojahn et al., 2016). This duality of thought can inhibit the transfer of research skills.

As a result of these challenges, rather than disconnect Google from the academe, connecting *inquiry* as a behavior that applies to searching databases, searching Google, and investigating the credibility of all sources may allow for transfer of the IL practice Research as Inquiry. Because many students are inadvertently taught that Google is bad research and databases are good research (Corbett, 2010), placing the focus on instruction in inquiry can avoid this divisive thinking and create a single positive practice: Research as Inquiry no matter what tool is utilized. Even Google searches can become circular and lead to increasingly complex questions and ideas if the practice of Research as Inquiry is engaged.

Further, incorporating inquiry as a learning outcome of the FYC classroom in reading, discussion, and writing can add metacognitive and self-reflective elements that many researchers assert enhances skills transfer from FYC to writing in the disciplines (Adler-Kassner et al., 2015; *Elon*, 2015; Wojahn et al., 2016). Because one of the 2016 Project Information Literacy Report's major findings is that our college graduates assert they're not being taught to question, and employers have made it clear that questioning is a desirable skill for college graduates (Head, 2016), using Research as Inquiry to transfer questioning skills from FYC to discipline-specific writing and beyond should be a priority. The ACRL IL *Framework* asserts: "inquiry extends beyond the academic world to the community at large, and the process of inquiry may focus upon personal, professional, or societal needs" (2015), which potentially makes the teaching of inquiry quite significant. Inquiry, which the following assignments will illustrate, can be incorporated in ways that engage students' metacognition and reflection practice and can prime Research as Inquiry for transfer.

RECOMMENDATIONS FOR FOSTERING INQUIRY

The following are applications that were developed for use in both community college and four-year college classrooms over two years while I was a recipient of a Reading Apprenticeship (RA) grant for faculty development through Assessment in Action (AIA). All of the work here derives from my study of RA; however, simultaneously I was studying transfer, and so I modified the classroom resources to reflect those transfer-focused studies. I found that the goals of RA closely align with those of transfer. Strong inquiry skills are at the heart of both reading critically and transferring knowledge from first-year composition into Writing in the Disciplines WID courses and beyond. Although these methods are malleable for several levels of composition, they were developed for second-semester or second-year English composition courses with an academic-research focus.

These inquiry-based assignments might be applied before and during the research process including in reading and synthesis of information, during in-class discussion of shared texts, in research question development, in database searches, and in research writing and reflection. By incorporating versions of the following assignments, students might increase their ability to frame Research as Inquiry and to create increasingly complex lines of inquiry during each stage of the research process. In their ability to be decontextualized, these applications lend themselves to transfer into writing in the disciplines courses and potentially to prepare students for inquiry in the workplace.

Reading and Questioning

Integrating questioning into reading is not a new concept, but the behavior of questioning during the reading process, popularized by Reading Apprenticeship (RA), makes a strong foundation for self-reflection and metacognition through inquiry. RA is an instructional framework that guides classroom applications to assist students to feel safe discussing the difficulty of texts and exploring metacognitive inquiry during the reading process, rather than after the fact (Greenleaf & Schoenberg, 2017). For more on RA see Box 7.1, "What Is Reading Apprenticeship?"

Inquire of the Text Bookmarks

Think aloud bookmarks (see Figure 7.1) are one such application beneath the RA framework. The original bookmarks created for RA

BOX 7.1
WHAT IS READING APPRENTICESHIP?

In 1995, Cynthia Greenleaf and Ruth Schoenbach, the founders of the current Reading Apprenticeship at WestEd, began the Strategic Literacy Initiative to research literacy and create an inquiry-based literacy model—now known as Reading Apprenticeship. The model was first tested at a San Francisco high school as a course called Reading Apprenticeship Academic Literacy (RAAL), and it resulted in two years of growth in student test scores in only seven months of classroom work. The bestselling 2012 book *Reading for Understanding: How Reading Apprenticeship Improves Disciplinary Learning in Secondary and College Classrooms* by Ruth Schoenbach, Cynthia Greenleaf, and Lynn Murphy introduces RAAL and the Reading Apprenticeship instructional framework for classroom practitioners with a particular focus on four-year and community college students (Schoenbach & Greenleaf, 2017).

Today, through federally funded studies, the effectiveness of RA is being tracked in high schools and colleges across the country. It was through one such program that the author was funded and educated in Reading Apprenticeship. For more on the Reading Apprenticeship Framework, visit https://readingapprenticeship.org/our-approach/our-framework/.

Talk Back to the Text

Question the author's intention

Identify your emotional reaction
Ask a Why question about it

Question the context of this text in a greater literary tapestry

Question the author's assumptions

Question the author's influences

Figure 7.1 Think aloud bookmark.

encourage various types of questioning as part of active reading. This update more closely reflects the intentions of a first-year composition course working under the Habits of Mind framework and includes metacognitive and reflective elements to engage transfer (Adler-Kassner et al., 2015). Encouraging students to use the bookmark not just in a composition course, but in all courses, can assist them in understanding that the concept of inquiry is highly transferable.

Play the Believing and Doubting Inquiry Game

First suggested by Peter Elbow and mentioned in subsequent textbooks, this inquiry game is described by John Bean (2011) as: "teaching students to simultaneously be open to texts and skeptical of them" (p. 176), which supports the ACRL Research as Inquiry practice: "monitor gathered information and assess for gaps or weaknesses" (2015). This activity can be developed into an inquiry grid to assist students in questioning reading materials and prepare them to practice Research as Inquiry with search results and source material during any research process. This extremely flexible application can be used in a large class discussion, in small groups, or individually.

Believing

What's the author's claim? Question their influences.
Question the author's intention as it aligns with your interpretation.
How does the claim relate to your experience?

Doubting

Question the author's claim.
Upon what might the claim be based? Can you question these premises?
Where can you question the author about something they might have overlooked—perhaps with which you've had personal experience?

Discussion and Inquiry

Victor Villanueva (2014) describes using dialectic in his classes, which address difficult issues of race and intolerance in order to trace their exigencies. Villanueva asserts that his students use dialectic as a method of inquiry. This practice might also be understood as sharing inquiry: looking at multiple senses of a text and being open to others' interpretations of a text. To encourage this type of inquiring discussion, a worksheet reminiscent of the intentionality of Villanueva's dialectic assignment might engage students in self-reflective inquiry. This type of assignment echoes the importance of inquiry as a component of critical thought and self-reflection and may assist students to meet the Research as Inquiry disposition to "maintain an open mind and a critical stance" and "demonstrate intellectual humility" (ACRL, 2015).

Inquiry Through Emotional Response

1. Question your emotional reaction to a text. Why did you respond to the text the way you did?
2. Question the origin of your emotional reaction to a text. What experiences have you had that made you feel the way you do?
3. Question the factors that contributed to your emotional reaction. What life experiences and values have led to your thoughts and reactions?
4. Question how others might have reacted to the text. How are others' experiences different from your own, and how can you consider them in our discussion?

Research and Inquiry

Yancey (2010) models incorporating inquiry into classwork in order to stress the importance of inquiry for inquiry's sake. She asserts that such assignments are exercises in thinking (p. 328) illustrating the shift from the K–12 model of claim and evidence to one that allows students to develop philosophical questions. The following assignment, inspired by Yancey's work and my development of an inquiring classroom, shows efforts to alleviate students' high levels of frustration with databases.

Question Creation

The Question Creation handout might be assigned after essay prewriting but prior to research, or during an informational library session in order to begin to meld students' home research behaviors with their school research instruction. Research, according to the ACRL, depends on creating increasingly complex questions (2015). Here, students are asked to narrow their research question and create a stronger, more specifically worded question for their research projects through inquiry.

- What is your general observation or idea?
- A question you have about this idea or observation is?
- Look at the specific language of your question. Can you create more concrete words?
- Now, ask a question about your question by including a WHY element.
- Look at how your question reflects on society. Can you question its relationship to our world, and what's important in our world?
- How can you further define the question elements for concrete, specific language?
- What ideas have you discovered or unveiled? Can you question those ideas?

Question Maps

The "timing of the research question" has been explored in various papers from Nutefall and

Ryder (2010) to Gregory and McCall (2016), but an exploration of *how* a research question *evolves* throughout the research process can assist students to understand research as circular and ever-developing. Yancey (2016) creates a map assignment for students in order to address the ACRL IL *Framework*. Using Yancey's concept and altering it for Research as Inquiry, the hope is that students shift their ideas into question form even if they have slipped away from such a practice during prewriting. This exercise is an excellent example of an application with high transferability to research in other courses. I often give my students several copies and encourage them to use them for other research projects in their other courses (see Box 7.2).

BOX 7.2
SAMPLE QUESTION MAP

Question: Why do we have so many strong female dystopian heroes?
Search terms entered: female dystopia* main character
Found: The Hunger Games review Analysis of Major Characters

New question: Besides Katniss, are there strong female leads in young adult dystopias?
Search terms entered: female lead young adult novel
Found: Reading Like a Girl: Narrative Intimacy in Contemporary American Young Adult Literature, a book of several analyses of YA novels and their intimacy and contradictory ideas

New question: What are contemporary, strong girls looking for in literature? Why?
Search terms entered: young adult novel contemporary literature strong
Found: no appropriate sources
Search terms revised: children's literature female strong
Found: "Talking About Books: Strong Female Characters in Recent Children's Literature"
Source to use: "Talking About Books: Strong Female Characters in Recent Children's Literature"

Writing and Inquiry

Researcher's Notebook

Numerous researchers have looked at ways to incorporate IL into research papers, but most focus on the issue of source credibility rather than process. But Wojahn and colleagues (2016) explore various ways to integrate information literacy into classroom teaching with strong metacognitive and reflective elements using "Research Diaries." The researchers assert that Research Diaries allow for reflection, which they report enhanced their students' research practices (p. 199).

A modified version offered here is the Researcher's Notebook, which asks for a paced, inquiry-heavy process and includes an end-of-semester self-reflection. The notebook is composed of process activities to be completed over six weeks, but they may be altered as appropriate for any FYC class.

Researcher's Notebook

Part 1 Question Creation Handout
_________/5

Part 2 Essay Proposal with new research question, research plan
_________/10

Part 3 Research Question Map and revised research question
_________/10

Part 4 Revised Proposal including draft thesis and revised research plan
_________/10

Part 5 First 3–4 annotated works cited
_________/10

Part 6 Finished annotated works cited sheet
________/10

Part 7 Outline of argument including anticipated sources
________/15

Part 8 Abstract of your argument; first three essay pages
________/10

Part 9 Peer draft of your paper
________/10

Part 10 Research Reflection: Your Research Theory
________/10

Your points total: ________/100

WHY INCLUDE INQUIRY?

In 2010, journalism professor Clay Shirky compared the advent of the Internet to that of the printing press and suggested that, much as society has created a literate culture by investing in teaching children to read, we must now "figure out what response we need to shape our use of digital tools." Composition instructors, Head (2016) notes, have the power to begin to address students' ability to question texts and multimedia in just this way. As it is the responsibility of instructors to teach reading skills, it is also the responsibility of FYC instructors to "assist students [to] learn to approach these texts as informed critical thinkers" (Schoenbach, Greenleaf, & Murphy, 2012, p. 11). Even if FYC instructors collaborate with librarians for enhanced IL instruction (Gregory & McCall, 2016), if students lack the ability to frame Research as Inquiry, they will be challenged in their ability to sort through the world of information. The research of Head and colleagues illustrates a clear lack of transfer of inquiry skills, and it's been shown that there's a "vital link between higher education, information literacy, and lifelong learning" (Head, Van Hoeck, Eschler, & Fullerton, 2013, p. 75). This leaves FYC instructors with an opportunity to teach Research as Inquiry as more than an IL skill. Let us teach inquiry as a transferable skill that can create a foundation of curiosity that will serve students in their discipline and beyond.

REFERENCES

Adler-Kassner, L., Clark, I., Robertson, L., Taczak, K., & Yancey, K. B. (2015). Assembling knowledge: The role of threshold concepts in facilitating transfer. In C. Anson & J. Moore (Eds.), *Critical transitions: Writing and the question of transfer* (pp. 17–47). Fort Collins, CO: WAC Clearinghouse and University Press of Colorado.

Association of College and Research Libraries (ACRL). (2015). *Framework for information literacy standards for higher education*. Retrieved from http://www.ala.org/acrl/standards/ilframework

Bean, J. C. (2011). *Engaging ideas: The professor's guide to integrating writing, critical thinking, and active learning in the classroom* (2nd ed.). San Francisco, CA: Jossey-Bass.

Brent, D. (2011). Transfer, transformation, and rhetorical knowledge: Insights from transfer theory. *Journal of Business and Technical Communication, 25*(4), 396–420. https://doi.org/10.1177/1050651911410951

Brown, S., & Walker, J. R. (2016). Information literacy preparation of pre-service and graduate educators. In B. J. D'Angelo, S. Jamieson, B. Maid, & J. R. Walker (Eds.), *Information literacy: Research and collaboration across disciplines* (pp. 193–218). Fort Collins, CO:

WAC Clearinghouse and University Press of Colorado.

Corbett, P. (2010). What about the "Google effect"? Improving the library research habits of first-year composition students. *Teaching English in the Two-Year College, 37*(3), 265–277.

Driscoll, D. L. (2011). Connected, disconnected, or uncertain: Student attitudes about future writing contexts and perceptions of transfer from first year writing to the disciplines. *Across the Disciplines: Interdisciplinary Perspectives on Language, Learning, and Academic Writing 8*. Retrieved from http://wac.colostate.edu/atd/articles/driscoll2011/index.cfm

Elon Statement on Writing Transfer. (2015). Retrieved from http://www.centerforengagedlearning.org/elon-statement-on-writing-transfer/

Fulkerson, R. (2005). Composition at the turn of the twenty-first century. *College Composition and Communication, 56*(4), 654–687.

Greenleaf, C. & Schoenbach, R. (2017). *Reading apprenticeship and the strategic literacy initiative-history.* Retrieved from https://readingapprenticeship.org/about-us/history/.

Gregory, A. S., & McCall, B. L. (2016). Building critical researchers and writers incrementally: Vital partnerships between faculty and librarians. In B. J. D'Angelo, S. Jamieson, B. Maid, & J. R. Walker (Eds.), *Information literacy: Research and collaboration across disciplines.* Fort Collins, CO: WAC Clearinghouse and University Press of Colorado.

Head, A. J. (2016) How today's graduates continue to learn once they complete college. *Project Information Literacy.* Retrieved from http://projectinfolit.org/images/pdfs/2016_lifelonglearning_fullreport.pdf

Head, A. J., Van Hoeck, M., Eschler, J., & Fullerton, S. (2013). What information competencies matter in today's workplace? *Library and Information Research, 37,* 74–104. Retrieved from http://www.lirgjournal.org.uk/lir/ojs/index.php/lir/article/view/557

Nutefall, J. E., & Ryder, P. M. (2010). The timing of the research question: First-year writing faculty and instruction librarians' differing perspectives. *portal: Libraries and the Academy, 10*(4), 437–449. Johns Hopkins University Press. Retrieved from https://muse.jhu.edu/article/398804

Purcell, K., Rainie, L., Heaps, A., Buchanan, J., Friedrich, L., Jacklin, A., & . . . Zickuhr, K. (2013). How teens do research in the digital world. *Education Digest,* no. 6, 11. Retrieved from http://www.pewinternet.org/2012/11/01/how-teens-do-research-in-the-digital-world/

Schoenberg, R., & Greenleaf, C. (2017). Reading apprenticeship and the Strategic Literacy Initiative. Retrieved from https://readingapprenticeship.org/our-approach/our-framework/

Schoenbach, R., Greenleaf, C., & Murphy, L. (2012). *Reading for understanding: How reading apprenticeship improves disciplinary learning in secondary and college classrooms.* San Francisco, CA: Jossey-Bass.

Shirky, C. (2010, June 4). Does the Internet make us smarter? *Wall Street Journal.* Retrieved from https://www.wsj.com/articles/SB10001424052748704025304575284973472694334

Stec, E., & Varleis, J. (2014). Factors affecting students' information literacy as they transition from high school to college. *School Library Research: Research Journal of the American School Librarians, 17,* 1–23. Retrieved from http://www.ala.org/aasl/sites/ala.org.aasl/files/content/aaslpubsandjournals/slr/vol17/SLR_FactorsAffecting_V17.pdf

Stockham, M., & Collins, H. (2012). Information literacy skills for preservice teachers: Do they transfer to K–12 classrooms? *Education Libraries, 35,* 59–72. Retrieved from http://les.eric.ed.gov/fulltext/EJ989514.pdf

Villanueva, V. (2014). For the love of language: A curriculum. In D. Coxwell-Teague & R. F. Lunsford (Eds.), *Lauer series in rhetoric and composition: First-year composition: From theory to practice.* Anderson, US: Parlor Press.

Wardle, E. (2012). Creative repurposing for expansive learning: Considering "problem exploring" and "answer-getting" dispositions in individuals and fields. *Composition Forum,* 26. Retrieved from http://compositionforum.com/issue/26/creativerepurposing.php.

Wojahn, P., Westbrock, T., Milloy, R., Myers, S., Moberly, M., & Ramirez, L. (2016). Understanding and using sources: Student practices and perceptions. In B. J. D'Angelo, S. Jamieson, B. Maid, & J. R. Walker (Eds.), *Information literacy: Research and collaboration across disciplines.* Fort Collins, CO: WAC Clearinghouse and University Press of Colorado.

Yancey, K. B. (2010). Attempting the impossible: Designing a first-year composition course. In D. Coxwell-Teague & R. F. Lunsford (Eds.), *Lauer series in rhetoric and composition: First-year composition: From theory to practice.* Anderson, US: Parlor Press.

Yancey, K. B. (2016). Creating and exploring new worlds: Web 2.0, information literacy and the ways we know. In B. J. D'Angelo, S. Jamieson, B. Maid, & J. R. Walker (Eds.), *Information literacy: Research and collaboration across disciplines.* Fort Collins, CO: WAC Clearinghouse and University Press of Colorado.

Zoellner, K., Samson, S., & Hines, S. (2008). Continuing assessment of library instruction to undergraduates: A general education course survey research project. *College and Research Libraries, 4,* 370.

CHAPTER 8

JOINING THE CONVERSATION

Using a Scaffolded Three-Step Information Literacy Model to Teach Academic Research at a Community College

Melissa Dennihy
Neera Mohess

Many college students lack the skills needed for academic research, and professors, more than ever, are increasingly concerned about their undergraduates' "inability to conduct research adequately" (Kueppers, 2016). However, if students lack the skills professors expect them to have, when and where will they learn to "conduct research adequately" if not in their college classrooms? In other words, who is responsible for teaching information literacy and academic research, and how much instruction are students really receiving in these areas? Can information literacy be taught in substantive ways that equip students with the skills they need, while still allowing instructors to cover all of their course content? These are some of the questions that concerned us when we first began collaborating several years ago to develop a cross-disciplinary model for teaching information literacy (IL) and academic research. As faculty at a City University of New York (CUNY) community college—one of us a librarian and the other an English professor—we were both responsible for teaching information literacy and academic research to largely underprepared students, and were experiencing similar problems and frustrations. Our efforts to collaborate with each other had been minimal, however, mirroring a broader lack of cross-disciplinary conversation between faculty in these two disciplines. At a certain point, we acknowledged a need for greater collaboration, and began developing a model for co-teaching academic research, one that sought to make instruction in information literacy a more sustained and successful part of students' learning.

This chapter discusses the scaffolded information literacy model we developed to teach general IL skills while also helping students learn to conduct discipline-specific research and enter scholarly conversations. Drawing upon five years of collaboration in which we have implemented this model in numerous sections of Professor Dennihy's English 102 course (a dual first-year writing and Introduction to Literature course), we will explain how we use this model to teach research skills specific to the discipline and more generally applicable to courses across the disciplines. Particular attention will be given to how we use *flipping*, *reinforcements*, and *incentives* to enhance our model's success. These concepts allow us to teach research in more substantive ways that help students move beyond approaches such as "Googling" or using a citation generator to become more discerning and discriminating in how they find and use sources. While faculty, especially those teaching subjects other than English or first-year writing, often explain that they don't cover research skills because they can't afford to take time away from course content, our experiences suggest not only that students can learn important research skills without "cutting" substantial time from content, but also that, when taught in substantive and effective ways, research and information literacy enhance, rather than detract or take time away from, students' abilities to learn and respond to course material. We see this as a particularly valuable learning experience for community college students, who are often underprepared and may have anxieties about academic research: by researching and joining a scholarly conversation, students think more critically and substantively about what they are studying, and become equipped to contribute in more informed ways to academic discussions.

ANOTHER WAY IN: TEACHING ACADEMIC RESEARCH TO UNDERPREPARED STUDENTS

The ability to do college-level research is dependent upon the more basic abilities to read and write about varied texts. A student needs to understand what she or he is reading in order to effectively conduct research: Is this source scholarly? Is it appropriate for my research? What is the author's thesis? Students also need to understand how to locate authoritative sources and then synthesize and write about these findings coherently. At Queensborough Community College (QCC), however, many students are underprepared not only with regard to research skills, but also more basic reading and writing skills: in the 2014–2015 academic year, 27.4% of incoming QCC students needed remedial writing instruction, while 23.1% required remedial reading instruction (*QCC FactBook, 2014–2015*). Additionally, a recent study of research habits among QCC students found that while a majority—68%—had written a college research paper, 60% had never taken an information literacy class (Kim & Dolan, 2015). This suggests that students are being asked to do college-level research without acquiring the requisite information literacy skills needed to successfully conduct research. Understandably, this can cause students to view the physical library and the prospect of research assignments with fear and anxiety (Mellon, 1986). Project Information Literacy's 2013 study of college freshmen, which included 10 community colleges, found that, indeed, a majority of students find college libraries daunting (Head, 2013). They also recognize that their often inadequate high school research skills need updating to accommodate college-level rigor. But without further instruction in research skills, students tend to default to what they already know, which often does not go beyond using search engines like Google or sites like Wikipedia to conduct research.

Thus, while professors expect students to utilize credible, authoritative information, many students approach research assignments with both a lack of skills and anxieties about library research. It should be unsurprising, then, that anecdotal conversations with our QCC colleagues indicate that many are unhappy with the quality of their students' research papers. Yet, even as professors are aware of and frustrated by students' lacking IL skills, many explain that because they have so much course content to cover, they cannot afford to cover research skills in much depth. A popular approach to addressing this dilemma is the "stand-alone" or "one-shot" information literacy session, in which instructors bring their students to the library to spend one class with a librarian, attempting to absorb as much information about research as it is possible to introduce in less than two hours. Students who attend a one-shot session do learn some research skills, and it is better for instructors assigning research assignments to schedule a one-shot class than to provide students with no instruction in information literacy at all. However, since much of the information and skills covered in a one-shot class is new to students—and often not reinforced by their instructors beyond this single session—students tend to forget much of what they learn. Many students find their way to the library reference desk at some point after the one-shot class, needing assistance with an IL component covered during the session such as evaluating sources or locating a specific database. The single-session library class, therefore, is ideal for *introducing* IL concepts, but is not structured to *reinforce* student learning.

We began our collaboration after several years of one-shot sessions in which Professor Dennihy brought English 102 students to the library once a semester for a class with Professor Mohess. Though students expressed that these one-shot sessions were helpful, many students' assignments were still inadequately researched, and their citation skills were subpar. We wanted to develop a model that would make it possible to extend and deepen IL instruction in a way that did not detract from course content or prove onerous to students. Since English 102 is both an Introduction to Literature course and a first-year writing course with a research component, there is a lot of content to cover, much of which is unfamiliar and intimidating to students. Instead of treating literary study and academic research as two separate hurdles to conquer throughout the course, we designed a scaffolded research model that allows students to learn about both in a complementary fashion.

The assignment we use is fairly straightforward: students write a literary research paper using two secondary sources, at least one of which must be a scholarly work of literary criticism, to support their analysis of a novel. Throughout the steps of the assignment, students learn a variety of research-related skills that also further their abilities to engage in literary study. These skills are comparable to the content covered in a typical one-shot session (differentiating various types of sources; learning about search mechanics and library databases; discussing citing and plagiarism; etc.). What is different is the *manner* in which IL instruction is deployed. Rather than trying to cram everything into a one-shot class, we "flip" and space the learning process by scaffolding instruction and having students complete some tasks on their own outside of the classroom. We then reinforce and add on to this learning during the library session, and give graded incentives to complete the work. Our flipped, scaffolded approach draws on educational research on student learning, namely the benefits of spacing, accumulated practice, and testing. Spacing refers to how "the same thing recurring on *different days*, in *different contexts*, read, recited, referred to again and again, related to other things and reviewed, gets well-wrought into mental structure" (Carey, 2014, p. 79). Accumulated practice addresses students' need for a sufficient quantity of practice in order for learning benefits to accrue (Ambrose, Bridges, DePietro, & Lovett, 2010, p. 133). Testing, in certain forms and contexts, can be equivalent to additional study and can reinforce and improve learning (Carey, 2014, p. 101). Embedding these research-based practices into a scaffolded model enables students to encounter the same IL concepts multiple times in different contexts; offers ample opportunities for practice at home and in class; and provides structured reinforcement of student learning beyond a single library session.

SCAFFOLDING INSTRUCTION IN ACADEMIC RESEARCH: A THREE-STEP MODEL

When working with students who are less familiar with academic research, scaffolding and flipping are particularly useful ways to allow for spacing and accumulated practice. If students are not given adequate time to learn and practice research skills, they are more likely to look for quick fixes when writing research papers, including Googling or even plagiarizing. Research assignments can cause underprepared students to experience "trepidation, anxiety, and confusion," accompanied by an "intense need to 'fix' this problematic assignment as quickly and easily as possible . . . [m]any students are doomed to failure under this scenario" (Leckie, 1996, p. 201). Instead, a scaffolded model, one that "flips" some responsibilities onto students prior to and after their library session, more effectively sets students up for success.

Our scaffolded model includes a series of cumulative tasks, some of which are flipped, requiring students to access IL content (video tutorials, research worksheets, and an MLA citation guide) from the course's online library subject guide or Blackboard site in order to complete at-home assignments and review material covered in class. While students have approximately five weeks in total to complete their research essays, most of the scaffolded instruction takes place within the first week after students receive the assignment. The steps of our model, which we will elaborate on in more depth below, are as follows:

Step 1: Pre–Library Class

- During the class prior to the library session, Professor Dennihy gives an introduction to the research process and QCC library databases.
- Students are assigned video tutorials to view for homework, with accompanying deliverables to be brought to the library session.

Step 2: The Library Class

- Students attend an IL session with Professor Mohess in the physical library, which includes (1) reinforcing of previously covered material; (2) introduction of more advanced research skills and strategies; (3) time for hands-on practice in IL skills and conducting research.

Step 3: Post–Library Class

Students:

- are assigned several short video tutorials to watch at home, which reinforce some of the more complex material introduced during the library session
- take an open-book quiz on research skills and concepts
- continue with independent research outside of class, directly applying the skills they have learned and practiced to a course assignment
- can request one-on-one meetings with Professor Mohess to receive further individualized instruction in conducting research and citing sources

It is important to emphasize that all of these steps in total require less than two full sessions of the course instructor's class time, and allow students much more intensive instruction in academic research than a typical one-shot session.

Step 1: Pre–Library Class

The in-class introduction to research begins with a video tutorial entitled "Picking Your Topic *Is* Research"[1] (Burke, 2013), which is only three minutes long, offering a quick introduction to the research process. The tutorial emphasizes the iterative nature of research, helping students to understand that the research process typically involves several cycles of selecting and refining a topic. As Leckie (1996) notes, college students often see the "ambiguity and non-linearity" of the research process as "quite threatening": "they do not think in terms of an information-seeking strategy, but rather in terms of a coping strategy" (p. 202). It's important to introduce students to the nonlinear nature of research and to assure them that ambiguity and nonlinearity are both natural and desirable. This can be done easily through a digestible video students can easily watch again later should they wish to. Students are also introduced at this time to library databases appropriate for literary criticism, though they are not instructed in how to develop search terms or find appropriate sources using these databases. Watching the video and introducing library databases requires, in total, only about 20 minutes of class time.

Flipping some of what would be covered *in* the classroom during a one-shot session, the next task requires students to complete at-home work prior to their library session. Students are assigned to select an appropriate library database and find one source related to their paper topic, bearing in mind that the research process may require adjusting or refining one's topic, and browsing through multiple sources to find a suitable one. Students are given some concrete strategies for searching databases by being assigned to watch a tutorial on "Library Database Search Tips" (QCC Library, 2013) before beginning their search. Assigning students to watch this tutorial and practice conducting a database search for homework frees time in both the previous class session and the upcoming library session. While watching the tutorial is important for students to learn database search strategies, the tasks of conducting a search and finding an appropriate source take this lesson several steps further, asking students to put the strategies they've learned immediately into practice. Having a deliverable—requiring that students not only locate but also bring a printed copy of a source to class—is also important: if asked only to watch a video and then do a search, students may not follow through with the tasks; but assigning students to bring printed sources to class in order to receive participation credit for that session provides a concrete *incentive* to complete these tasks. These low-stakes tasks also scaffold the learning process, ensuring students start their research early and conduct it in manageable steps, rather than becoming overwhelmed by last-minute efforts to research and write a paper days or hours before a deadline. Student writers, especially underprepared writers, benefit when instructors provide starting points and offer approachable steps for breaking down challenging assignments, and the scaffolding and flipping models effectively allow for this.

Step 2: The Library Class

Since students have already been introduced to the iterative nature of the research process, subject-specific databases, and how databases work, the library session both reinforces this material and further advances students' research skills. Students know they will be quizzed on the content covered during the library class, and, as a result, are also more attentive and engaged than students in a traditional "one-shot" class. Many students take notes and actively participate throughout the session. When certain IL concepts need only be reviewed, rather than introduced, this also leaves more time during the session for deeper, more substantive discussions about research. Students move on to more advanced skills, such as learning what makes a source scholarly or nonscholarly, a distinction our students initially have a hard time understanding. Students are often surprised to learn, for example, that a college textbook or *New York Times* article are not scholarly sources. Upon learning this, students will often ask if these sources are therefore not authoritative or appropriate for college research, which launches a discussion about what might make a source—scholarly *or* nonscholarly—reliable and relevant. During these conversations, some students even learn for the first time that their professors conduct research—in other words, they learn the qualifications that make someone an expert on a topic, which helps students understand how and why some sources can be more authoritative than others. When professors are concerned about the time it takes to teach research, they may not want to bother delving into distinctions between scholarly and nonscholarly sources; but a flipped model that covers some material outside of class allows for more advanced discussions of this nature.

Another topic that can be more substantively covered during our library session—one that confuses even those students more adept in library research—is how to determine if a source, whether scholarly or not, is relevant to one's paper topic and suitable for the assignment. Addressing these questions helps students become more discerning in how they assess sources and incorporate them into their writing: not only do they learn they can't rely on Google for academic research, but they also learn that just because a source is scholarly or available through a library database does not mean it is appropriate for the discipline, assignment, or argument. For example, when students in Professor Dennihy's course write literary research papers on the Vietnam War novel *The Things They Carried*, many students will initially struggle to understand why certain sources—such as a study of PTSD symptoms among Iraq War veterans—may not be directly relevant to an analysis of postwar trauma as experienced by fictional characters in the novel. These students are assuming that any scholarly source is a good one, and they need more substantive instruction to understand the different *types* of scholarship produced within different disciplines. Distinctions that are obvious to academics, such as the difference between a psychological study and a work of literary criticism, can be quite confusing to students who are new to academic research. When students are taught this information, they quickly understand it and are able to make better choices when selecting sources—but instructors cannot expect students to learn this on their own.

Similarly, students can benefit greatly from some instruction in formulating keywords, recognizing related search terms, and narrowing search results, another set of topics our model can cover in more depth than a one-shot session. For example, a student researching the theme of sexuality in Nella Larsen's novella *Passing* might, without the requisite IL skills, conduct a database search using only the word "passing" as a search term. This will yield an overwhelmingly large number of results, many of which will not be relevant to the student's paper. Students need to be taught, through a more substantive discussion of academic research, how to develop and recognize keywords that more specifically address their own paper topic. As Leckie (1996) notes, students often do not know how to find and narrow down sources related to their topic, and may even reject sources well suited to their research because "the words in the title did not [exactly] match the words they were using to describe their topic" (p. 204). While professors may think students know enough about searching the Web to effectively formulate search terms and narrow down results, these are actually challenging intellectual tasks that require students to understand the different ways their topic might be described and discussed. Students "have to be able to articulate the[ir] topic, preferably with some alternative words[,] an act which even graduate students have difficulty performing" (p. 205). To help students understand the importance of effective search terms, we often begin with a "real world" example, such as noting the differences in search results when Googling "how do I get money for school" versus "CUNY scholarships." Starting with a more relatable example helps students transition into thinking about how to develop effective search terms for their research. At the same time, students are also learning how IL skills can be applied not only to the research paper genre, but to everyday challenges they face outside academic contexts.

After substantive discussions about locating, assessing, and using sources, both scholarly and nonscholarly, the library session ends with approximately 30 minutes of hands-on time. This more individualized portion of the class, which we did not have as much time for during one-shot sessions, provides a much-needed opportunity for students to practice and receive further instruction in the skills most challenging for them: some students use this time to brainstorm or refine search terms; others read and evaluate potential sources; and still others practice writing citations or Works Cited pages. This gives students a chance to apply what they have learned and get help from both Professors Mohess and Dennihy with challenges specific to their own paper topics. Students are also invited to contact the librarian for further one-on-one help with research and citations.

All of these students are *accumulating practice* in aspects of research that may be new or challenging for them. In *How Learning Works* (2014), Carey discusses "time-on-task": "even if students have engaged in high-quality practice, they still need a sufficient *quantity* of practice for the benefits to accumulate." Practice should ideally be "focused on a specific goal or set of goals," which students tackle at "an *appropriate level of challenge*" (p. 136). Quantity of practice and appropriate levels of challenge are inherent within our model: students get an easy "warm-up" by watching video tutorials and locating an article in a literary database before the library session. This enables them to arrive at the session with some prior knowledge. During the library session, they further refine and build upon what they have learned about database mechanics, keyword searching, and refining a topic; then, they practice these skills during the hands-on time in a more sophisticated and independent way that allows each student to spend time on a task and work at a level appropriate to his or her needs.

Step 3: Post–Library Class

After the library session, students are assigned several more short tutorials to watch at home, which reinforce topics covered during the session and further prepare students for the short-answer quiz they will take in the following class. Students can use their notes to complete this "open-book" quiz, which gives them incentives to actively take notes during the library session and while completing the "flipped" work. Completing the quiz itself, which includes questions on citing as well as more complex questions on how to find, evaluate, and incorporate sources, serves as yet another way to reinforce the concepts students have been learning and practicing throughout this process. As Carey (2014) argues, certain forms of testing can be viewed more accurately as "equivalent to additional study. Answering does not only measure what you remember, it increases overall retention." Carey also notes that "some kinds of tests [can] improve later learning—even if we do poorly on them" (p. 101). To ensure that even students who may do poorly on this quiz have an opportunity to learn from it, we review the answers in class immediately after students take the quiz, and students are expected to fill in or correct answers to questions they had trouble answering before handing their quizzes in (taking the quiz and reviewing answers requires, in total, about 40 minutes of class time). The opportunity to assess and revise their answers before handing their quizzes in to be graded reinforces the material yet *another* time, and also makes students more cognizant of which IL skills they may need continued practice in. Writing out answers to the questions also gives students an additional set of notes they can later reference as they continue their research on their own. All of this makes students better equipped to move forward with the assignment: sustained, continually reinforced coverage of IL concepts more readily allows students to retain and employ what they have learned than would be likely in a one-shot session.

At this point, students are equipped not only with a stronger set of research skills, but in many cases, an increased sense of confidence, as they are better prepared to conduct research and write their papers. We have also noticed that, although the quiz marks the end of in-class instruction in information literacy, many students make an active effort to continue developing their IL skills on their own time. Some students make appointments to work on their research papers one-on-one with Professor Mohess, indicating how this model can facilitate greater student interaction with library faculty. That students know when and why they may want feedback or guidance from someone other than their professor suggests that this model also encourages students to more actively use campus resources—which can extend not only to the library, but other resources like the Writing Center. Leckie (1996) notes that even when mention of librarians and library resources are embedded into an assignment, students may not share their professors' sentiments that "librarians are there if you need them": they may be hesitant, skeptical, or nervous about asking librarians for help (p. 205). By co-teaching research with a librarian, however, professors help students to become familiar with library faculty and to better understand when and how librarians may be able to help them with aspects of their coursework. As Leckie argues, models for teaching information literacy should strive for "meaningful participation of librarians in the educational experience of students," and this seems to be one notable outcome of our model (p. 201). Another outcome is that many students seem to have a changed relationship to the library itself. After working in the library and with a librarian, the library is no longer perceived as an intimidating space where students feel uncertain of what to do, where to work, or whom to ask for help. Instead, the library becomes akin to a second classroom or study space: students know where it is; what resources it has; where to find books, computers, and quiet study spaces; and how to ask librarians for help with various aspects of research assignments.

IS IT WORTH IT?: THE ADVANTAGES OF ADOPTING A SCAFFOLDED IL MODEL

Our experiences using this model in multiple courses over several years suggest that, when given more sustained, substantive opportunities to learn and practice information literacy skills, even underprepared students can and do successfully tackle research assignments. Incorporating flipped components, incentives, and reinforcements into a scaffolded model helps students reach significantly higher levels of sophistication in how they conduct and produce research. Using our model, students are not just learning how to write citations or format a bibliography in ways that are disconnected from the topics they are studying and writing about. Instead, they use IL skills and resources to enhance their knowledge of specific topics and improve the quality of their written work. As such, teaching IL *adds to or enhances,* rather than detracting time from, students' engagement with and understanding of course content. Students learn new, more substantive and sophisticated approaches to both academic research *and* literary study, and both their research and literary analysis skills improve. For example, students learn how incorporating literary criticism into an analysis of a novel can strengthen the writer's argument, allowing him or her to consider multiple perspectives and acknowledge other textual interpretations. Developing the ability to effectively use scholarly sources also gives students increased confidence and capability to continue with scholarly research in future courses across the disciplines: they now know not just how, but why, to move beyond Googling in order to use library resources and more advanced research strategies. Indeed, we have observed fewer cases of both plagiarism and research anxiety once students have had a chance to learn substantive—not just superficial—research skills. Rather than feeling intimidated by the library and its resources, or resorting to Googling or plagiarism out of a desperate need for a quick fix, students know how to find, evaluate, and effectively use scholarly sources in their writing. Underprepared students also gain confidence in their ability to enter scholarly conversations: once they know how to find and use authoritative sources, students feel increasingly "authorized" to make scholarly arguments themselves and join academic discussions.

The model we use is easily adaptable across the disciplines. Professors can play a valuable role in enhancing students' research skills (and reducing research anxieties) by introducing them to library materials and personnel through an IL session; and by scaffolding and deepening the learning of IL concepts through flipping and reinforcing elements of IL instruction. Flipping some of this instruction effectively scaffolds new learning concepts without detracting significant time from course content or adding a burdensome workload for students (Roselle, 2009). Even a little can go a long way—our experiences echo Leckie's (1996) assertion that "even with minimal effort, faculty intervention can make an incredible amount of difference to the outcome of the research paper process" (p. 206). Since implementing our model, the quality of research papers submitted by Professor Dennihy's students—including reliability of sources; suitability of sources for the discipline and assignment; and how effectively sources are used to support an argument—has improved notably. When students approach research in scaffolded, manageable steps; are guided throughout the process by two faculty members from different disciplines; and have multiple opportunities to practice research skills in the classroom, in the library, and on their own, they are much better equipped for continuing this work independently and successfully in both current and future courses. The opportunity to learn and conduct research also helps students enter academic conversations, as they gain the confidence to research, read, and respond to scholarly debates.

NOTE

1. Our model uses a number of video tutorials, a format we find beneficial because students can watch—and rewatch—tutorials on their own time. Some of our tutorials were created by Professor Mohess, and some were developed by other university libraries, many of which conveniently post tutorials directly to YouTube.

REFERENCES

Ambrose, S. A., Bridges, M. W., DePietro, M., & Lovett, M. C. (2010). *How learning works: Seven research-based principles for smart teaching.* San Francisco: Jossey-Bass.

Burke, A. (2013). *Picking your topic IS research.* [video file]. Retrieved December 29, 2016, from https://www.lib.ncsu.edu/tutorials/picking_topic/

Carey, B. (2014). *How learning works: The surprising truth about when, where, and why it happens.* New York: Random House.

Head, A. J. (2013). *Learning the ropes: How freshmen conduct research once they enter college.* Retrieved December 29, 2016, from http://www.projectinfolit.org/uploads/2/7/5/4/27541717/pil_2013_freshmenstudy_fullreportv2.pdf

Kim, M., & Dolan, M. (2015). "Excuse me, but what is a research paper?": Embedded librarian program and information literacy skills of community college students. *Community & Junior College Libraries, 21*(1–2), 53–70. https://doi.org/10.1080/02763915.2016.1149001

Kueppers, C. (2016, April 4). *More professors say undergraduates need to hone research abilities, survey finds.* Retrieved December 29, 2016, from http://www.chronicle.com/blogs/ticker/more-faculty-see-a-need-for-undergrads-to-hone-research-abilities-survey-finds/109977

Leckie, G. J. (1996). Desperately seeking citations: Uncovering faculty assumptions about the undergraduate research process. *Journal of Academic Librarianship, 22*(3), 201–208.

Mellon, C. A. (1986). Library anxiety: A grounded theory and its development. *College & Research Libraries, 47*(2), 160–165. https://doi.org/10.5860/crl.76.3.276

QCC Library. (2013, August 14). *Library database search tips.* Retrieved December 29, 2016, from https://www.youtube.com/watch?v=D7HSR9CZYxU

Queensborough Community College FactBook, 2014–2015. Retrieved December 29, 2016, from http://www.qcc.cuny.edu/oira/docs/factbook-2014-15/FactBook2014-2015.pdf

Roselle, A. (2009). Preparing the underprepared: Current academic library practices in developmental education. *College & Research Libraries, 70*(2), 142–156. https://doi.org/10.5860/crl.70.2.142

PART III

Pedagogies and Practices

CHAPTER 9

PROMOTING SELF-REGULATED LEARNING IN THE FIRST-YEAR WRITING CLASSROOM

Developing Critical Thinking in the Selection of Tools and Sources

Robert Hallis

INTRODUCTION

Today's students never knew a time when the digital environment was not available and have a reputation for having mastered the Internet. When they need to find information for assignments in a first-year writing course, however, students face a perfect storm. They are new to the conventions of the academic conversation, new to the sources available through an academic library, and new to the critical thinking needed to evaluate information for college work. Students are then asked to write about a topic that interests them without the help of their most familiar tool, Google. This challenge is even more daunting when students need to tie academic sources together for interdisciplinary issues.

A seemingly innocuous writing assignment could ask students to pick a current issue from the news; use eight sources (five of which must be scholarly) and explain how this issue affects them. Certainly such assignments engage students in an authentic situation, but consider how the granular nature of scholarly information fits into the broad issue of current events. If the student wants to discuss alternative fuel cars, academic sources may range from engineering studies of lithium batteries to case studies of consumer behaviors. Even a seemingly focused thesis such as the use of therapy dogs in treating PTSD patients could retrieve sources ranging from how these animals are trained and paired with clients to the effectiveness of this therapy. Additionally, students need to make significant links between information aimed toward a general reader when using newspapers or magazines and specialized articles from the scholarly community. Students in first-year writing courses are generally brought to the library for an introduction to the available materials and services. This collaboration can nurture their introduction to the academic conversation as well as demonstrate how to link a broad discussion from a general source to relevant academic sources in a variety of disciplines.

There are a number of choices to be made when bringing academic disciplines together: which database to use, how to evaluate the information, which source to select, and how to integrate information into their assignments. In order to navigate these choices, students need to become self-regulated learners (SRLs). They need to develop an awareness of the range of available search tools, the variety of available sources, the diverse criteria for evaluating the appropriateness of each source, the task at hand, and then how to select an appropriate tool and method of evaluating information to complete their assignment. Self-regulated learning provides a structure for consciously selecting search tools and evaluating the resources they locate. Appreciative inquiry (AI) provides an approach for nurturing confidence in identifying and evaluating alternatives as students develop a broader range of skills.

Rather than "fixing" old habits, AI provides a way to build on students' experience through discovering their abilities, identifying what they want to be able to do, and closing the "is-ought" gap through implementing a plan of action (Harrison & Hasan, 2013, p. 71). Library instruction can play a vital role in developing these skills as students begin to find sources for their writing assignments. After a brief survey of SRL, the chapter examines how developing AI can improve students' performance on first-year writing assignments through examining how to coach students using this method in the context of a one-shot library instructional session.

SELF-REGULATED LEARNING

Self-regulated learning (SRL) refers to the ability of students to guide their own learning through developing an awareness of current skills and tools, an understanding of the assignment, and an ability to reflectively select the most appropriate way to complete the task at hand within their abilities (Zimmerman & Martinez-Pons, 1990). It involves developing *strategic knowledge*, which includes a familiarity with the different types of tasks; *knowledge about the cognitive task*, which includes understanding the task and the strategic knowledge needed to complete the task; and *self-knowledge*, which refers to the ability to judge which strategy would work best in a given situation (Nilson, 2013, pp. 2–3). Preparing students to locate appropriate material for their paper requires strategic knowledge, which includes an understanding of the functionality and content of various databases, evaluation criteria for vetting a variety of sources, and the conventions of citing used in an academic conversation. Knowledge about the task refers to the requirements of the assignment, and self-knowledge refers to the ability to select the most appropriate strategic knowledge to complete the assignment.

Instructing self-regulated learners is fundamentally different from demonstrating the functionality of a database, or providing an orientation to the sources available through the library. Rather, it involves making an informed choice from a range of familiar options. If the task involves finding background information on a source, the student could use the library's OPAC to find a book, the library's discovery tool to find a magazine, or even Google to find an article in Wikipedia. Each of these sources requires using a different tool to locate material and a different method of evaluation to assess its relevance. While editors assess books, magazines, and newspapers, there is no editorial control of social media, and Wikipedia's editors are not clearly evident. While scholarly articles have bibliographies and a peer-review process to check the credibility of the source, newspapers, magazines, and books undergo a different method of quality control. In addition to a familiarity with the various ways of evaluating sources, there is the issue of developing a familiarity with using a number of different search tools to identify and access relevant material.

Developing self-regulated learning is especially useful in working with interdisciplinary topics. Students tend to recycle methods used in high school and stick to a single routine from one assignment to the next (Head & Eisenberg, 2010, p. 3) "Whether they were conducting research for a college course or for personal reasons, nearly all of the students in our sample had developed an information-seeking strategy reliant on a small set of common information sources—close at hand, tried and true" (Head & Eisenberg, 2009, p. 3). Furthermore, students who had not developed a solid background in their issue "appeared to develop further erroneous habits as they continued[;] this may partly be due to frustration and fatigue as they worked with the challenging task" (Debowski, 2001, p. 378). Consequently, library instruction needs to expand the range of tools and sources students use.

Narrating the thought process of a self-regulated learner involves explaining the process, thinking aloud as one chooses among a variety of approaches to accomplish the task at hand. This is designed to develop an awareness of available techniques, explain the rationale for selecting sources best suited to the assignment, and critically evaluate the source, the tool, and the relevance of material. This activity is not "fixing" a search strategy, but rather explaining choices, demonstrating how one knowledgeably selects an appropriate tool from a range of known options, evaluating the source using criteria appropriate for that assignment, and effectively incorporating the source within the assignment. This instruction is not deliberate practice. Whereas deliberate practice involves breaking a task into components to perfect steps in a larger process, SRL involves the metacognitive task of selecting and employing appropriate procedures (Nilson, 2013, p. 6). Bridging the gap between how students searched for information and how they need to search for information involves adapting new skills.

APPRECIATIVE INQUIRY

Appreciative inquiry (AI) acknowledges the abilities students developed through previous searching activities, explores the skills needed to complete academic assignments, and provides a plan to bridge this gap. Cooperrider and Srivastva developed AI in the late 1980s as a tool for improving organizational effectiveness (Cooperrider, Stavros, & Whitney, 2008). Developed in a business environment, this method explores issues using the perspective of everyone in an organization within the categories of the 4-D structure of appreciative inquiry; Discover, Dream, Design, and Delivery. Discover encourages participants to acknowledge the best current practices within an organization. Dream encourages participants to envision what an ideal situation might be. Design organizes a plan for reaching these aspirational goals, and Delivery involves implementing and perpetuating these objectives. Bloom, Hutson, He, and Konkle (2013, p. 8) added two additional phases to the 4-D structure of AI: *Disarm* and *Don't Settle*. These two phases provide bookends around the 4-D structure by preparing a supportive environment at the beginning of the session, and motivating the student to continue using the techniques discussed after the session ends. The author will use all six elements of AI in an analysis of the content of instructional sessions for first-year writing students.

AI is far different from problem solving. Problem solving involves a postmortem of a situation with the intention of fixing something that is not working well. It involves analyzing what caused the problem, investigating possible solutions, and enacting a remedy. AI begins with appreciating the best features of current practices, envisions what might work better, designs a method for achieving these aspirational goals, and carries through with these plans (Cockell & McArthur-Blair, 2012, p. 15). Whereas problem solving is reactive and limited to a particular situation, AI is forward-looking, focuses on achievement, and is open ended. Rather than fixing a situation, one can improve a process through AI. AI practices have been adapted to an educational setting in a number of ways (Bloom et al., 2013; Cockell & McArthur-Blair, 2012; Harrison & Hasan, 2013). This approach is especially helpful in overcoming many of the negative mythologies labeling students, parents, and the educational process (Harrison & Hasan, 2013, p. 65).

Librarians can use AI in structuring the sessions as well as conducting the class. Examining the literature from an AI perspective reveals what the current situation is, articulates aspirational goals, and can lay the groundwork for reaching these goals. AI in the classroom provides positive reinforcement for what students know how to do, and offers a supportive environment in which to develop the skills needed to inform an academic conversation. Students build on their extensive Internet experience when learning to locate information for more sophisticated tasks, and librarians use these experiences as a foundation for developing more robust skills in locating and evaluating information. "AI can be utilized deliberately in shaping experiences and processes designed to focus student attention and reflection on both the dynamic complexity of their world and the agency of purpose available to them" (Harrison & Hasan, 2013, p. 71).

Disarm

The first phase of AI involves creating a safe environment (Bloom et al., 2013, p. 8). Students, faculty, and librarians come to instructional sessions with a number of preconceived notions. Creating a safe environment involves abandoning such characterizations as: students are Google dependent, faculty have unrealistic expectations, and librarians are little old ladies who constantly patrol the stacks of books reminding patrons to be quiet. In reality, professors are mentoring students in the conventions of an academic conversation. Rather than abandoning a familiar technique, students are developing more sophisticated search strategies and developing more rigorous evaluation skills to effectively participate in a new conversation. Librarians are not fixing defective searching strategies but rather mentoring successful strategies for managing information needed in an academic conversation. AI provides a framework for looking past negative sweeping overgeneralizations while searching for positive traits to continue and aspirations to meet (Harrison & Hasan, 2013, p. 65).

Discover

This phase involves learning other people's perceptions of their own personal strengths and the strengths of the organization of which they are a member (Bloom et al., 2013, p. 8). The literature provides a wealth of information about how students, faculty, and librarians view the library; resources available through the library; and the assistance provided by librarians.

Students appear to have always had problems finding sources for an academic conversation. In the 1990s, Jennie Nelson concluded, "Students tend to draw quotations from sources that they have not demonstrated they have read and understood and engage in 'patchwriting' rather than synthesizing information or creating their own understanding" (Fister, 2015, p. 98). Around the same time, Leckie (1996) concluded that students were desperately seeking citations. Twenty years later, students are still desperately seeking citations (Rose-Wiles & Hofmann, 2013). Blundell (2015, pp. 35–37) found that students used family, friends, and peers as primary sources of information, demonstrated a reluctance to change search strategies even following library instruction, exhibited a tendency to resort to minimal requirements of an assignment because of anxiety, and continued to experience difficulty when trying to locate relevant academic resources. Furthermore, these students believed they were more proficient in finding material than their skills demonstrated.

The challenge of engaging students has been studied by Linda Nilson and others. In describing how to create a "Self-Reflective

Learner," she summarizes an apparent apathy on the part of students that undermines efforts to engage them in the following way: "Specifically, these students take little or no responsibility for their own learning, blaming their shortcomings in achievement on their 'ineffective' instruction and the 'too advanced' or irrelevant course material" (Nilson, 2013, p. 20).

Porter (2011) found that millennials begin on Google, using natural language queries, and generally select a source from the beginning of the results list because they trust that the search engine has already prioritized the results. He contrasts the success students experience on popular search engine sites with the difficulties they experience on library database sites. Students also appear to make a number of careless mistakes as well. A number of studies report that students make rudimentary mistakes in logic and spelling, make errors in manipulating a database, and exhibit problems in citing sources (Debowski, 2001; Fidel et al., 1999; Ford, Miller, & Moss, 2002; Minetou, Chen, & Liu, 2008; Thatcher, 2006, 2008; Wildemuth, 2004). Might we be missing something? Townsend, Brunetti, and Hofer (2011) provide an interesting observation about the innate knowledge students appear to demonstrate.

> Students understand instinctively that you would not look in the school newspaper for a definitive one-page biography of Lincoln any more than you would check out a book of postmodernist film criticism to [find] this week's movie listings. Capitalizing on this understanding, instructors can guide students toward connecting what they understand through their own experiences with the underlying principle of why information formats are distinct entities. (Townsend et al., p. 861)

Clearly students have some "instinctive" knowledge. Numerous studies document the benefit domain knowledge has in the search process (Lazonder, Biermans, & Wopereis, 2000; Waniek & Schäfer, 2009; Wildemuth, 2004). Students who developed a familiarity with the broader issues of their topic use better keywords and select more relevant sources. The lack of such a background is perhaps the most difficult obstacle to overcome.

> Finding contexts for "backgrounding" topics and for figuring out how to traverse complex information landscapes may be the most difficult part of the research process. Our findings also suggest that students create effective methods for conducting research by using traditional methods, such as libraries, and self-taught, creative workarounds, such as "presearch" and Wikipedia, in different ways. (Head & Eisenberg, 2009, p. 1)

Faculty know that students experience problems when asked to find information for assignments, value the instructional support provided by librarians, and collaboratively work through a number of instructional initiatives (Wolff, Rod, & Schonfeld, 2016). The instructions for their assignments, however, may not provide adequate guidance in the techniques for searching for appropriate sources or evaluating the quality of the sources their students choose to use (Head & Eisenberg, 2010). Furthermore, faculty appear to use many of the same Internet tools their students use. Through social media, blogs, and Google, some faculty keep current in their field of research. After locating information on authors or sources, however, they turn to the library to access the needed material (Wolff et al., 2016).

Librarians have gone to great lengths to empower users to independently access the information they need. Their familiarity with resources and search tools, however, may cause librarians to overestimate the importance of particular techniques or sources. Badke provides three remarks that deserve special attention in relation to teaching first-year students. Badke (2010) says that librarians can demonstrate how to walk through the resources of a discipline. He believes that librarians can play the role of a mentor in deciphering an assignment (Badke, 2014b). Librarians can untangle the complications behind the enticing simplicity of Google searching (Badke, 2014a). Librarians may also need to rethink the selection process.

Librarians generally regard "satisficing" as settling; as accepting less than ideal information or locating it through an ineffective process. The notion that something is "good enough," however, means various things. As skills improve, expertise in a discipline develops, and requirements become more rigorous, one becomes more selective about the information gathered. Whereas faculty are satisficed only when they located the breadth and depth of sources relevant to a particular area, students look to the requirements of an assignment (Barrett, 2005; Nicholas, Huntington, Jamali, Rowlands, & Fieldhouse, 2009, p. 109; Prabha, Connaway, Olszewski, & Jenkins, 2007). "A satisficing search is 'thermostatic' in that it is turned on or off as the need arises; formal information seeking is never done without a proximate cause of specific question in mind" (Zach, 2005, p. 25). Librarians can effectively mediate between the professor's expectations and the student's performance by discussing where the thermostat is set in an instructional session. Librarians are not crafting little experts nor are we initiating them into a discipline. Rather, we are working with students to become "participants in the community of college graduates. More narrowly, they are apprenticing to the community of scholars in a particular discipline or to the community of a particular profession" (Kuglitsch, 2015, p. 461). Sources that are "good enough" for a first-year composition course are clearly different from sources that are "good enough" for a master's thesis. The tools that are used to locate these sources as well as the criteria used to evaluate them should reflect a growing sophistication as students progress through their academic career.

This brief survey reveals that students have a basic sense of the relation between different types of sources. Faculty may use the same tools as students but have more success in using the tools more effectively because of their superior domain knowledge, and librarians can act as a mentor while untangling a Google search or deciphering an assignment. Building on this foundation is the next phase of AI.

Dream

The goal of this stage is discovering the big picture ideas (Bloom et al., 2013, p. 9). Information overload is now a fact of life, and the goal of library instruction is to develop a student's ability to navigate these sources. Clearly the assignment sets the thermostat. If five sources are required, five relevant sources need to be included. If five sources within the field of psychology written within the past three years need to be included, then five relevant psychology sources written in the past three years need to be included. So articulating the quality and relevance of the sources becomes an important part of the assignment. Establishing a context for their topic, however, requires students to develop expertise in using a broader variety of search tools and more sophisticated evaluation criteria, and the language we use to pursue these goals is important. "Telling people they are capable and that their successes depend on them opens up opportunities for new thinking and positive action. Conversely, using judgmental language or language that diminishes self-respect is oppressive" (Samba, 2013, p. 57).

Librarians can verbalize the process of what adequate background means within the context of an assignment and show how to turn broad topics into more narrowly focused questions. These questions then provide descriptive keywords for a search as well as criteria for selecting relevant sources. If the source addresses a particular question, it should be selected. If it does not, it should be passed by. As students become more familiar with conventions within their discipline, perhaps instructions can assume a greater familiarity of expectations.

Design

This stage involves charting the journey from "is to ought" (Bloom et al., 2013, p. 8). It involves designing learning objectives. The unique attribute of AI is involving all stakeholders in the process. Students, however, have not been involved in the discussion to this point. Engaging students in the process becomes a critical element of designing an instructional session. As we move from Is (Discover) to Ought (Dream), we need to keep in mind the supportive atmosphere first discussed (Disarm). Students have likely used a search engine, and developed a familiarity with selecting items, placing results in a shopping cart, and downloading content. They may, however, have less familiarity with filtering their results, and may not have needed to distinguish between the types of sources they retrieve. Acknowledging what students know while emphasizing where they need to grow is an essential part of AI.

Preparing for an instructional session involves explaining the assignment, demonstrating how to use the tools available for locating sources, and explaining the rationale for selecting one tool over another. Furthermore, it involves explaining why one source in the list of sources is better than another. Following an instruction session, students should be able to locate background information about their topic, formulate a research question, use descriptive keywords in a search, make informed selections from the list of results, access their selections, and use the selected sources in their assignment within the citation conventions of the academic conversation. While this is an optimistic list of objectives, these become the goals we aspire to reach.

Deliver

This stage involves carrying out the plans created in the previous section (Bloom et al., 2013, p. 9). In this case, a class presentation incorporates the principles discussed above. Introductory remarks can create a supportive environment in which the students' previous search experience is acknowledged (Disarm). Linking the search process to what students may have done in Google provides a connection between what they have done (Discover) and what they need to do (Dream). The same bridge needs to be built between the terms they use, the process they apply to select results, and the method they use to access the selected material. Clearly they need to adopt more sophisticated methods of evaluation, develop an awareness of a broad range of databases, and adopt a more rigid method of documenting the sources they used and the way they use the source (Dream). Moving beyond the mere number of sources involves the last component of AI.

Don't Settle

This stage challenges one to revisit the process (Bloom et al., 2013, p. 9). In information literacy, this stage involves moving past locating three scholarly sources to finding three scholarly sources that are relevant to the assignment, integrating them into the assignment, and doing so within the conventions of the academic conversation. In Discover we've learned that students may resort to minimally acceptable sources, and faculty to assignments that do not emphasize the connection between sources and the academic assignment. Students need to understand the link between the research question, the descriptive words used in the search query, and the connection between individual sources and the original research question. The classroom environment provides an excellent forum in which to explain how each source relates to the research question.

Utilizing SRL in the Classroom

A brief survey of several common writing assignments illustrates the range of tools needed to complete an assignment and the variety of evaluation techniques required to select viable sources. Instruction needs to discuss the differences between academic sources and popular material, content type with publication cycles to determine currency, and free-range information on the Internet with material approved by an editor or peer review process. Writing about a contemporary issue requires students to pick an issue, locate enough background information to become familiar with the context of their topic, evaluate relevant information, and integrate sources into the assignment using appropriate citation conventions. The sources for current issues can be found in newspapers, social media, or broadcasts. One could use Google, a discovery tool, or a specialized database to locate the initial source. When evaluating these sources, students need to realize that there will be no bibliography to indicate the sources used in the story, and an editor checks the accuracy of the article before it is published.

Placing that event in a context involves accessing an understandable source for background. This could be a general news magazine, a book chapter of a book, or a feature article in a newspaper. The tools used to locate this could include a specialized database, such as *CQ Researcher*; a book, such as one from the opposing viewpoints series; a newspaper database; or a discovery tool (limiting the results to magazines or newspapers). Using the AI process in this instruction involves creating a safe environment through comparing this activity with those many students regularly do (Disarm), linking common procedures used in finding background information with the techniques commonly used in searching the Internet (Discover), identifying the more refined requirements needed for finding background information (Dream), creating the search (Design), executing the search and evaluating the results (Deliver), and ensuring the selected resources are relevant to the research topic (Don't Settle).

A different writing assignment involves analyzing a literary work. While the AI goals may be the same in an interdisciplinary investigation, the tools, sources, and method of evaluation are different. Students may find background information in SparkNotes or a Wikipedia article using Google but would need to use the library's OPAC to find books about the author or work. While these sources can provide background information, only the book would be considered a scholarly source, which could be used in the essay and included in the bibliography for the assignment. Additional scholarly information can be located through searching a specialized database, using a discovery tool, or citation chasing from the bibliography of a book. An interesting twist on a literary analysis involves investigating an issue raised in a course reading and comparing the historical context of an issue evident in the story with the current treatment of that issue. Examples include the status of women in Chopin's *The Story of an Hour*, or psychological illness in Faulkner's *A Rose for Emily*. This involves gaining a familiarity with the literary work as well as a historical perspective of an issue. One would use a literary database to explore issues discussed in the story, and a discovery tool to find background information concerning the issue when tying a historical perception to a present outlook, and any one of a number of databases when locating scholarly perspectives.

In *A Rose for Emily*, one could examine mental health. This would require students to find background information on the history of the treatment of mental illness and then find scholarly information about current practices regarding specific pathologies. Although the content may be unfamiliar, students would have some familiarity with the search process (Discover). Comparing results from Google and a discovery tool would reveal that the discovery tool helps refine searches through using filters for content type, date, and even discipline, and students would need to develop an understanding of the distinctions between newspapers, books and journal articles (Dream). A Wikipedia entry could provide some background, but would need to be validated through scholarly material for the assignment. The narrative in this assignment would discuss the role a Google search and Wikipedia could play in developing enough background so the student can understand the professional literature dealing with mental health, and then discuss how descriptive keywords would be used in a discovery tool to retrieve a set of results, which would then be filtered (Design and Deliver).

REFLECTIVE MENTORSHIP: CULTIVATING SRL THROUGH THE RESEARCH PROCESS

At the University of Central Missouri, six hours of the general education curriculum are devoted to two English composition classes, and a major assignment in the second-semester class involves writing an extended essay. The essays professors assign range from exploring current events to analyzing literary works. Library instruction generally consists of a single class period, and the author focuses the instruction on locating information to support the specific essay assigned. Classes generally have between 20 and 25 students, and usually meet in a hands-on environment. Learning objectives for library instruction focus on using a discovery tool, a literary database, and evaluating information when making selections. Appreciative inquiry guides a journey from search activities students are generally familiar with, to more sophisticated evaluation techniques and a wider range of search tools. The narrative uses principles of SRL in discussing the available options for selection along the way, and explains the rationale for those choices.

An interesting assignment involved integrating the university's common reader that year, Elizabeth Svoboda's *What Makes a Hero,* with a short story selected by the student. The essay needed to examine the heroic nature of a character from the story using several sources, five of which must be scholarly. Students need to have a familiarity with the common reader, the short story they chose, and an issue they want to use to tie these sources together, and integrate the granular information of scholar sources into the essay.

When class begins, students are in a computer lab, and the teaching podium projects computer images on a screen at the front of the room. Before coming to class, students are expected to have selected a story, formulated a topic, and prepared several questions from earlier class discussions. At the beginning of the class, the handout is distributed (see Appendix), and preliminary introductions and explanations of the assignment involve a few minutes and several PowerPoint slides (Disarm).

The narrative discusses the importance of having a context for the assignment. While the students have done this in class, the narration explicitly links this background information to finding sources and writing the essay. The discussion turns to finding background information using some nonscholarly material, including SparkNotes and even a well-written Wikipedia article. Students then follow the author on an analytical discussion of what the professor wants as we collaboratively work thorough the handout.

The first section of the handout addresses the thesis of the essay. It is phrased as a question so that it becomes a tool for evaluation. A question requires an answer, and serves to more precisely describe their essay. An academic database will provide access to dozens if not hundreds of peer-reviewed sources for practically any topic. If the source answers the question, it is relevant to the essay. If the source does not answer the question, it is not relevant. The next section of the handout involves an analysis of what Svoboda considers heroic. The class then considers Faulkner's Homer, and students analyze his character using Wikipedia and SparkNotes. These are not scholarly sources, but can provide background for understanding the context of the story, the time, and some of the issues. As the author uses Google, Wikipedia, and SparkNotes, students are encouraged to evaluate sources and identify what each source can provide. The class collaboratively looks for signs of scholarship and critically evaluates the information retrieved. For example, Wikipedia may have a bibliography but is not scholarly. Whereas Wikipedia prohibits original research, scholarly publications only contribute original research to the academic conversation. Whereas Wikipedia strives for consensus in the community contributing to an issue, academic conversation embraces unique, original, and controversial ideas in the conversation of a discipline. None of these popular sources count in the five scholarly sources required for the essay, but they can provide the needed context for evaluating the assignment and selecting relevant material. At this point, the narrative discusses attributes of a scholarly article: material written by professionals for professionals, extremely detailed and specific, and following the conventions of an academic conversation in a specific discipline. These conventions include how citations are formatted as well as the importance of the accompanying bibliography. If the article doesn't have a named author or a bibliography, it quite likely is not scholarly.

The class then collectively uses the research question to identify search terms that would be appropriate, and looks up words that may be unfamiliar, such as antebellum South. Through this diversion, students have the experience of working through a frequently encountered obstacle, unfamiliar terms. The class then investigates the different between Google and a discovery tool. On the worksheet, the two boxes below the search information inquire about some context for heroic expectations of the character and heroic expectations discussed by Svoboda. At this point, students have a research question, and they have selected keywords from that question to use in a Central Search, the discovery tool used at UCM. Following the search, they identifying the number of magazine in which journal articles are available. In this example, the author is looking for examples of heroism in the antebellum South. The search retrieves hundreds of journal articles, all of which are peer-reviewed scholarly sources, but not all of them are relevant to the questions raised on the worksheet. The first several titles have nothing to do with the topic. Using the research question to evaluate relevance, two sources are selected because they address that question, and MLA citation format is used to identify the selections. The narrative uses appreciative inquiry by tying past search experience to the present task while setting more rigorous goals to accommodate the requirements of the current assignment. This activity generally takes one of two sessions devoted to library work by this professor, and the second session provides time for individual consultation using the worksheet as a framework for focusing the search and selecting the results.

Appreciative inquiry identifies transferable knowledge that can be used on the task at hand. The basic mechanics of searching (Discover) are developed by building more sophisticated skills in describing and evaluating sources for use in academic work. The questions need to be more focused. The keywords need to be more descriptive, and skill in manipulating a database needs to develop to include filtering the results (Dream). The worksheet provides a framework for structuring the exercise (Design), and working through the exercise steps the student through the various stages of locating and evaluating material for the essay (Deliver). The process of selecting relevant material embraces the Don't Settle objective.

CONCLUSION

Instead of giving students a fish in the form of information contained in textbooks, reserve readings, or lectures, assignments force students to learn to successfully fish for sources through gaining proficiency in finding what they need. Creating SRLs involves familiarizing students with a number of different tools and techniques. This instruction cultivates an awareness of the task so students can effectively choose the technique suited to the task. Reflective mentoring in the classroom offers a "director's commentary" on the search process in which librarians verbalize the thought process involved in analytically evaluating the research question, selecting descriptive keywords, selecting a search tool, and evaluating results. Library instruction can effectively cultivate information management skills through reflectively mentoring the critical thinking needed to overcome crucial obstacles in the research process and begin the process of linking the sources to the assignment. In this context, the challenges of information overload and anxiety can be addressed through discussing how to filter and evaluate a seemingly overwhelming list of results. AI recognizes skills students may already have, but identifies these abilities as a foundation that needs to be developed to successfully complete the task at hand.

Stories provide a memorable way to communicate information (Devine, Quinn, & Aguilar, 2014; Klipfel, 2014). A director's commentary on why choices in the research process are made provides such a story. Narratives provide an explanation when selecting one search tool over other available options, and how one is working with aspects of an issue provides a bridge between parts of the research exercise and past the obstacles discussed above. SRLs are able to choose the most applicable tools for a task, provide a rationale for that choice, and have an awareness of their ability to decide which technique is more effective for a given situation. Modeling this behavior provides an example that students can follow in a narrative they can relate to. This approach to satisficing sets the thermostat according to what the professor wants in an assignment while explaining how to achieve it to students. It explores which search tool is appropriate and which attributes of the source need to be evaluated. An AI approach recognizes the abilities students have while setting aspirational goals for completing more rigorous tasks along the way, and students gain more sophisticated research skills as librarians reflectively mentor self-reflective techniques through verbalizing critical choices along the way.

APPENDIX. Example of Completed Worksheet

<table>
<tr><td>Name</td><td>Date</td></tr>
<tr><td colspan="2">What question(s) would you like to investigate?
What were the heroic tendencies of Homer Barron?</td></tr>
<tr><td>What are the traits of a hero:
[Use information from Svoboda's book]</td><td>What are the character traits of my character:
Need character analysis of Homer</td></tr>
<tr><td colspan="2">Turn one interest into a question for evaluating further information:
How strongly did Homer reflect a <u>heroic image in the antebellum South</u>?
/Unfamiliar terms/</td></tr>
<tr><td>Then:
<u>heroic/image/antebellum South</u></td><td>Now:
[Use information from Svoboda's book]</td></tr>
<tr><td colspan="2">What keywords would capture that question: <u>heroic/image/antebellum South</u>?
Using CentralSearch I found this number of responses: 10393 Total, 88 Magazine, 1420 Journal</td></tr>
<tr><td colspan="2">==== Scholarly Article 1 Article [MLA Citation]
Goldner, Ellen J. "The Art of Intervention: The Humor of Sojourner Truth and the Antebellum Political Cartoon." MELUS, vol. 37, no. 4, 2012., pp. 41–67 doi:10.1353/mel.2012.0059.
Why was this source selected?
Illustrates how political cartoons satirized heroic images
==== Scholarly Article 2 Article [MLA Citation]
Glenn, Myra C. "Forging Manhood and Nationhood Together: American Sailors' Accounts of their Exploits, Sufferings, and Resistance in the Antebellum United States." American Nineteenth Century History, vol. 8, no. 1, 2007, pp. 27–49 doi:10.1080/14664650601178932.
Why was this source selected?
Discussed how sailors' tales told of heroic deeds</td></tr>
</table>

REFERENCES

Badke, W. (2010). Information as tool, not destination. *Online Searcher, 34*(4), 52–54.

Badke, W. (2014a). Mythbusting. *Online Searcher, 38*(3), 22–26.

Badke, W. (2014b). Those baffling assignments. *Online Searcher, 38*(3), 71–73.

Barrett, A. (2005). The information-seeking habits of graduate student researchers in the humanities. *Journal of Academic Librarianship, 31*(4), 324–331. https://doi.org/10.1016/j.acalib.2005.04.005

Bloom, J. L., Hutson, B. L., He, Y., & Konkle, E. (2013). Appreciative education. *New Directions for Student Services, 2013*(143), 5–18. https://doi.org/10.1002/ss.20055

Blundell, S. (2015). A descriptive phenomenological investigation of the academic information search process experience of remedial undergraduate students (Order No. 3710087). Available from ProQuest Dissertations & Theses Global. (1700193255). Retrieved from https://login.cyrano.ucmo.edu/login?url=http://search.proquest.com/docview/1700193255?accountid=6143

Cockell, J., & McArthur-Blair, J. (2012). *Appreciative inquiry in higher education: A transformative* force (1st ed.). San Francisco: Jossey-Bass.

Cooperrider, D. L., Stavros, J. M., & Whitney, D. K. (2008). *Appreciative inquiry handbook: For leaders of change* (2nd ed.). San Francisco, CA; Brunswick, OH: Crown Custom Pub.

Debowski, S. (2001). Wrong way: Go back! An exploration of novice search behaviours while conducting an information search. *The Electronic Library, 19*(6), 371–382. https://doi.org/10.1108/02640470110411991

Devine, J. R., Quinn, T., & Aguilar, P. (2014). Teaching and transforming through stories: An exploration of macro- and micro-narratives as teaching tools. *Reference Librarian, 55*(4), 273–288.

Fidel, R., Davies, R. K., Douglass, M. H., Holder, J. K., Hopkins, C. J., Kushner, E. J., . . . & Toney, C. D. (1999). A visit to the information mall: Web searching behavior of high school students. *Journal of the American Society for Information Science, 50*(1), 24–37.

Fister, B. (2015). The social life of knowledge: Faculty epistemologies. In T. Swanson & H. Jagman (Eds.), *Not just where to click: Teaching students how to think about information* (pp. 87–99). Chicago, IL: Association of College and Research Libraries.

Ford, N., Miller, D., & Moss, N. (2002). Web search strategies and retrieval effectiveness: An empirical study. *Journal of Documentation, 58*(1), 30–48.

Harrison, L. M., & Hasan, S. (2013). Appreciative inquiry in teaching and learning. *New Directions for Student Services, 2013*(143), 65–75. https://doi.org/10.1002/ss.20061

Head, A. J., & Eisenberg, M. B. (2009). *What today's college students say about conducting research in the digital age.* Seattle: University of Washington Information School, Project Information Literacy. Accessed 5/13/2016. chrome-extension://oemmndcbldboiebfnladdacbdfmadadm/http://www.projectinfolit.org/uploads/2/7/5/4/27541717/2009_final_report.pdf

Head, A. J., & Eisenberg, M. B. (2010). *Truth be told: How college students evaluate and use information in the digital age.* Seattle: University of Washington Information School, Project Information Literacy. Accessed 10/13/2016. http://www.projectinfolit.org/uploads/2/7/5/4/27541717/pil_fall2010_survey_fullreport1.pdf

Klipfel, K. M. (2014). Authentic engagement: Assessing the effects of authenticity on student engagement and information literacy in academic library instruction. *Reference Services Review, 42*(2), 229–245.

Kuglitsch, R. Z. (2015). Teaching for transfer: Reconciling the framework with disciplinary information literacy. *Portal: Libraries & the Academy, 15*(3), 457–470.

Lazonder, A. W., Biermans, H. J. A., & Wopereis, I. G. J. H. (2000). Differences between novice and experienced users in searching information on the World Wide Web. *Journal of the American Society for Information Science, 51*(6), 576–581. https://doi.org/10.1002/(SICI)1097-4571(2000)51:6<576::AID-ASI9>3.0.CO;2-7

Leckie, G. J. (1996). Desperately seeking citations: Uncovering faculty assumptions about the undergraduate research process. *Journal of Academic Librarianship, 22*(3), 201–208. https://doi.org/10.1016/S0099-1333(96)90059-2

Minetou, C. G., Chen, S. Y., & Liu, X. (2008). Investigation of the use of navigation tools in Web-based learning: A data mining approach. *International Journal of Human-Computer Interaction, 24*(1), 48–67.

Nicholas, D., Huntington, P., Jamali, H. R., Rowlands, I., & Fieldhouse, M. (2009). Student digital information-seeking behaviour in context. *Journal of Documentation*, *65*(1), 106–132. https://doi.org/http://dx.doi.org/10.1108/00220410910926149

Nilson, L. B. (2013). *Creating self-regulated learners*. Sterling, VA: Stylus Publishing.

Porter, B. (2011). Millennial undergraduate research strategies in Web and library information retrieval systems. *Journal of Web Librarianship*, *5*(4), 267–285. https://doi.org/10.1080/19322909.2011.623538

Prabha, C., Connaway, L. S., Olszewski, L., & Jenkins, L. R. (2007). What is enough? Satisficing information needs. *Journal of Documentation*, *63*(1), 74–89.

Rose-Wiles, L. M., & Hofmann, M. A. (2013). Still desperately seeking citations: Undergraduate research in the age of Web-scale discovery. *Journal of Library Administration, 53*(2–3), 147–166. https://doi.org/10.1080/01930826.2013.853493

Samba, E. N. (2013). Appreciative inquiry: An alternative approach to applied theatre. *Matatu*, (43), 47.

Thatcher, A. (2006). Information-seeking behaviors and cognitive search strategies in different search tasks on the WWW. *International Journal of Industrial Ergonomics*, *36*(12), 1055–1068.

Thatcher, A. (2008). Web search strategies: The influence of Web experience and task type. *Information Processing and Management*, *44*(3), 1308–1329.

Townsend, L., Brunetti, K., & Hofer, A. R. (2011). Threshold concepts and information literacy. *Portal: Libraries and the Academy*, *11*(3), 853–869.

Waniek, J., & Schäfer, T. (2009). The role of domain and system knowledge on text comprehension and information search in hypermedia. *Journal of Educational Multimedia and Hypermedia*, *18*(2), 221–239. Retrieved from https://login.cyrano.ucmo.edu/login?url=https://search.proquest.com/docview/205853773?accountid=6143

Wildemuth, B. M. (2004). The effect of domain knowledge on search tactic formulation. *Journal of the American Society for Information Science and Technology*, *55*(3), 246–258.

Wolff, C., Rod, A. B., & Schonfeld, R. C. (2016, April 4). *Ithaka S+R US Faculty Survey 2015*. Retrieved July 18, 2016, from http://www.sr.ithaka.org/publications/ithaka-sr-us-faculty-survey-2015/

Zach, L. (2005), When is "enough" enough? Modeling the information-seeking and stopping behavior of senior arts administrators. *American Society for Information Science and Technology*, *56*(1), pp. 23–35.

Zimmerman, B. J., & Martinez-Pons, M. (1990). Student differences in self-regulated learning: Relating grade, sex, and giftedness to self-efficacy and strategy use. *Journal of Educational Psychology*, *82*(1), 51–59. https://doi.org/10.1037/0022-0663.82.1.51

CHAPTER 10

USING INFORMATION LITERACY TUTORIALS EFFECTIVELY

Reflective Learning and Information Literacy in First-Year Composition

Emily Standridge
Vandy Dubre

INTRODUCTION

As is common for librarians and composition instructors, the authors of this text, humanities librarian Vandy Dubre and assistant professor of English Emily Standridge, collaborated on various classroom projects. Our partnership was, though, what Rolf Norgaard (2003), a professor of English, calls "a partnership of convenience," characterized by the stereotypical "quick field trip, the scavenger hunt, the generic stand-alone tutorial, or the dreary research paper" (p. 124). We worked together as needs arose but did little in terms of "genuine intellectual engagement" (p. 124). That changed when tasked with the improvement of information literacy (IL) instruction for the students at a medium-sized regional university, the University of Texas at Tyler (UT Tyler), when the university created an Information Literacy Directive, which, in full, reads:

> Faculty members and professional librarians at The University of Texas at Tyler believe that the ability to evaluate and incorporate information strategically will be critical in creating a competitive advantage for students. Graduates will be skilled in locating, evaluating, and effectively using and communicating information in various formats. They will be aware of the economic, legal, and social issues concerning the use of information and will be able to access and use information ethically and legally. Within this comprehensive information literacy effort, the University will strive to develop the ability of its students to use information technology effectively in their work and daily lives. UT Tyler's information systems will be state-of-the-art and will serve as the central hub influencing, supporting, and integrating academic and administrative processes across the University. (The University of Texas at Tyler, p. 3)

This new directive provided the urgency to implement some of the ideas we had been discussing about improving pedagogical methods for library and composition interactions. The directive called for reaching students across multiple disciplines, and we wanted to do more than just disconnected lessons with little value placed on them. We also wanted to value the limited class time composition instructors had with their students. We were searching for a model that would teach the amount of information literacy dictated by the university, have flexibility for faculty and students in completion, and have the ability to maximize the impact of hands-on librarian instruction.

We knew "one of the major difficulties information literacy practitioners must contend with is how to make information literacy embodied, situated, and social for our diverse student body" (Jacobs, 2008, p. 259). We wanted to offer individualized and comprehensive lessons to all first-year composition students, but we lacked the time or resources to develop such lessons from scratch. The Muntz Library leadership at UT Tyler decided to start the IL program with purchased lessons from Research Ready-Academy (RR-A). RR-A was designed by information literacy librarians and aligned with the Association of College and Research Libraries (ACRL) information literacy standards (ACRL, 2000). The ACRL standards identify criteria for the "information literate" person and break each criterion into "performance indicators" and "outcomes." The desired learning outcomes and assessments of those outcomes provided

TABLE 10.1 *Courses Within the RR-A Levels*

Level 2	Sources, Sources, Sources	Website Evaluation	Conquer the Research Process	Cite It Before You Write It	Inquiring Minds Want to Know
Level 3	Source Identification	Databases & Open Web	Identifying Source Credibility	Ethical Research	Conquering Research

confidence that RR-A would have the rigorous content dictated in the IL directive. Additionally, RR-A reported multiple points of data about student performance, painting a nuanced picture of what students were learning as well as where they were having difficulties. RR-A is split into three "levels"; each level begins with a "Pre-Test" to assess what students know going in and ends with a "Post-Test" to assess what students have learned (or not learned) through that level. Each "level" is broken down into multiple "courses" (see Table 10.1), which cover specific areas of IL with quizzes and activities built in to assess learning of the concepts at each stage.

One of the main concerns in using RR-A was the information being too "canned," created to meet the ACRL guideline but not actually meeting the needs of our students in our courses. Jacobs (2008) notes similar concerns, stating, "because learning, teaching, researching, writing, and thinking are inherently messy processes, the neatness of ACRL-inspired rubrics does presses a certain allure. It is no wonder, then, that administrators turn to them as a way of managing the messiness of pedagogical reflection and curricular evaluation" (p. 258). Ultimately, RR-A made it clear that we could adapt the materials as needed to meet our needs and objectives while working within their tested and rigorous standards. They were happy for us to change text, examples, and the order of delivery of the lessons to work with our courses. With limited time and resources to develop fully individualized lessons, let alone be able to justify their assessments across situations, this was the best option available.

We also found that RR-A answered a call for a best-practices teaching method for IL. Bean (2011) notes the importance of engaging students at multiple points through multiple methods as a means of increasing critical thinking skills. RR-A does just what Bean calls for: each "lesson," a subset of a larger "course," includes several "quiz" questions reviewing the material immediately after it is presented; short answer questions appear at the end of each "lesson," reviewing the material as a whole. At the end of each "course," several short answer questions are presented to review material on a larger scale. When added to a course that often already instructed students on IL matters, RR-A further increased the multiple points and methods of instruction in IL. Plus, students and instructors are able to see students' scores on IL matters at multiple points and through multiple methods within RR-A, giving another window into how students are actually learning the material. This method of instruction was what we wanted to see across all sections, so we were encouraged to see it as part of this product from the beginning. We would only need to modify things slightly, if at all, based on our individual needs.

RR-A was also the ideal product from the perspective of implementation. All of the set answer quiz questions were graded automatically, including the pre- and post-test scores; they required no additional labor to process. The short answer questions did need to be graded individually, but Vandy argued that that job could easily be taken on by the librarians because they are experts in both IL and RR-A. RR-A did more than just collect information. Pre- and post-test scores were compared in the program itself, and a number of statistical analyses on all of the assessment data was provided through the RR-A platform. This allowed unprecedented insight into student work with a minimum of effort. Further, RR-A technology was convenient to integrate into the learning management system, so both on-campus and online university classes could use the materials easily.

We anticipated having to defend the use of RR-A against claims that it would be "disconnected from pedagogical theories and day-to-day practices, but it also begins to lose sight of the large global goals" of IL in higher education, becoming nothing more than an extra set of activities divorced from the content of the class (Jacobs, 2008, p. 258). Our goal was to start with the lessons RR-A had already created and, through our "genuine intellectual collaboration" (Norgard, 2003, p. 124), build something suited exactly to the needs of our institution.

Our Approach

This chapter traces our process from Research Ready-Academy's existing information literacy lessons to completely customized information literacy education for the University of Texas at Tyler's first-year composition classes. We offer what Jacobs (2008) calls "actual classroom practices and activities not, as Chris Gallagher has described, so that we may present 'replicable results' but to 'provide materials for teachers to reflect on and engage'" (p. 260). The information we present does support the idea that information literacy instruction is effective when provided through first-year composition using both a structured curriculum package created independently of any particular course with a reflective writing element that is particular to that FYC course.

This chapter traces our path to this conclusion by reviewing our pilot semesters using RR-A and the refinements to our approach as we proceeded. We conclude with evidence from student writings, which shows that they have achieved a new kind of thinking about their IL. This new thinking is indicative of their movement in Bloom's Revised Taxonomy.

DATA

Pilot 1: Lessons in One Semester of FYC

Model

In the spring 2015 semester, we started with one section of English 1302, the second semester of the FYC courses offered at UT Tyler. Our goal was for students to complete both Level 2 and Level 3 of RR-A and to increase their post-test scores. RR-A was used as an IL-focused supplement to the implied IL instruction of the other course materials. RR-A materials were graded mostly on completion as it was assumed that the "active learning" and "application" seen in the other areas of the course were more important to their learning (Porter, 2014).

Rationale

English 1302 was selected because it is a required course, whereas other FYC courses are optional in students' degree plans. Students from all majors take English 1302 and are not isolated by major, and the course was specifically designed to be interdisciplinary, a common goal among similar programs (Deitering & Jameson, 2008; Palsson & McDade, 2014).

Outcomes

We were encouraged about the possibility of instructing a large majority of students (we will never reach "all students" with implementation in only one course) since we saw such a large number of majors represented in this pilot: Nursing, Biology, Accounting, Spanish, Human Resources, and Education. However, many of the students failed to complete the RR-A materials; while 12 students completed the RR Level 2 pre-test, only 2 completed the post-test. Only 7 of the beginning 12 students did the Level 3 pre-test, and only 2 of those did the Level 3 post-test. This lack of completion was likely due to the language of instruction, which failed to say "take the post-test" directly. Still, students were not completing the materials and we felt that we would need to make some important changes in how the materials were presented in order to meet the directive's imperative to instruct "all students" with a "full range of instruction."

For the students who did complete the pre- and post-tests, Level 2 results showed an increase while Level 3 showed a decrease in scores. This result was perplexing because in-class discussions showed students were capable of fluent discussions of the new IL material in both levels of RR-A. The quiz scores helped illuminate the matter further: students were having trouble retaining what they learned. Students showed increases in the scores from the pre-tests to the quizzes at the end of each course in Level 2, demonstrating an ability to remember the material for the short term (see

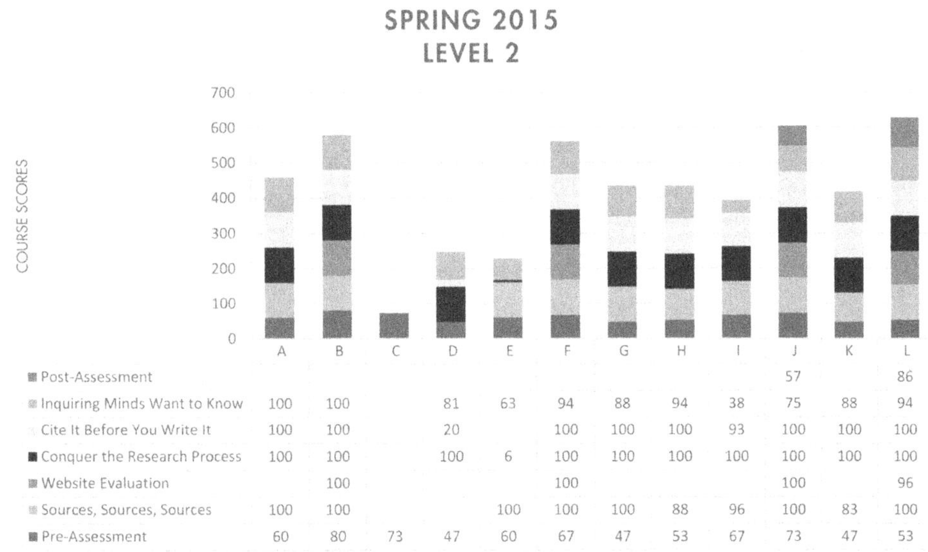

	A	B	C	D	E	F	G	H	I	J	K	L
Post-Assessment										57		86
Inquiring Minds Want to Know	100	100		81	63	94	88	94	38	75	88	94
Cite It Before You Write It	100	100		20		100	100	100	93	100	100	100
Conquer the Research Process	100	100		100	6	100	100	100	100	100	100	100
Website Evaluation		100				100				100		96
Sources, Sources, Sources	100	100			100	100	100	88	96	100	83	100
Pre-Assessment	60	80	73	47	60	67	47	53	67	73	47	53

Figure 10.1 Spring 2015 (Level 2) student scores on all courses. Students who did not attempt the course are left blank.

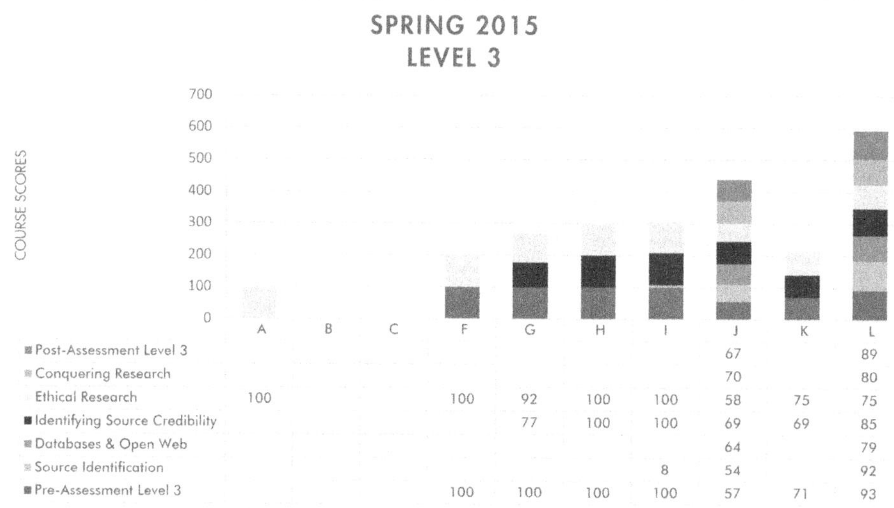

Figure 10.2 Spring 2015 (Level 3) student scores on all courses. Students who did not attempt the course are left blank.

Figure 10.1). A similar, although less marked, change in scores was also shown in Level 3 (see Figure 10.2). The lack of post-test scores and the decrease in post-test scores seen in Level 3 combine to show a picture of students not remembering the material beyond their moments within RR-A, likely because they were not applying the information beyond the immediate setting. Even though close analysis of student writing was beyond our original scope, specific trends seen in grading revealed that they were not applying what they were doing in the supplements to their "main" writing work.

Changes

Based on students' requests on satisfaction surveys for "more time to do" the work and more quizzes to process RR-A as well as the low completion rates, we knew that completing Level 2 *and* Level 3 in one semester was simply too much work. Splitting the levels over the two-semester FYC sequence made sense.

We also decided to change how the RR-A lessons were used. We wanted to make clearer the connection between the RR-A and the class material as students claimed RR-A was not "relevant to the subject matter." This meant revising both the RR-A materials and the course content. At the end of our first pilot semester, we were convinced of the potential of our project to meet many of the IL Directive goals using RR-A, but we also saw room for a great deal of improvement.

Pilot 2: Expanding to Two Semesters of FYC: English 1301

Model

With the new semester of our pilot study, we wanted to increase students' retention of the RR-A information by moving the RR-A lesson timing relative to class discussions and by including the language and terminology of RR-A within class discussions more consciously and purposefully. This semester, we worked with English 1301, the first of the FYC courses offered at UT Tyler, and included Level 2 courses as they best matched the course material.

In addition to the reconfiguring of the content delivered, the reporting of quiz evaluations was changed. Vandy agreed to compile scores from multiple choice and short answer questions and forward the information to Emily. Emily would incorporate this data into the class grading scheme. This grading arrangement eased the issues students encountered with their "proof" of completion while also increasing the importance of actually learning the material, as that knowledge would be reflected in their grades.

Our goal in the second pilot was to obtain higher completion rates, to see improvements in post-test scores, and to create improved engagement with the RR-A material among students as measured by in-class discussions.

Rationale

The guiding assumption of Pilot 1 was that highlighting the IL concepts inherent in the work students were doing through RR-A would increase students' IL abilities, but this was not seen to be accurate. More work was needed to "situate [IL] instruction in the lived academic and social lives" of our students (Norgaard 2004). By directly linking the RR-A lessons into class content, using shared vocabulary among the elements of the class, and grading on answers as well as completion in RR-A, we hypothesized that Pilot 2 would be more beneficial for our students.

Outcomes

Eleven students completed the pre- and post-tests and 91% of those students showed an increase in their post-test scores. This shows an increase in both completion rates and knowledge measured. We were satisfied that this increase in post-test completion revealed students were being exposed to all of the information we wanted, so we were well on the path to meeting the directive. We still had a disappointing eight students begin but not complete the work; our efforts to increase the importance and relevance of the RR-A courses were only partially effective. Student quiz grades were also consistent with our previous pilot: they showed an increase from pre-test to quiz, so students were remembering the information during the course of RR-A (see Figure 10.3).

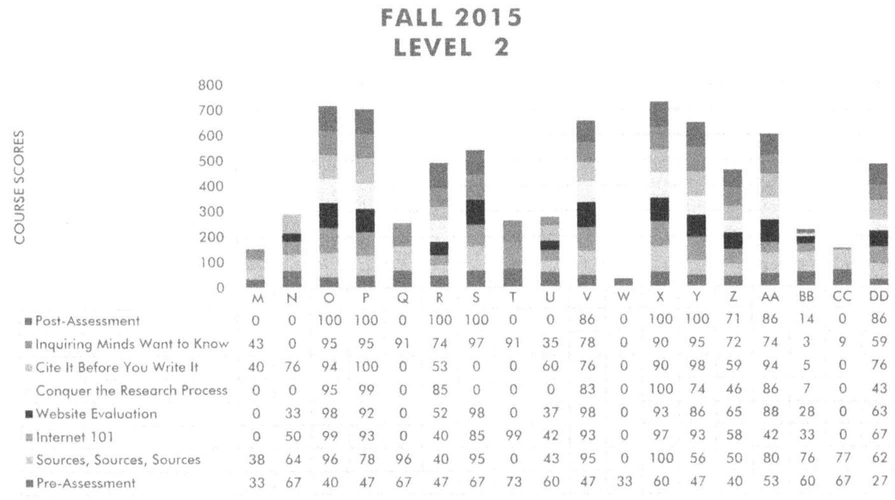

	M	N	O	P	Q	R	S	T	U	V	W	X	Y	Z	AA	BB	CC	DD
Post-Assessment	0	0	100	100	0	100	100	0	0	86	0	100	100	71	86	14	0	86
Inquiring Minds Want to Know	43	0	95	95	91	74	97	91	35	78	0	90	95	72	74	3	9	59
Cite It Before You Write It	40	76	94	100	0	53	0	0	60	76	0	90	98	59	94	5	0	76
Conquer the Research Process	0	0	95	99	0	85	0	0	0	83	0	100	74	46	86	7	0	43
Website Evaluation	0	33	98	92	0	52	98	0	37	98	0	93	86	65	88	28	0	63
Internet 101	0	50	99	93	0	40	85	99	42	93	0	97	93	58	42	33	0	67
Sources, Sources, Sources	38	64	96	78	96	40	95	0	43	95	0	100	56	50	80	76	77	62
Pre-Assessment	33	67	40	47	67	47	67	73	60	47	33	60	47	40	53	60	67	27

Figure 10.3 Fall 2015 (Level 2) student scores on all lessons.

A new trend emerged as we kept closer track of students' performance on the short answer questions versus the multiple choice answer questions. Students would score well on the multiple choice questions but failed to do well on the short answer–type questions. This pattern of scores indicated that even though students were viewing the information and able to remember it, they were not able to apply the information. Students were simply remembering the material from RR-A, and probably only for a short time; if we wanted to increase their ability to retain and apply the ideas, we would need to make further adjustments. In-class discussions showed students were more invested in this work than in Pilot 1, but they were not applying their learning as much as we wanted.

Changes

Something needed to be added to increase students' engagement with the material to move them past the remembering stage of learning. Students needed to do more writing in conjunction with the RR-A lessons to get this increased critical thinking (Bean, 2011). We decided to add reflective writings built on those already a regular part of the course, but with specific consideration of RR-A and IL; as Yancey (1998) states, reflection allows students the "articulating of what learning has taken place, as embodied in various texts as well as in the processes used by the writer" (p. 6). Reflective writings along with the other data points would provide a nuanced picture of students' IL skills while also helping them do more than just remember the lessons temporarily.

Pilot 3: Lessons in Two Semesters of FYC With Reflective Writing

Model

Pilot 3 occurred in spring 2016 with English 1302 and Level 3 of RR-A. The incorporation and pacing of the RR-A lessons was the same as in Pilot 2, but we built upon established reflective writing assignments by including questions about how the information presented in the RR-A lessons impacted writing throughout the semester and by creating a distinct writing assignment directly related to the RR-A lessons. Students completed reflection questions at the end of each writing project. The prompts asked them to consider how the RR-A information added to their work in the project. At the end of the semester and as scaffolding for their final exam paper, students were asked to "speak about the benefits and shortcomings of the Research Ready activities" using "specific elements in the Modules (lessons)" to "find at least one beneficial thing and one negative thing" in a separate paper. They were given a set of questions to consider in their writing:

What are the main things Research Ready was attempting to teach you?
How was Research Ready attempting to teach? (Using what methods?)
How much of Research Ready did you already know? How much was new?
Do you think you learned using Research Ready—why or why not?
What do you know about yourself as a learner because of Research Ready?

Students worked on drafts of this paper with teacher and peer feedback. Their writing received a final grade; students were familiar with this pattern of work as it was followed throughout the semester. The goal of this assignment was to help students learn the ways they were expected to perform "reflection" on the final exam paper: using specific examples from the lessons and thoughtfully answering the questions given, in addition to helping them retain and apply their IL learning from

RR-A. The questions were designed to help students postulate about the impact of RR-A information on their coursework as well as their future lives, which ,as Norgaard (2004) suggested improves learning and retention of material.

Rationale

While we knew the importance of writing in learning, we did not want to add what seemed like *another* required writing feature to English 1301 and 1302, especially since so many of the assignments already in place achieved what we wanted from information literate students. We also did not want to encounter the issues Palsson and McDade (2014) encountered in setting up a common assignment; namely, we wanted to keep instruction firmly situated in the hands of each instructor. Reflection, though, adds a common feature with common evaluative methods, which works for any classroom or goal (Yancey, 1998). We thus thought that it was time to add a reflective writing feature.

Outcomes

Seventeen out of the initial 30 students completed the pre- and post-tests in RR-A during the spring 2016 semester. Their scores were consistent with those in previous semesters, as shown in Figure 10.4.

Unlike previous results, just 82% of students showed an increase in their scores from pre-test to post-test. While this was initially concerning, as it seemed to indicate that students were learning less in the RR-A courses with the addition of written reflections, there are some potential explanations for the lowered score. First, since more students actually completed both the pre- and post-tests, there could have been some selection bias in the previous semesters. Students who knew much of the material to begin with may have been the ones to complete the tests rather than all students, making Pilot 3's percentage simply a better representation of this population's growth since more completed both tests. Second, since students were interacting with the material in more depth, they could have been less certain of what they knew. As students grapple with complexity, we know that they sometimes "drop" what they have previously mastered. Potentially the same is true here. Third, because this was such a small sample, the results from this class may just have been a fluke. Overall, there was a 35% increase in the scores between pre- and post-tests, which means the class as a whole was learning, whatever else was happening. While this drop was puzzling, the further data from the reflective writings eased some of our concerns.

Gleaning information from the reflections was more complicated than grading quiz questions. We did a two-round coding process on the reflective essays: first, reading the essays individually, creating coding categories based on the patterns noticed. We then compared categories and refined them to "suggestions," "how I learn," "already knew/ expanded knowledge/wrong information," "writing skills," and "topics" discussed. With the new set of coding categories, we recoded the essays together.

The "suggestions" and "how I learn" pieces of the reflections were responses to either the prompt or in-class discussion; they had little to do with meeting the IL Directive, but they were ultimately important in the ways discussed below. The code about what students knew or did not know was very revealing for the directive. One student wrote, quite impactfully, "Of course I knew what primary and secondary sources were, and basic information like that. What surprised me, however, was the amount of information I

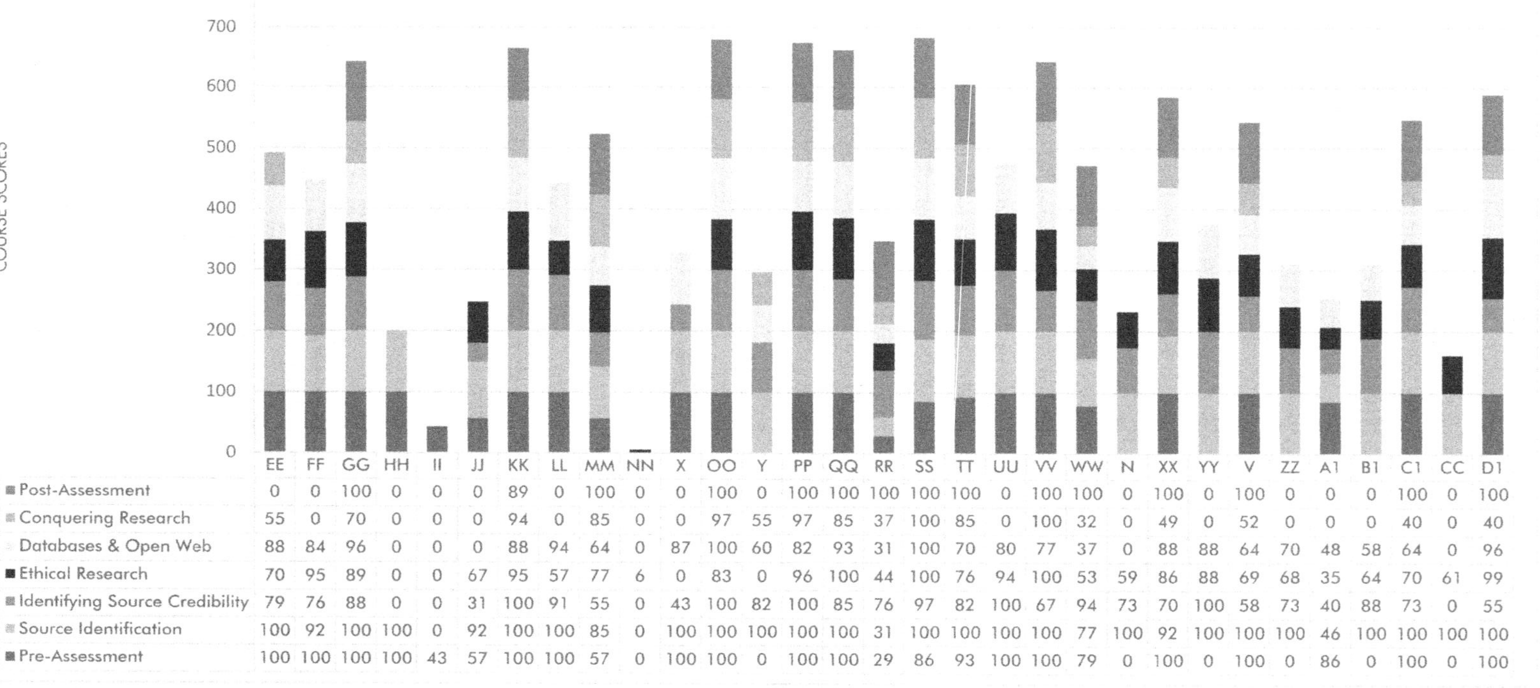

	EE	FF	GG	HH	II	JJ	KK	LL	MM	NN	X	OO	Y	PP	QQ	RR	SS	TT	UU	VV	WW	N	XX	YY	V	ZZ	A1	B1	C1	CC	D1
Post-Assessment	0	0	100	0	0	0	89	0	100	0	0	100	0	100	100	100	100	100	0	100	100	0	100	0	100	0	0	0	100	0	100
Conquering Research	55	0	70	0	0	0	94	0	85	0	0	97	55	97	85	37	100	85	0	100	32	0	49	0	52	0	0	0	40	0	40
Databases & Open Web	88	84	96	0	0	0	88	94	64	0	87	100	60	82	93	31	100	70	80	77	37	0	88	88	64	70	48	58	64	0	96
Ethical Research	70	95	89	0	0	67	95	57	77	6	0	83	0	96	100	44	100	76	94	100	53	59	86	88	69	68	35	64	70	61	99
Identifying Source Credibility	79	76	88	0	0	31	100	91	55	0	43	100	82	100	85	76	97	82	100	67	94	73	70	100	58	73	40	88	73	0	55
Source Identification	100	92	100	100	0	92	100	100	85	0	100	100	100	100	100	31	100	100	100	100	77	100	92	100	100	100	46	100	100	100	100
Pre-Assessment	100	100	100	100	43	57	100	100	57	0	100	100	0	100	100	29	86	93	100	100	79	0	100	0	100	0	86	0	100	0	100

Figure 10.4 Spring 2016 (Level 3) student scores on all lessons.

didn't know" (Student 14.004). Throughout the pilots students noted how they felt that RR-A was not new material, but, like this student, soon realized that there was far more depth to the topics than they had previously been introduced to. Eighty-nine percent of students thought the material in RR-A was familiar to them to some extent, claiming that they "already knew most of what was presented." Upon further analysis of the essays, though, we found that 79% of the students were able to name at least one area where they expanded their knowledge on a previously known topic or learned a new facet of those known topics. So students were "reviewing" their knowledge, but they were also expanding, refining, and gaining new knowledge in the process. The reflections revealed that students were deepening their understanding of the topics, which was important since it called for students to have a working knowledge of IL skills.

The "writing skills" elements showed students applying what RR-A was teaching to their work, with 25% discussing finding sources more effectively and efficiently than they previously had or other writing skills. For instance, one student said, "my writing is also improved after doing the research ready assignment because it informed me about researching a topic on the internet without wasting a lot of time such as using proper search engines for scholarly articles instead of spending an ample of time on the open web and finding the vague information" (Student 3.006). In addition to technology-specific writing skills, students wrote about how RR-A improved their writing skills more generally, such as, "this helped me in future writing as I am able to take essays and learning in small chunks rather than try to complete everything in one sitting" (Student 3.004). Students were thus using the information they learned as well as applying it to effective communication in multiple situations, an element of the directive not seen in any of the other pilots. Finally, the topics mentioned most often were about sources (79%) and plagiarism (54%), indicating that students were remembering, outside of RR-A quiz questions, information about finding and ethically using sources, another of the IL Directive elements not seen as clearly in previous pilots. Overall, students in Pilot 3 showed a much greater growth in their information literacy than in any other semester.

There was a small but important 11% of the students who claimed to know specific information from RR-A, but in the essay wrote information that was incorrect or not in the RR-A platform at all. For instance, a student wrote, "I learned that primary sources are usually peer-reviewed journals and secondary sources, like magazines usually have advertisements" (Student 4.004). This incorrect understanding of primary and secondary sources suggests a student who was just "clicking through to get completion" as it correctly identifies a topic of discussion in the tutorial. Some students are not going to engage with the material, no matter what. At least this student was considering types of sources in a way that would not harm him or her in the future. Another student wrote about improving grammar knowledge during RR-A, which was part of the course materials, not the RR-A. This student's response, despite not meeting the assignment, argues for the work we have been doing, as it shows that the student did not really distinguish RR-A from any other course material.

Overall, students were starting to connect the information from Research Ready and the course to create a cohesive idea of what information literacy means in practice and to think about how they will be able to apply those skills throughout their lives when they had both the RR-A lessons and the reflective essay incorporated in their course.

Benefits of This Approach

We had two main goals in our process: we wanted and needed to find a method for meeting the IL Directive set by our university, and we wanted to see students develop their critical thinking in multiple directions in order to impact their college careers and life after college. We were frustrated by our students' inability to apply learning from one course to another or one situation to another, especially as they used online resources. Through these pilots, we found that using a premade (but adapted to our situation) IL curricula along with reflective writing met our goals. The benefits of this model are seen through the lens of the IL Directive, Bloom's Revised Taxonomy, and students' reflective writing.

IL Directive

The IL Directive had three main components, in which students showed marked improvement during our third pilot:

1. Students are skilled in locating, evaluating and effectively using and communicating information.
2. Students are aware of economic, legal, and social issues concerning the use of information.
3. Students are able to use information technology effectively in their work and daily lives.

As discussed throughout, students were making progress toward meeting the elements of this directive from Pilot 1. In each iteration, we saw students interacting with the material, especially in locating information and being aware of the issues concerning the use of information. In Pilot 3, we saw students engaging in all areas of the directive. Students saw the information, were tested on it, and wrote about it. The student writing artifacts suggest they were both being instructed on and applying the information in their English classes, and students claimed to be able to use the information in other classes as well. Students developed the information literacy skills to have the "competitive edge" the directive asked for; with reflection, though, students were also developing their critical thinking skills in many areas, demonstrating growth along Bloom's Revised Taxonomy (see Figure 10.5).

Bloom's Revised Taxonomy

The quizzes, both multiple choice and short answer, included in RR-A primarily measured students' remembering skills—the lowest level. The set answer questions were drawn directly from the lessons, with wording nearly the same as in the lessons. The short answer questions, which drew more on contexts in which the information would be used, were aimed at the understanding element of Bloom's. The fact that students in Pilots 1 and 2 did not do as well on the short answer questions shows that they were not advancing in this area. When we moved to Pilot 3, students showed an increase in their short answer scores, demonstrating their growth from remembering to understanding. With the reflective writing, many students showed even more growth, up to the analyzing and evaluating stages.

Students were asked to "analyze" source information during RR-A; this analysis was seen in multiple courses including "Sources,

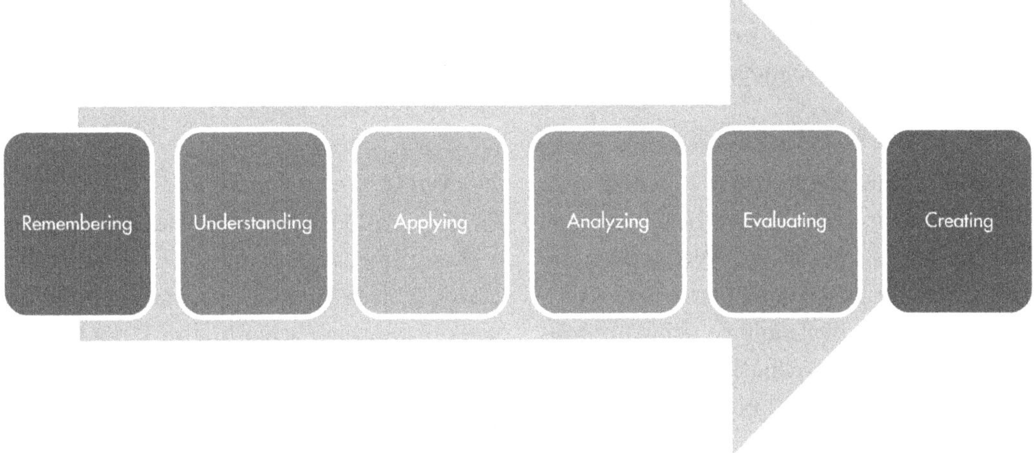

Figure 10.5 Bloom's Revised Taxonomy. (Data from Krathwohl, 2002.)

Sources, Sources" and "Identifying Source Credibility." The short answer quiz responses demonstrated some limited analysis, but students showed detailed analysis in their reflective writing on two levels:

1. Analysis of sources within their own writing. For instance, "Being taught how to use a database and what good sources looked like, I was able to differentiate the good from the bad to improve my papers" (Student 1.004). Additionally, another student discussed how RR-A helped him or her learn to "identify if [sources] are credible or not and also if they are considered primary or secondary sources that really helped me use those article in this class and other more effectively" (Student 11.004). Both of these examples reveal students' own awareness of how and when they "analyze" source material. Students then reported using that analysis to their benefit when writing papers. While we cannot be certain this portrayal of "analysis" is entirely accurate, the fact they write about it indicates this level of thinking is present.

2. Analysis in action is seen as they answered the question "What do you know about yourself as a learner because of Research Ready?" Students variously described themselves as "visual learner," "impatient learner," and "to the point learner" and discussed how "reflecting over what I gained from Research Ready encouraged me to not only understand what I learned, but to also recognize how I learned it" (Student 4.006). Many students really dug into how they retained information and how they write. For instance, Student 3.004 noted that RR-A "helped [*sic*] me in future writing as I am able to take essays and learning in small chunks rather than try to complete everything in one sitting." This student was able to recognize the pattern of instruction in RR-A as a pattern of writing that would help him or her be more successful. A student who claimed "although I personally prefer learning in a classroom with a professor" because he or she enjoyed personalized attention, argued that "doing Research Ready really helped me as a student by teaching and explaining the lessons in a different way" (Student 2.004). This student was able to see beyond personal preferences in order to analyze the learning elements and recognize the strength of them. Students enact "analysis" in their writing as well as discussing it as a process they have

completed. With both of those elements present in the reflective writing, it is safe to say that students have indeed expanded their thinking in this way.

"Evaluating" was seen as students spoke about the value of the RR-A experience. In Pilot 1, students claimed that the lessons were "boring" or "super cheesy." While these are critiques of the program that have some validity, they lack specificity and do not really evaluate the program as such. By Pilot 3, though, we were seeing students pointing to specific benefits and detraction leading to an overall evaluation of the entire learning experience. For instance, one student said, "because of the narrative, Research Ready made it personable, even if it was just cartoons with talking bubbles" (Student 6.006). This student, instead of calling the art "cheesy," discussed why that simple addition made his or her learning of the subject more effective. Similarly, another student lauded the use of clever examples and well-structured explanations to help him or her "personally understand what research ready was trying to explain" (6.004). The ability to tie the learning to specific examples and explanations and thus claim its overall usefulness is an excellent evaluation. Even the students who did not find the course useful showed elements of evaluation in their work. Student 13.006 stated, "I am not saying that this research academy work was a waste of time" even though it started to "feel like busy work" because the lessons were "drawing things out and doing cartoons for students who are in college." Even while noting that the style of instruction did not suit his or her learning preferences, this student thought that it encouraged a "focus on each subject" and that the lessons "do something different so that these topics that we have to do" feel less repetitive and stick to "just the facts." This evaluation points to a problem the student identified and looks to a solution for that problem, which fits into Bloom's "analysis" and "evaluation" levels.

Student Learning Preferences

As was mentioned above, student learning was a theme seen among many of the reflective essays. In addition to demonstrating students' ways of thinking according to Bloom's Taxonomy, discussions of their learning allowed us insight into how to revise the lessons for future use. Many students (14%) noted how the small chunks of information were useful for them. They noted that "this is a good way to teach as it is not overwhelming at any point" (3.004). Since students in Pilot 1 complained of not having enough time or interaction with the material, this statement was gratifying; splitting the levels over two semesters was a good choice. Also, students who feel overwhelmed will not learn as effectively, so students noting their comfort with the way information is presented indicates they are in a mindset to learn (Gute & Gute 2008). Students also noted that delivery of RR-A was helpful, with one stating it "allowed me to be more flexible with my learning styles and have some control of my environment" (Student 1.006). Control is another marker of student engagement with the material. We saw through the reflections that Pilot 3's model set students up to learn as much as possible.

Reflections also revealed that students need examples and applications in order to learn most effectively. Student 5.004 said, "I now definitely know that I will retain information better when I write the information given and actually put it to use" (Student 5.004). While this information does not come as a surprise to educators, allowing students to come to this conclusion through experience cements that learning principle for them. Whether that "writing things down" is done through independent written reflection or quizzes used in RR-A seems less important; 43% of students claimed frequent quizzes and other assessments aided in their work, indicating this practice helps them pay attention to the lesson and apply what they learn immediately. Keeping the application questions is important for RR-A's success, even if students voice complaints.

Students also valued the multiple modes of instruction as much as we theorized they would. Students need instruction to come in multiple verbal patterns, as evidenced by 36% of reflections noting the importance of definitions in conjunction with examples in their understanding of important topics. Working beyond just verbal patterns is crucial as well. Student 6.006 noted, "sometimes it can be difficult to understand what an educator or education program is trying to teach, but because of the narratives research ready made it personable even if it was just cartoons with talking bubbles." Adding a visual story, even a simplistic cartoon, can really change the impact of a lesson, helping students learn more effectively. This is supported by the fact that 21% of reflection noted the importance of added visuals in students' engagement with and processing of the material.

MOVING FORWARD

Problems With Large-Scale Implementation

In fall 2016, we offered a "soft start" to the program. Instructors were given the choice of incorporating the Pilot 3 model into their courses. Few chose to do so; many who did accept the invitation used methods that clearly misunderstood the goals of the project, sticking to inserting the "canned product" into their course with no consideration of how it fit into their teaching or grading schemes at a larger scale. For instance, one instructor did not want to change the planned class syllabus so added RR-A courses and reflections as "extra credit," thinking it would accomplish the same goals as the pilot with the incorporated reflection. These flawed adoptions were in spite of sharing the data from the pilots and a sample syllabus showing how and where the lessons could be placed.

We attempted full implementation to all sections of FYC courses in spring 2017. All English 1302 instructors on our campus were asked to use the model of courses and reflections used in Pilot 3. We saw 12 sections adopt the program, which was not full implementation, but did give us a bigger picture of the ways to work with faculty and the issues with student use of the lessons. Faculty struggled with technical concerns as well as ideological issues related to the importance of the work to their course. As in our "soft start," they assumed the "canned product" could not work for their individualized needs. We also heard repeatedly that the lessons were covering material that was already implied in the course and that it was "busy work" for students. This was all despite a workshop discussing the needs for the lessons as well as why they were best practices for diversifying instruction.

Additionally, the 12 sections created a great deal more work for Vandy than anticipated. She found herself managing all the technical problems and complaints without the support that she needed. Out of these issues, we created a focus group of five instructors teaching both FYC courses. The goal of the focus group was to increase faculty "buy-in" for the program while increasing understanding of the purpose of the lessons in meeting the directive while meeting faculty concerns. The discussion resulted in planned adaptations of the program in terms of faculty control and personalization. The Focus Group worked together to both improve the lessons and also align the lessons themselves with the topics presented in the sections (see Table 10.2). Looking at the types of concepts taught in English 1301 and English 1302, some lessons were moved between the two sections and some lessons were found to be redundant. The new collection better suits the faculty and the needs of each section. We removed short answer questions from the lessons since faculty felt grading of those by someone outside their class removed the importance and value of the work. Instead, starting in fall 2017, all faculty were given options for short answer questions to incorporate into their established quizzes and reflection during the course. This adaptation also relieved some of the extra work on Vandy and eased the complaints of students about the grading of the work. It also increased faculty's engagement with the lessons and the purpose of the program. We also decided to further revise all of the lessons using avatars resembling the diverse population at UT Tyler. While this was not directly requested by the focus group, we realized that making the lessons appear more personalized with these recognizable "faces" rather than the generic drawings originally used would increase the impression of the personalization that was already occurring but that seemed invisible to the faculty. We also thought that this change would help students engage with the material more as the lessons were "coming from the mouths" of faces they "knew." Avatars were created with the diversity of our student population as well as specific types of "majors" that reflect the different types of research needs, such as the differences in nursing, humanities, and engineering research. Using these examples helps the students understand how these concepts relate to them in their fields of study and careers. All of the skills were discussed in both academic and personal life settings, emphasizing how each skill could be used in the school/work environment and in everyday life. Ultimately, the focus group helped us think about ways of discussing and displaying our lessons that moved beyond the impression (however false it might have been) that these were "canned lessons" that could be added to a class with no engagement from the faculty.

Changing With the Times: When Your Product Disappears

After all of our efforts to learn the best way to work with Research Ready-Academy, we learned the company had been purchased and would no longer be available. Sadly, this is not an uncommon occurrence, especially

TABLE 10.2 *New Course Schedule Within the RR-A Levels*

Level 2	Internet Basics	Website Evaluation	Scholarly Thinking & Writing	Plagiarism Citations	
Level 3	Source Identification	Source Credibility	Using Databases	Ethical Research	Research Processes

when looking at digital tools. Because of our history with the company, though, we were able to use all of their course content with appropriate recognition, so we do not have to develop new lessons. If this kind of usage were not an option, we could have created our own lessons; however this would have forced a drastic time issue and would have delayed full implementation for possibly another year.

As we scrambled to adapt the material to a new platform (Softchalk, for us), we were able to adjust the materials along the way, taking into consideration the feedback students had given us. We are building in more content with a direct link to course materials. We are also incorporating the kinds of assignments used in English 1301 and 1302 into the courses. We are using the RR-A platform to springboard our program, adapting it completely to our campus's needs.

Importance of Reflection

The most important thing we learned in this process was the importance of the right kind of reflection. Simply using the product as marketed, even with short answer questions that required students to apply the material taught, did not result in the learning gains we hoped to see. When we added the reflective questions to the process of their papers and the independent reflective essay, we saw completion increase and engagement with the material increase. Students were able to make larger scale connections to the tutorial, their classwork for English 1301/1302, courses beyond English, and themselves as students and future professionals.

While the importance of reflection was indicated through all of our research, it was not until we saw the methods of reflection actually working through the students' own words that we were convinced of the ultimate success of this approach. With the evidence from these reflective pieces, we are able to fight the concern often raised about the use of a "canned product" for individualized learning.

CONCLUSION

Vandy and Emily started working together because Vandy could offer library lessons to Emily's classes, as was the standard procedure when Emily joined UT Tyler. We found, though, that we work well together and our ideas build on each other to improve the offerings we can give to students. When the Information Literacy Directive came down from the university, we realized we could use the directive to our advantage to make larger scale changes to IL instruction campus-wide. We felt as if we had a strong grasp on what was needed when we started, but our pilots allowed us to use our individual strengths together to create a data and theory–driven method of IL instruction and critical thinking skills that impacts students across disciplines and throughout their careers. We have devised a way to use a standard product as a starting point for truly individualized instruction without a huge budget or lengthy timeline. We continue to work together to address the needs of the students and the faculty. Even if the approach we have used here is ultimately discarded, which we believe and have evidence suggesting it should not be, we know this collaboration between the library and FYC faculty will continue to be fruitful because it is a true meeting of minds.

We share our results for several purposes. First of all, we have further evidence of the benefits of students' reflective writing in learning. More importantly, we have been able to show how our collaboration in refining our IL lessons and pedagogy have worked so others can see how such a development can occur. We took Jacobs's (2008) call to show such work to heart. Finally, we want to argue for the continued work of collaboration between libraries and composition.

REFERENCES

Association of College and Research Libraries (ACRL). (2000). *Information literacy competency standards for higher education.* Retrieved from http://www.ala.org/acrl/standards/informationliteracycompetency

Bean, J. C. (2011). *Engaging ideas: The professor's guide to integrating writing, critical thinking and active learning in the classroom* (2nd ed.). San Francisco, CA: Jossey-Bass.

Deitering, A-M., & Jameson, S. (2008). Step by step through the scholarly conversation: A collaborative library/writing faculty project to embed information literacy and promote critical thinking in first year composition at Oregon State University. *College and Undergraduate Libraries, 15*(1–2), 57–79.

Gute, D., & Gute, G. (2008). Flow writing in the liberal arts core and across the disciplines: A vehicle for confronting and transforming academic disengagement. *Journal of General Education, 57*(4), 191–222.

Jacobs, H. (2008). Information literacy and reflective pedagogical practice. *Journal of Academic Librarianship, 34*(3), 256–262.

Krathwohl, D. R. (2002). A revision of Bloom's Taxonomy: An overview. *Theory into Practice, 41*(4): 212–218.

Norgaard, R. (2003). Writing information literacy: Contributions to a concept. *Reference and User Services Quarterly, 43*(2), 124–130.

Norgaard, R. (2004). Writing information literacy in the classroom: Pedagogical enactments and implications. *Reference and User Services Quarterly, 43*(3), 220–226.

Palsson, F., & McDade, C. L. (2014). Factors affecting the successful implementation of a common assignment for first-year composition information literacy. *College and Undergraduate Libraries, 21*(2), 193–209.

Porter, B. (2014). Designing a library information literacy program using threshold concepts, student learning theory, and millennial research in the development of information literacy sessions. *Internet Reference Services Quarterly, 19*, 233–244.

Robert R. Muntz Library. (n.d.). *Mission and policies.* Retrieved from http://www.uttyler.edu/library/about/mission-policies.php.

The University of Texas at Tyler. (n.d.). *Inspiring excellence strategic plan 2009–2015.* Retrieved from https://www.uttyler.edu/president/docs/Strategic_Plan.pdf

Yancey, K. B. (1998). *Reflection in the writing classroom.* Logan, UT: Utah State University Press.

CHAPTER 11

USING OBJECT-BASED LEARNING TO ANALYZE PRIMARY SOURCES

New Directions for Information Literacy Instruction in a First-Year Writing Course

Crystal Goldman
Tamara Rhodes

The role primary sources play in research can be largely unknown to undergraduates. Though they are often required to use them, many students are unfamiliar with what they are, where they can be found, and how they can be used. With a large amount of research detailing information anxiety among undergraduates, the added complication of finding and using primary sources can set first-year students up for failure. Designing an information literacy workshop focused on primary sources can not only teach first-year students how they fit into the larger research conversation, it can increase engagement with research materials and enhance research skills to create more capable writers and researchers.

UNDERGRADUATES AND PRIMARY SOURCES

First-year writing programs are designed to be an introduction to academic research and writing. Traditionally, the introduction to research would chiefly include how to use secondary and tertiary resources, but there is growing recognition among instructors and librarians alike of the need to provide a more well-rounded view of and experience with information. For the case study outlined in this chapter, which was implemented at the University of California, San Diego (UCSD), this began with a foundational understanding of the information environment within which students find themselves. Reflecting its prominence within the education literature, the *Framework for Information Literacy for Higher Education* created by the Association for College and Research Libraries (ACRL) incorporates the concept of metaliteracy. Some library literature even heralds reframing more traditional information literacy as a metaliteracy (Mackey & Jacobson, 2011). In the ACRL *Framework* (2016), students are considered both consumers and creators of information. Mackey and Jacobson (2011) put this into context by highlighting that with the prevalence of participatory environments found on social media and in online communities, a metaliteracy frame ensures that information literacy is taught in a way that reflects the current Web 2.0 environment within which students interact. It relies on the belief that students should understand the intricacies of the relationship between the creation and consumption of information. If they do, they also understand that they are able to add their own analyses of materials to create new information and research. They then have the skills and knowledge to become contributors to the scholarly community and feel confident in doing so. Furthermore, when academic writing and research become more personal, students feel ownership over and interest in what they are being asked to do (Mackey & Jacobson, 2011). In a major study of the relationship between primary source use and undergraduate education, the Students and Faculty in the Archives (SAFA) project found that after students were able to engage with primary sources, they showed greater academic engagement represented by their level of interest and satisfaction (Anderson, Golia, Katz, & Tally, n.d.). Students also demonstrated better academic outcomes than their peers, represented by higher course grades and higher rates of course completion (Anderson et al., n.d.). Taking into account the current information environment students find themselves in, a focus on using primary sources has many benefits.

In addition to the benefits of increased engagement and better academic outcomes, the instruction of primary source use enhances critical thinking skills. A 2014 survey from the Association of American Colleges and Universities (AAC&U) reported that "95% of the chief academic officers from 433 institutions rated critical thinking as one of the most important intellectual skills for their students," and this was echoed among 81% of employers surveyed in 2011, who desired a stronger emphasis on critical thinking in colleges (Liu, Frankel, & Roohr, 2014, p. 1). The emphasis on the need for teaching critical thinking skills is there, but improving these skills has been a notoriously difficult outcome for instructors to meet. The analysis of primary sources is one way to fulfill that need. In some exercises, such as the one outlined later in this chapter, analyzing primary sources involves viewing a source, asking questions, and postulating what it could mean in a particular context. Such exercises require students to think critically about the materials and to use their own previous knowledge to make inquiries. Krause (2010) found this to be true in her study, testing student knowledge before and after a session involving primary source use. Using Yakel and Torres's (2003) archival intelligence mode, she created four objectives to measure knowledge of source analysis, one of which was critical thinking. Her results showed that those students who received archival instruction demonstrated an increase in critical thinking, asking questions regarding source validity, limitations, and strengths.

OBJECT-BASED LEARNING IN FIRST-YEAR WRITING

The workshop outlined in this chapter was grounded in an object-based learning approach, and this learning model aims to help students develop the skills needed to draw "conclusions based on an examination of evidence, together with an understanding of the limitations and reliability of evidence" (UCL, n.d., para. 6). It is well suited to facilitate the acquisition of the benefits enumerated previously. Implementing this model allows students to explore the sources for themselves and realize that their personal observations of a source translate and contribute to the scholarly conversation within which the source is included. While this kind of exploration can occur with any object, during the UC San Diego workshops, students interact with topic-relevant primary sources from the campus library's special collections, as well as digitized materials from other online collections, as needed. The exploration is paired with a worksheet that prompts students to make inferences about a chosen primary source, and think about how it relates to their prior knowledge and what questions it raises for them. The hands-on inquiry of these primary sources from the library collection, where possible, also facilitates teaching students how to find them in the library's collection and, subsequently, how to use them in academic research and writing.

STRUCTURING INFORMATION LITERACY WORKSHOPS IN FIRST-YEAR WRITING PROGRAMS

There are many elements to consider when embedding a primary source information literacy workshop into a course. In thinking about its structure, a single class may form a partnership with the library, or a programmatic partnership can be formed between a library's instruction program and a first-year writing program. Further, librarian roles in the workshops might differ based on a number of factors—in some cases, librarians may teach the workshops themselves; in other cases, librarians might be involved in instructional design for the workshops and help in train-the-trainer sessions so that faculty or teaching assistants (TAs) can teach the workshops. Depending on the university and library, the structure of the workshops might differ.

While there are always logistical concerns in instructional partnerships between the library and first-year writing courses, these concerns become magnified when the partnership is not between an individual course instructor and a single librarian, but between a library instruction program and a large-scale, multicourse writing program, such as it was in this case study. With more students, faculty, TAs, staff, and librarians involved, there were a greater number of obstacles that had to be navigated. The UC San Diego Library partnered with the Culture, Art, and Technology (CAT) writing program on campus, which included over 30 stakeholders and 1,000 students. With this number of students, a major consideration was how to facilitate these workshops. Bahde (2011) notes that small class sizes are best for special collections instruction as they make it easier for students to "gather around and share" what they are discovering (p. 77). This is one reason that discussion sections were used in the case study, as a way to achieve the smaller class sizes.

In addition to the concerns discussed above, this case study required the consideration of several other potential issues, including:

- Communication between stakeholders
- Creating unified information literacy workshop learning outcomes
- Primary source selection
- Training of workshop instructors

Many of these concepts may need to be addressed for a single workshop, and thus many of the following recommendations would be applicable to all primary source information literacy workshops for first-year writing courses, but in this context, due consideration will be given to the added planning and attention needed to implement such workshops in a large-scale program, as was the case for the UCSD workshops.

COMMUNICATION BETWEEN STAKEHOLDERS

In any collaborative effort, effective communication is key to success. The more stakeholders involved in a project, the more crucial communication becomes. Pivotal stakeholders are typically the writing program coordinator or course instructor and the librarian planning the workshop(s). Each of these stakeholders must then communicate with faculty, TAs, and students, or librarians, archivists, and library staff, respectively, to coordinate and confirm the logistics of scheduling the series of workshops so that everyone is aware of what will happen, when, and where.

Communication Between Library Stakeholders

The use of primary sources in information literacy workshops provides a rare opportunity for collaboration between instruction and special collections librarians, but it also presents several challenges. Special collections librarians or archivists often have expertise in teaching the analysis of primary sources in a variety of formats. However, they may not have experience designing instruction for or teaching in large-scale programs like a campus first-year writing program. In this instance, combining knowledge and skills of both types of librarians makes for a better workshop experience for writing students.

Communication Between the Library and First-Year Writing Program Stakeholders

If a single instructor is partnering with the library to create an information literacy workshop, he or she needs to work with students and TAs to make certain they understand the purpose and expected outcomes of the workshop. It is essential that students can relate the content of the workshop to the content of the course; indeed, if there is no course assignment that relates to the information literacy workshop, it can feel like "busy work for both students and the librarian" (Matthew & Schroeder, 2006, p. 63).

If a writing program is coordinating workshops for all first-year writing students, it is important to have buy-in from course instructors, otherwise there may be a sense that the workshops are "an imposition that infringed on their control of the course" (Dhawan & Chen, 2014, p. 419). Furthermore, if the workshops will take place outside of the usual classroom (i.e., in a library classroom), the complex logistics of scheduling means that faculty, TAs, and students need to be aware well in advance when and where the workshops will take place.

CREATING UNIFIED WORKSHOP LEARNING OUTCOMES

Writing programs may have a cohesive set of course learning objectives, but how each instructor approaches those objectives may differ. Further, disparate emphases in courses might be a specific feature offered by the program, allowing students to select the topic they prefer. The writing program courses included in this case study covered such topics as music, storytelling, history, religion, and science. This meant that the information literacy workshop content needed to be flexible enough to accommodate the varied sources necessary for diverse topics, while still fulfilling a common set of workshop learning outcomes.

Information literacy learning objectives can take several forms. They can align with course learning objectives, planned workshop activities, recognized information literacy standards (e.g., AAC&U Information Literacy Rubric; ACRL *Framework for Information Literacy for Higher Education*), or some combination of these options. A sample of the workshop learning outcomes for the case study is included in Table 11.1, which aligns the outcomes with specific workshop activities and threshold concepts from the ACRL *Framework* (2016).

PRIMARY SOURCE SELECTION

When considering a primary source–focused information literacy workshop, selecting appropriate sources for students to interact with and analyze is a crucial step in the planning process. The source or sources used in the workshop should reflect the focus of the class, and instructors should consider using sources in formats other than paper (e.g., sound recordings for a music-themed writing course). A close partnership between writing course instructors and campus librarians during the workshop planning process can

TABLE 11.1 *Learning Outcomes From the UCSD Primary Source Information Literacy Workshop*

Workshop Outcomes	Workshop Activities	ACRL Framework
Given a definition of types of sources and a list of sources, students will be able to determine if each one is a primary, secondary, or tertiary source	Think-pair-share exercise where students identify source type (primary, secondary, tertiary) for six provided sources	Authority Is Constructed and Contextual Information Creation as a Process
Given a primary source to study (e.g., photograph, song, postcard), students will be able to analyze the source, including describing the item in detail, identifying potential bias presented in the source, generating questions about the source, and evaluating how the source might be used in a college-level paper or project	Group activity where students are assignment a primary source and given a worksheet with questions to prompt analysis	Authority Is Constructed and Contextual Information Creation as a Process Information Has Value

assist enormously with source selection, as librarians have intimate knowledge of digital, print, and archival collections, all of which could provide relevant primary sources for any number of topics.

Preservation of Sources

When choosing between digital or physical sources for a primary source workshop, consideration needs to be given to security and preservation concerns for special collections materials, due to the large number of students who might be handling the items. For a single workshop in a small- or medium-sized class, librarians can often ensure the security of the sources, but for large lectures with more than 50 students or multiple classes using the same object, instructors might opt for a digitized surrogate of the item, a born-digital primary source, or a print reproduction of a fragile or rare physical source (Bahde, 2011). In the case study, stakeholders opted for digitized surrogates of more fragile archival items. An excerpt of one source used is included in Figure 11.1, along with the questions provided in its accompanying worksheet to help students begin analyzing the assigned source.

Format Variety

In this case study, a variety of primary source formats were used, including audio recordings, digital surrogates of pamphlets, differing biblical translations, paintings, and engraved illustrations. Students, instructors, and librarians alike may find analyzing—or teaching the analysis of—sources in nontext formats a disconcerting endeavor. Proper training, discussed in the next section, can help mitigate this discomfort for instructors and librarians, and there are a number of tools available to assist in designing effective information literacy instruction for nontext sources. The first priority should be selecting the most appropriate primary source(s) for the course content, which may or may not mean using nontext items. As mentioned above, preservation and security issues might impact source format as well. However, using nontext sources can offer many benefits to students. Objects such as sound recordings, film, maps,

Residence of Mrs. Mary S. Hodgson, Mt. Nebo

IDEAL SUBURBAN HOME PLACE

NESTLING among the foothills eleven miles from San Diego's business center, La Mesa possesses natural beauties of very striking character, and these have been enhanced by improvements of the most up-to-date and artistic kind. Its magnificent streets are kept in perfect condition, and many of them are flanked by attractive homes, with trees, flowers and lawns. There are many miles of cement sidewalks; ample water supply and sewer system; gas and electricity; telephones. Stores in all the principal lines, also bank, theatre, churches, school, ice plant, newspaper, etc. Connected with San Diego by fine boulevard and state highway. Ample train service, with 11-cent commutation fare. La Mesa residents are in touch with all the business and social advantages of the city, while enjoying the particular pleasures of suburban life.

Madame Schumann-Heink's Grossmont Home

Examine the source

- List three pieces of information the pamphlet provides its audience.
- What is the general ambiance of the pamphlet? What mood does it create? How does it do this (images, colors, fonts, word choice, etc.)?
- Who created this pamphlet?
- When was this pamphlet created?
- Where was this pamphlet created?
- Who is the intended audience of this pamphlet?

Inference

- Why do you think this pamphlet was created? What evidence in the pamphlet tells you why it was made?
- Do you notice any biases presented in the pamphlet?
- Based on what you have observed above, write down one thing you might infer about this pamphlet.
- Write down one thing the pamphlet tells you about life in the place and time it was created.

Questions

- Think about what you already know about the topic addressed in the pamphlet. How does this source relate to your prior knowledge?
- What questions does this pamphlet raise in your mind?

Figure 11.1 Scanned excerpt of a 1915 pamphlet brochure for La Mesa, California, along with sample questions from the UCSD workshops used to analyze the source. (From La Mesa Chamber of Commerce, 1915.)

visual art, and photographs can offer profound insight into the ways people thought and acted throughout history. Using a variety of source formats can assist with increasing student engagement in the classroom and, as with text-based primary sources, help give "students a powerful sense of history and the complexity of the past. Helping students analyze primary sources can also guide them toward higher-order thinking and better critical thinking and analysis skills" (Library of Congress, n.d., para. 2).

TRAINING WORKSHOP INSTRUCTORS

Teaching analysis of primary sources is often the purview of special collections librarians or archivists. If these experts are teaching the information literacy workshop(s) for a writing course, there may be no need for further training of instructors. However, if workshops are taught by librarians with other specialties, like instruction, reference, or subject expertise—as was the case at UCSD—then primary source analysis might not fall under their normal teaching duties. Likewise, if these workshops are taught by TAs or course instructors, information literacy instruction in general could be well outside their current skill set.

For workshop instructors unfamiliar with teaching primary source analysis, train-the-trainer sessions taught by special collections librarians would be highly advisable. These experts can walk the instructors through the workshop activities, and perhaps run a workshop simulation, with the instructors posing as students. Additionally, instructors new to teaching this type of workshop might consider investigating sources that provide tips and materials on teaching primary resources:

- Library of Congress, Teacher Resources: http://www.loc.gov/teachers
- National Archives, Teaching with Documents: https://www.archives.gov/education/lessons
- Using Primary Sources: Hands-On Instructional Exercises (Bahde, Smedberg, & Taormina, 2014): http://www.abc-clio.com/ABC-CLIOCorporate/product.aspx?pc=A4130P

ASSESSMENT

With any type of instruction, especially when using a new format, it is important to build assessment into the framework. Due to the one-shot nature of this kind of workshop, determining a useful assessment method can be a challenge. The UCSD workshop outlined here was the first part of a three-part course series, where different aspects of information literacy instruction was scaffolded over all three parts, so the consideration was whether to assess the primary source session on its own or as part of the whole series. The ultimate decision was to assess the progression of student knowledge over their three workshop/three quarter experience with the library. While it is commonly opined that assessing student knowledge directly at the conclusion of a course is not best practice, as demonstrated in Krause's (2010) study, useful data can still be learned by doing so.

In either case, a one-shot session or a series of workshops, a formative assessment method, specifically a pre- and post-test, could offer an idea of how closely the workshop aligns with the outcomes set for student learning and if student understanding of the concepts taught in the session improved by the end of the course or course series. The question used for this assessment presented students with a list of primary, secondary, and tertiary sources, and asked students to choose which ones were primary. Data analysis included determining how many primary sources were correctly identified, which primary sources were not identified at all, and which sources were incorrectly identified. After analyzing which sources were discussed in the workshop and to what degree, and comparing that to the data, the workshop can be improved in subsequent academic years.

SUMMARY

Embedding primary source–focused information literacy workshops into first-year writing courses, individually or as part of a large-scale program, is both challenging and rewarding. It can increase student engagement and academic outcomes, and provide tools for building critical thinking skills. By using an object-based learning model to relate the analysis of primary sources to students' previous knowledge, and asking them to use that previous knowledge to make inquiries about the sources, this type of workshop also helps students begin to question a source's validity, context, strengths, and limitations. This ultimately helps students understand their part in the relationship between creation and consumption of information. In acknowledging these many benefits, and offering the context of the UC San Diego Library as a case study, these guidelines allow anyone to create this kind of workshop, and in doing so, foster students who are better equipped to handle the current information-rich environment.

REFERENCES

Anderson, A., Golia, J., Katz, R. M., and Tally, B. (n.d.). *TeachArchives.org: Our findings*. Retrieved from http://wwww.teacharchives.org/articles/our-findings/

Association of American Colleges and Universities. (2011). *The LEAP vision for learning: Outcomes, practices, impact, and employers' view*. Retrieved from https://www.aacu.org/sites/default/files/files/LEAP/leap_vision_summary.pdf

Association of College & Research Libraries. (2016). *Framework for information literacy for higher education*. Retrieved from http://www.ala.org/acrl/sites/ala.org.acrl/files/content/issues/infolit/Framework_ILHE.pdf

Bahde, A. (2011). Taking the show on the road: Special collections instruction in the campus classroom. *RBM: A Journal of Rare Books, Manuscripts, & Cultural Heritage, 12*(2), 75–88.

Bahde, A., Smedberg, H., & Taormina, M. (Eds.). (2014). *Using primary sources: Hands-on instructional exercises*. Santa Barbara, CA: Libraries Unlimited.

Dhawan, A., & Chen, C. J. (2014). Library instruction for first-year students. *Reference Services Review, 42*(3), 414–432. https://doi.org/10.1108/RSR-04-2014-0006

Krause, M. G. (2010). Undergraduates in the archives: Using an assessment rubric to measure learning. *American Archivist, 73*(2), 507–534.

La Mesa Chamber of Commerce. (1915). *A few things you should know about La Mesa: The scenic suburb of San Diego County* [pamphlet]. Retrieved from http://roger.ucsd.edu/record=b6302708~S9

Library of Congress. (n.d.). *Using primary sources*. Retrieved from http://www.loc.gov/teachers/usingprimarysources

Liu, O. L., Frankel, L., & Roohr, K. C. (2014). Assessing critical thinking in higher education: Current state and directions for next-generation assessment. *ETS Research Reports Series, 2014*(1), 1–23. https://doi.org/10.1002/ets2.12009

Mackey, T. P., & Jacobson, T. E. (2011). Reframing information literacy as a metaliteracy. *College & Research Libraries, 72*(1), 62–78.

Matthew, V., & Schroeder, A. (2006). The embedded librarian program. *Educause Quarterly*. Retrieved from http://er.educause.edu/~/media/files/article-downloads/eqm06410.pdf

UCL Museums and Collections. (n.d.). *Introduction to object based learning*. Retrieved from http://www.ucl.ac.uk/museums/learning-resources/object-based-learning

Yakel, E., & Torres, D. (2003). AI: Archival intelligence and user expertise. *The American Archivist, 66*(1), 51–78.

PART IV

Classroom-Centered Approaches to Information Literacy

CHAPTER 12

COMMUNITIES OF INFORMATION

Information Literacy and Discourse Community Instruction in First-Year Writing Courses

Cassie Hemstrom

Kathy Anders

At many universities, information literacy is an integral part of the first-year composition course. The *Framework for Success in Postsecondary Writing* from the Council of Writing Program Administrators, the National Council of Teachers of English, and the National Writing Project explains that one of the primary goals of college composition instruction is to encourage a "Habit of Mind" of curiosity, which

> is fostered when writers are encouraged to: use inquiry as a process to develop questions relevant for authentic audiences within a variety of disciplines; seek relevant authoritative information and recognize the meaning and value of that information; conduct research using methods for investigating questions appropriate to the discipline; and communicate their findings in writing to multiple audiences inside and outside school using discipline-appropriate conventions. (2011, p. 4)

First-year writing (FYW) courses seek not only to introduce students to strong research methods, but also to help students understand the motivations for conducting research. Additionally, students learn how to frame appropriate questions for their field or topic, find and use credible sources, and synthesize their research. Since information literacy is just one aspect of composition instruction, FYW students often struggle with the complexities of information literacy given the limited amount of time for instruction. Therefore, FYW introductions to information literacy work best when thought of as a foundation that students will continue to build upon in subsequent academic pursuits.

However, for information instruction to be most useful, students need to learn how to transfer those skills into other areas. Recent composition studies have found that students have trouble transferring what they learn in one class, or even in one assignment, to the next. The *Elon Statement on Writing Transfer* explains that students do not think they will use the knowledge and skills from FYW courses in other areas (2013, p. 4). Writing instructors can help foster transfer by teaching concepts of composition and information literacy in context with each other as part of a research-writing process and in assignments that tie in with students' academic interests.

Additionally, both composition and information literacy theories (ACRL *Framework,* 2015; Townsend, Brunetti, & Hofer, 2011) hold that threshold concepts can be powerful learning tools for students. Recognizing the centrality of threshold concepts to learning transfer, the *Elon Statement* says that "Once educators identify threshold concepts that are central to meaning making in their fields, they can prioritize teaching these concepts, in turn increasing the likelihood that students will carry an understanding of these core concepts into future coursework and contexts" (2013, p. 3). Linking together the threshold concepts of composition, based in the theory of discourse communities, with those of information literacy enables students to see how research and writing are bound together, and how the practices of both apply to other disciplines.

Discourse communities are formed when a group of people use language in similar ways, with shared key terms, values, and assumptions. They use this set of shared language tools to build and achieve common aims, and to communicate internally and externally about those aims. Discourse community analysis assignments ask students to use multiple methods of research to identify and explain how a particular discourse community communicates their goals. Many FYW courses employ discourse analysis as a means to teach students about composition concepts like audience and genre. Discourse analysis promotes learning transfer, giving students a strategy instead of a template, and when instructors allow students to conduct analysis on an academic or professional discourse community that they are interested in, or plan on entering, students are both more prepared to conduct research in their chosen field, and are better able to see how the strategies they learn can transfer to future writing and researching situations. By extending the bounds of discourse communities to information literacy, instructors and librarians can create powerful connections between composition and information use. We adopt the criteria for discourse communities delineated by John Swales (1990). He outlines the six characteristics of a discourse community:

1. A discourse community has a broadly agreed set of common goals (Swales, 1990, p. 24).
2. A discourse community has mechanisms of intercommunication among its members (Swales, 1990, p. 25).
3. A discourse community uses its participatory mechanisms primarily to provide information and feedback (Swales, 1990, p. 26).
4. A discourse community utilizes and hence possesses one or more genres in the communicative furtherance of its aims (Swales, 1990, p. 26).
5. In addition to owning genres, a discourse community has acquired some specific lexis (Swales, 1990, p. 26).
6. A discourse community has a threshold level of members with a suitable degree of relevant content and discoursal expertise (Swales, 1990, p. 27).

By engaging students in an analysis of a particular discourse community with which they are already connected, or with which they wish to be connected, instructors can encourage students to ask: What does it mean to enter scholarly conversations? How can I (the student) conduct research that helps me to understand and enter into the discourse community? What does the lens of the discourse community help me (the student) to better understand about the community's work and methods of communication? How does that help me (the student) understand the information creation process and participate in it?

To make a discourse community assignment even more useful, instructors can give students the opportunity to research their choice of an academic community that they either are a part of now or are on the road to joining. For example, they might choose to conduct research on the discourse community of first-year writing courses, or first-year science courses, or they might choose to research the discourse community of the American Association for the Advancement of Science journal *Science* in preparation for reading, using, and eventually contributing to the research shared in that community. This approach makes the assignment relevant to students while also introducing them to the academic conventions in their field, making transferring knowledge of how to write *in their field* more likely.

DISCOURSE COMMUNITIES AND INFORMATION LITERACY

The artifacts of discourse (print texts, recordings, Web documents, etc.) are information, and as such fall under the umbrellas of both discourse communities and information literacy. Since the product of a discourse community is information, and in a FYW course students are both learning how to navigate and to join discourse communities, students should be taught about discourse communities and information as linked ideas. Another way to reframe the idea of discourse communities would be as information communities that share aspects of both Swales's definition and the *Framework for Information Literacy for Higher Education*. Not only do students learn about the features of different types of communication in a given field, they begin to think of the artifacts of that communication and how it is organized, shared, and created. While the notion of linking genre analysis and information literacy is not new (Simmons, 2005), our goal in this chapter is to give examples of how to explicitly draw together some of Swales's characteristics of a discourse community and the *Framework*. Here are three areas where discourse communities and information literacy overlap.

ACTIVE RESEARCHERS

Swales's second and third characteristics of a discourse community are that it "has mechanisms of intercommunication among its members," and that it "uses its participatory mechanisms primarily to provide information and feedback" (Swales, 1990, p. 26). In other words, in discourse communities members use agreed upon outlets to communicate with one another. For example, in academic discourse communities, those outlets are commonly conference presentations, posters, peer-reviewed articles, monographs, and, more recently, blogs and tweets. Notice how, in Swales's definition, intercommunication is a key feature of the discourse community. In order to be considered members of a discourse community, participants must communicate with one another in some fashion. Discourse community members are not passive; they share information and make active choices about how to explain the significance of that information in ways that support achieving their shared goals.

This idea of intercommunication is at the heart of the *Framework for Information Literacy for Higher Education* frame Scholarship as Conversation, which states that "communities of scholars, researchers, or professionals engage in sustained discourse with new insights and discoveries occurring over time as a result of varied perspectives and interpretations." Contemporary information literacy teaches that students should recognize that information often develops through dialogue, and that they are entering that dialogue with their research. For the librarian teaching information literacy in a classroom that is using discourse community analysis, this is a key component of showing how the skills learned in that analysis transfer to information literacy. In particular, the *Framework* also highlights the active nature of information-literate students, who "see themselves as contributors to scholarship rather than only consumers of it." Students should understand that with their research and writing they become active participants in the discourse community.

AIMS AND FORMATS

The frame Information Creation as a Process intersects with Swales's fourth criterion that "a discourse community utilizes and hence possesses one or more genres in the communication furtherance of its aims," particularly in how the *Framework* considers format. Swales's definition of discourse communities is in service of his larger project of laying out genre analysis, but in this particular case librarians can examine how the formats of information used in a discourse community work within larger definitions of genre. Students can map how information moves through different formats within a given community, and how those formats serve the needs of audiences within the community. Looking at format and genre provides an opportunity to teach not only traditional information literacy concepts like primary and secondary sources, but also allows for deeper exploration of how the information creation process can be shaped by the goals of the community itself. For example, in scientific communities where quick access to new information is a priority, scientists tend to publish journal articles, which allow for faster publication than monographs.

Tying together format and aims can be particularly helpful for promoting the knowledge practice that students "develop, in their own creation processes, an understanding that their choices impact the purposes for which the information product will be used and the message it conveys" (*Framework*). Another way of considering this would be to suggest that the purpose of the information product can determine its format. For writing instructors, too, linking together these ideas highlights the process by which information moves through different formats.

LEXIS AND SEARCH STRATEGIES

Swales's fifth criterion for a discourse community is that it "has acquired some specific lexis," and this is certainly one of the more challenging aspects for students seeking to join writing and research communities. Librarians regularly see how finding the right terms used to convey and retrieve information is a stumbling block for novice members of a discourse community. The *Framework for Information Literacy for Higher Education* recognizes that students should view Searching as Strategic Exploration, and that part of that threshold concept consists of helping students develop the ability to "use different types of searching language."

For librarians trying to emphasize the iterative nature of searching, discussing how terms are used and developed by communities can reveal how one comes to know the terms of a discourse community through the process of analyzing and joining it. Students, especially those attempting to join academic discourse communities, "try on" the language of the academy (Bartholomae, 1986). Likewise, students seeking information must "try on" different lexical terms and searching vocabulary and strategies.

CONSTRUCTING EFFECTIVE DISCOURSE COMMUNITY ANALYSIS ASSIGNMENTS

This sample assignment is a prompt for a three-part discourse community project that emphasizes information literacy by engaging students in learning about an academic community and guiding them through an iterative process of research and writing. Students conduct observations, analyze primary documents, and use their findings to draft effective interview questions. Next, they identify stakeholders in the community and conduct interviews with them. They mine the interviews for significant insights, vocabulary, and indications about the ideologies of the community. Finally, they compose a written or digital representation of their findings and the significance of their findings. Their final product demonstrates what makes the discourse community unique and serves as an introductory piece of information for people interested in entering or furthering their involvement in the community.

The three-part setup of the assignment places an emphasis on information literacy, and particularly on helping students to see how discourse communities create and use information. The iterative nature of the project empowers students to recognize how information creation is a process by asking them to engage in different types of research and to conduct research at multiple points in the project. It encourages them to see themselves as beginning researchers who are entering a scholarly field and conversation.

TAILORING AND SCAFFOLDING THE ASSIGNMENTS

This assignment can easily be adapted to serve different class needs. It can be used as a group project with a presentation aspect at the end or as a portfolio, with the separate pieces written throughout the class and revised for a final class project. The assignment could also result in a multimodal presentation, an infographic or poster, a fully written research article, and so on. Instructors can shorten an in-class or supplemental assignment by directing students to focus on only one of the six characteristics of a discourse community. Another option would be to make it an innovative full-class project to encourage collaboration—the whole class can choose a community (perhaps the campus, or the freshman class) and split the class into six groups, with each group responsible for focusing on one of the six aspects of the discourse community. The assignment can also be adapted for use in library instruction classes or interdisciplinary courses.

To further aid in learning transfer and to give the assignment higher stakes, instructors can require or recommend that students submit their analysis to an external audience. The following are just a few options that are available: Students can (1) submit to an Undergraduate Research Conference at their campus or another school, (2) submit to the journal *Young Scholars in Writing*, which has a special section for first-year writing, or (3) circulate their research projects to a wider audience online through a blog, website, YouTube video, and so on. There are many student-produced discourse analyses posted on YouTube that can show students how they might share their own work.

Sometimes students can feel anxious when asked to engage in such in-depth and nuanced research, especially about an academic community to which some students may not yet feel that they belong. To ease student anxieties, scaffold the assignment carefully by using some or all of the activities in order to give students confidence in their abilities. Reading Swales's definition and characteristics of a discourse community together as a class (it is written in academic language, for an academic audience, but is short and accessible for students) and discussing the reading before assigning the project gives everyone a shared vocabulary. It can also be very helpful to show examples of discourse analysis projects from YouTube or the *Young Scholars in Writing* archive and discuss how these examples relate to Swales's text and what they illuminate about a particular community.

THREE-PART DISCOURSE COMMUNITY ANALYSIS ASSIGNMENT SAMPLES

These materials can either be adapted for independent use or used to scaffold a larger assignment. In the latter case, use the materials in class or as homework assignments that students can build upon to compose an in-depth discourse analysis.

Discourse Analysis Assignment Overview

This assignment invites you to use your researching and rhetorical analysis skills to investigate a discourse community. A discourse community is a group of people who share the same goals, interests, genres, and ways of communicating: for example, a group of scholars or students in an academic field like biology or sociology, a group of workers who all work in the same office or for the same company, and so forth. To decide on a discourse community to investigate, pick a community that you are either involved in yourself or that you want to be involved in. In either case, make sure it's a community about which you are interested in learning more. The community needs to be connected either to an academic field or a professional community.

Purpose: The purpose of this project is to practice the "habit of mind" of curiosity by engaging in research as a process and entering into scholarly conversations in your field. To do so, you will conduct research about a discourse community that you are a member of, that you want to join, or that you want to learn more about. You'll present the results of this research in the form of a scholarly research article.

Rhetorical Situation: The primary audience for your Discourse Community Project is the academic discourse community of First-Year Writing students and teachers here on campus, and particularly the FYW students who are majoring in or interested in majoring in a program connected to the discourse community that you choose to study. The primary purpose for writing this assignment is to gain knowledge about the discourse community so that you and your reader will be better prepared to enter into the conversations in the community effectively. For example, if you are interested in entering a finance profession, such as accounting, your audience will be other FYW students who are interested in becoming accountants, and your goal will be to write an analysis that will help them understand an accounting discourse community (the language, genres, shared knowledge, information, etc.) so that both you and your reader will be able to use and create information as part of conversations in the field. You'll also have the option of circulating your Discourse Community Project to a wider academic audience.

Assignment Part 1: Identifying a Discourse Community

Choose a discourse community and identify your primary audiences. The discourse community should be one related to a field or discipline that you are studying or plan to study, or to a profession that you are part of or wish to enter. Draw on your own interests to choose a discourse community. Then, in 500–750 words, explain why you are interested in this community, how you are connected to the community, and why you think it will be a fruitful community to study. Is this community a discourse community?

Why? Does it meet the six characteristics of a discourse community? In what ways? Who is part of it? Why is it a significant community to study? How will learning more about the community, its values, its methods of communication, and the information it produces be worthwhile for you? For other students? Use 2–3 primary sources from the community to support and illustrate your explanation.

Next, in 500–750 words, identify and discuss your primary audiences. To whom will you write? What other students or student groups would benefit from learning more about this discourse community? Choose a group here on campus with whom you can share your findings. This might be students majoring in a particular field, students who are members of a professional club, or students who are interning at a specific company, for example.

Finally, draft questions that you can use to interview participants in the group. Write a list of 10–20 questions, and a 150–250-word rationale for why these are good questions, and what they will help you discover about how the discourse community functions.

Assignment Part 2: Identifying Stakeholders and Conducting the Interview

Building on what you found in Part 1 and on the research you have conducted, write a 500–700-word analysis of the people who make up the community, both generally and specifically. What groups of people are involved in the community? In what ways? How do they interact with the community? What methods do they use for communicating information? In which genres do they read or write? Which specific people involved in the community do you want to talk to? Why? What do you already know about these people? What do you hope to learn about their discourse community? Use 3–5 primary sources to illustrate and support your analysis.

Then, choose one of these people and conduct an interview. You can use the interview questions you wrote for Part 1, but tailor them to the specific person you are interviewing. Transcribe the interview into a Word document, and complete the Interview Analysis Table (Figure 12.1).

In-Class Activity: Compile a Lexis

Discourse communities use very specific terms to refer a given idea or thing. Sometimes these terms are the same across all communities, but more frequently different groups use different terms for the same thing or idea. For example, agricultural communities refer to a device that keeps a mother pig from her piglets as a "gestation crate," a "sow stall," or a "farrowing pen." Gathering information from any retrieval system, whether it be Google, a database search, or your library catalog, depends upon knowing the terms used by your discourse community.

For this assignment, create a lexis of the key terms used by your discourse community. You should come up with as many terms as possible, both popular and specialized, and identify which of the terms you find most often used in your discourse community. It is important to note that different discourse communities will likely use different terms to indicate the same things depending on the context and intended audience. For example, where community health organizers might say "heart attack," medical researchers will likely say "myocardial infarction."

Information: Transcript from key parts of the interview	**Student answers**
Analysis What it means: What do these quotes show? Why is the quote significant? What do you think it means? How are you interpreting it? What does it tell you about the community? Does it relate to the discourse community that you are studying directly or indirectly? If indirectly, how will you make the connection? If directly, what aspect of the discourse community does it connect to? Which of the characteristics of a discourse community does it relate to?	Analysis
Implementation How will you discuss this information? How will you write about this info to the appropriate audience? What section will you put it in? Will you use a direct quote, a paraphrase, or a summary? Do you need to support this point with examples from primary documents? What other pieces of your research does this section connect to?	Implementation
Further Research What other questions does this info raise for you? What terminology do you need to research for definition and context?	Further Research

Figure 12.1 Interview analysis table.

Generate a table that outlines the key terminology you have identified, the alternative terms for each key term, what that key term means when used by community members, and an example of use from one of the primary sources you found.

In-Class Activity: Identifying Genres and Sharing Information

Discourse communities use one or more genres to share information, build on knowledge, or make claims. For this activity, investigate what formats or genres your discourse community uses to disseminate information. For example, where does someone new to the community go to find the artifacts of discourse? Would that person go to encyclopedias, Web pages, scholarly articles, books, textbooks, documentaries, or other resources?

Compile your own mini-database (a corpus) of examples of the genre or genres used by your discourse community. Include 3–5 primary examples in your database, and write a 100–250-word discussion of why you think this (or these) particular genres are useful to the community.

Assignment Part 3: Discourse Community Analysis

Using your primary and secondary research sources, as well as your analysis of the interview you conducted, compose a 1,000-word written or the equivalent digital representation of your findings about the discourse community to help your audience understand how to successfully enter into and communicate with the community.

In your analysis, use support from primary texts and artifacts from the community, interviews with members, and secondary research to discuss how the community meets the six characteristics of a discourse community: What are the common goals of the community? The mechanisms for participation and intercommunication? How do members of the community provide information and feedback with each other? What genres do they utilize, and why? What are the key terms in the community's lexis and what do they mean? Who are the experts and authorities in the community, and what counts as expertise? What other key things does someone who is interested in joining the community need to know in order to enter into and communicate effectively with the group?

TAKEAWAYS

Creating interwoven information literacy and composition assignments that promote learning transfer requires finding the commonalities between the two disciplines. The theories and praxis of discourse community analysis intersect with information literacy at multiple points, thus providing a wealth of options for crafting meaningful learning experiences for students. When teaching this assignment sequence in our own classes, we have seen positive development in how capable our students are in conducting research, and this is a development they have also noticed and commented on in reflective letters at the end of the course. We have also seen that teaching our first-year writing courses with a long-term, scaffolded discourse community analysis assignment helps students to think of using and creating information as iterative processes. Returning to their initial research through different lenses at multiple points in the course helps students make stronger analyses and claims. Student reflection letters indicate that they independently recognize that they are gaining authority and entering into the scholarly conversations of the discourse community. They also identify nuances of primary and secondary research materials and discover that how sources are used depends upon the context and purpose of the author. Instructors can help students become more confident information users and creators by highlighting the interconnected nature of discourse and information practices.

REFERENCES

Association of College & Research Libraries. (2015). *Framework for information literacy for higher education*. Chicago: American Library Association. http://www.ala.org/acrl/standards/ilframework

Bartholomae, D. (1986). Inventing the university. *Journal of Basic Writing, 5*(1), 4–23.

Council of Writing Program Administrators, National Council of Teachers of English, and National Writing Project. (2011). *Framework for success in postsecondary writing*. Council of Writing Program Administrators, National Council of Teachers of English, and National Writing Project. http://wpacouncil.org/files/framework-for-success-postsecondary-writing.pdf

Elon Statement on Writing Transfer. (2013). Elon University. http://www.elon.edu/docs/e-web/academics/teaching/ers/writing_transfer/Elon-Statement-Writing-Transfer.pdf

Simmons, M. H. (2005). Librarians as disciplinary discourse mediators: Using genre theory to move toward critical information literacy. *portal: Libraries and the Academy, 5*(3), 297–311. https://doi.org/10.1353/pla.2005.0041

Swales, J. (1990). *Genre analysis: English in academic and research settings*. Cambridge: Cambridge University Press.

Townsend, L., Brunetti, K., & Hofer, A. R. (2011). Threshold concepts and information literacy. *portal: Libraries and the Academy, 11*(3), 853–869. https://doi.org/10.1353/pla.2011.0030

CHAPTER 13

A COOPERATIVE, RHETORICAL APPROACH TO RESEARCH INSTRUCTION

Refining Our Approach to Information Literacy Through Umbrellas and BEAMs

Amy Lee Locklear
Samantha McNeilly

It isn't unusual to hear discussions among college library and freshman-year composition instructors about the "one-shot" library session. In that traditional introduction to information literacy, a writing teacher might take a day out of the planned curriculum and set the students loose in the library lab, where they learn from the library instruction specialist about navigating database choices; using key search terms, Boolean operators, and the ILL system; and saving their findings. But this approach often leaves students with the sense that research is just "looking up stuff," rather than showing these new-to-the-university writers how research is really about *inquiry*, not just location, nor does the one-shot approach to information literacy instruction emphasize research as a creative behavior born of students' curiosity and a desire to explore—and later join—existing conversations on a subject. Finally, it often does little to help students learn how to *engage* with these sources, or how to think of them in ways that empower students to see themselves as active, contributing participants in an emerging discussion.

We wanted to find a better approach, one that created a shared research instructional space that incorporated a rhetorical approach toward, as well as ways to effectively engage with, the research materials found by our students. Therefore, in the spring of 2016, we set out to combine our writing and library instructional lesson planning to create more of a productive flow from the writing classroom to the library classroom and back again, lessening that silo-type feel of the previous "one-shot" model of instruction, and creating an extended, cross-classroom space informed by our respective disciplines' key beliefs about information literacy (ACRL, WPA) (see Figure 13.1).

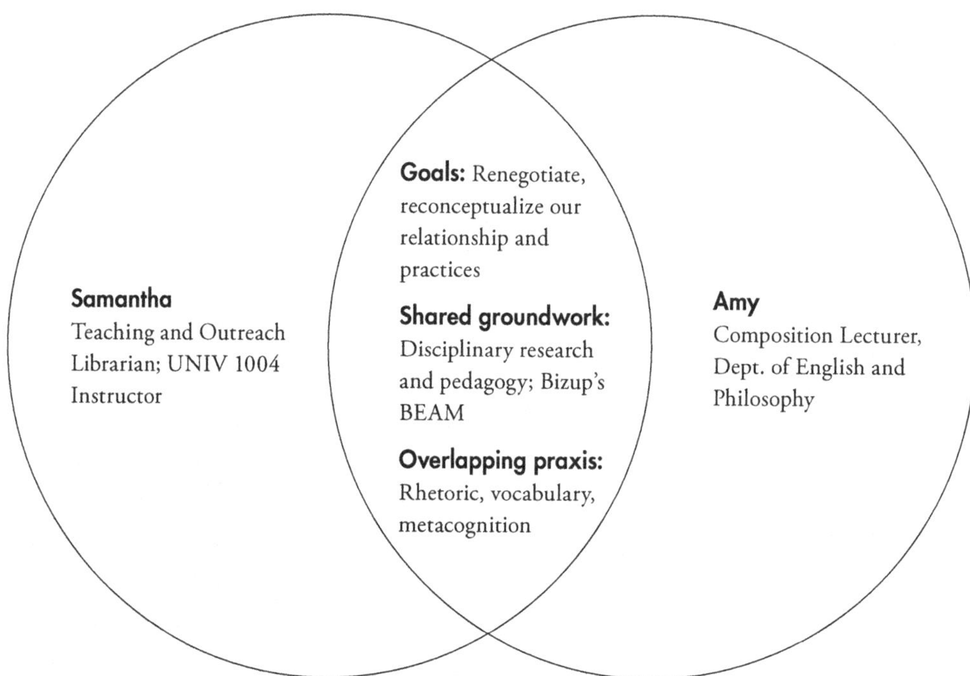

Figure 13.1 Collaboration Venn diagram.

Both our individual efforts as well as our collaboration were driven by the same goal: there has to be a better way than the "one shot" to teach students how to "do" research. We asked ourselves: How do we help students understand how to approach their research assignment and related search tasks as a process of inquiry, not just a quote-mining activity? How do we help our students re-see how they think about "doing research" as agency-promoting conversation exploration and building? The siloed nature of previous library instruction/writing classroom relationships has time and again proven unsatisfactory in addressing these questions. Our collaboration resulted in two tools that helped us enhance information literacy instruction through cooperative brainstorming and planning to help students think more about the *why* than merely the *what* when it comes to how they view research and source materials.

For our project, we operated from a definition of information literacy instruction as a practice that includes and incorporates the idea that research is more than just gathering bits of information. It is the search behaviors as well as how to critically evaluate and apply that found information. It is inquiry as a goal, not just a starting point, an idea shared by many scholars within our disciplines (D'Angelo, Jamieson, Maid, & Walker, 2016; Head & Eisenberg, 2009; Howard, Serviss, & Rodrigue, 2010; McClure & Purdy, 2016). We came at our individual tasks and tool development from our own disciplinary backgrounds, but we discovered that our thinking and efforts were linked by several common elements, foremost being Joseph Bizup's (2008) rhetorical classification framework, BEAM. This created a synchronicity of effort that not only provided us with a common vocabulary, but allowed us to create a set of instructional tools based on this common text as well as the shared goals of our respective disciplinary scholarship. Further, we discovered Bizup's work informs a variety of other library instructional publications such as Kristin Woodward and Kate Ganski's 2013 "Lesson plan," from which Samantha drew useful graphic summaries of core BEAM elements for her classroom session to reinforce the relationship between writing and library activities. For the writing classroom side, Bizup's rhetorical classifications approach to source material helped set up a much-needed shift in students' perceived relationships with sources, moving them from an extrinsic (source-as-authoritative-object external to student's ideas) to intrinsic (source-as-dialogic-partner-in-exploration) lens through which students might see themselves in a conversation (Bizup, 2008, pp. 73, 76). Extending this into the library instruction session, Samantha created an original conceptual visual metaphor designed to emphasize student agency in this relationship—the Umbrella—continuing the use of vocabulary and concepts that center the students' agency in relation to what their source materials do or offer them.

In our development of these two tools, we wanted to be sure we consciously and strategically created overlap and intersections made possible by existing disciplinary work. This was key to avoiding the siloed approach used in previous years, when the writing teacher simply passed the baton over to the library staff for "search instruction," then returned to the writing classroom lessons. We wanted to create a wider, more seamless frame by renegotiating not only how we taught information literacy as library search habits, but also students' own views of their research behaviors and—perhaps more importantly—their perceptions of and engagement with sources. Both the Umbrella and BEAM tools allowed us to "flip the lens" for students by transforming the way we talk about research and their source discoveries. The goal: to move them from seeing research and its results as a passive data-gathering performance—Burke's "extrinsic" relationship with information (as cited in Bizup, 2008, p. 73)—toward fostering a more organic, more "intrinsic" student-idea-driven relationship with sources and research-as-inquiry (ACRL).

PLANNING AND IMPLEMENTATION: THE KEY IS A RHETORIC OF CLASSIFICATION

Our collaborative work represents important overlaps reflecting the scholarship in our fields when it comes to information literacy and pedagogy. The two-course freshman writing sequence at Auburn University Montgomery (AUM) includes a second semester focused on research writing. In 2013, the composition program redesigned the course focus and assignment arc to better facilitate a more inquiry-based approach to research, moving from several stand-alone analytical papers to a series of scaffolded projects meant to promote students' critical and metacognitive thinking about their arguments and research best practices. These changes emerged from our work with the Citation Project in 2010. Our program was one of 17 national higher education institutions that contributed student research papers to examine how students actually integrated borrowed material into their own writing. What we learned changed our curricula, *and* fostered a new approach to/cooperation with library instruction specialists.

What emerged from the findings of the Citation Project for our own institution was how students perceive and use the sources they discover in their own writing. In a 2011 interview, Jamieson and Howard observed that their early stages of research data reflect on "what students are doing with their sources" (Jamieson & Howard, 2011). They remarked that most experienced academy writers believe "'research' is about the discovery of new information and ideas, and the synthesis of those ideas into deeper understanding." With that definition in mind, the data suggests that "the majority of the papers studied for the first phase of data analysis" failed. Only 6% of the citations are to summarized material. It is in summary that writers demonstrate comprehension of the larger arguments of a text, working from ideas rather than sentences. And in the papers we studied, students are not doing that." The underlying premise for our post–Citation Project course revisions and composition-library collaborative efforts—that is, why students may be engaging with sources on such a shallow basis—is that our students saw source material as an external object, some *thing* to use in pieces. Student-perceived agency in that meaning-making relationship with sources was therefore limited. This is where Bizup's (2008) rhetorical reframing of source material provides a way to re-see those conditions and gives us a way to help students rethink source materials and their research behaviors within the writing class *and* the library instructional classroom. The study's local results for our AUM writing program clearly suggested a lack of engagement with sources' ideas. These results not only changed our curriculum, they fostered a new approach to our cooperative efforts with library instruction specialists.

As part of our reframed approach to teaching information literacy, we became collaborative partners in developing ways to help students rethink their relationship to source materials, focusing on practices of inquiry that emphasized *why* and *how* their research discoveries were meaningful to their ideas—as opposed to simply *what* their sources were—to create more opportunities for metacognitive inquiry. To do this, we both relied on Bizup's (2008) BEAM acronym as our commonplace, giving us a shared touchstone vocabulary to renegotiate this relationship.

BEAMS AND UMBRELLAS: CONCEPTUAL TOOLS TO BRIDGE OUR CLASSROOM PRACTICES

Interestingly, we discovered Bizup's (2008) work independently. It was a happy moment of serendipity when we first met to discuss our collaborative library session planning that Samantha first mentioned BEAM as an influence on her lesson planning for my writing class's visit. For me, BEAM had crossed my path when I was conducting research on writing programs and WPAs. Our shared path of discovery was already influencing our respective approaches to transforming praxis.

The BEAM model (Table 13.1) provided us with a clear pathway to address the disciplinary (ACRL, WPA/NCTE, and PIL) calls for a *metacognitive* approach to information literacy instruction. Bizup (2008) pointed out in his article "BEAM: A Rhetorical Vocabulary for Teaching Research-Based Writing" that a contributing factor in students' troubles with engaging source material in a critical and academically accepted way is in many ways rhetorically based. As an illustration, he pointed out that our writing textbooks, library Web guides, and familiar instructional methods often rely on traditional terminology like "primary," "secondary," and "tertiary" to define for students what sources *are* (the "what"). Far too often, Bizup argued (and we agree), such labels have the power to create a rhetorical as well as relational distance between students and the source material.

Bizup's article offered us a useful resource to modify instructional vocabulary to better promote the disciplinary Frameworks' value of the metacognitive and inquiry-based approach to research. Our shared goal was to get students to think about sources differently, not approach searching as a type of "scavenger hunt" activity. Instead, we wanted them to see the sources in terms of what they *do* or *offer*. Bizup's article provided both of us with a "new" meta language that not only functioned as a filter to help us *rethink* and *reframe* not only teaching research writing, but opened new opportunities to create collaborative instructional spaces that would become the unifying undercurrent between the prelibrary writing classroom activities, the library instructional sessions, and back to the postlibrary writing classroom. In essence, BEAM and the Umbrella became unifying thematic and practical frameworks for our collaboration.

TABLE 13.1 *Bizup's (2008) BEAM Classification Categories*

Background/Background Source	"Materials whose claims a writer accepts as 'facts'" (p. 75) "Noncontroversial, used to provide context . . . facts and information"
Exhibit/Exhibit Source	"Materials a writer offers for explication, analysis, or interpretation" "Exhibit . . . is not synonymous with the conventional term evidence, which designates data offered in support of a claim." "Exhibits can lend support to claims, but they can also provide occasions for claims." "Understood in this way, the exhibits in a piece of writing work much like the exhibits in a museum or a trial" (p. 75).
Argument/Argument Source	"Materials whose claims a writer affirms, disputes, refines, or extends in some way" "Argument sources are those with which writers enter into 'conversation'" (pp. 75–76).
Method/Method Source	Materials "can offer a set of key terms, lay out a particular procedure, or furnish a general model or perspective" (p. 76).

THE "SETUP": USING BEAM PRINCIPLES IN THE WRITING CLASSROOM AS STAGE ONE OF REFRAMING SEARCH PRACTICES AND PERSPECTIVES IN THE WRITING CLASSROOM

Why is a rhetorical approach so important to teaching information literacy? The assumption at the heart of our answer to this question is that instructional terminology has the power to shape and frame our freshman writing students' approach to research behaviors and materials. A. Abby Knoblauch (2011) examined how composition textbooks' terminologies frame argument and research writing by "perpetuat[ing]" a specific "version" or approach to argument (p. 248). Her survey of several well-known textbooks suggests a rhetorically framed pathway to see and "do" argument (and research) writing, one that Bizup (2008) claimed "reflects a hierarchy of values at odds with the goal of teaching writing" (p. 74). The vocabulary employed has, then, the power to shape student attitudes toward and understanding of research materials. The terms used to discuss research, in other words, can shift the power of agency either toward the knowledge product or toward the knowledge builder (i.e., the student). To help students actively engage with sources rather than simply quote mine, we wanted to emphasize the role of the builder by using vocabularies that promoted their agency. This is where the rhetorical tools of BEAM and the Umbrella graphic prove useful in helping students thoughtfully engage with content by scaffolding activities that ask them to identify the functionality of the different types of information they wish to locate.

Using Bizup's framework, we moved the emphasis away from *what* the source is (tertiary, primary, etc.) to what students can do with it in their own researched argument by asking more *why* and *how* questions about the source content. Further, that lens can be flipped to become a way students can consider *how* their sources intended their materials to function rhetorically (e.g., Who was the target audience for such a publication? Why and how does such audience awareness affect the message?). Such considerations are key to framing the way students search and engage with these materials prior to attending the library session because of the potential to make explicit the potential for fundamental changes to the way they perceive not only their roles as researchers, but also how the knowledge offered *shapes* their thinking instead of what it *proves*. As Bizup (2008) put it, "If we want students to adopt a rhetorical perspective toward research-based writing, then we should use language that focuses their attention not on what their sources and other materials are . . . but on what they as writers might do with them" (p. 75).

During the early weeks of the term in the writing classroom, students work through topic exploration and preliminary inquiry activities. Prior to visiting Samantha's classroom, students had already submitted their Topic Exploration essay, a brief informal overview of what they know and what they want to discover—largely through in-class discussions and activities that frame research as a *conversation* within and between *discourse communities* and *stakeholders*. These terms create a conceptual and rhetorical framework through which to see their role and the role of sources they encounter through research. The in-class readings and activities emphasize inquiry and questioning to explore their topics as complex issues, not as pro/con arguments. The principles of BEAM are introduced through guided discussion of source materials (both provided and found through early searching using online Web browsers and news services). This allowed me to "prime the pump," as it were, so that prior to the library session, students are already using BEAM principles as a metacognitive lens through which to consider how sources function.

By the six-week mark, students had already received early feedback on their research ideas (their thesis admittedly still in a state of flux based on the assumption that further inquiry will help them refine their approach and thinking as they consider other conversational perspectives). Further, discussion had begun on how to evaluate source materials based on thinking of sources through the BEAM lens—what does the source *do* and *why*, not simply focusing on *what* it is. These discussions and early work produce materials students use to begin developing relevant key search terms (see the worksheet in the Appendix) as outgrowths of their own questions (what do they need, what do they want to do and why). The first six weeks, then, become a building phase based on focusing on the metacognitive, asking them to base their initial inquiry and exploration on questions and introducing other rhetorical factors: Who is my audience? Who is the audience of these early found materials? What is the purpose of these conversations? Why is this important to what I want to accomplish or discover? The lesson planning occurred with a conscious eye toward the upcoming session with Samantha, setting the stage for an instructional hand-off that played more like a duet than independent solo acts. This way, students were prepared for their time with Samantha, having already begun to think about their own informational goals.

Prior to the library session, students are provided with an infographic overview of the BEAM terminology (see Figure 13.2), which is incorporated into a discussion of the kinds of information students think they will need to move their ideas forward, address their early research questions (and variations of those questions), and represent the various views and needs of others involved in this conversation (aka stakeholders).

Students are then guided through a close reading of one or two short sample texts to explore these four classification categories, first by modeling, then in small group exploration and discussion, and finally individual blogging in which each student applies as many as possible of the BEAM features to one of their previously identified "conversation partner" source texts. Drawing from the sample questions provided by Woodward and Ganski's (2013) lesson plan (Table 13.2), students read a common reading text provided by the instructor and dissected it as a class. Students had a hard copy in hand while the same text was projected on the overhead screen. The guided discussion foregrounds the importance of student-centered inquiry—what do they want to know or discover about their topic—to shape the questions.

These lessons explicitly apply the BEAM acronym as a flexible rhetorical framework to show students how to engage with a source by asking questions about its rhetorical function from the student writer's perspective. Our own lesson designs integrate Bizup's (2008) explanation of such functionality: "Writers rely on background sources, interpret or analyze exhibits, engage arguments, and follow methods" (p. 76). During these close reading and group work activities, students were asked questions designed to help them think about their information needs as well as how sources

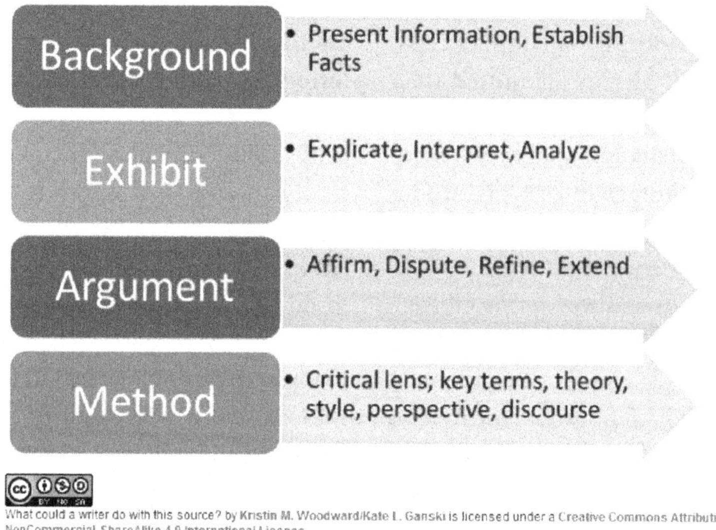

Figure 13.2 BEAM infographic. (From Woodward, K. M., & Ganski, K. L. [2013]. BEAM lesson plan. *UWM Libraries Instructional Materials*. https://dc.uwm.edu/lib_staff_files/1/. Used with permission.)

TABLE 13.2 *Questions Adapted from Woodward, K. M., & Ganski, K. L. (2013). BEAM lesson plan. UWM Libraries Instructional Materials. Paper 1; and Bizup, J. (2008). BEAM: A rhetorical vocabulary for teaching research-based writing.* Rhetoric Review, *27*(1), 72–86

B = Background	What information would you need to give your readers to establish key facts about [your topic or some feature of your topic]?
E = Exhibit	What could you analyze or interpret for your reader? Why might this be significant to your reader as you build your own claim?
A = Argument	What claims have your conversation partners (sources) made that you want to engage as part of building your own argument or deepening your inquiry? In other words, which of their claims do you want to agree with, disagree with, or build on somehow?
M = Method	How does this conversation partner (source) give you a model for a way or ways you might approach, analyze, or frame your own research question and/or contribute to this conversation?

might fulfill them. A few examples might be: How can you apply information provided by Source X as *Background* for your own ideas? What sorts of *Exhibits* will you want to provide and analyze to support your ideas, and how will you present or frame them? (It is important to distinguish between Evidence and Exhibit: Evidence might be seen as either/or, static proof that does not invite questioning or interpretation. Exhibits, on the other hand, require interpretation and analysis as a way to make meaning.) Why does the *Argument* presented in Source Y inspire you to push back or embrace its points as a way of affirming your own? How does the use of definitions by Sources L and M provide you with an example of a *Method* you might use to frame your own research questions? Such questions better prepare students to move into the library session because they help them see research as not just knowledge gathering, but an active engagement with and building upon others' ideas based on rhetorical inquiry practices. These questions also provided terminology for conducting preliminary searches in Google and Google Scholar as part of exploring existing conversations about their early topic ideas. These early key terms, as well as early research question(s), were recorded on an instructor-designed worksheet, a copy of which was provided to Samantha one to two weeks before our visit, along with the most recent assignment sheet (see Appendix). The worksheet's fill-in-the-blank prompts reflect the type of metacognitive questioning informed by the BEAM-inspired activities. This scaffolding serves as a guided note-taking device that helps not only to reinforce early research work, but to continue the common bridge between classrooms by creating a pattern of repetition picked up in Samantha's Umbrella graphic.

The students in a freshman writing classroom often struggle with their own agency as writers and knowledge builders; both BEAM and the Umbrella as conceptual tools help them to approach their sources as more than prepackaged bits of proof requiring nothing more of them than quote mining. Bizup's E of Exhibit is one of the more important (and often most difficult) of the tools as it requires them to take an intrinsic approach to their found material, to look at a source as more than "evidence" or "proof," labels that frame both the sources and the students' research behaviors as external. Many students seem to believe that they have to find sources that merely back up previously held beliefs, or they look to sources beyond their personal authority as the "real" (i.e., academically valid) knowledge builders as opposed to knowledge reporters. Such perspectives often do little to encourage students to embrace their own roles in new knowledge formation. Changing the vocabulary we use to discuss and practice research sets the stage for breaking down those perspectives. By asking students to apply this method of rhetorical classification to their thinking, planning, and search behaviors, we are asking them to consider how their sources-as-conversation-partners might add clarity, depth, and shape to their own ideas.

ON TO THE LIBRARY!

Many students, especially freshmen, struggle with research and its various components; being asked to write a paper and do research on a topic can be overwhelming. The Umbrella was created in an attempt to make the research process a little less daunting and a little more understandable for students. By breaking down a topic into its fundamental parts, students are able to go into a library database with topic-specific keywords and phrases and come back with useful and relevant sources. Research is not linear; there are lots of rabbit trails that can distract and derail students as they look for sources. Just as BEAM offers verbal/vocabulary "bumpers" (as in bowling) to help them manage the research process and their role in it, the Umbrella metaphor continues that effort into the library, offering a visual representation of their topic to help them stay on track.

The Umbrella is a fairly simple concept: the main part of the Umbrella is the fabric (the main topic), the framework of the Umbrella (the ribs) is the different aspects of the topic itself, and the handle represents the thesis or the core of the research (see Figure 13.3). For example, if a student is writing a paper on the topic of sports medicine, she would begin with the fabric of Sports Medicine, which is a very broad and generalized topic, and too big to plug into a database and expect relevant results. But by moving on to the ribs, or framework of the topic, she can begin to narrow down her topic. The framework is the sum of the parts of the topic—the questions students need to ask are: what makes up Sports Medicine, what is associated with that topic, what would someone who works in that field deal with on a daily basis, and so on. Once the students have narrowed down exactly what they want to find out about their topic, they can move down the handle. The handle represents what they want to pull out of their research, what they need to hold on to while looking for sources. If their goal in doing research is to find out more about the rate of concussions in high school football players, then they can look back to their Umbrella to find keywords, phrases, and concepts to help them in their research. In the database or some other research platform, they would start in the advanced search mode and use the broadest keyword in the first search box, followed by a narrower one, followed by another narrow keyword linked by Boolean operators AND or OR. For

Think of your research as an umbrella: Start broad with your main topic or theme, which would be the fabric of the umbrella.

Next, the framework, or supports of the umbrella, are what make up the fabric of the topic.

The handle of the umbrella represents your thesis, or what you want to grab hold of within the fabric.

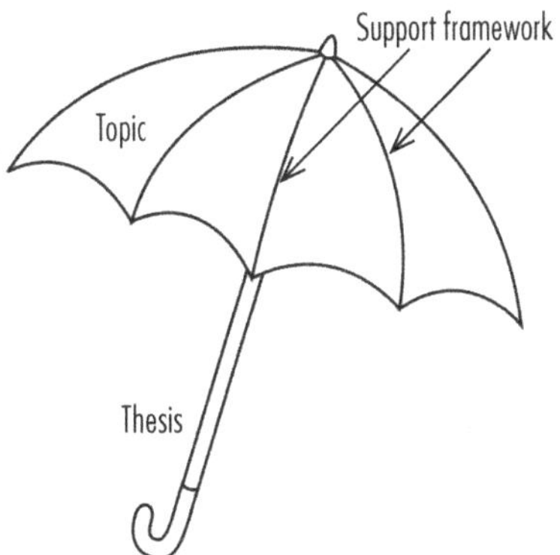

Figure 13.3 The research umbrella.

example: Sports Medicine AND Concussions AND Football.

This model can be used broadly for any research topic, and the process really is not very different from how most seasoned researchers conduct their own searches. However, what writing instructors and librarians need to keep in mind is that research, especially college-level research, is a foreign concept to most incoming students. They have grown up with Google, which reinforces their use of natural search language; they know they can just go to Google and ask it their questions. This approach, however, often leads to frustration when the student cannot find the scholarly, or even relevant, sources required for their assignment. This, in turn, can often lead to students changing their topic to what they feel is a more research-friendly topic, or complaining to the professor that there are no sources for their topic. Using the Umbrella and BEAM as a framework for their research changes the way students see and approach research and allows them to engage with sources on a deeper, more meaningful level. This approach allows librarians and writing instructors to help students produce better final products, as well as providing them with the tools they will need to be successful in future classes. The Research Umbrella graphic allows for more of an organic image of this process, as opposed to the more traditional linear metaphor of seek-and-find, and allows for more organic and inquiry-based thinking about doing research than the linear models that many students seem to cling to.

POSTLIBRARY: BACK TO THE WRITING WORKSHOP

The prelibrary classroom activities prime students with an introduction to BEAM vocabulary as a way to promote their engagement with source materials by emphasizing their roles as agents of knowledge building. Samantha's introduction of the Research Umbrella and review of BEAM principles during the library classroom session reinforced this, and combined it with an introduction to rhetorically driven search practices to support student engagement. Postlibrary, the two conceptual tools were then revisited in the writing classroom's activities and discussions, which were designed to explore how to best apply their library discoveries through more student-topic-focused BEAM-based questions. Moving forward into the research writing process, the BEAM and the Umbrella provide a powerful partnership of foundational concepts that offers the potential to deepen the connections between students' own thinking, reading, and inquiry efforts and the information literacy practices (i.e., search strategies and tools) presented during the library instructional session.

WHAT'S NEXT: RECOMMENDATIONS

Our goal for this collaborative teaching effort was to help our students approach research "as *strategic exploration*" ("Introduction," ACRL Framework), but in many ways we believe our approach to teaching and cross-disciplinary collaboration has been productively transformed as well. Both the BEAM's classification and the Research Umbrella metaphors provided lexical and conceptual tools for instruction as well as our own curriculum design practices. The BEAM and Umbrella are *metaphoric lenses* for *our* roles as well as the students as researchers . . . this is all about reframing the approach to research and student agency in that process. These tools provided us with a "new" meta language for our instruction: BEAM provided a rhetorical lens/filter to *rethink* and *reframe* not only teaching research but also collaborative possibilities. As teaching partners, we used these two tools in planning our instructional activities to create cohesion and transfer potential through the shared concepts and language they made possible.

There is room for revision, of course. In future collaborative sessions, we plan to address several areas:

1. Consider adjusting the timing of the library instructional session earlier or even a bit later in the research project arc. In this first iteration, the library session took place five weeks into the term, after students had begun working on their second project, a critical source evaluation and annotated bibliography project. Positioning the library instruction at this point allows students to think through their ideas independent of source materials; moving the session a few weeks later might promote more source-specific connections using the BEAM and Umbrella analysis, making it more relevant to students.
2. Incorporate more information literacy instruction throughout the course, not just one assignment. One possibility is the Embedded Librarian initiative proposed by Samantha, in which library instruction specialists would come into the writing classroom a few weeks after the initial library-based session. This would allow for expanded collaborative possibilities and additional one-on-one consultation between writing students and library instructional staff.
3. Many of our freshman students at AUM are first-generation college students (over 60% as of 2015). Most are local, and perhaps underprepared. Such categories may mirror many students who attend community colleges. This approach to collaborative information literacy instruction isn't just for a four-year institution like AUM. It can—and should—be successfully implemented in a variety of educational settings.

In the fall of 2016, we presented our work to a regional conference. Following the presentation, several writing and library instructors remarked that the BEAM and Umbrella materials could benefit their own student populations at smaller four-year institutions as well as community colleges. Such interest confirms that there is a real desire to find innovative ways to change how we teach information literacy, and such metaphoric/conceptual tools have the potential to contribute to this need.

4. This approach has the potential to be a bridge for underprepared students who have little background in research behaviors, but also can serve those in upper-level writing-intensive courses. Future collaborative efforts will focus on tailoring our approach to the needs of both.

This collaboration served as groundwork going forward, a collaborative partnership that promises much. We will tinker and adjust, but the main goal of widening the cooperative space for writing and library instructors, with common goals and a shared set of tools/perspectives, was achieved. William Butler Yeats once wrote that "Education is not the filling of a pail, but the lighting of a fire." We hope our work adds a spark to that ember.

APPENDIX. Library Day Worksheet

Complete the blanks below to help you think about the Types of Source Materials or Information you might need/want/find:

- Key Search Terms
  - ____________________
  - ____________________
- Key Definitions
  - ____________________
  - ____________________
- Historical/Background Information
  - ____________________
  - ____________________
- News Based/Facts (Dates, People, Numbers, Places)
  - ____________________
  - ____________________
- Analysis/Argument (Perspectives)
  - ____________________
  - ____________________
- Types of Publications or Websites that might have information on this subject
  - ____________________
  - ____________________
- Audiences who might weigh in? Be interested/invested/affected?
  - ____________________
  - ____________________
- Record below all of the resources you find during our Library Lab time. Even if you do not use them in your paper, it's a good idea to keep a Running Bibliography as you go.
  - ____________________
  - ____________________
  - ____________________
- Record the Questions That Arise:
  - *Should* ____________________?
  - *When/Where* ____________________?
  - *Why* ____________________?
  - *How* ____________________?
  - *What* ____________________?
  - *Who* ____________________?

REFERENCES

Association of College and Research Libraries. (2016). Introduction. *Framework for information literacy for higher education*. Retrieved from http://www.ala.org/acrl/standards/ilframework

Bizup, J. (2008). BEAM: A rhetorical vocabulary for teaching research-based writing. *Rhetoric Review, 27*(1), 72–86.

The Citation Project: Preventing plagiarism, teaching writing. (2010). http://site.citationproject.net/

Council of Writing Program Administrators, National Council of Teachers of English, and National Writing Project. (2011). *Framework for success in postsecondary writing.* Retrieved from http://wpacouncil.org/framework

D'Angelo, B., Jamieson, S., Maid, B., & Walker, J. (Eds.). (2016). *Information literacy: Research and collaboration across disciplines. Perspectives on Writing.* Fort Collins, Colorado: The WAC Clearinghouse and University Press of Colorado. Retrieved from http://wac.colostate.edu/books/infolit/

Head, A. J., & Eisenberg, M. B. (2009). *Lessons learned: How college students seek information in the digital age.* Project Information Literacy (PIL) at the University of Washington's Information School, Seattle, WA. Retrieved from http://projectinfolit.org/images/pdfs/pil_fall2009_finalv_yr1_12_2009v2.pdf

Howard, R. M., Serviss, T. C., & Rodrigue, T. K. (2010). Writing from sources, writing from sentences. *Writing and Pedagogy, 2*(2), 177–192.

Jamieson, S., & Howard, R. M. (2011). Unraveling the citation trail. *Project Information Literacy Smart Talk*, No. 8. Retrieved from http://www.projectinfolit.org/sandra-jamieson-and-rebecca-moore-howard-smart-talk.html

Knoblauch, A. A. (2011). A textbook argument: Definitions of argument in leading composition textbooks. *College Composition and Communication, 63*(2), 244–268.

McClure, R., & Purdy, J. P. (Eds.). (2016). *The future scholar: Researching and teaching the framework for writing & information literacy.* Association for Information Science and Technology (ASSIS&T).

Woodward, K. M., & Ganski, K. L. (2013). BEAM lesson plan. *UWM Libraries instructional materials.* Retrieved from http://dc.uwm.edu/lib_staff_files/1

CHAPTER 14

FOOD FOR THOUGHT

Writing About Culinary Traditions and the Integration of Personal and Academic Writing

Tom Pace

In their book *They Say/I Say: The Moves That Matter in Academic Writing*, Graff and Birkenstein (2010) challenge the assumption that writing for academic purposes can be separate from writing for personal reasons. In Chapter 9, "Academic Writing Doesn't Always Mean Setting Aside Your Own Voice," they remind readers that when writing for academic purposes, most students tend to assume that means they must subsume their own personal voice to the words and ideas of others they use from research. Graff and Birkenstein (2010), however, insist that students should not consider academic language as being mutually exclusive from other kinds of language. They stipulate that "Although academic writing does rely on complex sentence patterns and on specialized, disciplinary vocabularies, it is surprising how often such writing draws on the languages of the streets, popular culture, our ethnic communities, and home" (p. 128). This idea is often echoed in the experiences of many of my own first-year writing students. In a recent survey of student writers, one student claimed that most academic writing, especially writing that involves research, was "impersonal and quite frankly, boring." Whenever I teach this chapter to my students, many of them are suspicious that the personal can find a place in writing assignments that they have long assumed are reserved for what another student in the survey called "structured, fundamental, and basic." In other words, according to many of my first-year writing students, academic writing and personal voice, including a voice that emerges from writing about personal experiences, has little business in a college classroom where academic research is taught.

Indeed, moving between academic discourse and personal writing remains one of the most mysterious concepts for students. The experiences many young writers bring with them to their first-year writing classrooms usually involve writing assignments requiring them to pick one or the other. As such, many students fail to recognize how their personal stories can find a place in the context of academic research. Many in composition studies, though, have shown that writing for personal reasons is not mutually exclusive from learning how to write for academic ones. Gottschalk (2011) breaks through this either/or thinking by showing how a writing course on expressivism can coexist in Cornell University's writing-in-the-disciplines first-year program. She argues that the course provides for students "imaginative ways to enter into the conversation of the disciplines, when they are given ways to make the academic personal and the personal public" (2011). Similarly, Williams (2011) rethinks the legacy of Donald Murray to show that writing about the personal and writing about broader academic topics should be taught hand-in-hand. Williams (2011) insists that breaking through these dichotomies leads us "to respect student knowledge, to respect students as writers" (2011). In short, integrating students' personal experiences with academic writing and research should not be considered antithetical to what many, including students themselves, see as the primary work of the academy.

This chapter argues that requiring first-year students to integrate academic research with personal stories contributes to their stronger understanding of the broader social contexts of language use, contexts that allow them to complicate the role information literacy plays in their understanding of how to be a writer. I describe an assignment in which students write a personal essay about the role food plays in their family, investigating connections between familial culinary traditions and how those personal narratives connect to their understanding of broader social, historical, and cultural topics. Here, I draw from surveys with my student writers and from their essays to show how this project gives first-year writers rhetorical tools to be able to dismantle what Berthoff (1990) calls "killer dichotomies" when writing about personal experiences in academic contexts. This assignment challenges their understanding of personal and academic writing by addressing how academic conventions of research can be integrated into personal writing. While these students are not always able to negotiate this transformation successfully, almost all of them gained a clearer awareness of how their personal stories can be integrated with their academic literacy practices.

THE PERSONAL, THE ACADEMIC, AND FOOD NARRATIVES

The interaction between the personal and the academic is certainly nothing new in composition studies. Ever since the early process movement, writing teachers have routinely tried to get students to incorporate personal stories in an academic context. Yet, many students still enter their first-year writing courses under the assumption that their personal stories and narratives have little bearing on their academic work. As Berthoff (1990) insists, though, "There are no dichotomies in reality: dichotomizing is an act of mind, not of Nature" (pp. 13–14). In their edited collection, Holdstein and Bleich (2001) collect essays from several compositionists testifying to the way the personal intersects with professional lives. Specifically, they remind readers of how scholarly writing traditionally restricts first-person experiences and eschews the use of the dreaded "I" in scholarly writing: "Students are not taught that *sometimes* the first person is effective, or that one's own experience may well matter in one's announcing knowledge, but that it is actually *not acceptable* to use the I or to fold in personal experience in substantive ways in academic writing" (p. 2). Herrington (2002) reconsiders Peter Elbow's argument for getting students to render experience in their writing. Herrington applies Elbow's argument for rendering experience in academic as well as nonacademic writing so that when they leave her courses, first-year writers not only learn how to write for academic settings but learn something about themselves, too (p. 238). She also argues that if students are restricted from engaging the personal with the academic, their education lacks a certain richness of learning about themselves that otherwise might not take place:

> They are radically impoverished while at the university, as well, if they are cut off from a powerful way of continuing the ongoing work of composing themselves and, in relation to others, of bringing their knowledge to bear on topics pursued in their course work across disciplines. (p. 238)

This focus on work across the disciplines is reinforced in Gottschalk's (2011) research on the benefits of teaching personal writing in a writing-in-the-disciplines program and shows the success such a course can have on students' ability to integrate the personal with the academic, arguing that it "avoids the dichotomous trap of our asking for 'boring' academic writing or for 'interesting' personal writing" (2011). In short, encouraging students to integrate personal experience with academic knowledge and writing leads them to richer writing experiences, experiences that allow them to see their personal backgrounds as having a stake in their academic work.

One subject area where students have located the personal in the academic is food. Food narratives have become common genres for students to read, as well as to write. Indeed, *College English* once devoted a whole issue to writing about food. In that issue, Bloom (2008) compares the process of writing to the process of preparing a meal, quoting food historian Massimo Montanari:

> Food acquires full expressive capacity, thanks to the rhetoric that in every language is its necessary complement. Rhetoric is the adaptation of speech to the argument, to the effects one wants to arouse or create. If the discourse is food, that means the way it is prepared, served, and eaten. (p. 347)

Later, Bloom shows that food writing is accessible: "*Readers are looking for insight, entertainment, relaxation*, even more than for information (except in cookbooks), and can count on food writers to provide these" (p. 354). In that same issue, Waxman (2008) explores the role of food memoirs as a literary genre and argues "for the educational value and appeal of culinary memoirs in the literature classroom" (p. 381). Waxman's argument explores food memoirs as a genre to be read, consumed, and digested. Recently, Bedford St. Martin's published a reader entitled *Food Matters* (2014), a collection of food narratives and essays exploring the role of food production and consumption, designed for first-year writing classrooms. As such, food writing, as Bloom suggests and the Bedford reader demonstrates, can be an accessible genre for many first-year writing students. This chapter is an effort to extend Waxman's insistence on the value of the food writing genre, exploring what happens when food memoirs become something produced, cooked-up even, and not just consumed, in the first-year writing classroom.

INFORMATION LITERACY AND STUDENTS RETHINKING RESEARCH

The research skills students learn in the type of writing assignment I am about to describe are compatible with the development of information literacy skills outlined in the Association of College and Research Libraries' (ACRL) *Framework for Information Literacy for Higher Education* (2016). Specifically, the food narrative assignment engages students in three of the *Framework*'s six concepts: Authority Is Constructed and Contextual; Information Has Value; and Research as Inquiry. In addressing these three concepts, this chapter does not mean to suggest that the ACRL *Framework*'s other three concepts—Information Creation as a Process, Scholarship as Conversation, and Searching as Strategic Exploration—are not taught. They are. As explained in the "Introduction," the framework "is based on a cluster of interconnected core concepts, with flexible options for implementation, rather than on a set of standards or learning outcomes, or any prescriptive enumeration of skills" (2016). As such, my assignment focuses mostly on how students are able to construct writerly authority, to see how research leads to inquiry, and to discover the value in their information.

Integrating the personal and the academic allows students to transform their research and their understanding of what constitutes research in academic settings. This blending of the academic and the personal, as the food memoir assignment accomplishes in my first-year writing classroom, leads students to engage more fully in developing information literacy skills, skills that are increasingly taught, in collaboration with campus librarians, across the whole of the semester and not just in what Artman, Frisicaro-Pawlowski, and Monge (2010) call "one-shot" library lessons. Artman and colleagues (2010) argue that through collaboration and shared responsibility, writing teachers and librarians can integrate information literacy more fully and richly in student writing. "By helping faculty from across disciplines incorporate meaningful IL assignments and instruction in their courses," they write, "WPAs and their collaborative library partners can encourage the development of additional context-specific approaches to research writing beyond the composition program" (p. 105). Similarly, Nelson (2013) suggests that most students, in part because of the lack of integration between instructor and other university programs, still rely on a research process that she calls the "Compile Information Approach," an approach in which students see "their main task [being] compiling and presenting information 'to the customer neatly wrapped in footnotes and a bibliography'" (p. 89). Nelson discerns that many of these students rely on this "Compile Information Approach" despite the "recent advances in research technology and the growing emphasis on teaching information literacy" (p. 89). She quotes Bizzell and Herzberg (1987) in their assertion that "most faculty define student research as 'research-as-recovery,' not research-as-discovery" (Nelson, 2013, p. 105). In doing so, Nelson (2013) suggests that faulty need to design research assignments to "discourage the one-night-stand approach and require critical evaluation of sources and effective use of information to achieve self-determined goals, in other words, research-as-discovery" (p. 106). By incorporating information literacy instruction with the composition classroom, going beyond the "one-shot" lesson that Artman and her colleagues (2010) caution, while at the same time moving students beyond the "Compile Information Approach" and "one-night-stand" method that Nelson explores, my food narrative assignment encourages students to rethink not only their preconceived notions of research but also their preconceptions of the role the personal plays in the academic. It allows students to transform their traditional stance on research and, in so doing, transform their writerly selves.

THE SETTING

In the spring of 2012, and again in spring 2014, I taught a first-year composition course in which both times I taught an assignment on food memoirs. In the 2012 course, I revolved the course around the theme of "Cleveland." Most of the students come from Cleveland and the northeast Ohio region, and I believed a theme course on their hometown would generate interesting and vital papers that blended the academic with the personal. For the food assignment, I asked students to write an essay about the role food plays in the history and culture of Cleveland and in their own lives and families. To help them understand the role of food and culture in Cleveland, we drew from two main sources: one, Cleveland-native Michael Ruhlman's book *The Soul of a Chef*, specifically the section on Cleveland chef Michael Symon and his restaurant Lola. Two, students also read several articles on Cleveland food and culture by *Plain Dealer* food critic Joe Crea, who also visited the class and shared his wealth of knowledge and expertise on the Cleveland food scene. One of the assignment's options asked students to write a personal, first-person essay about the role food has played in their family, specifically investigating the connection between the food and the area or ethnicity in which they grew up. In addition to the readings from the sequence, I also asked them to conduct library research on those food traditions as secondary material to help them place their personal experiences in a broader, more public context. In the 2014 course, the focus changed a bit from a theme course on Cleveland to a theme course on popular culture, and the assignment changed a bit, too. I still kept the option to explore food traditions in their family and connect those traditions to broader contexts, but I also included an option where students were asked to pick a film or a popular television show that features eating and food and write an analysis of how that TV show and/or film portrays food. Again, students were required to combine library research with their analysis of the film or television program.

To help me with incorporating information literacy with this project, I worked closely with our library's liaison to the English department, Nevin Mayer. At my institution, information literacy is stated as a core competency for written and oral expression, and Nevin's work with the library reflects a larger information literacy outreach between academic programs and the library. Artman and colleagues 2010) argue that this kind of collaboration leads to better responses to research on the part of students. They stress that "librarians hope to provide information literacy instruction and support at multiple points during a project or a term, providing repeated opportunities in which students can practice a range of approaches to research" (p. 99). Indeed, Nevin and his library assistants not only offered one-on-one sessions, similar to the one-shot experiences in traditional research settings, but they also provided multiple sessions during a semester, both in class and in the library, where students could focus on anything from basic research strategies to more specific tasks, such as looking for a particular piece of supporting evidence for a project. For instance, Nevin and his assistants built a Subject Guide specifically for my Cleveland-themed course, and they also constructed a Web page of online resources and databases on the history of Cleveland and Ohio, including both academic and nonacademic—yet substantive—sources students pulled from for their writing assignments. For my popular culture course, Nevin provided a page of databases for pop culture studies. In addition, Nevin and I collaborated on the role information literacy would play in the course's different assignments, and Nevin visited the course two or three times to work with us on various aspects of finding materials using both traditional and online methods. Nevin also met one-on-one with students in both courses on a variety of information literacy strategies: understanding and developing an appropriate topic, accessing appropriate information, evaluating information for quality, using information critically. In response to a survey on his role in teaching research to students across the university, Nevin stressed "that critical thinking is closely aligned with information literacy. To that end, that is a value I see woven through the university's learning goals." This connection, therefore, between information literacy and critical thinking manifests itself in my food assignment and the process Nevin and I used to lead students to see research as an integration of scholarly sources and personal experience.

STUDENT RESPONSES TO THE ASSIGNMENT

Now, I would like to share some of my student writers' reflections on how incorporating personal experience with academic research in their food memoirs led some of these students to transform their relationship to research, highlighting the assignment's strengths and weaknesses. The feedback comes from a small group of students from the class, but it reflects the feedback in general that I received from students in both courses. These cases demonstrate the role that blending personal and academic research can have for different kinds of first-year writing students, bolstering their transformation from students who held rigid notions of research to writers who complicated the relationship between personal and public. Many of the students who responded to my survey noted that they rarely, if ever, considered much research when writing. Or, if they did, it was to gather as many secondary sources as possible and put them together as quickly as possible to satisfy a high school research assignment, echoing Nelson's (2013) "Compile Information" and "one-night-stand" approach (p. 89). As such, the food narrative assignment leads students to understand authority as constructed and contextual, to understand that information has value, and to see research as inquiry.

AUTHORITY IS CONSTRUCTED AND CONTEXTUAL

One of the benefits of the food narrative assignment is that it teaches student writers that writerly authority, and the decisions made about resources, depends on context. One of the threshold concepts developed by the ACRL (2016) insists that "Authority Is Constructed and Contextual." In other words, according to the ACRL, "Information resources reflect their creators' expertise and credibility, and are evaluated based on the information need and the context in which the information will be used" (Association of College and Research Libraries [ACRL], 2016). Yet, most students who come into my class assume that most research assignments are written for the same audiences and for the same purposes, if they are familiar with research methods or information literacy practices at all. In her response to the survey Trish, for example, emphasized that academic research was something she was not familiar with entering first-year composition: "In high school, I remember writing one big research paper but wasn't taught what in-depth research was. I remember using a few websites and a book. In college, I learned how to properly use all my resources online and in the library." Here, she suggests that, based on her experiences, most research projects lack a clearly defined rhetorical situation, that all she had to do was cite a few websites and maybe a book or two, and be done with it. Trish also noted that previous teachers—including college instructors—gave students "a number of required sources for a particular paper with the only instruction being: no Wikipedia." In other words, her previous experience with research and information literacy revolved around satisfying strict requirements for the number and type of sources used, without taking into consideration audience, purpose, or the overall context of the project.

In allowing students to integrate the personal with the academic, my food narrative assignment shows students how authority is constructed and that decisions about what information to include in a research assignment are context-bound. Because of the assignment's narrative bent, students build a writerly *ethos* through incorporating family stories and other personal anecdotes and connect them to information gathered through their academic research. In her paper, "The Irish Way," Trish explores her family's Irish roots and describes the various food traditions her family maintained, focusing on her family's tradition of enjoying brunch at her grandparents' house after mass each Sunday. In her narrative, she describes her Nana's boxty, a potato pancake popular in Irish breakfasts. Her grandparents emigrated from Ireland in their early twenties, and Trish depicts the different Irish dishes they served around the lunch table each Sunday. In doing so, Trish integrates her family's traditions with the history of Irish immigration to the United States and the impact of the mid-nineteenth-century potato famine on the Irish diet:

> When the potato crop replenished, it came back as more of a side dish than the main ingredient, because of its prior difficulties. Though, potato pancakes still remain one of the most precious items on Nana's list, and will continue to be one for my future family.

Here, through the integration of her personal stories from her family and through her research into the history of the Irish potato famine and its impact on Irish culture, Trish is able to connect her family's traditions to larger public and historical events. Later, Trish remarked in the survey that before this assignment, she "knew very little about incorporating credible and relevant research in my writing." After researching Irish food histories and connecting them with her family's experiences, she notes that "there is a correlation between the two. I remember writing about family traditions and researching different meanings to those traditions and understanding where it came from and why my family did that."

Another student who responded to the survey, Kelly, reflected that the integration of the personal with the academic in the food assignment challenged the way she considered context and authority in her writing. At her high school, Kelly remarked, "They taught us how to see if a source was credible or not. I briefly learned how to use a scholarly database, [and previous writing teachers] nearly always emphasized the importance of incorporating trustworthy research in writing." In other words, she recognized that the integration of the personal with the academic altered her previous assumptions about her paper. After writing about the harmful side effects of fast food in American diets, Kelly perceives that authority in research is largely dependent on the context of the research project. This assignment, on the one hand, led Trish and Kelly to engage in the kind of academic meaning-making that Gottschalk (2011) identifies when she argues that "Students and instructors alike are more engaged, more entertained, and more passionately involved when students are provided imaginative ways to enter into the conversation, . . . when they are given ways to make the academic personal and the personal public" (2011). On the other hand, the assignment also invited these students to construct a writerly authority and understand that information used in research is always bound by context.

INFORMATION HAS VALUE

In addition to constructing authority and context, this assignment also teaches students that using information from various sources adds value to a student's learning process. As the ACRL (2016) puts it, "Information possesses several dimension of value, including as a commodity, as a means of education, as a means to influence, and as a means of negotiating and understanding the world" (2016). In the food narrative assignment, students engage in different types of information acquired from both personal and academic sources, to negotiate and understand the world around them. Specifically, the ACRL stresses that "value may be leveraged by individuals and organizations to effect change and for civic, economic, social, or personal gains" (2016). This focus on numerous definitions of "value" may at first appear oversimplistic, or even contradictory. But the frame is careful to point out that "the individual is responsible for making deliberate and informed choices about when to comply with and when to context current socioeconomic practices concerning the value of information" (2016). In other words, my food assignment allows students to recontextualize information so that they see some kind of value in that information, value they may not have considered before—whether it is for "civic, economic, social, or personal gains" (2016).

Consider my student Zoe. Like most of my students, Zoe came to the course without much prior instruction in research, as she stated in the survey, and when she did use research in her writing, she assumed sources obtained from the library had little to nothing to do with information acquired from personal experience. To her, research was mostly "using databases and giving credit in the bibliography." At first, Zoe was unsure about integrating the personal with the academic: "I found it hard," she notes. "I wasn't sure how to go about conducting research when writing papers about personal experience." In her paper, Zoe chose the option of writing about a film and how it portrays food and food consumption, focusing on Morgan Spurlock's film *Supersize Me* (2008) and how fast food can have negative consequences for one's health. Although she did not focus on personal experiences and narratives as much as other students did in their papers, Zoe incorporated secondary sources she found from library research, mostly Michael Pollan's essay, "Escape From the Western Diet" (2012), an essay we had read as a class, as well as sources from economic and agricultural databases. Even though most of her essay summarizes these sources without connecting them to her own personal experiences and narratives, her narrative makes some moves toward writing about growing up overexposed to fast-food diets. In addition, the information she connected—Spurlock's film, Pollan's essay on Western diets, and the agricultural and economic sources—proved valuable to her, complicating the role of fast food in the American diet. Her essay focuses on how the food industry makes it difficult for Americans to escape a diet of processed and fast-food options, a perspective she learned through her research. Later, Zoe notes that even though she chose the film option, the topic was still personal because of the ubiquity of fast food and, as a result, the assignment challenged her previous understanding of the role personal experiences play in academic research. "It was easier to write papers about personal experiences, and finding research seemed a little easier because you're relating to yourself." Because students like Zoe, though the food assignment, are able to relate researched information to personal experiences, much of the information they gather and learn about has value.

In her response to the survey, Marissa also reflected on the value of information in her learning. Marissa expressed that she had little experience with information literacy instruction, pointing out she had little knowledge of research methods, stating that "even coming from a private liberal arts high school, we did more novel discussions than we did research writing." For the food narrative assignment, Marissa wrote a paper on the role her Mexican heritage plays in the food traditions her family enjoys during Christmas. Like Zoe, Marissa also struggled with integrating secondary sources with her personal stories. Indeed, the majority of her paper focuses on descriptions of her family's Christmas celebrations and her grandmother's cooking, with little library research incorporated; when she did use a secondary source, it felt more like an add-on than an integrated part of her writing. Yet even this clumsy attempt at integrating secondary sources proved valuable later in the semester for Marissa. The food assignment challenged her to connect family experiences with academic research, and although her food narrative was not as successful as it could have been, she later told me that the experience helped her with the semester's major research project, where students researched a topic associated with their major. In reflecting on the course's role in her learning, she mentioned that the food assignment had a significant impact on her research:

> I did my paper on public health and the study of infectious diseases and epidemiology. I'm not sure I ever thought the two papers were ever correlated but being able to write personally helped in leading to the big research paper as I was able to discover my voice and style. To me, using research in writing about personal experience is not always necessary but it adds value.

In other words, Marissa was able to complicate the integration of secondary research into personal experiences and, in the process, discover connections between personal experiences and academic research. As such, Marissa discovered the value such personal information holds. In short, while students such as Zoe and Marissa came to the assignment with little to no experience with research outside of a rigid, assignment-driven, "one-shot" experience that valued secondary sources only over any other kind of research, the assignment challenged their preconceived notions of research to show how different kinds of information can prove valuable to their learning and their writing.

RESEARCH AS INQUIRY

The food assignment, in addition to constructing authority and showing how information has value, also taught students Research as Inquiry. Research as Inquiry is one of the threshold concepts in the ACRL's *Framework*, where they state that "Research is iterative and depends upon asking increasingly complex or new questions whose answers in turn develop additional questions or lines of inquiry in any field" (2016). By starting with their own family food traditions, my students used those experiences as a starting place to begin questioning larger social, cultural, and historical conditions. Kelly's paper, for instance, is a good example of how students in my class were able to use research as inquiry. Kelly, an honors student who came into the class better prepared to conduct research than most other students, had never considered research playing a role in writing about personal experience. After her experience with the food memoir assignment, however, she responded in the survey that she "can turn personal experience into more than just stories. You could share information, and intertwine stories with facts to share good information with readers." Although she had a fairly strong grounding in research from high school and other prior experiences, Kelly noted that the food assignment led her to invert her research process, leading her to consider Research as Inquiry. "It changed the way I created a piece of writing," she reflected. "I revamped my whole writing process, which now begins with research rather than writing." In other words, Kelly let the research guide her writing process.

This focus on letting her research questions guide her writing process manifests itself in her food narrative. Kelly had spent much of her high school years living in Scandinavia with her family, and this experience led her to question American diets and what she saw as the overreliance on processed foods. Like Zoe, Kelly was interested in the harmful effects of Western diets, but unlike Zoe, Kelly researched the question further, and her paper reflects how this assignment leads students to ask, as the ACRL states, "simple questions that depend upon basic recapitulation of knowledge to increasingly sophisticated abilities to refine research questions" (2016). Kelly's research process began with responding to Pollan's essay, "Escaping the Western Diet." Here, she expanded Pollan's definition of "Western diet" and narrowed her focus to industrial farming. She drew from sociology resources to expand her understanding of the West to include Europe and other countries with significant European origins. In doing so, she combined her family history with various academic resources to write a paper that expanded Pollan's argument to show how industrial farming is not just impacting American diets but European ones, as well. In doing so, not only did Kelly connect personal experiences to academic resources, but she put into practice the ACRL's focus on inquiry, which, as they note, "extends beyond the academic world to the community at large, and the process of inquiry may focus upon personal, professional, or societal needs" (2016). Later, in reflecting on her experience researching and writing the paper, and its impact on research she performed later in her college career, Kelly observed that, "depending on the research I am able to do, sometimes my whole piece of writing may have to change from my original idea in order to incorporate the research properly." In short, Kelly's food narrative on industrial farming, Western diets, and her own experiences living in Europe and the United States exemplifies Research as Inquiry.

SUMMARY

In her brief essay, "Writing Is Informed by Prior Experience," Lunsford (2016) points out that when students identify clear connections between writing assignments or from one writing situation to another, prior knowledge assists them in solving the new rhetorical situation (p. 55). But, she adds, "when they simply rely on a strategy or genre or convention out of habit, that prior knowledge may not be helpful at all" (p. 55). As I have demonstrated here, an assignment that leads students to break down the dichotomies between personal experience and academic research illustrates this use of prior knowledge. Even though some of the papers were a mixed bag—some were quite good, like Kelly's, while others merely dropped secondary research into the personal story, like Marissa's—the assignment altered the way most of these students considered the role of research in their writing process. In doing so, the assignment engaged students in the ACRL's threshold concepts for learning information literacy. The assignment taught students how authority is constructed dependent on context, such as Trish's realization that her family's Irish food traditions connect to larger historical, public contexts and that her personal experiences give her an authorial credibility she might not have otherwise appreciated. The assignment also led students to see the value of information, such as Marissa's awareness that personal experience, combined with academic research, can lead not only to further understanding of family traditions but, in her case, led her to a richer understanding of her eventual major field of study, public health. Finally, the assignment also leads students to see Research as Inquiry, as when Kelly used her family experiences dividing time between Sweden and the United States to begin questioning the Western world's reliance on industrial farming and other kinds of processed foods. The combination of asking students to write food memoirs, of asking them to consider a more integrated model of learning information literacy, and of breaking down the dichotomy between personal and academic, transformed these students' relationship to research and writing.

REFERENCES

Artman, M., Frisicaro-Pawlowski, E., & Monge, R. (2010). Not just one shot: Extending the dialogue about information literacy in composition classes. *Composition Studies, 38*(2), 93–110.

Association of College and Research Libraries. (2016). *Framework for information literacy for higher education.* Retrieved from http://www.ala.org/acrl/standards/ilframework

Berthoff, A. E. (1990). Killer dichotomies: Reading in/reading out. In K. Ronald & H. Roskelly (Eds.), *Farther along: Transforming dichotomies in rhetoric and composition* (pp. 12–24). Portsmouth, NH: Heinemann.

Bizzell, P., & Herzberg, B. (1987). Research as a social act. *The Clearing House, 60*(7), 303–306.

Bloom, L. Z. (2008). Consuming prose: The delectable rhetoric of food writing. *College English, 70*(4), 346–361.

Gottschalk, K. L. (2011). Writing from experience: The evolving roles of personal writing in a writing in the disciplines program. *Across the Disciplines, 8*(1). Retrieved September 20, 2016, from http://wac.colostate.edu/atd/artiles/gottschalk2011.cfm

Graff, G., & Birkenstein, C. (2010). *"They say/I say": The moves that matter in academic writing* (2nd ed.). New York: W. W. Norton.

Herrington, A. J. (2002). Gone fishin': Rendering and the uses of personal experience in writing. In P. Belanoff, M. Dickson, S. Fontaine, & C. Moran (Eds.), *Writing with elbow* (pp. 223–238). Logan, UT: Utah State University Press.

Holdstein, D., & Bleich, D. (2001). *Personal effects: The social character of scholarly writing.* Logan, UT: Utah State University Press

Lunsford, A. (2016). Writing is informed by prior experience. In L. Adler-Kassner & E. Wardle (Eds.), *Naming what we know: Threshold concepts of writing studies* (pp. 54–55). Logan, UT: Utah State University Press.

Nelson, J. (2013). "It takes a whole campus": Information literacy in composition and across the curriculum. *Journal of Teaching Writing, 28*(1), 85–116.

Pollan, M. (2012). Escape from the Western diet. In G. Graff & C. Birkenstein (Eds.), *They say/I say: The moves that matter in academic writing, with readings* (2nd ed., pp. 434–441). New York: W. W. Norton.

Waxman, B. F. (2008). Food memories. *College English, 70*(4), 363–382.

Williams, B. T. (2011, November 10). Dancing with Don: Or, waltzing with "expressivism." *Enculturation: A Journal of Rhetoric, Writing, and Culture, 13*. Retrieved September 20, 2016, from http://www.enculturation.net/dancing-with-don

CHAPTER 15

CREATING A MULTIMODAL ARGUMENT

Moving the Composition Librarian Beyond Information Literacy

M. Delores Carlito

Interacting with the world has never happened in one mode, and it certainly does not now. Advertisements have words and images if they are in print, and television commercials include voice and music. MTV brought music and video together for the television audience. Even before mass media, orators combined text using language, an image of the speaker, voice and tone, and gestures.

Educators are realizing that composing in more than one mode is necessary. In 2016, the Association of College and Research Libraries (ACRL) published its *Framework for Information Literacy for Higher Education*. The *Framework* emphasizes threshold concepts, or ideas that are central to understanding a discipline,[1] and cross-modality creation and assessment. The Council of Writing Program Administrators, the National Council of Teachers of English, and the National Writing Project (2011) collaborated to publish the *Framework for Success in Postsecondary Writing*, which emphasizes that writing is no longer dominated by pen and paper. Both guidelines are used by academic faculty, including teaching librarians, in addressing new forms of discourse in freshman composition.

Librarians are an integral part of any instruction team, and they should be involved specifically when addressing assignments that involve information literacy, visual literacy, multiliteracies, and copyright. Since students must rethink the meaning of reading and text, librarians must reevaluate how they conduct instruction for composition classes in both context (how they teach) and content (what they teach) by becoming co-instructors with faculty when a multimodal assignment appears in the curriculum. Composition programs are undergoing a pedagogical shift from emphasizing modes to writing for the public sphere, including multimodal texts for students to evaluate and create. Librarians are already well versed in many literacies, including information, visual, and media. In addition, they are familiar with the ethical issues related to using images, videos, and sound files in multimodal tools. Therefore, academic librarians should take the lead in collaborating with composition instructors to become the primary resource on campus for creating multimodal artifacts by teaching faculty and students to locate, evaluate, use ethically, and cite various modes.

BACKGROUND ON MULTIMODAL DISCOURSE

Multimodal discourse has been a major topic in composition studies for over 20 years, but the library literature has only taken it up recently. In the groundbreaking work "A Pedagogy of Multiliteracies: Designing Social Futures," the New London Group (1996) emphasized the challenges students faced in interacting with the digital world, and they described future literacies. They specified several modes of meaning: visual, aural, gestural, special, and multimodal. Of the meaning-making modes, they stated:

> The Multimodal is the most significant, as it relates all the other modes in quite remarkably dynamic relationships. For instance, mass media images relate the linguistic to the visual and to the gestural in intricately designed ways. Reading the mass media for its linguistic meanings alone is not enough. (p. 80)

Therefore, multimodality is not one way of reading, but it incorporates many "languages," or, as Frank Serafin calls it, "Words married to images, sounds, the body, and experiences" (2014, p. xi).

Multimodality first appeared in the library literature in a 2009 talk at the International Federation of Library Associations and Institutions (IFLA) World Congress in Milan, Italy. In his talk and consequent paper titled "Broad Horizons: The Role of Multimodal Literacy in 21st Century Library Instruction," Sean Cordes (2009) emphasizes:

> Although reading and writing are still the foundation of knowledge, literacy in this age means more than the ability to read and write; it requires a complex set of skills including: access analysis, synthesis, evaluation, and use of information in a variety of modes. (p. 1)

Cordes also describes multimodal literacy as requiring "in part a new sensibility, one that promotes a self responsibility for the acquisition and use of knowledge that is flexible, exploratory, and ethical" (p. 4). Cordes believes understanding many modes was important to library patrons because of information literacy's role in lifelong learning. Technology both helped and hurt libraries and patrons, but, to Cordes, the crucial point was that library instruction would aid patrons in both understanding and creating knowledge. He emphasizes that reading and producing material with more than one design element could be complex, and he praises librarians for being both creators and those who enable innovation. He ends with a call for more research.

In *A Writer's Reference*, Diana Hacker and Nancy Sommers (2016) describe multimodal "writings" as "those that draw on multiple (multi) modes of conveying information, including any combination of words, numbers, images, graphics, animations, translations, sounds (voice and music), and more" (p. MM-6). According to Serafin (2014) in *Reading the Visual*, multimodal "refers to texts that utilize a variety of modes to communicate or represent concepts and information" (p. 12). Both books use the term "modes." Kress and Van Leeuwen (2001) define *mode* as "that material resource which is used in recognizably stable ways as a means of articulating discourse" (p. 25). In other words, modes are the resources, or tools, used.

The research provides many lists of modes. The book *Writer/Designer: A Guide to Making Multimodal Projects* lists five:

- Linguistic
- Visual
- Aural
- Spatial
- Gestural (Arola, Sheppard, & Ball, 2014)

According to Cordes (2009), a literacy framework includes the modes of

- Linguistic (oral and written)
- Visual
- Audio
- Gestural
- Spatial
- Cultural
- Multimodal

In the library literature, understanding modes is often referred to as metaliteracy. In their seminal article in *College and Research Libraries*, "Reframing Information Literacy as a Metaliteracy," Mackey and Jacobson (2011) list six frameworks that contribute to a literacy for addressing all student needs:

- Information Literacy
- Media Literacy
- Digital Literacy
- Visual Literacy
- Cyber Literacy
- Information Fluency (pp. 63–67)

For the purposes of this chapter, the primary modes that will be covered are linguistic (words), visual (images), technology (tools and media), aural (voice and music), and spatial (organization).

At its core, "multimodal" is about communication. It is another way to communicate with others and relay information. It is also a way to interpret meaning. It relies on hybridity, or the ways that different modes interact, and intertextuality, or how the container changes the meaning. Multimodality allows its users to communicate across cultures and languages, thus making people multilingual. Multimodal also includes an aspect of creation that may not be present in the other literacies; it not only involves interpreting the data in the form of letters, number, images, or symbols, but creating it using the various modes.

Students are already creating these texts without giving it a name. When they send an instant message with a selfie that they have modified using stickers, they are using their multimodal skills to convey a particular meaning to the receiver. The speed at which information is delivered and seen means that lifelong learning literacy outcomes must address multimodal skills such as evaluating news videos on Facebook or creating presentations. Librarians and instructors need to help students understand that the same set of skills they already use can be adapted to create academic multimodal artifacts.

LITERATURE REVIEW OF CURRENT RESEARCH

As stated earlier, the first article to address multimodal instruction as it relates to information literacy was a presentation given by Cordes at IFLA. Most of the literature on multimodal literacy, new literacy, multiliteracy, transliteracy, multimodal discourse, or Web 2.0 literacies does not involve library instruction.

The greatest number of works on multimodal composition come from the writing discipline, and authors view multiple literacies as important in a writer's arsenal (D. Anderson et al., 2006; Archer, 2006; Cope & Kalantzis, 2009; Eyman, 2015; Fraiberg, 2010; Jewitt, 2005; Mikulecky, St. Clair, & Kerka, 2003; Vasudevan, 2013). Takayoshi and Selfe (2007) address composition teachers who might question whether they are actually teaching rhetoric and composition when they concentrate on multimodal texts. They state that multimodality has existed for a while and is not a creation of the 21st century so, yes, teaching multimodality is teaching composition (pp. 7–8).

Authors recognize the changed, and changing, nature of literacy and communication (Kress & Van Leeuwen, 2001; Walsh, 2009). Writing in many modes, because it can be read not just by those in the language of creation, has become a skill for political purposes (J. Anderson, 2006).

Library literature centered on the academic library's role in multimodal discourse has emphasized the importance of librarians being well versed in various literacies (Berndston, 2010; Hattwig, Bussert, Medaille, & Burgess, 2013; Koltay 2011; Lippincott, 2007; Mackey & Jacobson, 2014; Marcum, 2002). In fact, Marcum (2002) states, "The profession must expand its definitions of librarianship to include new forms of expertise . . . and must recast the model of information literacy to embrace multiple literacies and sociotechnical competencies" (p. 202). Koltay, Spiranec, and Karvalics (2015) believe the shift in information literacy "enable[s] researchers to create, annotate, review, re-use and represent information in new ways and make possible a wider promotion of innovations in the communication practices of research" (p. 89).

Visual literacy is viewed as a vital literacy, whether taught by the school or by the library (Avgerinou, 2009; Harris, 2010; Hattwig et al., 2013; Spalter & Van Dam, 2008; Thomas et al., 2007). The Association for College and Research Libraries (2011) has set forth a set of competency standards for visual literacy in higher education, the *ACRL Visual Literacy Competency Standards for Higher Education*. These standards include the skills of finding, interpreting, evaluating, using, and creating images.

While much has been written about multimodal composition, little has been written about the academic library's role in supporting this modality. The traditional academic reference librarian has evolved into a teacher librarian, collaborating with professors on assignments and assessment. ACRL's *Standards for Proficiencies for Instruction Librarians and Coordinators* was updated in 2017 to the *Roles and Strengths of Teaching Librarians in Higher Education* (2017). The document states, "Teaching librarians have many opportunities to collaborate in different instructional settings with teaching faculty . . . [and] these relationships aspire to be partnerships rather than support services" (Teaching Partner). Therefore, librarians are not solely at the university to support others' teaching, but to actually teach students, themselves.

WAYS LIBRARIANS CAN COLLABORATE WITH WRITING PROFESSORS

The *ACRL Visual Literacy Competency Standards* (2011) coupled with the ACRL *Framework for Information Literacy for Higher Education* (2016) place librarians at the center of multimodal instruction. Due to these two documents, librarians are in the unique position of being knowledgeable about and having the professional guidelines to be fluent in, and recognize the fluidity of, multiliteracies. Librarians easily navigate the literacy worlds, jumping from one participatory skill to another, able to distinguish the differences yet also able to see the connections and translate them between the modalities.

Information literacy is a way of reading the world, evaluating in context the messages and discourses going on around us, and contributing to these conversations. It was originally codified in ACRL's *Information Literacy Competency Standards for Higher Edu*cation (2000) but was superseded by ACRL's *Framework for Information Literacy for Higher Education* (2016). Information literacy's most basic (and most used) definition is that it is the ability to recognize an information need and then locate, evaluate, and use that information effectively and ethically. With the *Framework*, information literacy still respects its foundations, but the definition has been expanded to be based "on a cluster of interconnected core concepts . . . rather than on a set of standards or learning outcomes or any prescriptive enumeration of skills" (Introduction). In part, it was created because "Students have a greater role and responsibility in creating new knowledge, in understanding the contours and the changing dynamics of the world of information, and in using information, data, and scholarship ethically" (Introduction). At various points in the *Framework*, the frames refer to formats besides print, such as "a short blog post," "all media types," "in any format," "dimensions of value," and "an appropriate level, such as local online community" (Authority Is Constructed and Contextual; Information Creation as a Process; Information Has Value; Scholarship as Conversation). Even using the term "creators" rather than "authors" implies that different modes can be used or valued depending on the context.

In addition to initiating and perfecting information literacy, librarians have been at the forefront of classifying and cataloging visual literacy outcomes. According to Hattwig and colleagues (2013):

> The *Visual Literacy Standards* are the first of their kind to describe interdisciplinary visual literacy performance indicators and learning outcomes. These learning outcomes provide a framework for student visual literacy learning and offer guidance for librarians, faculty, and other academic professionals in teaching and assessing visual literacy. (p. 62)

Visual literacy is similar to information literacy in that it asks the user to determine a need, locate material, and then interpret, analyze, and use it effectively and ethically. The *Visual Literacy Standards* extend information literacy's traditional definition to include the ability to "understand and analyze the contextual, cultural, ethical, aesthetic, intellectual, and technical components involved in the production and use of visual materials" (Visual Literacy Defined). With the visual literacy standards, established information literacy outcomes are extended to images.

Thomas Mackey and Trudi Jacobson (2011) expand on the different literacies defined in both the library and other literatures. They recommend combining all literacies into one metaliteracy that encompasses them all, but they see the single metaliteracy based in information literacy. They state, "Information literacy is the metaliteracy for a digital age because it provides the higher order thinking required to engage with multiple document types through various media formats in collaborative environments" (p. 70). They emphasize that information literacy "prepares individuals to adapt to shifting information environments," helps them learn how to learn, and allows them to apply the information they learn from all sources and modalities to become "participatory learners" (p. 70). Mackey and Jacobson recognize that information is not static and that learners must be able to adapt to current and future technologies.

While the literature of rhetoric and composition has focused on composing in many modes, librarians are uniquely equipped not only to teach these modalities, but to evaluate and assist with multimodal creation. Librarians have been working with formalized information literacies for 17 years, and the *Visual Literacy Standards* (2011) and the *Framework for Information Literacy* (2016) have only solidified their position as the leader in understanding various literacies and modalities and being able to convey this information to students and faculty. Librarians understand that multimodal instruction does not just mean finding an image and using it, but it involves learner-centered production coupled with conscious and thoughtful evaluation.

In order for librarians to have a framework for teaching multimodal texts and combining multiple literacies, I refer to Kress and Van Leeuwen's (2001) four "strata," or the "four domains of practice in which meanings are dominantly made" (p. 4). The four strata, with no hierarchy, are discussed below (pp. 4–8).

Discourse. Discourse is a "socially constructed knowledge of some aspect of realty" (p. 4). Socially constructed contexts relate to the group as a universe of discourse, and no one can know everything in any universe. Discourse is independent of genres but not of the audience's knowledge and experiences.

Design. Design is "[use of] semiotic resources, in all semiotic modes and combination of semiotic modes" (p. 5). It changes "socially constructed knowledge into social (inter-) action" (p. 5). Therefore, with design, communication becomes a conversation *with* rather than *at*.

Production. Production is creation. It is the "organization of the expression, to the actual material production of the semiotic artefact" (p. 6). Production involves tool skills, or the ability to manipulate the medium.

Distribution. Distribution facilitates "the pragmatic functions of preservation and distribution" (p. 7). Distribution is dissemination.

Kress and Van Leeuwen's strata work very well as a model for multimodal communication. They break down each part of a multimodal assignment into its respective parts, each with its own decisions to be made. It can be difficult for students to understand multiple layers of meaning, but hopefully Kress and Van Leeuwen's strata can help (see Figure 15.1).

In this model for multimodal composition, the same four strata are used but the content is specialized to library instruction to support multimodal creation in composition. Composing with multimodal texts has the same outcome as composing solely in print, because "composing has always served to capture, save, and deliver ideas, messages, and meanings" (Hacker & Sommers, 2016, p. MM-7). The format is different, and this model can help students walk through the process of thinking about and creating multimodal texts.

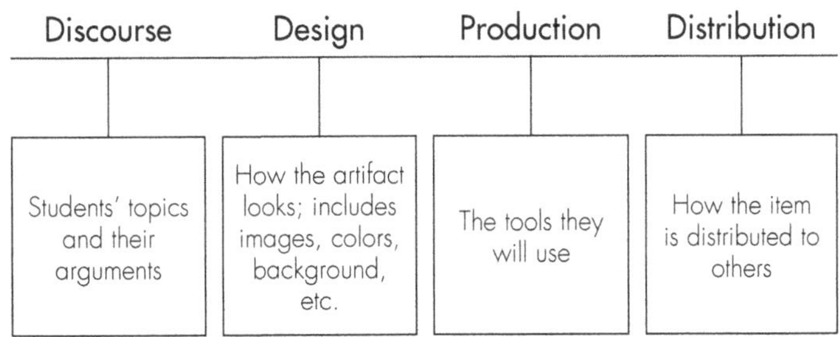

Figure 15.1 Strata for multimodal communication.

Discourse

While discourse is socially constructed, in the library instruction and freshman composition context discourse refers to students' topics and arguments. Hopefully students have written a paper or created the text of their discourse, but sometimes they have not. If they have not, the librarian must make sure that the students have a clear view of their topics and have researched all viewpoints in order to create a well-versed multimodal composition. The *Framework for Information Literacy* (2016) emphasizes that searching is strategic and scholarship is a conversation, so students must look for the debate and not just one side; students must find what has been argued on a topic and realize that their viewpoints can impact the search. If the audience is not aware of the context, it is the student's responsibility to make sure that the audience understands it. The discourse will also guide students in determining what type of image to use (*ACRL Visual Literacy Competency Standards*, Standard One). If the student is not aware of the debate, then that person also does not have the ability to decide what type of visual will advance the argument, so a useless or ineffective image may be used. A good argument can put the reader and the writer in the same place of empathy and understanding.

Design

Design is the "language" the student will use to communicate the argument or point. Design may be the use of colors, music, images, video clips, or other modes, and it is important because it lays out the tone of the presentation. Librarians can assist students with locating and evaluating these modes, or they can help students with citing and using them ethically and effectively.

Librarians can use search tools that emphasize open access materials. The Creative Commons search (https://search.creativecommons.org) allows students to search for materials that are covered under a Creative Commons license for sharing and adapting. Rather than having students search for any image on a topic, the librarian can use worksheets that make students contemplate their potential images. For example, if a student was attempting to locate an image to describe how global warming affects emperor penguins in Antarctica, using a worksheet and thinking about the image can prevent the student from choosing an image of any penguin floating on a piece of ice anywhere in the world. Requiring students to think strategically about the type of image, music, or font they want to use also makes them approach their multimodal design with the same methodology they use for research (looking at a topic, choosing keywords, searching those keywords, and either using what they find or modifying the search). The *Framework* (2016) addresses multimodal design in the disposition for Information Creation as a Process: The learner will "value the process of matching an information need with an appropriate product." The product can be of any design as long as considerable thought has been given to *what* the product should be. *Visual Literacy Competency Standards* (2011) Five and Six provide visual literacy instruction outcomes: The visually literate student "uses images and visual media effectively" (Standard Five) and "designs and creates meaningful images and visual media" (Standard Six). Librarians can accomplish these outcomes by utilizing the aforementioned worksheet to ask students to think about the most effective mode for their argument. The book *Visual Literacy for Libraries: A Practical, Standards-Based Guide* (Brown, Bussert, Hattwig, & Medaille, 2016) has some excellent activities that can be used as-is or modified to a specific assignment.

Citing and using images and other modes effectively at the point of design can emphasize to students the importance of attribution. Copyright and attribution are two different issues; being able to use an image is one matter while attribution is needed whether copyright is in place or not. Both the *Information Literacy Framework* (2016) and the *Visual Literacy Competency Standards* (2011) emphasize the importance of attribution. Phrasing citation and the ethical use of images in the students' language can help explain attribution and copyright; for example, if the librarian asks students whether they want someone to use the item they are working on without giving them credit, they will usually reply in the negative. Using citation in their multimodal essay allows students to recognize that a creation belongs to someone and thus has value.

Production

Production involves the tools that are used. An audience may react positively or negatively to the same message depending on the tool. There is meaning *in* meaning; each discourse and design has multiple layers. For example, if the tool is PowerPoint (one mode of communication with meaning), there are other choices in design such as colors, fonts, images, and the inclusion of any sound, that also convey meaning. Communication does not happen in a bubble; there must be a communicator with a message and a receiver—articulation and interpretation. When the message is received, it is translated through the receiver's mind of biases, background, and other filters. Kress and Van Leeuwen (2001) emphasize, "We constantly import signs from other contexts (another era, social group, culture) into the context in which we are now making a new sign, in order to signify ideas which are associated with that other context by those who import the sign" (p. 10). In the *Framework* (2016), Information Creation as a Process asks that students recognize "an understanding that their choices impact the purposes for which the information product will be used and the message it conveys."

Matching the right tool to the right job may sound easy, but the student must take into account the message, the audience, the message's tone, any software or hardware issues, whether the information dissemination will be in real-time or asynchronous, and any costs to use the tool. The *Visual Literacy Competency Standards* (2011) lists performance indicators of "uses technology effectively to work with images" including using "appropriate editing, presentation, communication, storage, and media tools and applications" and "Edits . . . as appropriate for quality" (Standard 5). The librarian can help the student choose the tool based on some short questions, or the librarian can help the instructor by creating a list of student-friendly tools.

Distribution

Distribution, in multimodal composition, is simply how the final assignment will be disseminated to the audience. The *Framework* (2016) underscores audience and distribution in several of its frames. Authority Is Constructed and Contextual asks students to "understand the increasing social nature of the information ecosystem"; Information Creation as a Process asks students to "understand that different methods of information dissemination with different purposes are available for their use"; and Scholarship as Conversation states that students should "contribute to scholarly conversation[s] at an appropriate level, such as local online community, guided discussion, undergraduate research journal, [or] conference presentation/poster session." The *Framework* clearly emphasizes that information-literate students should know how and where to deliver their message.

Some questions for the student, professor, and librarian to consider when deciding on message distribution are: Will the student be present or will the assignment have to stand on its own without the student? Will sound be available? If this is being presented at a meeting, will the software/hardware requirements be available? Students even need to think about poster presentations, such as whether the poster will have a stand.

ACTIVITIES

The following activities are ways for librarians to insert themselves into multimodal instruction. They were created with a 50-minute class in mind. They touch on various aspects of the *Framework for Information Literacy.*

Audience + Tone = Tool

This activity has two parts. First, the librarian chooses two similar Web pages for different audiences. For example, the librarian would show the "about us" page for a more conservative clothing store and for a trendy clothing store. The audience and librarian discuss the design of each page and how the images, fonts, texts, and even layout set a certain tone and appeal to their audiences. This activity can be a starting point for the students thinking about the tools they will use in their composition.

For part two of this activity, the librarian and students brainstorm a chart for some of the tools they would use with different audiences. The librarian then shows students some of the free online tools available to them (Figure 15.2).

Multimodal Toolkit

The instruction librarian creates a guide (or toolkit) with some of the resources students can use for their multimodal assignment. Possible tools for creating sound and image files are word clouds, infographic tools, charts, timelines, cartoons and animations, presentation software, and sound, image, and video editors and manipulators. This toolkit should also point to information on citing material such as images, music, videos, and infographics. Purdue's Online Writing Lab (OWL) has a page of resources for citing electronic sources (https://owl.english.purdue.edu/owl/resource/747/08/).

Evaluating Infographics

Infographics can be an exciting and eye-catching way to express data. Nevertheless, the information in an infographic needs to be evaluated just like any Web page or print set of statistics. Using one of the major infographic sites (visual.ly: http://visual.ly/view; Infographic of the Day: http://visual.ly/view; Knowledge is Beautiful: http://www.informationisbeautiful.net), the librarian locates an interesting infographic on a topic the students are researching and discusses the author, sources, and argument. The librarian should remind students that just because

Audience	Tone	Tool
Classmates	Casual	Cartoon
Community group	Formal	Slide presentation
Community group	Casual	Infographic
Professor	Formal	Charts and graphs

Figure 15.2 Audience, tone, and tool chart.

information is pretty does not mean it is any more valid than if it is in spreadsheet or paragraph form.

Finding Relevant Images

This activity is adapted from one in the book *Visual Literacy for Libraries: A Practical, Standards-Based Guide* (2016).

The librarian provides students with a worksheet to help them locate an image for their multimodal essay. The image should relate to their topics in as many ways as possible. For example, if students are creating multimodal presentations on poverty in the United States, they should not be using an image of poverty in India (unless they are drawing a similarity between the two countries).

This activity is best done in class rather than as a homework assignment. If the students have also completed a similar worksheet to brainstorm research terms for a database search, they can easily see the similarities of research for any format material.

The worksheet can ask the following questions:

- What is your topic?
- Why are you looking for an image (what is your purpose)?
- Brainstorm some words related to your topic.
- Circle the words that best describe your topic.
- Search for those words in the Creative Commons.
- Did you find an image or video?
- If not, what terms could broaden or narrow your search?
- Does your image or video have:
    - Meaning?
    - Clarity?
    - Layout?
    - Style?
    - What is the overall design?

The worksheet should also include a fill-in-the-blank section noting what information students will need for citing; students will be more likely to cite correctly if they have a model to follow.

Evaluating Advertisements

Students should locate an advertisement to evaluate. The librarian can provide a list of websites that have vintage and modern images (a list is available at http://guides.library.uab.edu/English101/findingimage). The students research how the image illustrates an idea from its cultural or intellectual context and how the image is persuading a specific audience. This activity requires students to think about and research culture at the time the advertisement was created (the historical mindset) and the advertisement's audience. The research causes students to think outside of their own universe to see how the argument was made.

CONCLUSION

As students advance in their university careers, they will continue to create presentations, posters, and other visual material. After they leave college, they will use visual literacy skills in their work. Not only does multimodal instruction early in their college careers help them with upcoming assignments, but it also contributes to their information literacy lifelong learning. The one consistent, unifying force in students' university careers is the librarian. Whether students are sending a tweet or giving a presentation at a large sales meeting, multimodal literacy matters. Instruction on information and other literacies led by a librarian in collaboration with a composition instructor can lead to critical-thinking students and future leaders who can create meaning successfully.

NOTE

1. For more information on threshold concepts, see the chapter "Threshold Concepts and Troublesome Knowledge: An Introduction" (Meyer & Land, 2006).

REFERENCES

Anderson, D., Atkins, A., Ball, C., Millar, K. H., Selfe, C., & Selfe, R. (2006). Integrating multimodality into composition curricula: Survey methodology and results from a CCC research grant. *Composition Studies*, *34*(2), 59–84.

Anderson, J. (2006). The public sphere and discursive activities: Information literacy as sociopolitical skills. *Journal of Documentation*, *62*, 213–228. https://doi.org/10.1108/00220410610653307

Archer, A. (2006). A multimodal approach to academic "literacies": Problematising the visual/verbal divide. *Language and Education*, *20*, 449–462. https://doi.org/10.2167/le677.0

Arola, K. L., Sheppard, J., & Ball, C. E. (2014). *Writer/designer: A guide to making multimodal projects*. Boston, MA: Bedford/St. Martin's.

Association of College and Research Libraries. (2000). *Information literacy competency standards for higher education*. Retrieved from http://www.ala.org/acrl/standards/informationliteracycompetency

Association of College and Research Libraries, (2011, October). *ACRL visual literacy competency standards for higher education*. Retrieved from http://www.ala.org/acrl/standards/visualliteracy

Association of College and Research Libraries. (2016, January 11). *Framework for information literacy for higher education*. Retrieved from http://www.ala.org/acrl/standards/ilframework

Association of College and Research Libraries. (2017, April 28). *Roles and strengths of teaching librarians*. Retrieved from http://www.ala.org/acrl/standards/teachinglibrarians

Avgerinou, M. D. (2009). Re-viewing visual literacy in the "Bain d' Images" era. *TechTrends*, *53*, 28–34. https://doi.org/10.1007/s11528-009-0264-z

Berndston, M. (2010, August 14). *Libraries promoting multimodal literacy in an intercultural society*. Paper presented at 76th IFLA General Conference and Assembly: Open Access to Knowledge, Gothenburg, Sweden. Retrieved from http://www.ifla.org/en/ifla76

Brown, N. E., Bussert, K., Hattwig, D., & Medaille, A. (2016). *Visual literacy for libraries: A practical, standards-based guide*. Chicago, IL: ALA.

Cope, B., & Kalantzis, M. (2009). "Multiliteracies": New literacies, new learning. *Pedagogies: An International Journal, 4*, 164–195. https://doi.org/10.1080/15544800903076044

Cordes, S. (2009, August 24). *Broad horizons: The role of multimodal literacy in 21st century library instruction*. Paper presented at 75th IFLA General Conference and Assembly: Libraries Create Futures: Building on Cultural Heritage, Milan, Italy. Retrieved from http://conference.ifla.org/past-wlic/2009/94-cordes-en.pdf

Council of Writing Program Administrators, National Council of Teachers of English, National Writing Project. (2011, January). *Framework for success in postsecondary writing*. Retrieved from http://wpacouncil.org/framework

Eyman, D. (2015). *Digital rhetoric: Theory, method, practice*. Ann Arbor: University of Michigan Press.

Fraiberg, S. (2010, September). Composition 2.0: Toward a multilingual and multimodal framework. *College Composition and Communication*, *62*, 100–126.

Hacker, D., & Sommers, N. (2016). *A writer's reference for the University of Alabama at Birmingham*. Boston, MA: Bedford/St. Martin's.

Harris, B. R. (2010). Blurring borders, visualizing connections: Aligning information and visual literacy learning outcomes. *Reference Services Review, 38*, 523–535. https://doi.org/10.1108/00907321011090700

Hattwig, D., Bussert, K., Medaille, A., & Burgess, J. (2013). Visual literacy standards in higher education: New opportunities for libraries and student learning. *Portal: Libraries and the Academy, 13*, 61–89. https://doi.org/10.1353/pla.2013.0008

Jewitt, C. (2005). Multimodality, "reading," and "writing" for the 21st century. *Discourse: Studies in the Cultural Politics of Education*, *26*, 315–331.

Koltay, T. (2011). The media and the literacies: Media literacy, information literacy, digital literacy. *Media Culture, 33*, 211–221.

Koltay, T, Spiranec, S., & Karvalics, L. Z (2015). The shift of information literacy towards research 2.0. *Journal of Academic Librarianship, 41*, 87–93. https://doi.org/10.1016/j.acalib.2014.11.001

Kress, G., & Van Leeuwen, T. (2001). *Multimodal discourse: The modes and media of contemporary communication*. London, UK: Arnold.

Lippincott, J. K. (2007, November/December). Student content creators: Convergence of literacies. *Educause Review, 42*(6), 16–17.

Mackey, T. P., & Jacobson, T. E. (2011). Reframing information literacy as a metaliteracy. *College and Research Libraries, 72*(1), 62–78.

Mackey, T. P., & Jacobson, T. E. (2014). *Metaliteracy: Reinventing information literacy to empower learners*. Chicago, IL: American Library Association.

Marcum, J. W. (2002, April). Beyond visual culture: The challenge of visual ecology. *Portal: Libraries and the Academy, 2*, 189–206. https://doi.org/10.1353/pla.2002.0038

Meyer, J. H. F., & Land, R. (2006). Threshold concepts and troublesome knowledge: An introduction. In J. H. F. Meyer & R. Land (Eds.), *Overcoming barriers to student understanding: Threshold concepts and troublesome knowledge* (pp. 3–18). London, UK: Routledge.

Mikulecky, L., St. Clair, R., & Kerka, S. (2003). *Multiple literacies. A compilation for adult educators*. Columbus: Ohio State University Center on Education and Training for Employment. Retrieved from http://eric.ed.gov/?id=ED482361

New London Group. (1996). A pedagogy of multiliteracies: Designing social futures. *Harvard*

Educational Review, 66(1), 60–92. https://doi.org/10.17763/haer.66.1.17370n67v22j160u

Serafin, F. (2014). *Reading the visual: An introduction to teaching multimodal literacy.* New York, NY: Teachers College.

Spalter, A. M., & Van Dam, A. (2008). Digital visual literacy. *Theory into Practice, 47*, 93–101. https://doi.org/10.1080/00405840801992256

Takayoshi, P., & Selfe, C. L. (2007). Thinking about multimodality. In C. L. Selfe (Ed.), *Multimodal composition: Resources for teachers* (pp. 1–12). Cresskill, NY: Hampton Press.

Thomas, S., Joseph, C., Laccetti, J., Mason, B., Mills, S., Perril, S., & Pullinger, K. (2007). Transliteracy: Crossing divides. *First Monday, 12*(12). Retrieved from http://journals.uic.edu/ojs/index.php/fm/article/view/2060/1908/

Vasudevan, L. (2013). Literacies in a participatory, multimodal world: The arts and aesthetics of web 2.0. *Language Arts, 88*, 137–154.

Walsh, M. (2009). Pedagogic potentials of multimodal literacy. In L. T. Hin & R. Subramaniam (Eds.), *Handbook of research on new media literacy at the K–12 level: Issues and challenges* (pp. 32–47). Hershey, PA: IGI Global/Information Science Reference.

CHAPTER 16

PROJECT-BASED LEARNING

How an English Professor and a Librarian Engaged Hispanic Students' Emerging Information Literacy Skills

Dagmar Stuehrk Scharold
Lindsey Simard

The University of Houston–Downtown (UHD), a designated Hispanic-Serving Institution and Minority-Serving Institution, self-describes its student body as "many first generation college students, students who work full or part time, students who may have family obligations and students who transfer from community colleges and other higher education institutions" ("About UHD," 2012). Given the diverse student population of UHD[1] (primarily urban and first-generation students), information literacy approaches need to deviate from the standard. In this chapter, we explore how a faculty-librarian information literacy collaboration benefited freshman students through leading and participating in a campus-wide Human Trafficking Awareness Day. While we recognize that our approach to information literacy benefits all students, in this chapter, we will concentrate on why this approach specifically addresses the needs of Hispanic students and reinforces key information literacy concepts in this group.

THE NEED FOR A DIFFERENT APPROACH

While the librarian community has acknowledged that many researchers view the "one-shot" library instruction as flawed, it is still a common instruction model and the one UHD librarians use for almost all information literacy sessions. In this model, students receive one session of library instruction, usually around an hour long. This is their only interaction with a librarian unless they seek research assistance on their own. However, one short interaction is not enough to allow students to absorb information literacy skills into their long-term memory (Artman, Frisicaro-Pawlowski, & Monge, 2010). Given the relationship between information literacy and writing, it follows that "Through collaboration and shared responsibility, writing teachers and librarians can better incorporate information literacy instruction within composition programs and improve students' research options and behaviors," as Margaret Artman, Erica Frisicaro-Pawlowski, and Robert Monge attest (2010, p. 93). Plus, it is easier to extend library instruction into a course with a research focus than it is to incorporate information literacy into the curriculum of the university (Artman et al., 2010). Clearly, the "one-shot" approach is not used because it is most effective. However, at UHD the "one-shot" approach lessens the strain on librarians and allows faculty members to devote class time to the topics of the course. Having a librarian co-teach or assist a professor throughout a course is not feasible given the overall staffing it would require. In our project, the librarian taught a traditional information literacy session, followed up in the classroom for four to six classes, and participated in the Human Trafficking Awareness Day programming with the students.

THE NEED FOR INCREASED EXPOSURE TO LIBRARIES AND LIBRARIANS

The increased librarian presence as a participant in the project serves as library outreach as well, which is an important goal when targeting students who have had limited experience with school librarians. In our project, the librarian, Lindsey, represented the library at the Human Trafficking Awareness Day, demonstrating the library's commitment to student-created events, and she furthered her role as library ambassador by assisting in the classroom. By including a librarian in the college classroom, students have the opportunity to build a personal relationship with a librarian and receive individual attention. Considering Dallas Long's (2011) confirmation that "library use is strongly linked with student persistence in higher education, and Latino students have lower rates of academic library use and proficiency than other racial/ethnic groups of students" (p. 511), it is reasonable to include more librarian exposure outside of the library (in this case, the classroom) to encourage library use at UHD and boost student graduation rates, specifically with regard to Hispanic students.

Outreach is also important for UHD students because they may not understand the role of the academic library and are likely to have had limited exposure to school librarians before attending UHD. According to Long (2011), the academic library "does not translate easily to [Hispanic students'] personal experiences with libraries in other contexts of their lives" (p. 510). Long also highlights an individual Hispanic student who noted that white students are more likely to use the library because "they grew up with better libraries" (2011, p. 508). While this is one individual's opinion, it is true that UHD students may not have had access to an adequate school library. Many of UHD's feeder schools are located within the Houston Independent School District (HISD) ("Gear Up," 2010). However, HISD employed only 118 librarians in 2011, less than one librarian for every two schools (Radcliffe, 2011). According to HISD data cited by Jennifer Radcliffe (2011) in the *Houston Chronicle*, "More than 80 percent of HISD libraries fail to meet state guidelines for staffing and book collections, and an additional 20 percent of the district's 289 schools don't even have functioning libraries" (para. 2). Although HISD participates in the robust TexShare resource-sharing program, it is unlikely, given the shortage of librarians and information resources, that UHD students have had access to a librarian or librarian-led information literacy instruction. Indeed, UHD professors have lamented to librarians that they are alarmed at incoming students' inability to perform basic research, noting accidental plagiarism and use of nonacademic sources as specific problems.

Another factor contributing to the need for librarian outreach at UHD is the number of Hispanic students who are first-generation college students. Arturo Gonzalez (2011) highlights that "Hispanic college students stand out as being primarily first-generation college students—65% of all Hispanics—even when compared to blacks (50%)" (p. 95). First-generation college students experience disadvantages when compared to their peers and are more likely to not complete a bachelor's degree within six years (Gonzalez, 2011). One of the Hispanic students mentioned in Long's (2011) study also commented on the lack of parental urging to use the library as opposed to white students' parents. Clearly, the library can be overlooked as an academic support service without one generation to pass down information about college library use to the next generation. When students lack information literacy skills due to their inexperience with library support, there is a good chance that this also can prevent students from being successful in their freshman-level writing courses, possibly preventing them from completing their college degree.

THE ENGLISH COMPOSITION COURSE

At UHD, English 1302: Composition II is the second course in a two-course composition sequence and is a required course for the General Education core curriculum.[2] In Composition II, the primary focus is to teach students to write an argumentative, researched essay through a series of scaffolded assignments. Layered onto students' nascent academic writing skills introduced in Composition I, students are also expected to become proficient in information literacy skills in Composition II. Given the complexity of managing all these new skills, students often fail to complete the course. It becomes a "barrier" course, causing many students to either repeat the course multiple times or, in extreme cases, drop out of college altogether. Given the percentage of Hispanic students at UHD, according to Silas Abrego (2008):

> The keys to improving access to college for more Latinos and retaining those who enroll through to graduation are (1) an understanding of their educational background coupled with strong academic and financial services; (2) a learning environment that encourages active learning; (3) and role models and activities that promote self-confidence. (p. 78)

As the composition professor, Dagmar had students in the course choose the course reader from a list of nonfiction selections at the beginning of the semester. Students research each book and then vote on the one they want to read. By a clear majority, students chose *The Slave Next Door: Human Trafficking and Slavery in America Today* by Kevin Bales and Ron Soodalter.[3] Dagmar's idea to help retain more students in the course was to implement a project-based learning approach that would not only give students agency but also provide them with an opportunity to connect their research to a real-life situation. Dagmar contacted Lindsey to see if she was interested in doing something different with the course, and she then assigned the Community Awareness Project, which would showcase freshman students' work to the university community at large. Lindsey and Dagmar both felt that students would gain confidence in their writing and researching skills and be better able to transfer those skills to other courses in the curriculum through the project. We also wanted to engage the students collaboratively in the course, which often can be perceived as a solitary endeavor.

THE COMMUNITY AWARENESS PROJECT

In pursuing the opportunity to fully engage students with the course and the library, we grounded our project in Jean Lave and Etienne Wenger's (1991) study of masters and apprentices. In Lave and Wenger's (1991) study of five different types of apprenticeships, they analyze the social dynamics of the master and apprentice relationship with regard to the communities of practice in which they function. Lave and Wenger (1991) created the term "legitimate peripheral participation" to encompass a way of studying the modern form of apprenticeships. Lave and Wenger define legitimate peripheral participation as follows:

> Learning viewed as situated activity has as its central defining characteristic a process we call *legitimate peripheral participation*

> [*sic*]. By this we mean to draw attention to the point that learners inevitably participate in communities of practitioners and that the mastery of knowledge and skill requires newcomers to move toward full participation in the sociocultural practices of a community. (p. 29)

For Lave and Wenger, the learning that takes place in a master/apprentice relationship is determined by the production of knowledge through a given activity. In our case, the given activity of the Community Awareness Project would create opportunities for students to become "legitimate peripheral participants" and move them toward integration within the academe by giving them a voice in shaping the course and making their research visible as newcomers to the university community.

The Community Awareness Project was student directed, allowing them to decide how they wanted to present what they learned in the course. The only caveat was that they had to showcase their research in a way that would attract their peers at the university as well as the surrounding community since the event would also be open to the public. Given the topic of the course, human trafficking and modern-day slavery, students decided to coordinate a Human Trafficking Awareness Day on campus. In groups, they organized the schedule of events, created and distributed promotional materials, and contacted guest speakers from within the UHD community and local nonprofit agencies affiliated with human trafficking awareness. Students would also showcase the research they were working with for their researched argument papers. To facilitate the logistics of coordinating the event, Lindsey and Dagmar arranged for the facilities at the university needed to host the event, parking for guest speakers, and technology needs, as well as sending student-generated promotional materials to printers and contacting the appropriate university personnel to promote the event to the public.

The research component for the course began with the "one-shot" delivery of library resources by Lindsey, including traditional print sources and multimedia sources. Students then formed topic-specific groups and decided what they wanted to do to contribute to the event. As the students worked on the research in preparation for their researched argumentative papers and the event, Lindsey would join the class on the days when we were workshopping the various aspects of the program. We hoped that Lindsey's presence in the classroom would, according to Anne C. Moore and Gary Ivory (2003), change the perceptions of librarians that Hispanic students hold. Moore and Ivory (2003) note:

> All students should find librarians friendly and supportive, but because Latinos and other minority students have often found the university unfriendly, we must make particular efforts with them. . . . With close relationships, librarians can join faculty in the classroom to connect with students. (p. 228)

We employed a team-teaching approach to demystify the library's role at the university. Both Dagmar and Lindsey assisted the groups with all aspects of their projects, ranging from basic information literacy skills, such as finding reliable sources, using the UHD databases, and citing appropriate images for promotional materials, to locating Houston-area anti–human trafficking organizations as a source for potential speakers, to figuring out how to create a QR code. We also assisted students with communication skills, such as providing feedback on individual students' topic-specific "elevator speeches," helping students to practice what they would say about their research during the event. In this aspect of the project, we facilitated students in making the connection between what they were writing for an audience in print to interacting with the larger audience of their peers and other members of the university community.

For those students who decided to showcase their research, they accomplished this through a variety of ways. This part of the event was staged near a high-traffic student area. Some students chose more traditional routes, creating poster presentations and looped PowerPoint presentations. Some students, being more outgoing, had tables with samples of fair trade chocolate and locally grown fruit from the farmer's market as a way to engage their peers in discussions about fair trade and human trafficking. Others had laptop computers available so that students could take a human trafficking awareness survey through the website slaveryfootprint.org. Their peers could interact with the website and then talk about their survey results with the student group. Students in the course also created and distributed cards with a QR code for the slaveryfootprint.org website to those who were not interested in stopping at the event. No matter the method for delivering the information, all groups were required to create some sort of handout, providing a summary of information about their particular topic and websites for more information.

Other students chose to participate in organizing a structured program for the event that was held in the university's auditorium. This part of the event consisted of a screening of *Call + Response*, a human trafficking awareness documentary, and various guest speakers. Students who participated in this part of the event chose research topics that focused on the effectiveness and limitations of what can be done to help the victims of human trafficking. Students contacted local Houston human trafficking awareness groups and individuals associated with the City of Houston's task force on human trafficking as well as professors in UHD's criminal justice program and arranged for them to speak. On the day of the event, students also introduced the speakers they contacted and facilitated the question and answer sessions following each speaker.

Overall, the project was a success in many ways. Over the course of the day, we had over 200 participants attend the auditorium program, with professors bringing entire classes to hear speakers and/or to view the film. A head count for the research showcase was not taken, but we can assume this was successful because students ran out of handouts before the end of the event. Students found that participating in the event helped to solidify the research they had been reading and further reinforced what they learned through listening to the guest speakers. During the question and answer sessions, students in the course asked substantive questions based on their research, thereby creating a high-quality group discussion. Since students had not yet written their final paper, talking to others outside the course provided opportunities for them to be open to new ideas or alternative viewpoints that could extend their research. This translated into the final version of their papers and persistence in the course. Finally, students maintained the connection they established with Lindsey after the event was over, with many continuing to work with her on the final paper.

THE BENEFITS OF OUR COLLABORATION

The collaborative approach allows students the opportunity for guided reinforcement of information literacy concepts and better satisfies the Association of College and Research Libraries (ACRL) *Framework for Information Literacy for Higher Education.* While students engaged with all six frames during our approach, Searching as Strategic Exploration, Information Has Value, and Scholarship as Conversation were especially relevant to our approach. The librarian can assist students when they cannot find sources and encourage them to persevere in their search for the best information, rather than take the first source they find, thereby supporting dispositions associated with Searching as Strategic Exploration: "persist in the face of search challenges," "understand that first attempts at searching do not always produce adequate results," and "seek guidance from experts." By participating in presenting a campus event, students were able to interact with the topic on a deeper level, thus developing the Information Has Value and the Scholarship as Conversation dispositions. Students become information authorities during Human Trafficking Awareness Day; that is, they "see themselves as contributors to the information marketplace rather than only consumers of it" and learn firsthand about the "skills, time, and effort needed to produce knowledge" (Association of College and Research Libraries, 2016, p. 6). Likewise, students see how information has power by meeting people in their community who use findings similar to the students' research results to create their approaches to ending human trafficking and gain support for their efforts.

In addition, students "[contributed] to scholarly conversation at an appropriate level," one of the tenets of Scholarship as Conversation, by interacting with professionals working against human trafficking within their city, presenting posters and papers to campus, and discussing the topic with their peers during Human Trafficking Awareness Day (p. 8). The combination of our approach and the seriousness of the topic requires students to think about the issue of human trafficking in a local and personal context; they must consider their values while they interact with their research results and analyze sources to be informed participants. Ideally, students "understand the responsibility that comes with entering the conversation through participatory channels" when they present information during the event on a human rights issue and "recognize they are often entering into an ongoing scholarly conversation and not a finished conversation," one they can continue to participate in within their community because of their high-quality research and resulting synthesis of information (Association of College and Research Libraries, 2016, p. 8).

Our approach further engages students through project-based learning, and could also be perceived as a service learning opportunity, brought about by the topic of human trafficking, a noted issue in Houston, to further these goals (Texas Advisory Committee to the U.S. Commission on Civil Rights, 2010). Margit Watts (2006) believes that service learning provides the opportunity for real-life problem solving and notes that real-life experiences make students more engaged with what they are learning. In addition,

Watts (2006) notes, "An important learning objective is to develop information literacy skills from the perspective of the student as an end user in real-life situations" (p. 43). As students research human trafficking, they develop the skills to research similar social issues locally and globally that affect their lives. Through our collaboration between faculty member and librarian, we guided freshman students into the university community by providing them with a real-life venue to showcase their research. This partnership is essential to mentoring and supporting Hispanic students through the first year of their university career. As Abrego (2008) asserts:

> A support network comprised of staff, faculty, and peers is crucial to the student's ability to successfully navigate the campus. . . . Almost all of us who have successfully graduated from college can identify one faculty member who made a difference in our educational career, either by inspiring us, believing in our potential, or being a role model. (p. 88)

We would like to think our collaboration through this project has succeeded in inspiring all of our students to continue to take action on a real problem within the Houston community,[4] believing in our students' potential to organize and deliver a successful program, and becoming role models for our students.

NOTES

1. According to the 2012–2013 UHD Fact Book, all students enrolled by ethnicity are as follows: American Indian .6%, Asian or Pacific Islander 9%, Black 27.5%, Hispanic 40.2%, White 19.5%, International 2.3%, and Unknown .9%. See http://www.uhd.edu/about/irp/documents/Fact_Book_2012-2013.pdf
2. In 2014, a revision to the Texas core curriculum will be implemented in all public universities across Texas. UHD will maintain a two-course sequence for freshman composition. For more information on the Texas General Education Core Curriculum see: http://www.thecb.state.tx.us/index.cfm?objectid=6AB82E4B-C31F-E344-C78E3688524B44FB
3. For the past four years, students overwhelming chose this book, and continue to do so, over any others offered.
4. As a direct result of this course, one student was able to secure an internship with the City of Houston's Office of International Communities. Through his internship, the student participated in planning a citywide human trafficking awareness event, "Shine a Light on Human Trafficking," held September 24, 2013. See http://houstonsvoice.com/2013/09/23/live-streaming-shine-a-light-on-human-trafficking/

REFERENCES

About UHD. (2012). University of Houston–Downtown. Retrieved September 18, 2013, from http://www.uhd.edu/about/

Abrego, S. H. (2008). Recent strategies to increase access and retention. In L. A. Valverde (Ed.), *Latino change agents in higher education* (pp. 77–92). San Francisco: Jossey-Bass.

Artman, M., Frisicaro-Pawlowski, E., & Monge, R. (2010). Not just one shot: Extending the dialogue about information literacy in composition classes. *Composition Studies, 38*(2), 93–110.

Association of College and Research Libraries. (2016). *Framework for information literacy for higher education.* Retrieved September 25, 2016, from http://www.ala.org/acrl/sites/ala.org.acrl/files/content/issues/infolit/Framework_ILHE.pdf

Gear up. (2010). University of Houston–Downtown. Retrieved September 18, 2013, from http://www.uhd.edu/academic/colleges/university/gu.htm

Gonzalez, A. (2011). Is there a link between Hispanics and first-generation college students? The importance of exposure to a college-going tradition. In D. L. Leal & S. J. Trejo (Eds.), *Latinos and the economy.* Retrieved from SpringerLink database.

Lave, J., & Wenger, E. (1991). *Situated learning: Legitimate peripheral participation.* Cambridge, UK: Cambridge University Press.

Long, D. (2011). Latino students' perceptions of the academic library. *Journal of Academic Librarianship, 37*(6), 504–511. https://doi.org/10.1016/j.acalib.2011.07.007

Moore, A. C. & Ivory, G. (2003). Do Hispanic-serving institutions have what it takes to foster information literacy? One case. *Journal of Latinos and Education, 2*(4), 217–231. https://doi.org/10.1207/S1532771XJLE0204_3

Radcliffe, J. (2011). Despite $10M allocation, story of HISD libraries looks grim. Retrieved September 15, 2013, from http://www.chron.com/news/houston-texas/article/Dozens-of-school-librarians-lost-to-budget-cuts-2279655.phpet-cuts-2279655.php

Texas Advisory Committee to the U.S. Commission on Civil Rights. (2011). Human trafficking in Texas: More resources and resolve needed to stem surge of modern day slavery. Retrieved September 29, 2013, from http://www.usccr.gov/pubs/TX_HT_Report--ver%2050--FINAL.pdf

UHD Fact Book. (2013). University of Houston–Downtown. Retrieved September 15, 2013, from http://www.uhd.edu/about/irp/documents/Fact_Book_2012-2013.pdf

Watts, M. (2006). Becoming educated: Service learning as mirror. In C. Gibson (Ed.), *Student engagement and information literacy* (pp. 33–54). Chicago, IL: American Library Association.

CHAPTER 17

ADAPTING FOR INCLUSIVITY

Scaffolding Information Literacy for Multilingual Students in a First-Year Writing Course

Emily Crist

Libby Miles

In early 2015, this author team witnessed and participated in two major shifts at the University of Vermont. The first shift was a new institution-wide foundational writing and information literacy requirement (known as "FWIL"). Remarkable for the sole reason that there had been no university writing requirement until the fall of 2014, this new FWIL creature was also significant in its combining of information literacy and writing into a single one-semester requirement.

The second shift was the university's embrace of international students as an attempt to both diversify our predominantly white campus and to tap a new revenue stream. When both converged in the fall of 2014, longtime faculty at the university were reeling with new responsibilities for writing and information literacy, compounded by linguistically diverse student audiences whom they felt underprepared to teach. Both of us were hired into this context as the FWIL requirement entered its second semester.

Prior to our arrival, writing faculty and instructional librarians had collaborated on what they hoped would be a shared, standard curriculum for graduate teaching assistants (GTAs) and instructors teaching English 001, Written Expression. It was a smartly integrated curricular design, moving students through personal inquiry, question-posing, researched literature reviews, and public writing (see Box 17.1). This curriculum addressed the first challenge: how to support faculty efforts in teaching both information literacy and foundational writing in a one-semester course. To address the second challenge, the layering in of international students, we created parallel sections of English 001 designed for our new international students (for a justification of parallel sections, see Braine, 1996). Such courses emphasize the same essential curriculum and student learning outcomes of the standard sections, but often have smaller enrollments to compensate for the labor-intensive nature of responding to multilingual student work. In keeping with the collaborative nature of our program, we collaborated with six other Multilingual Writing Faculty Fellows to alter the standard curriculum in ways that would benefit our growing international student population. This was particularly important in a course with substantial expectations for information literacy.

BOX 17.1
STANDARD ENGLISH 001 AT A GLANCE

Project 1: Social Narrative
Essayistic exploration into multiple perspectives on a social issue in which students have a personal stake

- emphasizes Research as Inquiry

Project 2: Question-Posing
A series of explorations to investigate a researchable question arising from Project 1 from the perspective of expert discourses

- emphasizes Searching as Strategic Exploration
- secondarily addresses Authority Is Constructed and Contextual

Project 3: Literature Review
Literature review using sources from the annotated bibliography; articulating patterns, themes, and trends; and putting those sources in conversation with one another

- emphasizes Scholarship as Conversation

Project 4: Public Researched Writing

- emphasizes Information Creation as a Process
- secondarily addresses Information Has Value

The term *multilingual students* indicates a wide range of writers with various linguistic backgrounds, both domestic and international. We like the term for its inclusiveness and for the way it focuses our attention on all students as potentially multiliterate. That said, at our university, the vast majority of our multilingual students are rather newly arrived international students from China. Reid (1998/2011) characterizes students such as ours as having learned English "principally through their *eyes*, studying vocabulary, verb forms, and language rules" (p. 85). When they arrive in our classes, the majority of our multilingual students have not yet had much experience learning English experientially and through their *ears*. Thus, English as a first language (L1) pedagogies that assume students are already surrounded by oral discourse in English, and hence have a "feel" for how language flows, are especially challenging for non-native English speakers (L2), particularly those who are new to North America. The Conference on College Composition and Communication (CCCC) provides useful guidelines for designing and teaching writing assignments, which include the following statement:

> Discussions on assignment design might include scaffolding, creating benchmarks within larger projects, and incorporating additional resources such as the writing center. Discussions might also include methods for teaching students the multiple rhetorical elements that influence a text's rhetorical effectiveness, as well as reflections on students' negotiations between composing in a home country language (including variations of English) and composing in academic English. (Updated in 2009, reaffirmed in 2014)

Supported by these recommendations, we recognized that our situation presented an opportunity to revise the standard curriculum with an aim toward reaching all linguistically diverse students, regardless of their background, their other spoken languages, or their relationship to the United States. Further, we saw the Association of College and Research Libraries (ACRL) *Framework for Information Literacy for Higher Education* (ACRL, 2015) as especially generative in considering the needs of our multilingual writers. Whereas all six of the ACRL frames align well with Writing Studies (see especially the CWPA *Outcomes Statement*, 2014, and NCTE's *Framework for Success in Post-Secondary Writing*, 2013), three frames resonated particularly strongly for us as we embarked on this work: Research as Inquiry, Searching as Strategic Exploration, and Scholarship as Conversation. Our efforts involved providing additional scaffolding for multilingual students—and then we found that our changes benefited all students, regardless of their language background (see also Reid & Kroll [1995] on the importance of scaffolding with L2 writers).

SOCIAL NARRATIVE TO PROMOTE RESEARCH AS INQUIRY

The traditional version of the course begins with a "social narrative"—a genre that originates as personal inquiry into a significant issue for the student and imbues it with social and cultural analysis. Throughout the process, students are encouraged to avoid too-easy endings and clichés, probing instead for "un-answers" and "non-conclusions." Thus, as a first major project, the social narrative functions to establish and begin practicing a number of the dispositions found in the ACRL frame of Research as Inquiry, particularly to engage in "open-ended exploration," to "value intellectual curiosity in developing questions" and "intellectual humility," to "seek multiple perspectives" and "appropriate help," and to "appreciate that a question may appear to be simple but still disruptive and important" (ACRL, 2015).

Second Language Writing scholars have long urged the Writing Studies community to be wary of uncritically adopting pedagogies designed for native English-speaking students (see especially Atkinson & Ramanathan, 1995; Silva, 1993). In particular, they note that many L1 pedagogies require culturally specific knowledge that our multilingual students may not yet possess, and they make Westernized assumptions about the nature of knowledge-making and revision as an individualistic, competitive, and self-oriented process. Ramanathan and Atkinson (1999) passionately argue that such so-called expressivist pedagogies "advantage those who have been socialized into these practices from an early age according to a highly child-centered, middle-class form of socialization" (p. 64). Further, they contend that in promoting such pedagogies, we make

> the tacit assumption that *everyone is fundamentally like us, so everyone must want what we want.* Or, to formulate it differently: Everyone is an individual, *but they are individuals on our terms.* Surely, this is not a principle that will help us to understand [L2s] *on their terms*, or that will allow us to use this understanding to help negotiate the complex demands of academic literacy in North American, British, or Oceanic universities. (p. 66)

For our multilingual learners, we felt that the social narrative was crucial not only for avoiding a Westernized personal narrative, but also for shifting students' expectations away from writing and researching to prove a point; we sought instead to guide them toward writing and researching to inquire and explore. Mindful of the critiques, we designed additional scaffolding that would help our multilingual students practice important foundational information literacy dispositions that we hoped would set up their inquiry research in the next two projects without replicating L1 biases.

In the standard version of English 001, the pedagogy supporting the social narrative is mostly draft-feedback-revise coupled with readings. It has little emphasis on invention, the creation and mining of material prior to drafting. It also demands sophisticated peer review of full texts and repeated commentary on full drafts by the instructor. Spending five to six weeks out of 14 on this first project seemed out of alignment when there were three more projects rich with information literacy to be taught. Thus, our first alteration was to rebalance the sense of scale in order to move on more quickly from narrative to information literacy.

All told, we made three major alterations to the course in order to better scaffold the foundational practices that would lead to a fuller engagement with information literacy in subsequent projects (Table 17.1). The first was logistic: shorten the time span from four to five weeks to three. The second was to build in smaller practices of peer review throughout the project, often as in-class activities, as advocated by Hu (2005). The third was the most radical shift in that it introduced students to a variety of low-stakes invention activities designed to generate multiple

TABLE 17.1 *Social Narrative—Standard and Multilingual*

	Standard Course Design	Multilingual Writers' Redesign
Week 1	Reading multiple models and freewriting/loopwriting	Memory inventory, developed to a paragraph, 1 model reading per class; peer feedback on ideas
Week 2	More models, descriptive writing + full draft	Practicing social analyses of a personal story, 1 model reading per class; peer feedback on analysis and idea development
Week 3	Areas of development + full draft revision	Organizational patterns, non-endings; guided peer review on full drafts
Week 4	Editing and style + another full draft revision	Full revision due; Project 2 begins

possibilities rather than asking them to dive into full drafts right away. For example, on the first day of class, students were asked to mine their memories for three moments at different time periods in their lives (birth–6, 7–12, 13–present) in which they experienced some sort of discomfort, cognitive dissonance, or culturally embedded lesson. This simple inventional task prompted them to think beyond their recent adjustment to college abroad, to dig deeper into their memories, and to produce three very different brief paragraphs. Other invention activities followed the same pattern: generate more ideas than you can use, get feedback on them from your peers in class, and build on them with your next assignment. We hoped these curricular changes would help students develop the habit of iterative inquiry.

ANNOTATED BIBLIOGRAPHY TO PROMOTE SEARCHING AS STRATEGIC EXPLORATION

The next section of the standard course centers around "question-posing," with the information literacy components focusing on students gathering and evaluating sources with the aim of learning to pose better questions. To understand the complexities of their chosen research topics, students explore and report on researchers' and experts' discussions occurring in the scholarship. Through this exploration, research questions are not expected to be answered, but rather investigated and refined through information searching. During this section of the standard course, students receive a one-shot library instructional session and keep a research log asking them to track and reflect on their literature searches. This section encourages several of the dispositions in the ACRL frame Searching as Strategic Exploration, including the ability to "identify interested parties . . . who might produce information about a topic," to "design and refine needs and search strategies as necessary, based on search results," to "use different types of searching language appropriately," and to "manage searching processes and results effectively" (ACRL, 2015).

In the new multilingual course sections, we reconsidered the approach to information literacy instruction and introduction to library resources. An increasing awareness exists that information literacy should not be viewed as one size fits all for the different populations of students that librarians encounter in the classroom. Aytac (2016) found that one-shot information literacy sessions are inadequate for L2s' information literacy acquisition, and calls exist for greater collaboration between librarians and instructors in order to enhance information literacy instruction for these students (Bordonaro, 2015). Furthermore, librarians have suggested that curriculum should take into account students' language proficiency levels (Amsberry, 2008), cultural backgrounds (Martin, Reaume, Reeves, & Wright, 2012), and past experiences with information (Johnston, Partridge, & Hughes, 2014).

For the multilingual sections of the course, we decided to have students produce an annotated bibliography showcasing their best sources discovered through their searching explorations. In addition to clarifying the end product, we identified two pedagogical moments in need of additional scaffolding: building topical discourse and reading comprehension (Table 17.2).

BUILDING TOPICAL DISCOURSE THROUGH TERTIARY SOURCES

Asking our multilingual students to immediately immerse themselves in academic discourse surrounding a research question appeared problematic for several reasons. Not surprisingly, language is repeatedly identified as impacting information literacy (Johnston et al., 2014) and obstructing L2s' library use (Amsberry, 2008; Conteh-Morgan, 2002), and due to their language proficiency levels and past experiences with information, we found that students had neither the vocabulary nor the disciplinary knowledge to delve into information searching. The use of tertiary sources provided one way for our multilingual learners to immerse themselves more gently into the discourse of their topic. For students to understand how and why they might make use of these resources, we first built on their previous understandings of information by discussing their own personal processes for quickly finding information about a topic. Students revealed that they often began the search process with Wikipedia and Google,

TABLE 17.2 *Question-Posing—Standard and Multilingual*

	Standard Course Design	Multilingual Writers' Redesign
Week 1	Forensic readings of a range of researched writing; proposal draft	Keywords from Project 1, tertiary source readings, model annotated bibliographies; begin library online tutorials
Week 2	Keywords and research logs; primary, secondary, and tertiary sources; library online tutorials	Library online tutorials; library visit; revised keywords and research logs; popular and trade sources; more annotated bibliography models
Week 3	Library visit; reverse outlining of sources found	Summaries, paraphrases, and annotations; workshop for clarity
Week 4	Storyboard and process folder	Annotated bibliography drafted, workshopped, and revised

and this provided an excellent starting point for discussions of the merits of these tools, such as their supply of background information, good organization, ease of reading, and accessible length. Next, students were introduced to tertiary sources—a mix of encyclopedias and reference collections that also contained these identified merits—and as a class, we modeled using them together. The class chose a broad topic (e.g., eating disorders), which was then written on the board. After the group brainstormed any words they already knew related to the topic, students independently explored the different tertiary sources. Any time a student found another word, topic, subtopic, question, or related point within the sources, they added it to the group brainstorm. When the activity was finished, we discussed the new and different entries written on the board and reflected on the development and growing intricacy of our basic knowledge and vocabulary surrounding the topic after allowing ourselves more room and time for lexical exposure. The goal was not yet to explore a question; rather, the goal became to strengthen the grasp of the discourse surrounding the question or the topic in order to more thoroughly prepare students to explore it later in the unit.

SOURCE SELECTION FOR INCREASED READING COMPREHENSION

In the standard course sections, students explore the work of specialists writing about their topic through scholarly articles—a process that librarians illustrate in the one-shot information literacy instructional session. However, the majority of the multilingual learners did not have the reading comprehension to delve into scholarly texts. At this point, our multilingual students had already used tertiary sources to build topical discourse, but another step was necessary before students were asked to engage with academic texts. Therefore, we decided to have our students first explore their topics through popular and trade sources. In this step, students were introduced to the debates of experts engaging in scholarship around the topic, but through a more accessible and approachable genre that aligned more closely with students' reading comprehension levels. Activities such as practice summarization and reverse outlining of the resources helped to further scaffold student understanding of the sources' strategies and main points. We also reinforced the importance of intermediary evaluation steps to ensure that students were reading beyond the abstract, as Martin and colleagues (2012) observed is a common practice arising from L2 students' difficulties with academic texts. After this step, we found that some of our highest achieving multilingual students were able to mine information from peer-reviewed scholarly texts.

LITERATURE REVIEW TO PROMOTE SCHOLARSHIP AS CONVERSATION

The ACRL frame of Scholarship as Conversation asks students to "seek out conversations taking place in their research area," to "critically evaluate" these contributions, to "see themselves as contributors to scholarship rather than only consumers of it," and to do so through appropriate citation and attribution (ACRL, 2015). From the second course unit, the annotated bibliography, students had gathered, read, and summarized sources on their research question. The challenge now came for students to take these sources from their isolated, alphabetically ordered summaries and put them into conversation with each other in the form of a literature review—arguably one of the most difficult and important types of synthesis writing in nearly any discipline.

For many of our multilingual learners, this genre was entirely new, and it required an elevated level of source synthesis and critical thinking from the annotated bibliography assignment. Here, too, we identified three scaffolding moments not found in the standard curriculum: using a storyboard to map conversational themes and gaps, re-researching in response to those gaps, and repeated workshopping of conversational chunks for textual integrity (Table 17.3).

Before asking students to attempt drafting a full literature review, we spent significant time exploring and mapping the thematic organization of literature review examples. In small groups, students collaboratively mapped a course reading and assigned a corresponding number to each source utilized in the text. Then, they gleaned the reading for the main points that the author used to present the story of her research to the reader and wrote each main point on a sticky note along with the corresponding source number(s) illustrating that main point. Students then organized the sticky note main points to reflect how the author organized them in her essay, including headings for each grouping of points. After discussing the organizational strategies used, students considered other possible options for organization that the author might have utilized. Through this visual display, students began to see organizational strategies and had a graphical representation of the source integration throughout the essay to support this organization. Next, students began making storyboards to represent the scholarly conversations arising from their own research. They identified key points from their research, finds such as particular facts, definitions, trends, developments or controversies, and translated these to sticky notes. Then, they experimented with organization, moving the notes around in multiple ways: tracking trends or developments over time, mapping points of support or contrast, or areas of agreement or disagreement, for example. Students were encouraged to try different arrangements, to discuss the impacts of these organizational choices, and to describe the most effective ways to present the scholarly conversations forming around their research questions.

As students began considering the organizational choices involved in integrating their research into a literature review, they also needed to consider the gaps in their research that required additional inquiry and exploration. From their storyboards, students identified where sources failed to "talk" to each other and discussed how these instances pointed to potential research gaps. Students then re-researched in response to these gaps. This process provided students with a more targeted research goal while introducing strategies for identifying weak spots in research and improving them through the iterative research and writing processes.

Whereas storyboards provide an excellent method for helping students visualize thematic connections and disagreements, also revealing gaps that iterate back to researching, they stop short of crafting a blend of researched sources into conversational prose. Putting sources into conversation in prose form presented an important leap, one requiring quite a bit of facility with written English. Here too, extra scaffolding helped our multilingual students

TABLE 17.3 *Literature Review—Standard and Multilingual*

	Standard Course Design	Multilingual Writers' Redesign
Week 1	Developing themes and debates from storyboard.	Using annotated bibliography, make a storyboard of common themes and conversations; reading model literature reviews; revise storyboards; re-researching as necessary
Week 2	Summarizing, quoting, paraphrasing	Grouping sources, paragraphing by theme rather than source; more model literature reviews, workshop conversational chunks
Week 3	Workshopping and revising full drafts	Continue workshopping conversational chunks for relationships among sources within paragraphs; developing a stance, using transitions

get to where they needed to be, so we developed a three-step in-class workshop.

In the workshop, the class first examined the literature review sections in various articles we had read throughout the semester, which also functioned to model purposeful rereading. Students were each assigned to specific paragraphs and asked first to identify those paragraphs that included more than one source, then share with a partner. Full class discussion began with their simple description: how did they know when a paragraph discussed more than one source? Quickly, they became adept at noticing important markers like parenthetical citations. This may sound patronizingly obvious, but for both L1 and L2 students, parentheses often seem to indicate material they don't actually have to read—so they skip over it. This simple yet powerful class activity trains their eyes not to skip what is in the parentheses, but rather to make appropriate meaning of it. If the information in one set of parentheses is different from the information in another, then at least two different sources are under discussion. It takes very little time, and once they get it, it sticks (see also Silva, 1997, on the importance of explicitly teaching citation conventions).

After the simple identification of the mere existence of multiple sources in a single paragraph, students looked more carefully at the *relationship* between those sources. Do they support one another, with one offering further evidence of the other? Do they disagree with one another, with one offering a counterpoint to the other? Do they build on one another, with one agreeing at first and then diverging with new information? In the workshop, students focused on the word choices that indicated the relationship among the sources in that paragraph and reported to the rest of the class by pointing to the exact words and phrases, projected on the big screen.

Beyond the relationship between the sources comes the relationship of the *writer* to those sources. The third and final step in this in-class workshop asked students to identify the additional framing the author provides around the source material in that paragraph. Where is the setup, and what does that look like? Where is the analysis, and what does that look like? At this moment in the text, is the author presenting multiple views, or is the writer asserting his or her own point?

Class wrapped up with the students returning to their own drafts and color-coding based on what they practiced in the workshop. They highlighted their parenthetical citations, circled the phrases that demonstrated relationships among sources, underlined the setup, and italicized their analysis. With this visual, they could see if they were missing any of the elements, and they left class with a very clear revision plan.

CONCLUDING THOUGHTS

Although it was not directly relevant to information literacy, we enacted one additional, crucially important alteration to the course: a true final portfolio. The standard curriculum required students to submit "portfolios" of their work at the end of each unit, which were essentially folders of the work completed. In a true portfolio system, students have the opportunity to reflect on work completed throughout the semester and to revise one more time in light of lessons learned and experiences integrated. True portfolios involve writers' choices, as they select which pieces to revise in order to showcase and reflect upon a varied range of their abilities and growth (see especially Reynolds, 2014). This final opportunity to revise is particularly crucial for multilingual writers (Leki, 1992; Song & August, 2002).

The purposeful, pedagogical redesigns we have described here afforded our team of Multilingual Writing Faculty Fellows the space and time to devote to collaborative information literacy and writing instruction. As a team, we utilized expertise from a writing scholar, English faculty, ESL faculty, and a librarian to modify the curriculum from a number of different yet connected disciplinary viewpoints. By using ACRL's *Framework for Information Literacy for Higher Education*, specifically the frames Research as Inquiry, Searching as Strategic Exploration, and Scholarship as Conversation, as a lens to ground and guide our curricular modifications, we sought to strengthen the information literacy experiences of our multilingual composition students. This resulted in a redesign rooted in the existing FWIL curriculum but incorporating additional activities in support of students' language proficiency levels and past experiences with information and writing.

We argue, as do many others before us, that linguistic diversity is a constant in all of our courses, through many of our students. Although our project began as a way to bring international students into our university curriculum, it quickly grew into a way to make our university curriculum more appropriate for all of our students, regardless of their language backgrounds. As Chiang and Schmida (1999) conclude, our too-easy labels and distinctions between native and non-native speakers of English "are inadequate when it comes to capturing the literacy journey of students whose lived realities often waver between cultural and linguistic borderlands" (p. 66). Ultimately, the additional scaffolding designed for both our writing and information literacy pedagogies make these concepts more accessible to all students with wide ranges of linguistic and cultural backgrounds.

REFERENCES

ACRL. (2015). *Framework for information literacy for higher education*. Retrieved September 8, 2016, from http://www.ala.org/acrl/standards/ilframework

Amsberry, D. (2008). Talking the talk: Library classroom communication and international students. *Journal of Academic Librarianship, 34*(4), 354–357. https://doi.org/10.1016/j.acalib.2008.05.007

Atkinson, D., & Ramanathan, V. (1995). Cultures of writing: An ethnographic comparison of L1 and L2 university writing/language programs. *TESOL Quarterly, 29* (3), 539–568.

Aytac, S. (2016). Use of action research to improve information literacy acquisition of international ESL students. *New Library World, 117*(7/8), 464–474. https://doi.org/10.1108/NLW-03-2016-0017

Bordonaro, K. (2015). Scholarship as a conversation: A metaphor for librarian–ESL instructor collaboration. *Collaborative Librarianship, 7*(2), 56–65.

Braine, G. (1996). ESL students in first-year writing courses: ESL versus mainstream classes. *Journal of Second Language Writing, 5*(2), 91–107.

Chiang, Y. C., & Schmida, M. (1999). Language identity and language ownership: Linguistic conflicts of first-year university writing students. In L. Harklau, K. M. Losey, & M. Siegal (Eds.), *Generation 1.5 meets college composition: Issues in the teaching of writing to U.S.-educated learners of ESL* (pp. 81–96). New Jersey: Erlbaum.

Conference on College Composition and Communication. (2009, reaffirmed 2014). *Statement on Second-Language Writing and Writers.* Retrieved December 16, 2016, from http://www.ncte.org/cccc/resources/positions/secondlangwriting

Conteh-Morgan, M. (2002). Connecting the dots: Limited English proficiency, second language learning theories, and information literacy instruction. *Journal of Academic Librarianship, 28*(4), 191–196. https://doi.org/10.1016/S0099-1333(02)00282-3

CWPA. (2014). *WPA Outcomes Statement for First-Year Composition (3.0).* Retrieved December 16, 2016, from http://wpacouncil.org/positions/outcomes.html

Hu, G. (2005). Using peer review with Chinese ESL student writers. *Language Teaching Research 9*(3), 321–342.

Johnston, N., Partridge, H., & Hughes, H. (2014). Understanding the information literacy experiences of EFL (English as a foreign language) students. *Reference Services Review, 42*(4), 552–568. https://doi.org/10.1108/RSR-05-2014-0015

Leki, I. (1992). *Understanding ESL writers: A guide for teachers.* Portsmouth, NH: Boynton/Cook-Heinemann.

Martin, J. A., Reaume, K. M., Reeves, E. M., & Wright, R. D. (2012). Relationship building with students and instructors of ESL: Bridging the gap for library instruction and services. *Reference Services Review, 40*(3), 352–367. https://doi.org/10.1108/00907321211254634

NCTE. (2013). *Framework for success in postsecondary writing.* Retrieved December 16, 2016, from http://www.ncte.org/positions/statements/collwritingframework

Ramanathan, V., & Atkinson, D. (1999). Individualism, academic writing, and ESL writers. *Journal of Second Language Writing, 8*(1), 45–75.

Reid, J. (2011). "Eye" learners and "ear" learners: Identifying the language needs of international student and U.S. resident writers. In P. K. Matsuda, M. Cox, J. Jordon, & C. Ortmeier-Hooper (Eds.), *Second language writing in the composition classroom: A critical sourcebook* (pp. 82–94). Boston: NCTE/Bedford. (Reprinted from *Grammar in the composition classroom: Essays on teaching ESL for college-bound students*, pp. 3–17, by P. Byrd & J. Reid, Eds., 1998, New York: Heinle)

Reid, J., & Kroll, B. (1995). Designing and assessing effective classroom writing assignments for

NES and ESL students. *Journal of Second Language Writing, 4*(1), 17–41.

Reynolds, N. (2014). *Portfolio teaching: A guide for instructors*. Boston, MA: Bedford/St. Martin's.

Silva, T. (1993). Toward an understanding of the distinct nature of L2 writing: The ESL research and its implications. *TESOL Quarterly, 27*(4), 657–677.

Silva, T. (1997). On the ethical treatment of ESL writers. *TESOL Quarterly, 31*(2), 359–363.

Song, B., & August, B. (2002). Using portfolios to assess the writing of ESL students: A powerful alternative? *Journal of Second Language Writing, 11*, 49–72.

PART V

Making a Difference

CHAPTER 18

ARE THEY REALLY USING WHAT I'M TEACHING?

Applying Dynamic Criteria Mapping to Cultivate Consensus on Information Literacy

Nicholas N. Behm
Margaret Cook
Tina S. Kazan

AAC&U's 2015 report "Trends in Learning Outcomes Assessment" notes that institutions have prioritized research skills, as 76% of member institutions reported student learning outcomes for information literacy. The effectiveness of this emphasis is complicated by studies conducted by Project Information Literacy (PIL), which suggest students experience difficulty initiating research projects, determining information need, and evaluating sources (Head, 2013). As institutions emphasize information literacy, writing instructors and librarians must collaborate to determine what curricular revisions are needed to enact best practices in both information literacy instruction and composition pedagogy. Such collaboration and curricular work have been inhibited by disciplinary jargon (Carter & Alderidge, 2016); by a paucity of scholarship exploring theoretical articulations between information and library sciences and rhetoric and composition (Mazziotti & Grettano, 2011); and by writing instructors' lack of exposure to scholarship on information literacy (D'Angelo & Maid, 2004; Deitering & Jameson, 2008; Mazziotti & Grettano, 2011).

This chapter contributes to an interdisciplinary conversation regarding the dynamic interrelationship between information literacy and writing by describing a collaborative assessment project at a small liberal arts college in the Midwest in which a librarian partnered with a writing program administrator and an assessment scholar as part of the American Library Association's "Assessment in Action" initiative. This ongoing, IRB-approved project applies dynamic criteria mapping (DCM), a qualitative, constructivist method of writing assessment where librarians and writing faculty defined information literacy and engaged in interdisciplinary conversations, developing consensus on what they value when they read first-year writing projects in light of research skills and information literacy and reconciling disparate disciplinary terminology. This chapter frames the DCM performance-based method for assessing information literacy that counters methods, like rubric scoring, prevalent within information and library sciences (Belanger, Bliquez, & Mondal, 2012), and that aligns "form and content of the assessment method" with "instructional goals" within both information literacy and writing programs (Oakleaf, 2008 p. 242). First, this chapter presents DCM as an assessment methodology and describes how it was applied at Elmhurst College. Then, the chapter explains important products of the process: a criteria guide and a criteria map. Finally, it describes how the project presents important interdisciplinary implications.

DYNAMIC CRITERIA MAPPING

Assessment of information literacy (IL) instruction concerns teaching librarians attempting to understand the effect of their instruction on student learning (Gilchrist, 2009). However, since IL instruction often occurs in "one-shot" sessions (Artman, Frisicaro-Pawlowski, & Monge, 2010) and since librarians rarely have access to student artifacts, authentic assessment of IL instruction remains difficult. Assessment, though, provides unique opportunities for collaboration among librarians and writing instructors, for highlighting the importance of IL, and for acquiring evidence of student learning (Belanger, Zou, Mills, Holmes, & Oakleaf, 2015). Research on best practices in IL instruction describes the positive impact of collaborative efforts between librarians and classroom faculty (Barratt, Nielsen, Desmet,

& Balthazor, 2009; Belanger et al., 2012), suggesting the need to conceptualize assessment as an important component of best practices.

In considering appropriate assessment methods, practitioners should consider dynamic criteria mapping, a site-based, locally controlled process that responds to the needs and circumstances of a community (Broad, 2003). Writing assessment scholarship frames DCM as organic, generative, and qualitative. As an organic assessment process, it engages the experience and knowledge of practitioners rather than outsourcing assessment to a commercial testing corporation, like Pearson. It is fundamentally focused on a specific community, encouraging practitioners to articulate and then cultivate consensus on what they value when they evaluate and assess student products in individual courses and/or during programmatic assessment processes (Broad, 2003). Underlying dynamic criteria mapping is social-constructivist theory, which privileges an epistemological framing of knowledge as constructed through social processes, like intensive discussion sessions, involving competing perspectives, values, power relations, and levels of expertise. DCM purposely addresses these complexities to identify how disciplinary knowledges and social dynamics influence the evaluative process. It contrasts sharply with traditional assessment processes, which are informed by a positivist psychometric epistemological framework that conceptualizes knowledge as precisely discernible and reality as distinctly stable and objectively known and knowable (Huot, 2002).

As a generative and qualitative practice, DCM encourages participants to verbalize and understand the specific criteria they apply when evaluating student products, identify textual features of student products fulfilling privileged criteria, and link criteria to learning outcomes for courses and programs (Broad, 2003). Enriching the generative process, participants think critically about the respective value of each and make articulations among evaluation criteria, textual features, and learning outcomes. DCM is also framed as a qualitative method of assessment because it elicits a variety of qualitative data, like marginalia on student artifacts, participant notes, and transcripts of small- and large-group discussion sessions. One key product of the DCM process is the creation of a visual representation that not only identifies privileged criteria but also conveys the dynamic relationships among them (Broad, 2003). This visual representation, or criteria map, portrays participant consensus regarding what they value; what criteria matter and why; and how criteria interrelate when participants apply them when evaluating student artifacts (Appendix A).

DCM AT ELMHURST COLLEGE

DCM's site-based, organic focus makes it adaptable to a variety of institutional contexts, ranging from community colleges to flagship state universities (Broad et al., 2009). For several reasons, DCM was a particularly compelling methodology to cultivate consensus on IL at Elmhurst College, a liberal arts institution with approximately 3,200 undergraduate and graduate students. One, precipitated by the financial stresses of the Great Recession and by the implementation of a corporate model of administration, distrust and skepticism permeated institutional dynamics and interdepartmental relationships, causing many faculty to presume that assessment enacts ulterior motives, like the curtailment of programs. It is impossible to develop a culture of assessment if faculty not only devalue assessment but also perceive it as a means to ominous ends (Behm, 2016; Janangelo & Adler-Kassner, 2009). Two, resulting from a long history of indifference to assessment, the college lacked empirical evidence of student learning, a deficiency gently admonished by a 2009 Higher Learning Commission (HLC) report. Three, across campus, practitioners have heretofore neither asserted ownership of assessment nor cultivated consensus on learning outcomes and criteria related to IL. This institutional context provided a unique crucible, then, in which to implement DCM and realize its benefits (see Box 18.1), because it privileges collaborative discussion, ultimately building trust, collegiality, and consensus.

Lacking consensus regarding learning outcomes and criteria related to IL, the most logical starting place was to engage English faculty and librarians in the process of clarifying their diverse understandings of IL: how they conceptualize it as a disposition and practice, what features distinguish IL within written products, and what aspects of IL they value and why. To do this, we designed a three-day DCM process that progressed inductively from individual close reading of student artifacts to successive small- and large-group intensive discussions during which 11 participants (six librarians and five writing instructors) articulated their disparate conceptions of IL but ultimately reached consensus on a shared understanding of IL and vocabulary, building a bridge across our disciplinary division. Students in six sections of first-year writing signed informed consent forms and submitted their academic argument essays. The 11 faculty participants of the DCM process also provided informed consent. Since essays were used only to springboard discussion as part of clarifying participants' expectations, we chose six essays for review. Though we delineate the steps sequentially below, in actual practice, DCM methodology functions recursively as participants generate ideas, identify and negotiate criteria, find common ground, and foster community.

The first step of our DCM process involved a brief introduction conceptualizing the project and explaining dynamic criteria mapping methodology. Participants then individually reviewed six student artifacts. To elicit participants' preconceptions of IL and how IL is demonstrated by written artifacts, participants provided marginalia on the artifacts, took notes, and completed a worksheet with the following questions: (1) Does this text demonstrate information literacy (Y/N)? Why? (2) What rationale can you provide for deciding as you did? (3) What aspects or characteristics of the sample texts do you value, privilege, or emphasize? (4) Why do you value those aspects/characteristics? (5) What do they reflect, represent, and/or demonstrate? The review of student artifacts not only fostered discussion of IL but also grounded and focused that discussion. For

BOX 18.1
BENEFITS OF DYNAMIC CRITERIA MAPPING (DCM)

- Privileges Qualitative Writing Assessment
- Conceptualizes Assessment as a Social Process
- Reveals What a Community Values
- Renders Evaluative Dynamics Visually
- Clarifies the Semantics of Criteria
- Facilitates Professional Development
- Builds a Culture of Assessment

(Data from Broad, 2003.)

instance, it was students' demonstration of IL that served as the impetus for participants to articulate and think critically about how they conceptualize IL. Also, if discussion veered unproductively, we could always return to the artifacts. The writing of marginalia, taking of notes, and responding to questions was critical in encouraging participants to express their respective definitions of IL, provide a rationale supporting that definition and their interpretation of the student artifacts, identify textual features that exhibit IL, and describe why they privileged those features and what those features represented within student writing.

The second step involved participants working in groups of three or "trio groups." With 11 participants, we divided participants into three groups of three and one group of two. In DCM methodology, small- and large-group work is framed as articulation sessions. Noting evaluative comments, criteria, and textual features delineating IL, the trio groups provided space for participants to discuss their respective interpretations of each text. Each trio group audio-recorded their discussion and participants took notes as well. Trio groups labored to generate consensus on a conception of IL, on what comprises it, and on what specific textual features and characteristics of student artifacts demonstrate IL.

The third step involved an articulation session with all participants during which each trio group presented their privileged comments, criteria, and textual features and described how each group cultivated consensus. The focus of the large-group discussion was to identify comments, criteria, and textual features; group synonymous comments and criteria together; and categorize them as constellations, a process of describing and framing the data in a way that makes it more amenable to visual representation as a map. Through this work, participants fostered consensus on a framing of IL as a developmental process and disposition toward information and knowledge that is active and engaged. The group also generated consensus on what comments and criteria ought to be emphasized and how we could combine and categorize them appropriately (see Appendix A).

After cultivating consensus as a large group, we moved to the fourth step: collaborating in the construction of a useful visual representation of that consensus that accurately portrayed how the group defines and describes IL, a rendering that could be shared with the Elmhurst College community, particularly students, to clarify the expectations of librarians and writing instructors. Another critical part of this step was to foster consensus among the group regarding the dynamics of how our privileged comments, criteria, and textual features interrelated to portray our framing of IL. With dynamic criteria mapping, not only is it critical to articulate privileged criteria, but also to convey visually the relationships among those criteria as they are applied when practitioners review and evaluate student artifacts.

The last step consisted of a debriefing session where participants discussed their experience with our dynamic criteria mapping methodology, noting challenges and providing feedback on how the exercise might be modified and improved in the future. The group also discussed how the criteria guide could inform future IL sessions, improve student learning, enrich strategies for teaching IL in first-year writing courses, and influence future assessment practices.

FROM CRITERIA TO MAP

The primary purpose of DCM is to make explicit, through small- and large-group discussion and critical reflection, what a community really values when assessing and evaluating student work (see Box 18.2 for the data analysis procedure). The criteria lists generated during our articulation sessions present a comprehensive, yet messy, view of what our community values in terms of IL (Appendix A). Criteria that were repeated frequently, like source/s, complicated/complexity, and integration, reflected what group participants considered important. Some of these criteria were more "honored in the breach," in that participants felt the papers lacked the quality/criteria rather than demonstrated it. In our large-group discussion, we worked on grouping the criteria into constellations that reflected both the importance of the criteria and also the group's conceptual consensus about their underlying significance. Ultimately, the constellations articulated by the large group were the following:

- **Process**: awareness of information need, searching, source choice
- **Praxis/Enactment:** synthesis/deployment of sources, awareness of context/perspectives/conversation, awareness of bias
- **Engagement**: cognition/metacognition, persistence, disposition of inquiry
- **Attribution:** mechanics of citation, paraphrasing

The sorting of the criteria into the constellations provided some interesting perspective. As the investigators sorted criteria into the constellations, it became apparent that two constellations, Praxis/Enactment and Engagement, were privileged, gaining the most criteria. We also noted that Attribution, though a necessary constellation, drew the fewest descriptors. Once the constellations and criteria were analyzed, we visually represented the relationships among the constellations. Our map uniquely represents the values expressed by the community and reflects how we see the constellations as overlapping. Though we initiated the map-making process during a large-group articulation session, time constraints necessitated that we construct the map after closely analyzing the data.

The elements of the map consist of the constellations (Process, Praxis/Enactment, Engagement, Attribution), as well as elements that connect and flow between

BOX 18.2
DATA ANALYSIS

Data Collected

- Workshop participant worksheet responses
- Marginalia respondent notes collected from sample papers
- Recording of trio- and large-group discussion (transcript)

Initial Analysis

- All material transcribed to Google docs
- Text search used to identify and locate relevant IL words/descriptors
- Each investigator also engaged in close reading of the texts

Constellation-Building Process

- Investigators compiled lists of criteria words/terms/concepts
- Word/term/concept groupings
- Themes emerge
- Themes become "constellations"

A note on analytic software: Although we had access to NVivo, the learning curve was steeper than anticipated given time constraints.

them—Sources, Synthesis, Cognition, and Writing are the means by which these concepts are enacted. These terms were repeated in our criteria enough that we felt they needed to be explicitly part of the map itself. They seemed to us to be structurally integral to explaining the relationships between the constellations, and added a representation of movement between the constellations.

The map itself (Figure 18.1) came out of discussions between the investigators and data analysis, and resulted from an intuitive leap by one of us while trying to articulate the movement and relationship among the constellations and the process-oriented elements. In DCM, the development of the map is a creative process. We benefited from allowing time for thoughtful processing. Several of the meetings between investigators were spent drawing things on paper and then throwing them away. This was a crucial part of the process and led to our having a map that really reflects our process and our community values. Our map portrays IL as a fluid process-oriented activity that students move through in a recursive way.

INTERDISCIPLINARY IMPLICATIONS OF THE PROJECT

Our process of applying DCM generated three important interdisciplinary implications: that writing and research are interrelated, that the DCM process can generate a

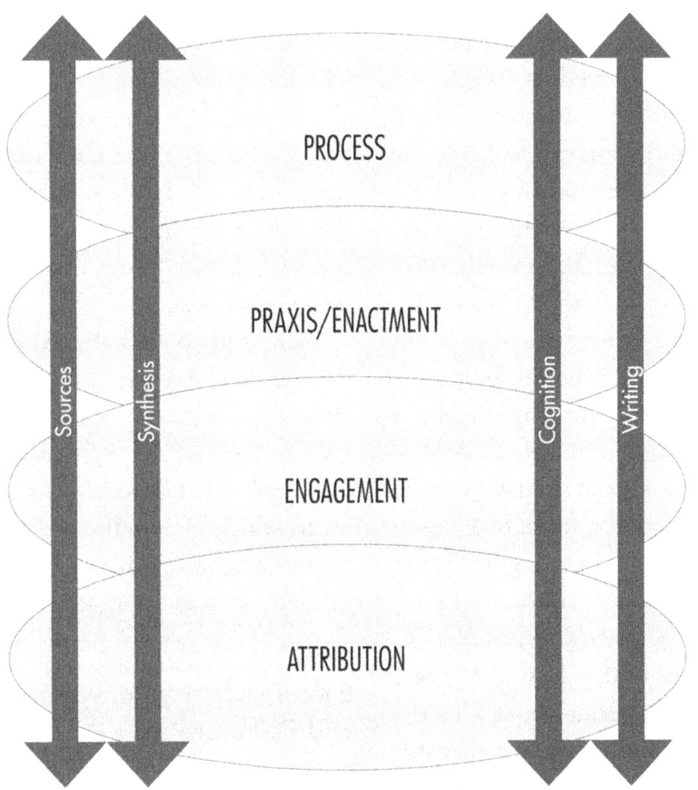

Figure 18.1 Dynamic criteria map.

shared language describing IL, and that disciplinary documents can possibly enable interdisciplinary collaborations and coalitions.

Writing and Research Are Interrelated

Participants agreed that writing and IL are interrelated and that student writing is useful in assessing IL. These essays were a valuable resource for assessing IL in terms of students' process and product. For instance, participants determined the extent to which students were comfortable with complexity and were aware of how research and writing enriched their perspectives and influenced their understanding of audience awareness and research needs as the projects unfolded. This exploration of student writing was particularly useful to the librarians. Because librarians typically don't have access to student products, they tend to focus on process. Having the opportunity to read student papers and see the enactment of the research process in student work helped librarians explicitly see that connection between writing and IL. The IL and writing criteria were inextricably linked so that while the constellations (Appendix A) developed with a focus on IL, the writing faculty and librarians could not separate the writing from the research. One librarian remarked on the "firm agreement in quality and criteria amongst a small pool of reviewers, as it illustrates and validates that we have a pretty common definition of a 'good' research essay." Similarly, a writing instructor did not see "a considerable amount of conflict between what we have articulated as IL and how it functions in the classroom. There appears to be some discussion about what the level of proficiency should be in first-year students; however, I have found the discussion to be incredibly useful and illuminating."

By its very nature as a radically situated process, DCM resulted in participants' experiences paralleling students' struggles with the academic research essay. Participants needed to experience the DCM process to understand the complexity of what we were asking students to do within a limited time period and what we valued in that process and those products. Students can't "pre-answer" their research questions just as practitioners can't subscribe to an ideal text that students are not developmentally ready to produce. Our initial review of essays applied our respective ideal texts. The insights emerging from the cross-disciplinarity of our group discussions, however, made us recalibrate our expectations so that we reviewed the essays as first-year students' initial attempt at entering an academic community, a reflection of the developmental nature of cultivating proficiency in IL and writing. One writing instructor observed how "during this workshop, it seems that we arrived at the right questions and became aware of the gap between our standards and student performance." For instance, we observed that students were using at least some library sources. Works Cited lists included many books, encyclopedia entries, and articles both scholarly and popular gleaned from databases. But one developmental marker for us was that, although students found sources, their writing revealed their inability to understand and skillfully deploy that material in service of an argument, which may indicate that students lack the metacognitive skill required to successfully integrate sources in support of an argument.

Interdisciplinary Conversation and Collaboration

Librarians and writing faculty both facilitate student learning, though their approaches and disciplinary jargon vary. However, DCM enables useful interdisciplinary conversation. Participants discovered that although the vocabulary/language we used to describe and articulate student demonstrations of IL differ, our group discussions allowed us to unpack semantics and revealed that we value similar demonstrations of IL, even if we initially used different words to articulate criteria. For example, one criterion that emerged revolves around the "why" of IL. Both librarians and writing faculty assign value to students understanding the intellectual underpinning of IL practices, like source citation. Librarians and writing instructors value the correct use of citation, but the different disciplinary approaches lead to different "whys." Librarians often use citations as a locator: the accuracy of a citation dictates its usefulness in harvesting additional sources. However, for writing instructors, citation reflects students' location in a discourse and recognition of a source's authority within a discourse. A writing instructor checks sources to ensure students are maximizing their rhetorical agenda. Our discussions allowed us to consider disciplinary perspectives, deepening our understanding of how we can work concertedly to develop student learning. A veteran librarian noted that "while we are speaking of terms from two different disciplines of librarianship and teachers of English, we have the same goals and many overlap. We may also view these goals through different lenses but our end point is the same." A shared—and expanding—vocabulary also emerged from this assessment project. One librarian intended "to be more purposeful in what I say to students."

Some participants attributed this shift to the shared meanings and varied synonyms that represent and clarify the constellations (see Appendix A), and others commented that hearing the perspective of someone in another discipline helped them see and name things they couldn't before. One writing instructor used the simile of a ball. She imagined that "if what we're talking about is like a ball, I'm looking at this part of the ball and the librarian might be looking at *this* part of the ball—the lenses—and it's really helpful for me for the librarian to describe what I'm looking at." She explained how this librarian perspective "forces me to re-prioritize in my own head what it is that students are supposed to get out of my class. Now I have a better image of what other expectations are and what other understandings of the subject are." This different perspective—and different language—expands one's approach. And a librarian, who had previously described the criteria as "cumbersome," in fact agreed that "I feel the same way from a library science perspective."

Articulations Between the Framework(s)

Before this DCM process, practitioners were aware of the national conversation about IL and writing as they have been enshrined in disciplinary documents, like the *Framework for Information Literacy for Higher Education* (IL Framework; ACRL, 2016) and the *Framework for Success in Postsecondary Writing* (Writing Framework; CWPA, 2011). While not anticipated, our criteria guide closely corresponded with and easily revealed discernible connections between these disciplinary documents. We identified *Framework* categories as speaking to our initial list of criteria (see Appendix B), and believe that highlighting the connections between the documents could initiate productive interdisciplinary collaborations and coalitions. For example, the IL Framework articulates lenses that generally correspond to the Writing Framework, like practices and dispositions. This approach—what students do and their orientation toward the process—parallels the "habits of mind" that "refers to ways of approaching learning that are both intellectual and practical and that will support students' success in a variety of fields and disciplines" (p. 1). Thus, the intellectual/disposition components of the process and practices/practical aspects encompass both an approach to writing and research and an enactment. Both frameworks emphasize metacognition with the Writing Framework devoting a section to it and the IL Framework founded on "these core ideas of metaliteracy, with special focus on metacognition, or critical self-reflection, as crucial to becoming more self-directed in that rapidly changing ecosystem" (p. 3). Our criteria include characteristics, like curiosity, recursivity, and persistence, that speak to the necessity for awareness and reflection on the part of the student writer.

Unlike the Writing Framework, the IL Framework talks explicitly about issues of power. In our reading of student papers, we found that the research frequently overpowered student writers in terms of their inability to understand and synthesize material as well as their facility in maintaining a strong voice and stance. The IL Framework maintains that even though "novice learners and experts at all levels can take part in the conversation, established power and authority structures may influence their ability to participate and can privilege certain voices and information" (p. 8). Writing instructors and librarians felt that students lacked "fluency in the language and process of a discipline," but rather than allowing this inexperience to disempower their "ability to participate and engage" (p. 8), our job as educators is to highlight entry points for students. For librarians, that might mean showing students encyclopedias that can facilitate access to the more in-depth scholarly conversation. For writing faculty, that might mean asking students to incorporate narrative elements, like personal anecdotes, into their arguments, or helping students formulate research questions that connect to their lived experiences, which allows students to understand their place in the scholarly conversation while still possessing the confidence to participate. Developmentally, students are being asked to "appropriate (or be appropriated by) a specialized discourse, and they have to do this as though they were easily and comfortably one with their audience" (Bartholomae, 1986, p. 9). While "their initial progress will be marked by their abilities to take on the role of privilege, by their abilities to establish authority" (Bartholomae, 1986, p. 20) this process may, ironically, be characterized by inconsistencies and false steps. Thus, given the place of first-year writing in the curriculum and in a student's undergraduate career, students may come to the institution with extensive learning needs regarding IL and writing. The criteria that practitioners generate through DCM must not ignore the institutional context and students' positions within that structure.

At the disciplinary level, the articulations between the IL Framework and the Writing Framework, particularly the dual emphasis on dispositions and practices, serve as an opportunity for future scholarship in both library science and rhetoric and composition. There is much that both disciplines could learn from each other, and the articulations between the respective frameworks could generate productive collaborative relationships among librarians and writing instructors, providing a shared discourse with which to not only unpack and understand disciplinary pedagogical and theoretical differences but also cultivate an awareness of the complex intercalations of IL and writing. At the programmatic level, this shared discourse and understanding could springboard discussions of how to design effective information literacy instruction; demystify the complex relationship between writing and information literacy for students; articulate pertinent, measurable learning outcomes; and construct programmatic professional development opportunities. For us, getting to know our colleagues in library science and rhetoric and composition through the DCM experience of assessment and the process of comparing the two disciplinary frameworks was one of the most rewarding outcomes, enabling us to find theoretical and pedagogical common ground. What is more, the iterative nature of the DCM discussion gave us the opportunity to think through the messiness of the evaluative process, helping us discover values we might not have recognized and requiring us to consider them critically as part of generating consensus about criteria and developing clear expectations that both librarians and writing faculty hold. Ultimately, applying DCM methodology, we generated consensus on how to conceptualize information literacy and engaged in interdisciplinary conversations that strengthened coalitions among librarians and writing faculty and initiated additional assessment projects.

NOTE

We would like to thank Ted Lerud, former Associate Dean of the Faculty; Susan Swords Steffen, Director of the A. C. Buehler Library; and Ann Frank Wake, Chair of the English Department, for their ongoing support of this project and the following participants: Librarians Donna Goodwyn, Jacob Hill, Elaine Page, and Jennifer Paliatka; and writing faculty members Erika McCombs, Michelle Mouton, Mary Beth Newman, Bridget O'Rourke, and Kathy Veliz.

APPENDIX A. IL Criteria Guide for English Composition Researched Arguments

Process	Praxis/Enactment	Engagement	Attribution
Library (Re)sources Range of Sources Number of Sources Source Genre Academic Sources Scholarly Sources Analytical Awareness Relationships among Source Material Appropriateness of Source Material Relevance Knowing Information Need Credibility/Credible Quotes Cite/Citation/Cites Digging Deeper Grappling with Viewpoints Curious Researcher Inquiry Recursive Complexity of Topic Curiosity	Command of Research and Argument Thesis Facilitate an Argument Analytical Awareness Bias Awareness Resisting Confirmation Bias Cherry Picking Conversation Explore Conflicting/Complex Integration/ Incorporation Claim Facts, Evidence, & Examples Support Synthesize Sources Contextualizing Source Material Grouping Sources Acknowledging Perspectives Discerning the Credibility of Sources Paraphrase Quote Synthesis Agency Demonstration of writing skills and of Being Informed about an Issue	Persistence Inquiry Grasp Engaged Curious Recursive Understood Interpret Inability to Distinguish Information from Opinion Accommodation of Alternative Perspectives Contrast Sides Dialogue Complexity Rhetorical Awareness Demonstration of Critical Thinking Demonstration of Being Informed about an Issue Possessing the Requisite Background to Enter the Conversation History Context Grasp Comprehension of Source Material Common Ground Representation	Cite Sources Works Cited Quotations Paraphrasing Attribution Tag Introduce/Introducing Not Traceable Authority Background Terms Quality of Source Material Quantity of Source Material Type of Source Variety Range of Source Material Conversation Visual Representation of Source Material Demonstration of Methods

APPENDIX B. The *Framework for Information Literacy for Higher Education* as Corresponding to the IL Criteria Guide for English Composition Researched Arguments (Appendix A)

<table>
<tr><th>Process</th><th>Praxis/Enactment</th><th>Engagement</th><th>Attribution</th></tr>
<tr><td colspan="3">Frame #1: Authority Is Constructed & Contextual</td><td></td></tr>
<tr><td>Frame #2: Information Creation as a Process</td><td></td><td>Frame #2: Information Creation as a Process</td><td></td></tr>
<tr><td></td><td></td><td colspan="2">Frame #3: Information Has Value</td></tr>
<tr><td></td><td colspan="2">Frame #4: Research as Inquiry</td><td></td></tr>
<tr><td></td><td>Frame #5: Scholarship as Conversation</td><td></td><td></td></tr>
<tr><td colspan="2">Frame #6: Searching as Strategic Exploration</td><td></td><td></td></tr>
</table>

REFERENCES

Artman, M., Frisicaro-Pawlowski, E., & Monge, R. (2010). Not just one shot: Extending the dialogue about information literacy in composition classes. *Composition Studies, 38*(2), 93–110.

Association of American Colleges and Universities. (2015). *Trends in learning outcomes assessment: Key findings from a survey among administrators at AAC&U member institutions.* Washington, DC: Hart Research Associates. Retrieved from https://www.aacu.org/sites/default/files/files/LEAP/2015_Survey_Report3.pdf

Association of College and Research Libraries. (2016). *Framework for information literacy for higher education.* Retrieved from http://www.ala.org/acrl/standards/ilframework

Barratt, C. C., Nielsen, K., Desmet, C., & Balthazor, R. (2009). Collaboration is key: Librarians and composition instructors analyze student research and writing. *portal: Libraries and the Academy, 9*(1), 37–56. Johns Hopkins University Press. Retrieved December 21, 2016, from Project MUSE database.

Bartholomae, D. (1986). Inventing the university. *Journal of Basic Writing, 5*(1), 4–23. Retrieved from http://wac.colostate.edu/jbw/v5n1/bartholomae.pdf

Behm, N. (2016). Strategic assessment: Using dynamic criteria mapping to actualize institutional mission and build community. In J. Janangelo (Ed.), *A critical look at institutional mission: A guide for writing program administration* (pp. 40–58). Anderson, SC: Parlor Press.

Belanger, J., Bliquez, R., & Mondal, S. (2012). Developing a collaborative faculty-librarian information literacy assessment project. *Library Review, 61*(2), 68–91. https://doi.org/10.1108/00242531211220726

Belanger, J., Zou, N., Mills, J. R., Holmes, C., & Oakleaf, M. (2015). Project RAILS: Lessons learned about rubric assessment of information literacy skills. *portal: Libraries and the Academy, 15*(4), 623–644. Johns Hopkins University Press. Retrieved December 21, 2016, from Project MUSE database.

Broad, B. (2003). *What we really value: Beyond rubrics in teaching and assessing writing.* Logan, UT: Utah State University Press.

Broad, B., Adler-Kassner, L., Alford, B., Detweiler, J., Estrem, H., Harrington, S., . . . Weeden, S. (Eds.). (2009). *Organic writing assessment: Dynamic criteria mapping in action*. Logan, UT: Utah State University Press.

Carter, T. M., & Alderidge, T. (2016). The collision of two lexicons: Librarians, composition instructors and the vocabulary of source evaluation. *Evidence Based Library and Information Practice, 11*(1), 23–39.

Council of Writing Program Administrators, National Council of Teachers of English, & National Writing Project. (2011). *Framework for success in postsecondary writing*. Retrieved from http://wpacouncil.org/files/framework-for-success-postsecondary-writing.pdf

D'Angelo, B., & Maid, B. (2004). Moving beyond definitions: Implementing information literacy across the curriculum. *Journal of Academic Librarianship, 30*(3), 212–217.

Deitering, A. M., & Jameson, S. (2008). Step by step through the scholarly conversation: A collaborative library/writing faculty project to embed information literacy and promote critical thinking in first year composition at Oregon State University. *College & Undergraduate Libraries, 15*(1), 57–79. https://doi.org/10.1080/10691310802176830

Gilchrist, D. L. (2009). A twenty year path. *Communications In Information Literacy, 3*(2), 70–79.

Head, A. J. (2013). Project Information Literacy: What can be learned about the information-seeking behavior of today's college students? In D. M. Mueller (Ed.), *Imagine, innovate, inspire: The proceedings of the ACRL 2013 Conference, April 10–13, 2013, Indianapolis, IN* (pp. 472–482). Association of College and Research Libraries. Retrieved from http://www.ala.org/acrl/sites/ala.org.acrl/files/content/conferences/confsandpreconfs/2013/papers/Head_Project.pdf

Huot, B. (2002). *(Re)articulating writing assessment for teaching and learning*. Logan, UT: Utah State University Press.

Janangelo, J., & Adler-Kassner, L. (2009). Common denominators and the ongoing culture of assessment. In M. C. Paretti & K. Powell (Eds.), *Assessing writing* (pp. 11–34). Tallahassee: Association of Institutional Research Press.

Mazziotti D., & Grettano, T. (2011). "Hanging together": Collaboration between information literacy and writing programs based on the ACRL Standards and the WPA Outcomes. In D. M. Mueller (Ed.), *Declaration of interdependence: The proceedings of the ACRL 2011 Conference, March 30–April 2, 2011, Philadelphia, PA* (pp. 180–190). Chicago, IL: Association of College and Research Libraries. Retrieved from http://www.ala.org/acrl/sites/ala.org.acrl/files/content/conferences/confsandpreconfs/national/2011/papers/hanging_together.pdf

Oakleaf, M. (2008). Dangers and opportunities: A conceptual map of information literacy assessment approaches. *portal: Libraries and the Academy, 8*(3), 233–253. Retrieved from Project Muse. https://doi.org/10.1353/pla.0.0011

CHAPTER 19

GOOGLE, BAIDU, THE LIBRARY, AND THE ACRL FRAMEWORK

Assessing Information-Seeking Behaviors of First-Year Multilingual Writers Through Research-Aloud Protocols

Lilian W. Mina

Jeanne Law Bohannon

Jinrong Li

Recent years have witnessed a rapid development of information technologies and their increasingly significant, though ubiquitous, impact on academic information literacy. Writing in the *Handbook of Reading Research*, educational scholar Don Leu (2000) argued that technology will change the pace, form, and function of literacy, and that digital technologies are rapidly and continuously redefining the nature of literacy. He further discussed how quickly classrooms will become irrelevant if instructors cannot keep up with students as they explore digital technologies and their associated writing spaces. Leu hit on the fact that we have come to embody almost 20 years later: we must provide students with opportunities for writing and research that embrace the Digital. To better prepare students for the opportunities and challenges in their navigation of the world of academia mediated by information technologies, researchers and practitioners have moved from simple bibliographic instruction or one-shot library instruction (Spievak & Hayes-Bohanan, 2013; Wang, 2016) to an ecological approach where information literacy skills are fully integrated into writing curricula (Bohannon, 2015; Brown, Murphy, & Nanny, 2003; Kress, 2003; Pinto, Antonio Cordón, & Gómez Díaz, 2010; Purdy, 2010; Valmont, 2003). Defined as a set of skills to locate, evaluate, and use information effectively for various purposes in academic settings (Behrens, 1994; Bruce, 1997; Doyle, 1994; Huston, 1999), information literacy skills have been shown to be essential for students' success in academic writing in various disciplines (Jordan & Kedrowicz, 2011; McDowell, 2002). More importantly, there is growing awareness that effective access and use of information resources indicate students' abilities to learn and are an indispensable skill in the production of new knowledge (Leu, Kinzer, Coiro, & Cammack, 2004; Markauskaite, 2006).

However, most of these studies focus on native English speakers, and with growing numbers of multilingual students in U.S. universities, it is important for both writing instructors and librarians to better understand and to scaffold the development of information-seeking behaviors of these students, particularly in the first-year writing (FYW) classroom, their gateway to academic writing and research. These classrooms are typically the environment where most college students are introduced to information literacy as they prepare to write an argumentative or research essay. A few studies have examined the information literacy of multilingual students. For example, in their survey study of 27 international undergraduate students, Mina and Walker (2016) examined the extent to which information literacy instruction may benefit students' information-seeking behavior, and found that there were important gaps between what students said they were learning and what they were expected to do. Although most students reported that they had received adequate instruction, they felt their information literacy skills were inadequate for many of the academic tasks. Other studies have also identified unique information literacy challenges facing international students (e.g., Zhao & Mawhinney, 2015). Nevertheless, most previous studies in this field are generally based on students' self-reported experiences from surveys or interviews. To examine students' actual experiences with information-seeking behaviors, the LILAC (Learning Information Literacy across the Curriculum) Project collects and analyzes screen-captured data containing a video record of screen activity and students' voice narrative while conducting online bibliographic research on a topic. LILAC researchers collect this qualitative data in addition to survey data that aims to unpack students' experiences, attitudes, and evaluation of their information literacy. As a networked component of the LILAC Project, this chapter uses three frames from the *Framework for Information Literacy for Higher Education* produced by the Association of College and Research Libraries (ACRL) as points of reference to examine perceived information-seeking behaviors and possible challenges multilingual students face. We also discuss pedagogical implications by addressing these research questions:

1. What are the information-seeking behaviors of multilingual writers in first-year writing courses?
2. What are the gaps in information-seeking behaviors of multilingual writers as plotted against three ACRL frames and their knowledge practices?
3. How can these findings inform specific pedagogical approaches to improve information-seeking behaviors of multilingual writers in first-year writing courses?

In answering these questions through an empirical study, we describe students' information-seeking behaviors and summarize the findings based on selected ACRL threshold concepts in an effort to help both writing instructors and librarians see where students are in the trajectory of information literacy development and provide effective instruction and assistance accordingly.

METHODOLOGY

Over the course of two semesters (spring and fall 2015), Lilian collected data for the LILAC Project from multilingual students in a Midwestern research-intensive university. At the time of data collection, that institution was a partner in the LILAC Project, with a special interest in exploring multilingual students' information literacy skills and behaviors. The deliberate focus on that student population was bicausal: the relatively large population of multilingual students in that institution (about 2,000 in 2015), and Lilian's teaching of FYW classes designated for multilingual students. This context made it possible to recruit students to participate in the LILAC Project. Participating in the LILAC Project comes in two consecutive parts: completing an online survey about the participant's training, experience, and self-assessment of information literacy skills, followed by a RAP (Research Aloud Protocol) screen recording session. The screen recordings contain a video recording of screen activity and students' voice narrative while conducting online research on a topic. The average length of every screen recording is 15 minutes.

Students were recruited and these research sessions were held when students were beginning the unit on argumentative writing that required bibliographic research to construct a research-based argument on a given topic. This unit is part of the program-set curriculum and it was known to start around week seven of the semester. By the time students came to participate in the study, they had selected a topic for their argumentative essay. At the beginning of the research session, students were informed that they would conduct online research on the topic they were writing about in their writing class. The timing of the research session was deliberate because it meant students wouldn't waste time thinking about a topic or fabricating a topic to research during the RAP session. Although we acknowledge that this setting isn't ideal for collecting extensive or more situated data, the authenticity of students' topics and the reality that students were indeed engaged in researching these topics for argumentative essays in their FYW classes compensated for the short time and relatively controlled situation of data gathering.

Data for our study come from 50 RAP recordings, with a total of about 650 minutes of screen-captured data. The recordings were collected from Chinese undergraduate students enrolled in the Midwestern university, most of whom were recruited from Lilian's FYW classes at the time of data collection. At the beginning of the data analysis process, our team calculated the intercoder reliability to ensure reliability of findings: we converted the questions and notes on the LILAC RAP Coding Scheme into a series of codes that each of us used later to code five RAP recordings (10% of the total data) independently; we then calculated the Cronbach alpha of the three sets of codes to be 0.86, a high reliability. After establishing the interreliability using the coding scheme, we coded the 50 RAP recordings, taking copious research notes that we later used for qualitative analysis of participants' information-seeking behaviors. As an integrated part of coding, each of us also took into account the fact that these participants were first-year writers, who would not be expected to possess a command of or fluency in all aspects of information literacy. Instead, we sought trends in how participants' information-seeking skills could be mapped against specific frames and knowledge practices of the ACRL *Framework*.

Upon comparing our research notes, we plotted the information-seeking behaviors identified in the RAP recordings against seven knowledge practices under three frames of the

TABLE 19.1 *A Synergy of the ACRL Framework and the LILAC RAP Coding Scheme*

ACRL Frames	LILAC RAP Coding
Searching as Strategic Exploration	First Search Source Type of Search
Research as Inquiry	Determining Search Scope Refining Search Scope Using Search Results
Authority Is Constructed and Contextual	Evaluating Search Results Evaluating Sources

2016 ACRL *Framework*: Searching as Strategic Exploration (p. 9), Research as Inquiry (p. 7), and Authority Is Constructed and Contextual (p. 4). Table 19.1 illustrates the synergy we created between the three ACRL frames and the LILAC RAP Coding Scheme. We decided to use the three frames as our thematic discussion points under which we will present a synergy of the seven knowledge practices selected and the LILAC RAP Coding Scheme. Our implications are outgrowths of both the findings as well as acknowledged limitations of the controlled nature of our Research Aloud Protocols (RAPs).

Searching as Strategic Exploration

The ACRL (2016) frame Searching as Strategic Exploration centers around the cognitive processes that drive information-seeking behaviors. This frame distinguishes between a novice and an expert searcher. While the expert searcher is expected to be more understanding of the context surrounding the search process with its limitations and challenges, the novice searcher may not always acknowledge the context of his or her search or the limitations of the search process. Another key difference between an expert and a novice searcher is the range of search strategies utilized by each of them; an expert searcher attempts a wide range of search strategies and may "search more widely and deeply" before deciding on the most suitable sources that have the information needed (p. 9). On the other side, a novice searcher employs only a few search strategies and resorts to "a limited set of resources," thus demonstrating little flexibility during the search process (p. 9). The following discussion of participants' broad scope of search, difficulty of accessing sources, and reliance on limited research types clearly demonstrates that most participants in this study are more on the novice than the expert end of this frame.

Broad Scope of Search

The first knowledge practice states that "[l]earners who are developing their information literate abilities determine the initial scope of the task required to meet their information needs" (ACRL, 2016, p. 9). Even though this knowledge practice does not have a corresponding question from the LILAC RAP codes, we were able to capture it in participants' RAP sessions. Most participants started their searching process by identifying the topic they were researching for a particular assignment in their FYW class. The topics were articulated in mostly broad terms, such as "[m]y topic is the global warming and the greenhouse effect." While very few participants used indirect questions to express the scope of their search, most of these questions were still so general. For example, one participant stated that his topic is "how digital technology affect our health." Such a loosely identified search scope may offer an interpretation of why most participants were not clear about the type of information they needed for their essays or the best sources to locate that information (as we discuss later); both are features of novice searchers.

(Access to) Sources of Information

When participants started their online search, Google was the first choice for almost half of them (48%), while the school library was the first stop for online information for half that number (24%), as Figure 19.1 illustrates. Although Wikipedia was not the first place participants searched for information, it was a preferred place to participants searching for definitions of their keywords or difficult terms relevant to their search. Surprisingly, many Chinese participants turned to Baidu, the major Chinese search engine, to understand the basics of the topic they were researching. Although these participants acknowledged that they wouldn't use the information they found through Baidu in their research papers, most of them explained that reading sources in Chinese was an essential stage for them in order to understand more about their topics. As one participant put it, "Chinese information gets me thinking before I search in English" (21028).

These participants' choice to use Baidu for better understanding of the topics and key terms they were searching highlights a serious access problem for multilingual students in this study. The linguistic barrier many students appeared to face may have resulted in their following unexpected and nontraditional search strategies, such as using a Chinese search engine, reading sources in Chinese, and using Google Translate for assistance with difficult terms in search results. When Mina and Walker (2016) examined the survey data collected from a portion of participants in this study, they found that "most students resort to using the web for their research

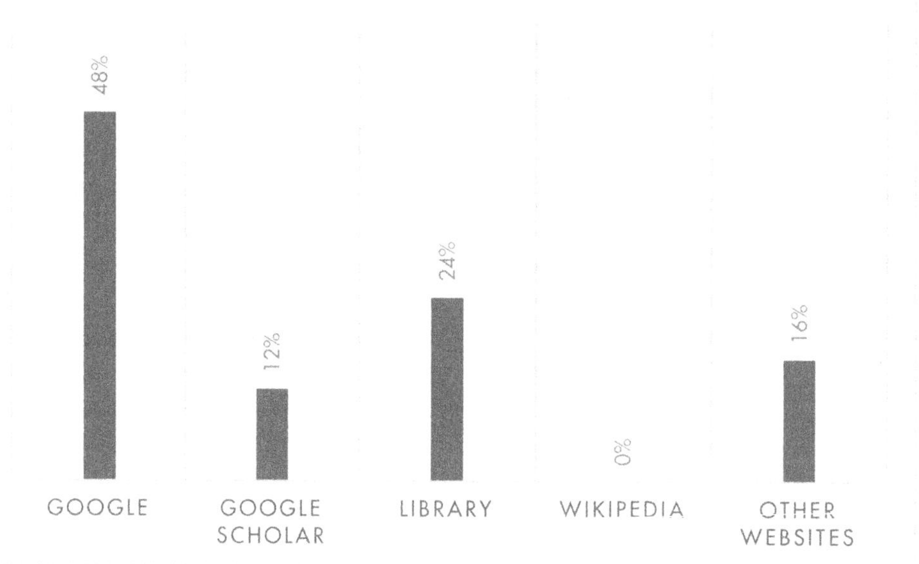

Figure 19.1 Sources of information.

needs," and they concluded that "many websites offer translation services" that multilingual students may have found easier to use because of the language barrier (p. 70). Not only does our finding support and consolidate Mina and Walker's, but it extends their finding and provides examples of those websites and help tools multilingual students utilize.

Another access problem that we identified in this study is the confusion about the technicalities of the search process. Many participants showed a good deal of confusion about locating and accessing various sources of information. Several participants, for instance, didn't know how to locate the school library website to start their search. A few participants used Google to search for the library website, whereas others started from the school home page to search for the library. When on the library website, many participants were puzzled about which tab to choose from the multiple ones available to start searching. While some participants searched the article database directly, many participants struggled between using the catalog and journal tabs and were frustrated when their keyword searches did not yield enough or any sources at all. In one particular case, a participant gave up on the library and switched to Google because his search wasn't yielding relevant results due to the fact that he was searching under the "Catalogue" instead of the "Articles and more" tab. One of the fundamental information literacy abilities expert learners should possess is to understand the organization of sources "in order to access relevant information" (ACRL, 2016, p. 9). When multilingual students know they should use their school library to find good and credible information for their writing assignments but they struggle with locating and accessing that information, instructors and librarians should intervene with explicit instruction and specially tailored materials that can facilitate students' access to sources of information.

Search Type

As Figure 19.2 displays, almost all participants in this study (90%) relied on keywords in their search for online information for their assignments in FYW classes. Being aware of Mina and Walker's (2016) study cited earlier, we didn't expect participants to use Boolean operators because only 4% of the multilingual participants in their study said they used this type of search in their responses to the LILAC survey. However, the minimal reliance on natural language query (6%) among participants in this study was quite surprising because we expected participants to use questions or natural-language phrases in their searches. One interpretation of this finding may be that most participants didn't have a specific question to guide their online search, as we noted earlier. Another interpretation may be that participants didn't trust their linguistic abilities to be able to correctly articulate natural-language phrases that they can employ in their searches, preferring simple one or two keyword searches instead. Most participants used relatively simple keywords that were very similar, if not identical, to the topics they said they were researching. Keywords included phrases such as "digital cameras," "food price," and "healthy food."

Regardless of the type of search a participant may have used, we noticed two issues. First is the spelling errors in search words. Despite the simplicity of keywords participants used in their searches, many of them struggled with the spelling of these words. Some students appeared to utilize Google's suggestions and would select the words they wanted but struggled with their spelling. When a student used another search source (e.g., school library database), search suggestions were not available, and if the student was not able to spell a keyword correctly, the search didn't yield results and the student would assume that there were no sources available on that topic. The student then would either try a new search source (e.g.,

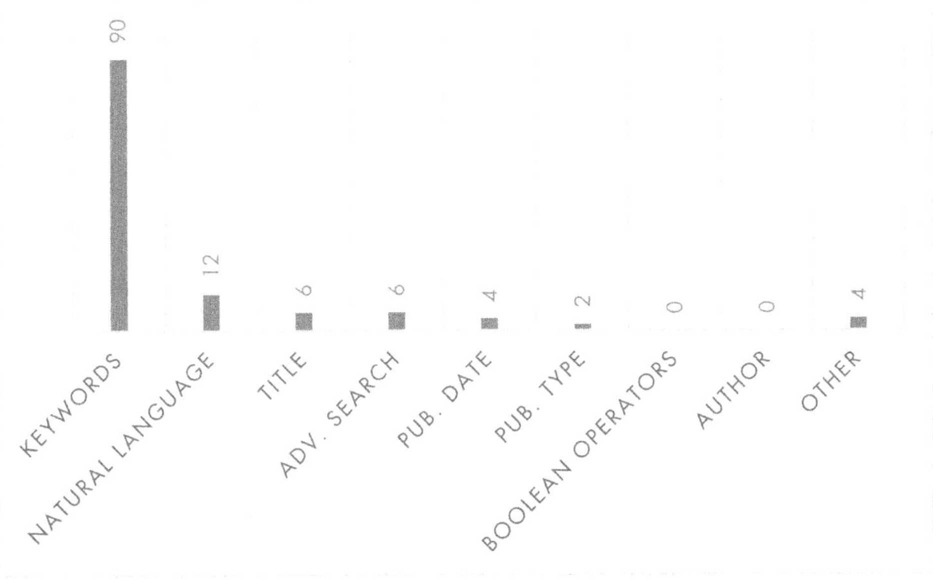

Figure 19.2 Type of search.

library database to Google) or come up with new search terms that might or might not be correct.

The second issue we noticed was literal translation. Some keywords students used appeared to be literal translations of words in the student's native language. These words and phrases did not always make much sense in English and thus would not return good or relevant results. This can be frustrating for the students because they wrongly thought there were no resources on their topic. One student, for instance, used "shopping by computer" as her keywords to search for information for her project on online shopping. Another student who was researching the negatives of online shopping used "shopping online judge" as her search phrase. Both searches yielded mostly irrelevant sources, and the two students sounded puzzled by the scarcity of sources on their popular topic.

Research as Inquiry

Another important frame for first-year multilingual writers is Research as Inquiry. Specifically, the ACRL emphasizes that it is critical for students to understand the iterative nature of research and to be able to ask "increasingly complex or new questions whose answers in turn develop additional questions or lines of inquiry in any field" (p. 7). Some major differences between experts and novices in this aspect can be observed in their abilities to (1) determine and refine the scope of investigation and (2) synthesize ideas from multiple sources. Whereas the experts demonstrate effectiveness in managing the iterative process of research by adjusting research scope and synthesizing information from multiple sources, the novices usually lack the understanding of research and the abilities to navigate the process. Segments of RAP videos coded for the corresponding questions on the LILAC coding scheme were used to describe the participants' abilities and challenges in this area (see Table 19.1).

To look at the participants' abilities to refine the scope of their research, we examined the changes between the initial scope of research determined by the students and that of the additional search(es). An overwhelming majority of the participants started with a general research purpose and broad scope, as we discussed in the previous section, which was usually taken from the instructor or the requirements of an assignment. After the 15-minute research session recorded in the RAP videos, most of these students made little progress toward refining the research scope. A few students attempted to narrow down the research scope, but all these attempts either ended with a quick answer or a complete change of direction. In other words, instead of trying to further refine research scope and/or search terms based on an evaluation of the search results, the students would choose to give up and switch to a new direction. For instance, when seeing no relevant sources from one search, a participant tried to carry out more searches on different websites (i.e., Google, *New York Times*, TED Talk videos, and YouTube), but she kept using the same search term (#21038). To understand the participants' abilities to synthesize information from multiple sources, we examined the extent to which they were able to manage the search process and to keep track of the information they found for future use. In coding the RAP recordings, we first evaluated and characterized the participant's entire search process: (1) did the participant demonstrate effective control of the process; and (2) was the participant looking for quick answers.

Among all the participants, only two (4%) demonstrated that they were in effective control of the search process, and the rest had encountered different degrees of various challenges. Language-related issues have caused some problems in choosing search engines, formulating and varying search terms, and understanding sources, but more importantly, such issues and the lack of information literacy skills seemed to have collided, resulting in ineffective search(es).

Perhaps one of the most important factors underlying the futile search process is the participants' understanding of the nature and purpose of research. As indicated by our observation of the characteristics of the participants' search process, 15 of the participants (30%) seemed to believe that research should be a straightforward path that links a question directly to an answer and that their search process was very much driven by the desire to seek quick answers.

The participants' plan for using the sources identified further confirmed this inclination: only two participants (4%) attempted to paraphrase the information identified; four (8%) indicated that they would copy and paste what they found onto their own papers; and none of the participants took the time to identify more specific sections to quote or to summarize, or to consider how relevant information from the sources can be *integrated* into their own writing. Although we do not have enough information to make valid inferences regarding how the students may actually use the information in their own writing, it is likely that their desire to seek quick answers during the research process will lead to patchwriting (Pecorari, 2008) or plagiarism concerns.

In terms of the management of the research process, 19 participants (38%) indicated some awareness of the need to keep track of their research. However, it is clear that some explicit instruction will help students develop their ability in managing the research process for the purpose of writing. Only a few students employed some strategies to help keep track of the research process: three (6%) copied and pasted the URL of the sources onto a Word document, and two (4%) used bibliography generators. The rest of the participants would either download the full text, note down the title of the article, or simply indicate that they would bookmark the webpage when doing research on their own computer. Among all 50 participants, none used or indicated that they would use reference management programs. Two alternative explanations may also account for the inadequate use of strategies in keeping track of the research process. First, the time constraint (15 minutes) in the RAP session did not allow the participants to fully demonstrate the actual process of research and writing. Second, the participants might not have access to all the record-keeping tools they need when conducting research on someone else's computer.

Authority Is Constructed and Contextual

In plotting how LILAC data align with ACRL practices through this frame's knowledge practices, we specifically focus on questions five and six of the RAP coding scheme: "Evaluating Search Results" and "Evaluating Sources." Findings from these two questions can help us better understand how students determine the credibility of sources and use their own information-seeking mental toolboxes to scan search engine result lists for sources, evaluate those sources (both multimodal and print), and determine markers of credibility. These data can also help us understand how students practice their judgment of credibility, specifically as they search for and analyze a range of sources in their research processes.

Drawing first from one of this frame's knowledge practices, that learners "use research tools to determine the credibility of sources" and that they further understand "the elements that might temper this credibility" (ACRL, 2016, p. 4), we found participants to have displayed shallow and simple behaviors that did not necessarily point to an understanding of tempering of source credibility. For example, when choosing a source from search engine results lists, participants were 47% more likely to choose a source from that list based on the source's title than they were to choose a source that might have relevance to their topic. This relationship was the closest relation from the data, which is visualized in Figure 19.3 and shows the frequency of source selection based on participants' choices from their results lists. In fact, participants were 63% more likely to choose Title as a valid source selector factor than Popularity of search results based primarily on a keyword search. This finding is significant because anecdotal research and scholarly "stories around the campfire" have long speculated that students choose sources based on list popularity. It's the "Google thinks the source is important because it's number one on the list" phenomenon. Our data show those stories may not be true, at least in the frequencies we thought. The most distant significant relationship between the factors participants use to choose sources from results lies between the data sets of Title and Brief Summary of Search Results, which we also call metadata, the information that authors code into their webpages that summarizes their content and includes relevant keywords. We found that participants were almost twice as likely to choose a source based on that source's title than its metadata. What this means to instructors and librarians is that

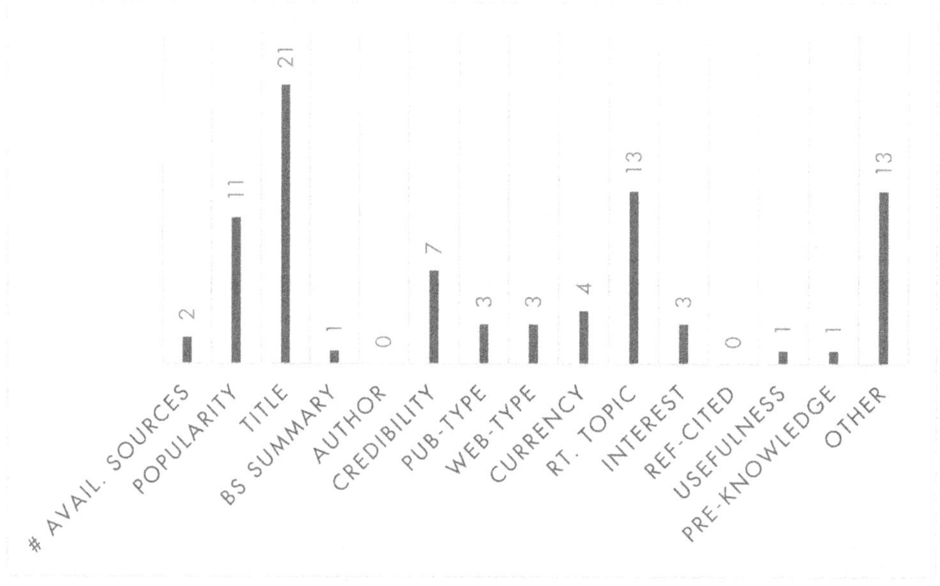

Figure 19.3 Evaluating search results.

students either are not considering metadata from websites at all, or do not consider that information to be relevant to credibility in their digital information-seeking practices.

Our findings further inform ACRL's knowledge practices in how participants evaluated sources they chose from search results. Figure 19.4 shows in what frequencies participants evaluated sources they chose. These information-seeking behaviors are depicted as findings from LILAC's coding template question six. Out of 50 participants, 38 (76%) evaluated sources they found based on the "relevance to topic" category on LILAC's coding scheme. This finding suggests that self-perceived topic relevance plays a primary role in source evaluation. Although we have no means of measuring what participants considered relevant, many of them actually articulated the word "relevance" and its synonyms as they evaluated sources during RAP sessions. We coded this finding based on verbal cues from participants, so we can conclude that participants did express their intent to evaluate a source based on self-perceived relevance.

Interestingly, the frequency data in Figure 19.4 also show that participants evaluated sources based on credibility 9% of the time during recorded RAP sessions and evaluated sources based on titles 7% percent of the time. We see a clear decrease in use of titles in terms of source evaluation versus search results evaluations, a statistical decrease of 20%, which is significant both because it marks a clear reduction as well as a clear distinction in behaviors. Curiously, this finding also points out how participants may view metadata and source abstracts (summaries) differently, with more ethos being placed on abstracts than metadata from websites. We noted only one instance in which a participant evaluated search results based on metadata, while we logged 13 instances of using abstracts to evaluate sources. This finding may point toward lack of digital literacy, that is, knowing how

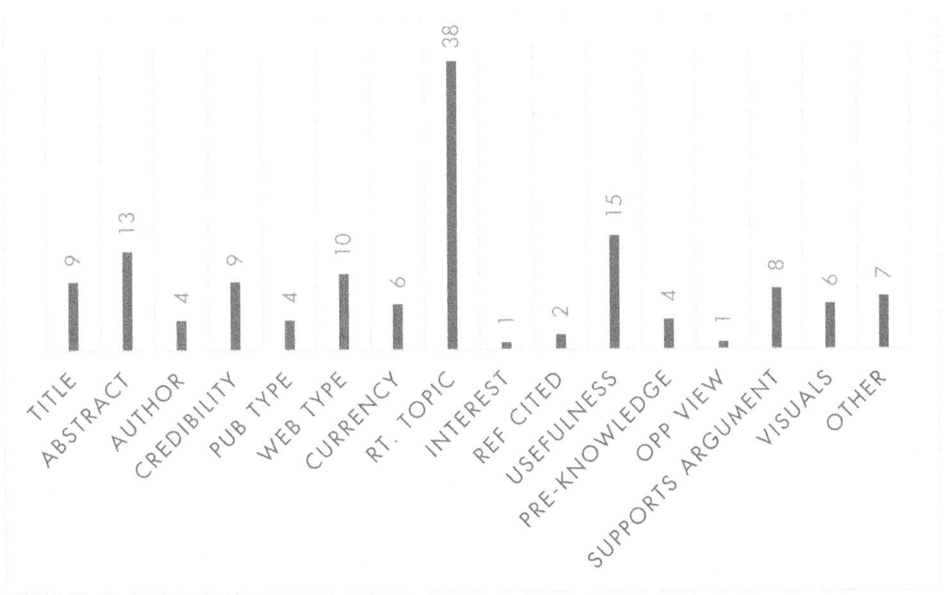

Figure 19.4 Evaluating sources.

to use metadata in digital spaces. It could also imply that participants are quickly skimming search results instead of evaluating them more deeply. These findings could also suggest that FYW students may, indeed, act on instruction they have received regarding the effective use of abstracts to evaluate a source's argument.

Further, participants differentiated between sources that supported their arguments and sources that represented opposing views by two to one. This finding may indicate a need to encourage FYW students to seek viewpoints that oppose their stated argument. Self-perceived credibility between search results and source evaluation sits at a frequency of seven and nine, respectively. This is the most consistent finding between the two questions in terms of what participants articulated in RAP sessions as "credible" search results and sources. We might be able to infer, then, that students have a notion of what credibility means as it relates to digital bibliographic research.

Drawing from another notable knowledge practice in this frame, that learners "recognize that authoritative content may be packaged formally or informally and may include sources of all media types" (ACRL, 2016, p. 4), we found that more than 8% of participants in our case study verbally asserted the credibility of visual sources. These sources included YouTube videos, Instagram images, specific image searches in Google, and TED Talk videos. For example, participant 21023 chose a YouTube video as a foundational (first) source and was even able to analyze one such video source in her own words when she had trouble doing so for textual sources. This participant, like many others, also recognized credible information on blogs, both professional and academic ones. Further, participant 21025 articulated the importance of videos not only in source selection but also as part of a more in-depth research process, saying: "TED is a really credible video and website. It is a good resource to support my claim." This participant also scrolled through search results to click on a link to videos and photos of her topic. Participant 21032 searched specifically for videos as sources for her topic, titled "Race Issues in America," from YouTube's website. Using keywords, she generated a results list on YouTube. She chose a speech from President Obama as a credible source. She also articulated that Facebook pages from nonprofit organizations were credible sources. We may view this RAP session as a lesson in how students seek multimodal sources, both informal and formal, to curate credible information for bibliographic research.

PEDAGOGICAL IMPLICATIONS

This study aimed to examine the information literacy skills of 50 international multilingual students enrolled in first-year writing courses through analyzing their recorded RAP sessions. Creating a synergy between the LILAC Project and the ACRL *Framework* (2016) has enabled us to plot these participants' information-seeking behaviors against three ACRL frames and their knowledge practices. Our findings indicate that these participants are situated on the novice end of the information literacy continuum with very few exceptions that move toward the expert end. Participants demonstrated narrow search scope and had difficulty accessing the information they needed for their writing projects. They also used limited search strategies without being able to refine or modify their searches. Further, most participants lacked strong search and source evaluation skills that resulted in their determining credibility randomly rather than systematically or consistently. These results add to the empirical evidence concerning multilingual writers' information literacy, and contribute to the ongoing discussion on integrating IL in the writing curriculum. Another interesting finding of this study is that many participants showed appreciation of multimodal digital sources while diligently seeking those sources to use in their FYW writing assignments. Not only do these findings answer the first two research questions, they also become the springboard for pedagogical implications for both librarians and instructors dealing with international multilingual students in FYW courses in U.S. universities. These implications address our third research question and offer what we hope to be points of consideration for both groups. Although we discuss these implications by the place where they are most likely to be applied, we don't mean to separate librarians from writing instructors while training this growing and important student population on information literacy skills. On the contrary, we hope these implications can be a starting point for valuable and meaningful conversations and collaborations between the two groups for more solid, situated, and reinforced skills.

In the Library

When instructing students on information literacy regarding the library itself, instructors and librarians should provide students with easy ways to access library websites. Many school libraries set the home page of computers housed in the library to the library website, and librarians start their instruction from that page without adequate information or navigational direction on how to locate and access that website from other computers. We observed that LILAC participants sometimes struggled with nonintuitive navigation on library websites. A key partner that is often overlooked in these situations is the university's information technology services. Many universities have Web designers who specialize in ease of instructional navigation. Regardless of school size, we assert the importance of collaborating across work units, including those that we might not usually work with but that can bring specialized expertise to our students' learning.

Furthermore, preparing print or digital handouts as well videos and podcasts that demonstrate the different search processes on a school library website would be helpful and reach diverse learners and digital natives, who often obtain their instructional information in multimodal ways. Examples of possible instructional resources should include catalog search, database use, journal results, and interlibrary loan services.

Information literacy classes provided to students in FYW classes should not be limited to the traditional one session per class or the "one-shot library sessions" as Artman, Frisicaro-Pawlowski, and Monge (2010) described them (p. 99). Extending the offering of these sessions and spreading them out through the course of the semester instead of offering it once before students start their research-driven papers should address students' different writing, research, and rhetorical needs pertaining to information literacy. These multiple sessions are particularly important for multilingual students whose information literacy needs and challenges can severely impede their information-seeking efforts and the desired outcomes of these efforts as seen in the findings of this study.

For more success in these multiple sessions, we'd like to encourage librarians to collaborate closely with language instructors or specialists who may better understand how language barriers may complicate the task of navigation. For many multilingual writers enrolled in first-year writing courses, both the information literacy concepts and the technical terms that are used to encode the concepts can be fairly foreign. Therefore, a one-shot library instruction session may not be effective for multilingual writers. Instead, librarians can work with language instructors to create materials and offer regular workshops to help these students map technical terms to information literacy concepts and strengthen their information literacy skills in the process.

In the Classroom

Writing instructors are encouraged to create curricula that "bridge students' prior and future experiences" (Albert & Sinkinson, 2016, p. 120). These curricula should not only include digital composition assignments that require research, but should encourage students to consider novel approaches to online searching for sources in different modes and media to complete those projects. These digital assignments should require students to "evaluate and reflect upon how scholarship is communicated in these formats" (Kalker, 2016, p. 220). Furthermore, incorporating digital composing projects is likely to introduce students to new information literacy conceptions and practices that they will increasingly need in their academic and professional futures. Our research shows the importance of implementing information literacy instruction across modalities of sources. As students search for new genres of sources, they should be "attentive to the fluidity of emerging communication formats" (Albert & Sinkinson, 2016, p. 120). Throughout their online searches examined in this study, many multilingual learners were keen on finding visual sources (videos, images, TED Talks) to support their arguments, demonstrating two significant dispositions: their recognition of the validity and authority of visuals in a research paper, and their understanding of the fluid concept of authority and credibility.

As instructors and librarians collaborate to better understand how students process information literacies in digital spaces, we must consider the results of our findings that point toward a need to instruct students on how to process credible visual sources. Instructors also need to consider how information literacy instruction meets students at the point of need, regarding the reality that they do, indeed, search for visuals as academic sources. How writing instructors approach this specific knowledge practice is especially significant, given our findings that students search for multimodal sources and consider those sources relevant inclusions in their research process and end products.

An essential part of recognizing the iterative nature of the research process is to be able to reflect upon and learn from failed research attempts. For example, students may start a research process with the goal of trying to identify differences in educational systems between two different countries. When students cannot identify self-perceived "useful" sources in these cases, instructors may find it important to help them evaluate the process challenge and assist them in making decisions on cause, such as ineffective use of search terms or library databases; other technical issues; or simply that students are trying to find answers to research questions in just one or two sources. This type of intervention may then lead to a discussion of how to refine the scope of research based on search results. Through large group, instructor-led class talks on effective evaluation of search results, complemented by small group experiential learning with revision of questions and purposes, students will learn to understand that research involves much recursiveness and that it is through such iterative processes that they advance their own research.

Our findings further demonstrate the need to train students on the use of Boolean operators as effective search strategies that are likely to help them find more relevant online search results. Learning to use Boolean operators to yield more focused search results would not only minimize the frustration we observed many participants articulate during their search processes, but such instruction would also result in more effective and efficient information-seeking behaviors. Accordingly, learning which words should go together and which words or phrases should be left out of a search is a valued and required critical thinking skill that instructors and librarians should encourage students to practice.

CONCLUSION

The above discussion and implications indicate a clear purpose for empirical information literacy research across academic fields as well as a need to continue this type of work in tandem with classroom and library instructional applications. During the course of this study and as we were engaged in data analysis and interpretation, we were able to identify some future directions for research other scholars may consider. Examining bibliographic research behavior extensively beyond the 15-minute RAP sessions is an important endeavor that will reveal more about the reality of online research strategies (or lack of) multilingual students utilize. Similarly significant is unpacking students' thinking process of online research behavior through interviews and focus groups after the research sessions and as a triangulation research method that would help us understand more about the students' conceptualization of online information-seeking behaviors. Another possible direction is to track the sources students identify in research sessions, as the ones captured in RAP, to study how students use them in their writing.

LILAC researchers continue to conduct studies at diverse institutions with participants of varying matriculations, ranging from first-year writers to graduate students, in order to gain better understanding of the information literacy skills of students at different levels of academic institutions. Given the collaborative, multi-institutional nature of the LILAC Project, we invite instructors and librarians to network with our group. Check out LILAC projects, presentations, publications, and collaboration opportunities on our website: http://lilac-group.blogspot.com/, or by following us on Twitter: @LILACProject.

REFERENCES

Albert, M., & Sinkinson, C. (2016). Composing information literacy through pedagogical partnerships. In R. McClure & J. P. Purdy (Eds.), *The future scholar: Researching and teaching frameworks for writing and information literacy* (pp. 111–129). Medford, NJ: Information Today.

Artman, M., Frisicaro-Pawlowski, E., & Monge, R. (2010). Not just one shot: Extending the dialogues about information literacy in composition classes. *Composition Studies/Freshman English News, 38*(2), 93–110.

Association of College and Research Libraries. (2016). *Framework for information literacy for higher education.* Retrieved from http://www.ala.org/acrl/standards/ilframework

Behrens, S. J. (1994). A conceptual analysis and historical overview of information literacy. *College and Research Libraries, 55*(4), 309–322.

Bohannon, J. (2015). Not a stitch out of place: Assessing students' attitudes towards multimodal composition. *Bellaterra Journal of Teaching & Learning Language & Literature, 8*(2), 33–47.

Brown, C., Murphy, T. J., & Nanny, M. (2003). Turning techno-savvy into info-savvy: Authentically integrating information literacy into the college curriculum. *Journal of Academic Librarianship, 29*(6), 386–398.

Bruce, C. S. (1997). The relational approach: A new model for information literacy. *New Review of Information and Library Research, 3*, 1–22.

CWPA, NCTE, & NWP. (2011). *Framework for success in postsecondary writing.* Retrieved from http://www.ncte.org/positions/statements/collwritingframework

Doyle, C. S. (1994). *Information literacy in an information society: A concept for the information age.* Syracuse, NY: ERIC Clearinghouse. ED 372763.

Huston, M. M. (1999). Towards information literacy: Innovative perspective for the 90s. *Library Trends, 39*(3), 187–362.

Jordan, J., & Kedrowicz, A. (2011). Attitudes about graduate L2 writing in engineering: Possibilities for more integrated Instruction. *Across the Disciplines, 8*(4). Retrieved November 20, 2016, from http://wac.colostate.edu/atd/ell/jordan-kedrowicz.cfm

Kalker, F. (2016). Digital/critical: Reimagining digital information literacy assignments around the ACRL framework. In R. McClure & J. P. Purdy (Eds.), *The future scholar: Researching and teaching the frameworks for writing and information literacy* (pp. 205–222). Medford, NJ: Information Today.

Kress, G. (2003). *Literacy in the new media age.* New York: Routledge.

Leu, D. (2000). Literacy and technology: Deictic consequences for literacy education in an information age. In R. Barr, M. Kamil, P. Mosenthal, & D. Pearson (Eds.), *Handbook of reading research* (pp. 743–770). New York: Routledge.

Leu, D. J., Kinzer, C. K., Coiro, J. L., & Cammack, D. W. (2004). Toward a theory of new literacies emerging from the Internet and other information and communication technologies. In R. B. Ruddell & N. Unrau (Eds.), *Theoretical models and processes of reading.* Newark, DE: International Reading Association.

Markauskaite, L. (2006). Towards an integrated analytical framework of information and communications technology literacy: From intended to implemented and achieved dimensions. *Information Research, 11*(3).

McDowell, L. (2002). Electronic information resources in undergraduate education: An exploratory study of opportunities for student learning and independence. *British Journal of Educational Technology, 33*(3), 255–266.

Mina, L. W., & Walker, J. R. (2016). International students as future scholars: Information literacy skills, self-assessment, and needs. In R. McClure & J. P. Purdy (Eds.), *The future scholar: Researching and teaching the frameworks for writing and information literacy* (pp. 63–88). Medford, NJ: Information Today.

Pecorari, D. (2008). *Academic writing and plagiarism: A linguistic analysis.* New York: Continuum.

Pinto, M., Antonio Cordón, J., & Gómez Díaz, R. (2010). Thirty years of information literacy

(1977–2007): A terminological, conceptual and statistical analysis. *Journal of Librarianship and Information Science, 42*(1), 3–19.

Purdy, J. P. (2010). The changing space of research: Web 2.0 and the integration of research and writing environments. *Computers and Composition, 27*(1), 48–58.

Spievak, E. R., & Hayes-Bohanan, P. (2013). Just enough of a good thing: Indications of long-term efficacy in one-shot library instruction. *Journal of Academic Librarianship, 39*, 488–499.

Valmont, W. J. (2003). *Technology for literacy teaching and learning.* Boston: Houghton Mifflin.

Wang, R. (2016). Assessment for one-shot library instruction: A conceptual approach. *Libraries and the Academy, 16*(3), 619–648.

Zhao, J. C., & Mawhinney, T. (2015). Comparison of native Chinese-speaking and native English-speaking engineering students' information literacy challenges. *Journal of Academic Librarianship, 41*, 712–724.

CHAPTER 20

YOU GOT RESEARCH IN MY WRITING CLASS

Embedding Information Literacy in a First-Year Composition Course

Elizabeth Brewer
Martha Kruy
Briana McGuckin
Susan Slaga-Metivier

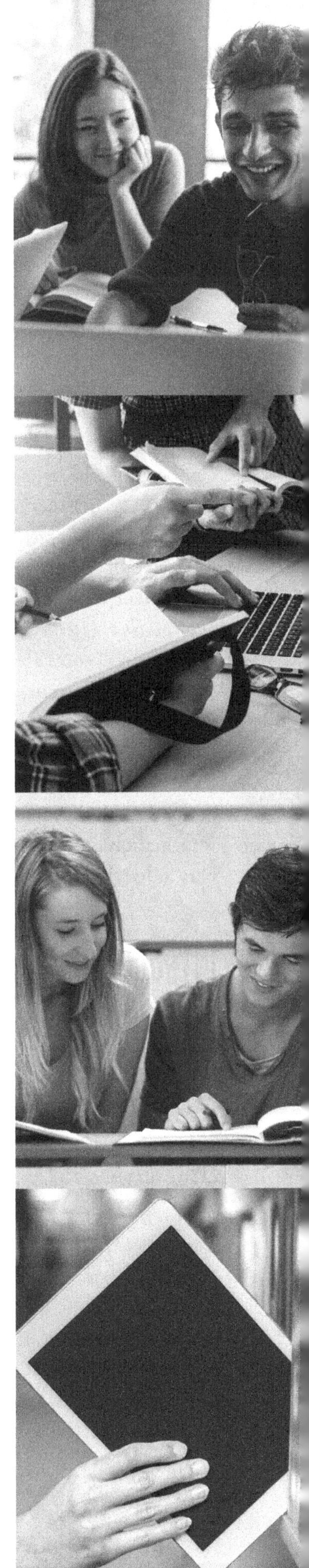

This chapter reflects upon a faculty-librarian partnership, guided by similarities between the ACRL *Framework for Information Literacy* (2015) and the WPA *Framework for Success in Postsecondary Writing* (2011), designed to teach information literacy skills alongside writing skills at a four-year university. It details a classroom-based embedded librarian model created to encourage knowledge transfer and support student research in first-year composition classes, as an alternative to one-shot library instruction. This profile of our program design is meant as a model for others interested in building a similar collaboration. Assessment data, collected via the AAC&U *Information Literacy VALUE Rubric* (2013) and surveys, compares information literacy learning in the embedded program to information literacy learning from a single session with a librarian. Assessment data shows that students do benefit from the embedded program, though they tend to self-report stronger information literacy skills than faculty members judge them to possess.

INTRODUCTION

Information Literacy Necessitates Embedded Librarianship

Librarians have many concerns about the *Framework for Information Literacy*, namely whether it's teachable, assessable, or even if it should have fully replaced the *Information Literacy Competency Standards for Higher Education*. Most of the controversy has to do with the introduction of threshold concepts, the "light bulb" moments we have about information and research that alter our searching, evaluating, and citing practices (e.g., Research as Inquiry). Such moments are difficult to teach and measure, even over several classes. But these threshold concepts articulate the complex challenges with which librarians grapple: namely, that information literacy is the possession of many discrete skills and attitudes, and cannot be taught, wholesale, during a single-session (or "one-shot") library class.

Information literacy, as a central value in academic life, is typically taught through the study of another content area. In order for it to make sense, there must be some common information about which to become literate; otherwise, the tools of information literacy have no application. A course on information literacy alone will not necessarily result in more savvy and responsible student research. One of the most common disciplines to partner with librarians teaching information literacy is composition studies; as students learn writing processes and skills, research strategies can be taught as part of a responsible and responsive writing process.

A perusal of commonly assigned textbooks in first-year writing classes (*The Allyn and Bacon Guide to Writing* [Ramage, Bean, & Johnson, 2009], *Everything's an Argument* [Lunsford, Ruskiewicz, & Walters, 2016], *The Norton Field Guide to Writing* [Bullock, 2013], *The St. Martin's Guide to Writing* [Axelrod & Cooper, 1991], *They Say/I Say* [Graff, Birkenstein, & Durst, 2009], *The Prentice Hall Guide for College Writers* [Reid, 2011]) shows significant chunks of text provide guidance on research. All have at least one chapter devoted to some aspect of research, whether on finding sources, evaluating sources, integrating sources into an argument, avoiding plagiarism, or citation. Many have more than one such chapter, and the *Norton Field Guide* has nine.

Embedded librarianship, which we used in the composition courses we detail in this chapter, functions as a middle ground through which students can be introduced to the *Framework*. The name is borrowed from embedded journalism, in which "journalists become a part of [a] military unit, providing a perspective, 'a slice of the war' from their vantage point" (Schulte, 2012). In the case of information literacy, an embedded librarian observes to understand the material being covered in a classroom, as well as the concerns of the professor and the students. The embedded librarian can integrate information literacy skills and threshold concepts, as appropriate, to shed new light on the material being covered.

A Tale of Two Frameworks

In order for an embedded program to be of real help, instead of intrusive or disruptive, the goals of the librarian teaching information literacy should match those objectives outlined for the course. Luckily, the *Framework for Information Literacy* and the Council of Writing Program Administrators' (WPA) *Framework for Success in Postsecondary Writing* have a lot in common. The *Framework for Information Literacy* challenges us to teach Research as Inquiry, that Authority Is Constructed and Contextual, and to frame Searching as Strategic Exploration (Association of College and Research Libraries Board, 2015). The WPA *Framework* urges the development of "critical thinking through writing, reading, and research," challenging students to generate questions, conduct research, and evaluate sources. Source evaluation shows up again in the WPA *Framework* under "Develop rhetorical knowledge," drawing attention to the ideas of audience, purpose, and context—information literacy concerns surrounding the research process (Council of Writing Program Administrators, 2011). As evidenced from the national disciplinary conversations about composition and about information literacy, research has a strong presence in composition courses, which makes them a natural environment in which to cover information literacy concepts.

Of course, the *Framework for Information Literacy* aims higher than to simply impart skills for library use within composition. It "envisions information literacy as extending the arc of learning throughout students' academic careers and as converging with other academic and social learning goals" (Association of College and Research Libraries Board, 2015). Under the threshold concept Information Creation as a Process, one of the Knowledge Practices is to "transfer knowledge of capabilities and constraints to new types of information products." Instead of modeling simple, linear behaviors for students to emulate in the library, this model encourages librarians to focus their students on metacognition and metaliteracy, to examine how they get information in their lives, how they evaluate its credibility, and how it may be of use to them. And metacognition is a shared focus in composition studies. Many teacher-scholars (Gorzelsky, Driscoll, Pazcek, Hayes, & Jones, 2016; Smit, 2004; Yancey, Robertson, & Taczak, 2014) similarly emphasize that students need to articulate their choices and processes if they hope to generalize their knowledge to other tasks and situations. Strengthening these understandings is useful in their academic, political, and personal lives.

Assessing Information Literacy: A New Challenge

The history of measuring information literacy learning in higher education is brief. The original *Information Literacy Competency Standards for Higher Education* (approved and introduced by the ACRL in 2000, and rescinded in 2016) were presented as a set of skills that were more easily measured. For example, students' abilities to properly cite sources in a given writing style has been achieved to some extent with standardized tests, such as Kent State's Tools for Real-time Assessment of Information Literacy Skills (TRAILS) open-access test (http://trails-9.org/index.php?page=home) and the Project SAILS (https://www.projectsails.org/) proprietary model test. Both standardized tests measure student information literacy levels pre- and postinstruction for benchmark and conclusive data sets. However, Carrick Enterprises has now assumed control of these information literacy tests and will soon launch the Threshold Achievement Test for Information Literacy (TATIL), a standardized test to measure students' comprehension and attainment of the Information Literacy Threshold Concepts (Radcliff, Cunningham, Hannon, Harmes, & Wiggins, 2018).

While these tests do provide methods for efficiently capturing data on student research, they also add to the burden of cost (to either the school or the students) as well as that of time management on all stakeholders' parts: the librarian who must encapsulate as much content as possible in an hour; the instructor, who must carve out time for research instruction; as well as the students, who tend to suffer from test fatigue. In Janine Lockhart's study of online information literacy skills assessment instruments (2014), standardized tests using multiple-choice questions have been critiqued by Megan Oakleaf as not testing "higher-level thinking skills" and lacking "the ability to assess students' authenticity" in the application of information literacy skills (p. 37). It is this specific issue of assessing authentic learning pertaining to the abstract concepts of information literacy threshold concepts that informed our decision to assess student writing from our embedded librarian program using the AAC&U's *Information Literacy VALUE Rubric*. The *VALUE Rubric* requires scorers to assess discrete skills, such as citation, but importantly locates these skills within the context of the student's entire paper (Association of American Colleges and Universities, 2013). In other words, it is a more contextual measure of information literacy applied in a paper than are the skills-based tests like TRAILS and SAILS.

Assessing students' information literacy, much less their ability to generalize their knowledge about research, is difficult and complex. As intimidating as the *Framework for Information Literacy* has been to understand and apply in the classroom, assessing a curriculum based on threshold concepts has proven to be even more daunting. First, faculty members often struggle with the burden of assessing programmatic curricula due to time constraints and perhaps some anxiety about the assessment of their curricula (and therefore their instructional capabilities). Second, the process of quantifying students' understanding of the more difficult abstract concepts, such as synthesizing the information from sources to support their thesis or accessing needed information, has yet to be fully developed. Two of the most significant barriers in measuring the effectiveness of any information literacy curriculum are the process-oriented nature and abstract quality of threshold concepts. Given that only one threshold concept could be taught or grasped within a one-hour period, capturing the full spectrum of information literacy learning outcomes is particularly challenging.

In response to these challenges, we developed an embedded librarian model that afforded us the opportunity to teach multiple threshold concepts over the course of three to five classes. Our design is by no means perfect; we expect it to evolve with our evaluations of our experiences and the assessment data. We share our structure and experience in this chapter to inspire similar partnerships and invite improvements of our program.

DESIGNING AN EMBEDDED LIBRARIAN PROGRAM IN FIRST-YEAR WRITING CLASSES

At our institution, a regional, comprehensive public university, the instruction librarians and the director of composition designed a new voluntary program for first-year composition instructors to include embedded librarians in their classes. Each librarian met with her respective composition instructor(s) to develop a plan of action for embedding information literacy into the composition curriculum. These meetings included discussion of student needs, syllabi, and possible research assignments, and librarians and instructors met several times and discussed the students' needs, the syllabus, assignments, and class schedules.

Rather than have librarians embedded throughout the entire semester, we concentrated librarian support on research assignments, scaffolding lessons as steps in the research process and incorporating relevant threshold concepts. These steps included shorter assignments on discrete skills, such as searching for scholarly journal articles and evaluating sources for annotated bibliographies. For evaluation we used the CRAAP test (Meriam Library, 2010) and for determining how to use information we incorporated BEAM (Bizup, 2008). The 3–5 embedded librarian class sessions included active learning assignments in class, as well as practical homework assignments.

The focus of the embedded librarian support differed slightly for each instructor. While all classes focused on the information literacy skills listed below, each class benefited from its own tailored lessons. In short, we designed flexibility into our embedded librarian program to respond to unique student needs and instructor priorities. For example, depending on the instructor, some students had flexibility in choosing research topics, and some did not. One class was limited to topics dealing with immigration in the United States.

We began by having the students search for background information on their topics using online encyclopedia databases or newspaper databases so they could become more familiar with their topics. After that, we moved on to performing effective search strategies using many of the library's online resources, since many underclassmen are not familiar with databases and think they function similarly to search engines. Other instruction sessions included evaluating and learning the difference between primary and secondary sources, and between popular and scholarly sources; students reviewed examples of different sources and evaluated them in large-group discussions. We also provided specific instruction in evaluating websites. Finally, we taught students about citing sources using MLA style, focusing on distinguishing between periodical and book citations, and becoming familiar enough with correct MLA citations so that they did not have to rely on citation generators.

In one first-year writing section that allowed students to choose their own topics for their research papers, the embedded librarian designed a lesson on brainstorming research topics. She showed the students an advertisement for a hair product and used that to inspire topic ideas, such as portrayal of women in fashion advertisements; feminism in advertising; women and body image and self-esteem. Using this advertisement as a shared example for the class, students searched for articles in the databases while the embedded librarian encouraged them to notice the database subject terms and differences between popular and scholarly sources. It is important for students to not only learn the skills and concepts in these sessions, but to be able to apply them to their final papers and hopefully to other classes with similar assignments. (For an example of one librarian's embedded lessons' progression, see the Appendix.)

Because of our emphasis on building information-literate students, not just teaching discrete skills, we used a shared vocabulary of terms meaningful to both composition and information literacy. The terminology that was emphasized differed for each librarian-instructor partnership. For example, one of the composition instructors and her embedded librarian introduced students to the term *exigency.* This term was used in lessons to discuss the reasons authors have for writing and their resulting biases. When choosing a source for their research, students had to evaluate it, including the author's exigency for writing, as well as their own. Finally, in a reflection following their research paper, students were asked to write about the concept of exigency and its role in their writing. Our goal in incorporating shared terminology was to reinforce threshold concepts in both fields and encourage metacognition about one's research and writing process.

OUR ASSESSMENT DESIGN

Our assessment of information literacy learning as a result of the embedded librarian program was modeled on both the Multi-State Collaborative to Advance Learning Outcomes Assessment (MSC) program (http://www.sheeo.org/projects/) and best practices for composition assessment. The process used in this collaborative model collects data from direct measures (scoring of student essays from composition classes), and we added an indirect measure of student information literacy learning (student surveys). The direct assessment of student writing measurably demonstrates the degree to which students transfer learned concepts of information literacy to their academic research and writing. The measurement of student learning outcomes through these methods provides better contextual evidence of information literacy than standardized tests have offered.

All student research papers were deidentified for blind assessment by a panel of first-year composition instructors and embedded librarians. We read and scored a total of 45 student papers: five randomly selected student papers each from six embedded classes, and three nonembedded classes as a control group, from two different semesters. We used the AAC&U *Information Literacy VALUE Rubric* (Association of American Colleges and Universities, 2013), but we did not score for students' ability to "Access Needed Information" because this criterion was not clearly demonstrated within the students' papers. This rubric focused our scores on the following aspects of a student's paper: (1) the ability to determine the extent of information needed by defining the scope of the research question/thesis/key concepts and using types of sources that relate to the paper's focus appropriately;

(2) the ability to evaluate information and its sources critically by using a variety of relevant sources with an awareness of audience and the bias/point of view of the source; (3) the ability to use information effectively and to accomplish a specific purpose; and (4) the ability to access and use information ethically and legally through proper citation and attribution.

In addition to directly assessing the information literacy skills demonstrated in student writing from different first-year writing courses, we also used a survey to ask students for self-reported growth and metacognitive reflection on their learning. This survey was only given to students in classes with embedded librarian support, so we do not yet have comparative data from nonembedded classes. Our surveys utilized a Likert scale with scores from 1 to 5 for each question, and asked students to rate their ability to complete a variety of information literacy activities as a result of their first-year writing course with embedded librarian support. The data from this preinstruction exercise will be assessed in the semester following our writing of this chapter and will be used to inform our instructors' lesson plans and research assignments.

We have not yet reached a conclusion as to how much overlap of curricular language, theoretical applications, and assessment methods occurs between introductory college writing and information literacy practices. Both librarians and composition faculty were encouraged by the similarities we discovered across the disciplines and intrigued by the differences; the differences suggest that there is still more to learn from one another, and the similarities confirm a shared academic goal that makes this partnership—and possible collaborations with other academic departments—promising.

FINDINGS: DIRECT AND INDIRECT MEASURES OF STUDENTS' INFORMATION LITERACY

Direct Assessment: Student Research Papers

The scores in all four categories of the AAC&U *Information Literacy VALUE Rubric* were slightly higher, approximately .3, for students in classes with embedded librarian support (see Table 20.1). Students in both embedded and nonembedded composition classes scored the highest in their ability to determine the extent of information needed, and they scored the lowest in the category of accessing and using information ethically and legally. Because ethically managing sources requires both a conceptual understanding of academic values and a mastery of distinct skills (summarizing, paraphrasing, quoting, choosing signal phrases, adhering to citation styles, etc.), this collection of skills provided particularly complex and challenging for students—and the rubrics sets the bar high for excellence in this category. As Table 20.1 shows, our first-year students are near the 2-range across categories of the AAC&U *Information Literacy VALUE Rubric*, which provides a sense of how much development is needed by the time they graduate. (When students graduate, they should be demonstrating information literacy in their writing at the 4-level of the rubric.)

Indirect Assessment: Student Surveys

Table 20.2 shows the distinct skills that students were asked to self-assess and the average scores they reported on the surveys. The survey asked students to rate their ability in

TABLE 20.1 *Aggregate Scores of Information Literacy in Student Writing Using the AAC&U Information Literacy VALUE Rubric*

	Determine the Extent of Information Needed	Evaluate Information and Its Sources Critically	Use Information Effectively to Accomplish a Specific Purpose	Access and Use Information Ethically and Legally	Average Score
Embedded Librarian Classes	2.43	2.08	2.12	1.86	2.11
Nonembedded Librarian Classes	2.13	1.83	2.07	1.43	1.80

TABLE 20.2 *Aggregate Scores for Student Self-Reported Information Literacy Abilities*

As a result of your composition class with embedded librarian support, how well are you able to do the following, on a scale of 1–5?	Average Score
Use the library to search for a range of popular and scholarly sources?	4.03
Understand the difference between popular and scholarly sources as we discussed them in class?	4.51
Understand the difference between databases, journals, and articles?	4.14
Evaluate the credibility of a source?	4.16
Evaluate the usefulness of a source?	4.26
Put multiple sources and your own perspective "into conversation" in your writing?	4.04
Use MLA style for in-text citations?	4.17
Create a Works Cited page using MLA style?	4.46
Use online citation tools (RefWorks, EasyBib, etc.) correctly?	4.34
Find books using the library's classification system?	3.20
Find materials in the library as a result of the tour?	3.18
Overall, how useful were the classes held in the library for your work on your research paper?	3.92
How useful do you believe the classes held in the library will be for your future classes?	3.89
Has your confidence increased for seeking out help with future research projects?	3.82

each discrete skill/concept on a 5-point Likert scale, 5 being the highest score, as a result of their composition course with embedded librarian support.

The first five survey questions prompt students to reflect on their skills related to searching for and evaluating different types of sources. Our curriculum emphasizes the difference between popular and scholarly sources, and we encourage students to use a wide range of sources responsibly and for different purposes. Students noted that they understood the difference between types of sources more than they were able to utilize search strategies, distinguish between databases/journal/articles, or evaluate the credibility and usefulness of a source.

The next six survey questions ask about students' ability to synthesize sources within their writing, document their sources, and make use of the library to locate sources. Students highly rated their ability to document sources and use tools to do so. They rate their ability to use the library lower than other categories, but we believe this is due to a few factors: (1) the classification system was not emphasized throughout the sessions as other skills were; (2) students used online sources more than print sources; (3) not all classes had a tour of the library, so some should have responded N/A, but instead rated this lower, skewing the scores. In any case, we do believe that these basic library use skills are weak for students, at least relative to their other information literacy skills.

The final three questions ask for students' responses on their general learning and impressions of the library support in first-year writing. Because we are interested in preparing students to be information literate across courses and we know they need to transfer their knowledge from first-year writing to other contexts, we asked how useful students believe their learning would be for the future. The scores were just under 4, indicating that students believe, though not as strongly as they might, that the library support will help them in their future endeavors as students.

Discussion

Though the AAC&U rubric cannot be compared apples-to-apples to the Likert survey (the former uses a scale of 0–4, while the latter uses 1–5, and they ask for slightly different skills), it appears that students have a higher estimation of their information literacy skills than the faculty scorers do. This may indicate that students simply don't know what they don't know, but it also may be their attempt to represent their significant learning over the course of the semester.

In our direct assessment of student writing we scored students' *cognition*, or the thinking involved in completing a task. We can judge this by the task itself. However, in this indirect assessment of students' self-reported skills, we also attempted to access their *metacognition*, or their reflection on what they know and the efficacy/outcomes of their choices. These definitions come from Gwen Gorzelsky and her co-authors who are undertaking a longitudinal study, the Writing Transfer Project, on students' ability to transfer knowledge about writing. One of the key points that Gorzelsky and her team make, as do others in composition studies who are interested in knowledge transfer, is that students are more likely to transfer skills when they can reflect on them and articulate them. We feel that this survey is a good start for getting students to articulate what they can do and what they know.

CONCLUSION

We see two concrete outcomes from this project. First, it helps our composition faculty to see where our students are and to view their information literacy learning as a journey that spans their entire lives. When we know that students are ending just above a 2 (the lower milestone level of the AAC&U rubric), we know that our goals for student achievement should be around that level instead of at the 4-level. If we see information literacy as a spectrum and consider students within zones of proximal development (Vygotsky, 1978), then we can present discrete research skills as not correct or incorrect, but as moving toward being a more responsible information user and creator.

Second, we learned that our students' weakest area in their writing was "Accessing and Using Information Ethically and Legally," and we learned that we can devote more in-class support to this. Most of our instruction on these skills comes early in the writing process, and it gets revisited as an issue of correct adherence to conventions. Once students have the other parts of their papers constructed, we should dedicate more class time to discuss the choices writers make about how they use information.

As our embedded librarian in composition program continues, we strive to improve our assessment design and support for composition instructors. One of our most recent developments is the addition of a pretest and posttest of students' information literacy skills, so that we can better gauge student development over the course of a semester. We have also used our assessment data as a feedback loop to inform lesson plans for embedded librarian composition classes, as well as a LibGuide that contains information on particularly challenging aspects of information literacy, such as "Accessing and Using Information Ethically and Legally."

It is our hope that this chapter inspires other partnerships like this one, especially those that use our experience to improve upon our model. We recommend that programs building a similar model of embedded librarians in composition courses consider the following: collecting open-ended survey responses from students about their learning; administering pretests and posttests, as well as survey responses, from one-shot classes and embedded librarian classes; and, if possible, conducting a longitudinal study of student writing and information literacy skills to better measure students' knowledge transfer across classes.

APPENDIX. Example: Embedded Librarian Lessons Progression Over Three Composition Class Periods

1. The Research Process/Examining Source Types

Exercise 1: Rethinking the Research Process

On board: *Some say happiness is about attitude; others say that happiness depends upon outside circumstances. Write a short paper on happiness and choice, using outside sources to support your argument.*

"What would you have to do first, next, last?" Common response: (1) pick a side, (2) research, (3) write.

Point out that, following directions in this order, conclusion is drawn at step 1, and step 2 (the research) has no purpose. Introduce research as inquiry, instead, and flip steps 1 and 2.

Exercise 2: Examining Source Types

Provide a popular article to half the class, scholarly article to the other half, on the same topic; students read, pay special attention to: (1) what the article is about, (2) who the intended audience is, and (3) why this article was written (purpose).

On board, chart differences. Introduce evaluation (CRAAP method). Distinguish between "popular" and "scholarly" sources.

2. Library Resources/Searching and Finding

After library tour: what is a database? What is the difference between catalog and electronic databases?

Come up with keywords around a topic; run a search; use Boolean operators; access full-text and citation information. Explain abstracts, interlibrary loan. Give students independent search time.

3. #subjectterms, Citations as Maps

Ask about hashtags—what happens if you click? misspell? They are unforgiving, but helpful. Relate to subject terms.

Demo a database search; pull subject terms from records. Check references for more related sources. Give resources for checking citations, and more independent search time.

REFERENCES

Association of American Colleges and Universities. (2013). *Information literacy VALUE rubric.* Retrieved from www.aacu.org/value/rubrics/information-literacy

Association of College and Research Libraries Board. (2015). *Framework for information literacy for higher education.* Retrieved from www.ala.org/acrl/standards/ilframework

Axelrod, R. B., & Cooper, C. R. (1991). *St. Martin's guide to writing* (3rd ed.). New York, NY: St. Martin's Press.

Bizup, J. (2008). BEAM: A rhetorical vocabulary for teaching research-based writing. *Rhetoric Review, 27*(1), 72–86.

Bullock, R. H. (2013). *Norton Field Guide to writing* (3rd ed.). New York, NY: W. W. Norton.

Council of Writing Program Administrators, et al. (2011). *Framework for success in postsecondary writing.* Retrieved from wpacouncil.org/framework

Gorzelsky, G., Driscoll, D. L., Pazcek, J., Hayes, C., & Jones, E. (2016). Cultivating constructive metacognition: A new taxonomy for writing studies. In C. Anson & J. Moore (Eds.), *Critical transitions: Writing and the question of transfer* (pp. 217–249). Fort Collins, CO: WAC Clearinghouse.

Graff, G., Birkenstein, C., & Durst, R. K. (2009). *"They say/I say": The moves that matter in academic writing.* New York, NY: W. W. Norton.

Lockhart, J. (2014). Using item analysis to evaluate the validity and reliability of an existing online information literacy skills assessment instrument. *South African Journal of Libraries & Information Science, 80*(2), 36–45. https://doi.org/10.7553/80-2-1515

Lunsford, A. A., Ruskiewicz, J. J., & Walters, K. (2016). *Everything's an argument* (7th ed.). Boston, MA: Bedford.

Meriam Library (2010). Evaluating information—Applying the CRAAP Test. Retrieved from http://www.csuchico.edu/lins/handouts/eval_websites.pdf

Radcliff, C., Cunningham, A., Hannon, R. H., Harmes, C., & Wiggins, R. (2018). The test. *Threshold Achievement.* Retrieved from https://thresholdachievement.com/the-test

Ramage, J. D. , Bean, J. C., & Johnson J. (2009). *Allyn and Bacon guide to writing* (5th ed.). New York, NY: Pearson Longman.

Reid, S. (2011). *Prentice Hall guide for college writers* (9th ed.). Boston, MA: Prentice Hall.

Schulte, S. (2012). Embedded academic librarianship: A review of the literature. *Evidence-Based Library and Information Practice, 7*(4), 122–138. Retrieved from ejournals.library.ualberta.ca/index.php/EBLIP/article/view/17466

Smit, D. (2004). *The end of Composition Studies.* Carbondale, IL: Southern Illinois University Press.

Vygotsky, L. (1978). Interaction between learning and development. From *Mind and Society* (pp. 79–91). Cambridge, MA: Harvard University Press.

Yancey, K. B., Robertson, L., & Taczak, K. (2014). Writing across contexts: Transfer, composition, and sites of writing. Logan, UT: Utah University Press.

CHAPTER 21

TEACHING FOR TRANSFER?

Nonexperts Teaching Linked Information Literacy and Writing Classes

Marcia Rapchak
Jerry Stinnett

Both writing studies (WS) and information literacy (IL) have the pedagogical objective of developing in students ways of thinking, researching, and writing that can transfer to other contexts. In recent years, scholars in both fields have increasingly embraced teaching the threshold concepts of their respective disciplines as a means of helping students at once recognize the situated, rhetorical character of research and writing practices but also identify those ideas, processes, and perspectives that can transfer across a range of research and writing contexts. In WS, this has taken the form of helping students study and analyze writing as compositionists do. Since "the study of writing involves consistent analysis of relationships between contexts, purposes, audiences, genres, and conventions," when students "learn to conduct that analysis, they are both participating in the epistemological practices of the discipline and [are] likely . . . to be more adaptable writers" (Adler-Kassner, Majewski, & Koshnick, 2012, para. 3). IL has expressed this pedagogical emphasis in the Association of College and Research Libraries' (ACRL, 2015) recent adoption of the *Framework for Information Literacy for Higher Education* with its six frames that position information literacy as "an overarching set of abilities in which students are consumers and creators of information who can participate successfully in collaborative spaces" (para. 3).

The close conceptual and institutional relationship shared by IL and WS has initiated scholarship identifying connections between the two and theorizing how these can be applied in college and university courses on research and writing (Maid & D'Angelo, 2016; McCracken & Johnson, 2015; Purdy & McClure, 2016). While such work is necessary, introductory research and writing courses in higher education face constraints that rarely allow the implementation of theoretical or pedagogical ideals. Such courses are often taught by nonexperts, instructors who may possess terminal degrees in historically related fields but have little formal training in the threshold concepts of either IL or WS. Thus, while it is important to identify and spell out the connections between the threshold concepts of IL and WS, such work must be done with an eye for who will implement any resulting pedagogical insights and how to prepare those instructors to do so. What threshold concepts of IL and WS do nonexpert instructors (typically trained in literary studies) teach when they teach introductory research and/or writing courses? What training, support, and professional development will nonexperts need to make use of theoretical developments in their pedagogy?

This chapter will examine whether linking an IL and WS course together, taught by a nonexpert teacher, allows instructors to teach for transfer, or whether the threshold concepts of WS and IL prove to be more elusive. Conducting an analysis of two focus group sessions with nonexpert instructors who taught the same groups of students in a three-credit first-year writing course and a one-credit introductory information literacy course, this study identifies what threshold concepts of IL and WS such instructors are likely to teach and to what extent. Based on our findings, we make recommendations for how to train nonexpert writing instructors to better teach and link the threshold concepts of WS and IL in their courses.

DESCRIBING THE CONTEXT; FORMING THE FOCUS GROUPS

We conducted our focus group sessions at an R2, private, mid-Atlantic Catholic university serving 9,000–10,000 students. As part of a broader CORE curriculum at the university, a number of first-year classes are grouped into learning communities in which the same group of first-year students take three classes grouped under a predetermined concept that serves as the theme of the community. Learning communities always include a first-semester composition course. The first-year writing course attached to each community is the first course in the first-year writing course sequence, a course focused on rhetorical analysis and argumentative writing. Students in the College of Liberal Arts are all enrolled in a learning community unless they are in the Honors College.

While tenure-stream faculty, part-time faculty, and graduate student teachers do teach learning community writing courses, instructors for learning community writing courses are typically drawn from full-time teaching faculty who are employed on contract for a set number of years, but who are not eligible for tenure. Full-time teaching faculty typically teach two sections of first-year writing, capped at 15 students each, in a learning community. As part of a pilot program beginning in the fall of 2016, full-time teaching faculty (and one experienced part-time instructor) were assigned to teach the required, one-credit information literacy course made up of the combined rosters of their learning community first-year writing classes. This meant that in these learning communities the same teacher would teach two sections of first-year writing and one section of information literacy taken by the students of their learning community writing courses. While many first-year writing instructors may not teach a separate information literacy course, our study provides a unique view into how first-year writing instructors view IL concepts when considering them separate from but still linked to writing, which can inform training for those teaching traditional writing courses since these often include lessons and assignments involving secondary research and the literate use of information sources as an integral part of the curriculum.

The instructors teaching both the first-year writing courses and information literacy courses in learning communities were the focus of our study since they represented nondiscipline instructors teaching introductory writing and research courses. We invited these instructors to participate in two focus groups, one at the beginning of the semester and one at the end of the semester, in which we asked them a number of questions about their plans, experience, and sense of preparation in these courses. Five instructors participated in the first focus group, four of whom received their formal professional training in literary studies programs (all hold PhDs), while one had completed a master's of fine arts. The second focus group at the end of the semester included three instructors who had been a part of the first focus group and one instructor who had not attended the first focus group meeting. All of these instructors hold PhDs in literary studies.

The focus group questions were designed to elicit instructors' views of the goals of both courses, how they defined writing and information literacy both explicitly and in pedagogical practice, and what kinds of connections the instructors saw between the subject matter of the courses and the courses themselves (questions for both focus groups are included in Box 21.1). We allowed the participants to respond to each question as they saw fit, offering guidance or direction only when it was requested, believing that the instructors' interpretations of the questions themselves could be

BOX 21.1
FOCUS GROUP QUESTIONS

Focus Group 1: Early Semester

1. What are the most important aspects students need to learn about writing and information literacy? What is good researching and good writing? How will you show students the link between researching and writing?
2. What concepts do you think will be most difficult for students to grasp in both UCOR 101 and UCOR 100? What makes those concepts so difficult? What approaches will you use to try to help students overcome this cognitive difficulty?
3. Where do you see UCOR 101 and UCOR 100 intersecting? What distinguishes one from the other?
4. What concepts from UCOR 101 and UCOR 100 transfer to other contexts and why do they do so? What concepts do not transfer and why not?
5. What are the benefits of having UCOR 101 instructors teach UCOR 100? What are the disadvantages?
6. What kinds of training, knowledge, or skills do you still feel you would like to have going into teaching in these courses?

Focus Group 2: End of Semester

1. What are you trying to teach students in UCOR 101 and UCOR 100 about writing and information literacy? How did you show students the link between researching and writing?
2. What concepts are most difficult for students to grasp in both UCOR 101 and UCOR 100? What makes those concepts so difficult? What approaches do you use to try to help students overcome this cognitive difficulty?
3. Where do you see UCOR 101 and UCOR 100 intersecting? What distinguishes one from the other?
4. What concepts from UCOR 101 and UCOR 100 transfer to other contexts and how do they do so? What concepts do not transfer and why not?
5. What were the benefits of having UCOR 101 instructors teach UCOR 100? What were the disadvantages?
6. Should UCOR 100 continue to be taught by UCOR 101 instructors in the Learning Communities? Why or why not?
7. What kinds of training, knowledge, or skills would you like to have if you were to teach these two classes together again?

revealing about their perspectives on writing, information literacy, and the overlap between the two. We recorded both focus group sessions in their entirety and later transcribed the recordings. After transcription of each focus group recording, we coded the transcripts, identifying the IL threshold concepts and WS threshold concepts stated or implied by the participant respondents. IL threshold concepts were drawn from the ACRL framework and were identified by the director of Research and Information Skills, while the director of First-Year Writing identified the WS threshold concepts, calling primarily on the recently published *Naming What We Know: Threshold Concepts of Writing Studies* (Adler-Kassner & Wardle, 2015) as a representation of widely agreed upon threshold concepts for WS.

THRESHOLD CONCEPTS AND NONEXPERT INSTRUCTORS

Analysis of the coded transcripts revealed patterns that seem unsurprising at first but reveal important insights about what training methods are likely to prove effective for preparing nonexpert instructors who are likely to teach overlapping courses or even traditional composition courses in which research "skills" form a significant pedagogical component. Based on the data collected, the participants' recognition and deployment of threshold concepts in both IL and WS was complicated and uneven. Generally speaking, participants did not typically identify or employ IL and WS threshold concepts in their pedagogy for either course as they represented it in the focus group discussions.

Rather than a genuinely rhetorical view of writing or research, participants tended to advance more universalist descriptions of composing and information literacy practices, relying on tropes of writing as self-expression and citing sources as granting a universally identifiable "credibility." Participants used much of the terminology that might surround specific threshold concepts without pursuing the implications that would demonstrate full understanding or implementation. A particularly striking example would be the ACRL frame of Scholarship as Conversation, which is implied through a number of WS threshold concepts, identified in some recent scholarship (McCracken & Johnson, 2015; Purdy & McClure, 2016) such as "Writing is a social and rhetorical activity" (Roozen, 2015); "Writing mediates activity" (Russell, 2015); "Writing invokes/address/creates audiences" (Lunsford, 2015); "Writing is a way of enacting disciplinarity" (Lerner, 2015); and "Disciplinary and professional identities are constructed through writing" (Estrem, 2015). Each of these concepts in WS points to the ways in which writing in academic settings operates as a means of identifying and intervening in discipline-, and even subdiscipline-, specific conversations. Indeed, Douglas Downs and Elizabeth Wardle (2007) identify helping students see Scholarship as Conversation as a primary goal of their threshold concept–focused Introduction to Writing Studies first-year pedagogy.

Participants consistently took up the teaching of research and the deployment of sources in writing in terms of joining an existing conversation. For instance, one participant in the first focus group stated, "I'm trying to sell them this concept of entering a larger conversation actively, you know and that part of research is an active engine running toward it." Another noted he would approach the class with the idea that students are "not necessarily researching to learn mastery of material, they're researching to enter into an existing conversation, recognize the broad strokes of a debate or of an argument or of an issue . . ." in an attempt to give students opportunities to "react and respond that they can then write about as opposed echoing or repeating those good facts or good pieces of information that they found." In the second focus group session, one participant said, "I was able to ask a bit more for especially the final paper in terms of putting the subject matter that we were sort of talking about in class . . . now ok, how do you put all of these resources together and think about this as a conversation?" These examples reflect a common consideration of conducting research and writing with sources as the practice of joining a larger conversation.

But while these comments exhibit an approach to teaching composition and information literacy using threshold concepts, the conceptual foundation for attending to conversations aligned less with socially understood visions of writing and research and more with expressivist conceptions of writing as the communication of individual ideas. This was most clearly expressed in the goals stated by participants for student writing. One participant noted, "The thing I try to emphasize is, this idea of their writing to create their own knowledge, not repeating my knowledge back to me. . . . You know you have to find your own thing." The key challenge for students, then, was not identifying the values, conventions, and widely recognized sources of authority for specific communities—disciplinary or otherwise—but finding the courage to express one's own, individual ideas. Linked directly to this more individualized sense of what marks good writing were more generalized rules or universal strategies for what defines good writing and research. Another participant thus noted, "every paragraph, you really need to have 75% of that paragraph really your ideas your words because there's that question of like how do you not let the voice get drowned out on the sentence to sentence level?" Another affirmed that the starting point of writing and research instruction involved "getting [students] into their own thinking and, 'can I, can I be me?'" While, again, there is certainly some truth to these assertions that students need to see the writing they do as genuine and meaningful, the strategies implied by participant comments framed authenticity and meaning as the result of students affirming their individual selves rather than situating themselves within a community of practice in which their utterances might serve as a meaningful intervention.

Invention for these participants seemed to be an individual act that occurs when writer and topic are brought together and the individual writer is willing to move beyond repeating accepted information. Certainly helping students gain the confidence to make an argument is important and necessary and requires challenging much of their training in school situations to become passive receptacles. But framing this practice as simply a matter of identifying one's own opinion and being willing to express it overlooks the ways in which scholarly conversations (and more public conversations) establish exigence for particular topics and not others, legitimize certain topics and not others, and demand a familiarity with particular sources, research, or intertextual traces and not others. The term "audience" was used by participants only twice in the first focus group session and not at all in the second. Related terms like "reader," "community," or "discourse" were as rare if not more so. So while "authority is constructed" through source use, the practice of constructing authority is the same for all discursive situations and the authority constructed thus applies to any situation.

In a similar way, the ACRL frame of Authority Is Constructed—which corresponds in many ways to the WS concept that "Disciplinary and professional identities are constructed through writing" (Estrem, 2015)—seemed superficially embraced rather than completely understood or implemented by participants. Source use was widely recognized as a means of establishing one's authority to speak on a given topic, but how sources granted such authority depended on a view of authority as resting with objectively established associations with academe rather than with the perceptions of a particular audience. A representative view was expressed by one participant in the second focus group session when she described the work on evaluating sources in her information literacy course: "[W]e spent a lot of time talking about 'this is what a scholarly journal looks like, this is what a scholarly book looks like,' and I took them a lot of time like doing very simple, fine, like this is how you know it's credible, right? And things like, look at where it's published, google the author, um, you know. If it's a university press it's automatically pretty much going to be fine." The notion that authority or identity is constructed through source selection and writing is evident here, but like the concept of Scholarship as Conversation, the participants' understanding reflects a narrow perspective of the dynamics of constructing authority and, thus, the implications of this concept likewise seem limited. Librarians would not be surprised to hear that some of the instructors required students to use "at least two books" or that they could not use certain Web sources; these requirements tend to ignore disciplinary or contextual situations surrounding the topics students would explore in their researched writing and to focus instead on notions of authority that tend to reflect humanities expectations.

A noteworthy exception was MLA formatting which, when discussed, was understood by all participants as narrowly applicable to humanities discourse and a problematic focus when teaching students who were generally not likely to pursue studies or careers in the humanities. Likewise, library database usage was recognized, particularly in the second focus group, as highly context- and discipline-dependent, leading participants to express doubts about their capability to teach students how to use databases for disciplines like nursing or chemistry even though database search practices may have some similarities across disciplines. Participants consistently interwove a strong sense of the contextual nature of research and citation practices throughout their discussions of the assignments they used and skills they taught in the one-credit-hour information literacy course, so much so that they did not focus as much on some of the more transferable aspects of Searching as Strategic Exploration or Information Has Value threshold concepts.

This speaks to the more interesting revelations apparent in the data. On the whole, participants lacked a sense of confidence in teaching information literacy skills despite the fact that they all identified themselves as expert researchers and many commonly teach research practices as part of their composition courses. This lack of confidence correlated directly with participants' widespread recognition of their lack of expertise in the disciplinary knowledge of information literacy. One participant explained, "I will say, I felt like I was sort of underwater and not necessarily very prepared. It's a whole . . . I mean . . . people you know have master's degrees and everything in [information literacy]. It's . . . to not have that background and to sort of jump in was difficult." Another described the difficulty in adjusting to teaching the course and explained about his own training in multiple research methods courses that he "stretched whatever I retained from those courses, which I don't know was a lot, until it broke [in the Information Literacy course]." The lack of confidence and desire for more expertise was such that all of the participants of the second focus group called for more training in information literacy, particularly the conceptual framework. One participant stated that she "would love to take a kind of summer crash course by librarians who've done library science just so I could be a little bit more like you guys" and added that she would like training on "some of the conceptual frameworks and what is currently in the discourse of library science right now." Participants' sense of acquired expertise over the semester primarily took the form of greater experience with course logistics, classroom management, and hands-on use of pedagogical tools unique to the course rather than increased confidence in teaching research.

This was not, however, the case with discussions of the composition course and the WS threshold concepts. Apart from not noting that master's degrees and PhDs are awarded in the discipline of WS just as they are in IL, participants seemed also to equate teaching first-year composition with expertise in WS. Certainly a reflective and conscientious teacher can develop significant expertise about composition and teaching composition, expertise that can include not only practitioner knowledge of classroom management but also significant insights into what writing and research are and how they work. Nor should we imagine that these instructors have no contact with WS research or do not seek supplements to their knowledge about writing and writing instruction. But the participants of our study exhibited a limited understanding of the counterintuitive, research-based knowledge of WS without a correlating recognition of those limitations or lack of confidence in their knowledge about writing or writing pedagogy. This seems easily explainable given their definitions of good writing as deriving from an assertion of one's own opinions as well as the ways in which "writing" in most English department–based first-year writing courses is typically figured as writing according to the conventions of literary studies discourse or, at least, the humanities more generally. Given these definitions, these participants are experts in composition and are, thus, uniquely qualified for composition instruction and are unlikely to see a need for further training.

RECOMMENDATIONS FOR TRAINING NONEXPERT INSTRUCTORS

The results of our focus group point to specific directions that are likely necessary for training teachers to instruct students in the threshold concepts of IL and WS and the points of overlap between each. Perhaps the most obvious direction for further training demonstrated by the data is helping instructors fully understand what the overlapping threshold concepts of IL and WS are, as well as what the implications are for teaching writing and research in ways that are accurate and transferable across contexts.

As the data suggests, such training is likely to prove challenging for a number of reasons. Since threshold concepts represent the distinguishing, often counterintuitive expertise of specific disciplinary practices and ways of thinking, acquiring threshold concepts amounts to joining a discipline (Meyer & Land, 2006). Ushering nonexpert instructors into a disciplinary paradigm through limited training and professional opportunities is a tall order for trainers and trainees alike. The challenge of accomplishing this work suggests that training resources would be better focused on helping nonexpert instructors learn those concepts that most clearly align, theoretically and practically, between IL and WS.

Another important challenge to developing training that helps instructors teach the overlapping threshold concepts of IL and WS is the ways in which the language and experience of these instructors can obscure the difference between their existing approach and disciplinary perspectives. As we demonstrated above, study participants typically used language similar to the ACRL framework and WS threshold concepts but deployed that language in rather narrowly defined and traditional ways. For participants, Scholarship as Conversation described the need for possessing differentiated opinions as a means of intervening in an existing debate but did not seem to indicate the connections between specific conversations and specific communities, the state of an existing conversation and the constraints it puts on identifying exigent topics, or the socially determined limitation on how a writer should frame one's discussion of a given topic. Likewise, authority was seen as constructed through the use of sources but in ways that naturally derive from using scholarly sources on any topic and universally apply to any writing situation. Such appropriation of new terminology for more traditional misconceptions of writing and research is unsurprising since we all integrate new knowledge through the terministic screens in which we assess and construct meaning, but this does raise challenges for effective training.

This reality points to the usefulness of beginning training with an emphasis on the ACRL framework and then drawing out implications for writing as a similarly rhetorical practice. The National Research Council–sponsored 2000 study *How People Learn: Brain, Mind, Experience, and School* suggests the importance of recognizing the limits of expertise in acquiring new skills and knowledge. The authors note that a view of experts as "accomplished novices" better supports initial and continued learning than a view of expertise as a destination at which one can finally arrive, stating, "Accomplished novices are skilled in many areas and proud of their accomplishments, but they realize that what they know is miniscule compared to all that is potentially knowable. This model helps free people to continue to learn even though they may have spent 10 to 20 years as an 'expert' in their field" (Bransford, Pellegrino, & Donovan, 2000, p. 29). Learning is thus much more likely to happen—for both the first-year college student or the long-time college teacher—when the learner perceives him- or herself as inexpert and open to the acquisition of new knowledge.

Because of participants' recognition of the limits of their expertise in relation to the information literacy course, perhaps writing instructors would be better able to begin acquiring the necessary IL concepts than those of WS. Our participants' recognition of a distinct, formal expert training in IL that they themselves did not possess and their failure to recognize distinct, formal expert training in WS as a reality points further to the likelihood of an openness to the ACRL framework than WS threshold concepts. To support training in both for nonexpert instructors, we would recommend focusing explicit training on the integrative aspects of the ACRL framework to show the interdependence of the framework to the practice of writing. For instance, a participant who has fully grasped how the selection of specific sources and intertextual traces constructs authority for the writer to a specific community of practice by indicating to that community that the author is not only familiar with the relevant research but knows how to manipulate it in discursively acceptable ways can be led to consider how other features of a particular text—its genre, terminology, sentence-level features, citation style, formatting, and so on—also work to construct authority for the author. In short, research and writing are part of the same socially defined practice of communicating effectively with a particular audience to mediate a specific activity (Russell, 1995).

But this itself may be a problem insofar as participants seemed to highly value the way teaching information literacy and composition as two different courses allowed them to "compartmentalize" their teaching. In other words, the separate classes seemed to allow for instruction to focus on one or the other despite conscious efforts by participants to integrate the two courses through assignments, lesson activities, and class discussion. Valuing this kind of distinctness speaks to a view of the two practices as separate. Even for institutions where writing instructors teach information literacy as part of the writing curriculum, compartmentalization can occur in the form of a one-shot session or a series of research workshops taught by a librarian. This suggests the beginning of any training for writing instructors teaching information literacy should focus on where IL and WS threshold concepts overlap. This connection will likely challenge preconceived notions regarding writing and shift the instructors' perceptions so that they are more open to viewing writing and research as contextualized, radically rhetorical practice.

While our study is limited due to the inclusion of a small number of participants teaching at a single institution, these instructors reflect the typical population of first-year writing instructors. Often, writing instructors teach information literacy concepts, and while they may not teach a separate IL course, first-year writing is traditionally used as an introduction to IL because of the overlap between IL and WS. Our study suggests future research evaluating the effectiveness of the training we have proposed—using IL TCs as a way to introduce writing instructors to some of the more "troublesome" WS TCs—could provide further recommendations for program directors in information literacy and writing studies. We envision that such training would enable nonexpert instructors to teach for transfer so that their students would see the integrative and rhetorical nature of research and writing, allowing pedagogical possibilities to overcome our institutional realities.

REFERENCES

Adler-Kassner, L., Majewski, J., & Koshnick, D. (2012). The value of troublesome knowledge: Transfer and threshold concepts in writing and history. *Composition Forum, 26*, 1–17. Retrieved from http://compositionforum.com/

Adler-Kassner, L., & Wardle, E. (2015). *Naming what we know: Threshold concepts of writing studies*. Boulder, CO: University Press of Colorado.

Association of College and Research Libraries (2015). *Framework for information literacy for higher education*. Retrieved from http://www.ala.org/acrl/standards/ilframework

Bransford, J. D., Pellegrino, J. W., & Donovan, M. S., eds. (2000). How people learn: Brain, mind, experience, and school: Expanded edition. Washington, D.C.: National Academy Press.

Downs, D., & Wardle, E. (2007). Teaching about writing, righting misconceptions: (Re)envisioning "first-year composition" as "Introduction to Writing Studies." *College Composition and Communication, 58(4)*, 552–584.

Estrem, H. (2015). Disciplinary and professional identities are constructed through writing. In L. Adler-Kassner & E. Wardle, *Naming what we know: Threshold concepts of writing studies* (pp. 55–56). Boulder, CO: University Press of Colorado.

Lerner, N. (2015). Writing is a way of enacting disciplinarity. In L. Adler-Kassner & E. Wardle, *Naming what we know: Threshold concepts of writing studies* (pp. 40–41). Boulder, CO: University Press of Colorado.

Lunsford, A. A. (2015). Writing addresses, invokes, and/or creates audiences. In L. Adler-Kassner

& E. Wardle, *Naming what we know: Threshold concepts of writing studies* (pp. 20–21). Boulder, CO: University Press of Colorado.

Maid, B., & D'Angelo, B. (2016). Threshold concepts: Integrating and applying information literacy and writing instruction. *Information literacy: Research and collaboration across disciplines.* Fort Collins, CO: WAC Clearinghouse and University Press of Colorado.

McCracken, I. M., & Johnson, B. (2015). Sustainable partners: Librarians and instructors using threshold concepts to reinforce information literacy. *Georgia International Conference on Information Literacy.* 40. Retrieved from http://digitalcommons.georgiasouthern.edu/gaintlit/2015/2015/40

Meyer, J., & Land, R. (Eds.) (2006). *Overcoming barriers to student understanding: Threshold concepts and troublesome knowledge.* Abingdon, UK: Routledge.

Purdy, J. P., & McClure, R. (Eds.) (2016). *The future scholar: Researching and teaching the frameworks for writing and information literacy.* Medford, NJ: Information Today.

Roozen, K. (2015). Writing is a social and rhetorical activity. In L. Adler-Kassner & E. Wardle, *Naming what we know: Threshold concepts of writing studies* (pp. 17–19). Boulder, CO: University Press of Colorado.

Russell, D. R. (1995). Activity theory and its implications for writing instruction. In J. Petraglia, *Reconceiving writing, rethinking writing instruction* (pp. 51–78). Mahwah, NJ: Erlbaum Press.

Russell, D. R. (2015). Writing mediates activity. In L. Adler-Kassner & E. Wardle, *Naming what we know: Threshold concepts of writing studies* (pp. 26–27). Boulder, CO: University Press of Colorado.

CHAPTER 22

ADDRESSING THE SYMPTOMS

Deep Collaboration for Interrogating Differences in Professional Assumptions

Donna Scheidt
William J. Carpenter
Holly Middleton
Kathy Shields

Writing faculty and librarians often collaborate with one another in the teaching of research in first-year writing (FYW). In doing so, they share a common aim, namely helping first-year students develop as researchers so that they may effectively incorporate their research into their learning and writing. Trained professionally with respect to research practice, writing faculty and librarians respectively carry with them certain theoretical and operating assumptions about research—what it is, what it involves, how it works, how to pursue it most effectively, and so forth. These professional working assumptions about research inevitably have implications for how research is taught to first-year students.

Despite differentiation and debate, it is nevertheless possible to get some sense of how those who work in writing studies and information literacy understand research from their respective recent professional statements. The sense one gets initially is that librarians and FYW faculty share several aims and interests. As just one example, the Association of College Research Libraries' (ACRL) *Framework for Information Literacy for Higher Education* (IL Framework; ACRL, 2015) includes the frame Research as Inquiry, which details knowledge practices in terms familiar to writing faculty: identify gaps or conflicts in information, determine the appropriate scope of a project, ask good questions, analyze and interpret the work of others in order to draw reasonable conclusions, and organize and synthesize ideas and sources (p. 9). In fact, these practices are similar to what the Council of Writing Program Administrators (CWPA) articulates as certain outcomes and experiences in its *WPA Outcomes Statement for First-Year Composition* (Outcomes; CWPA, 2014) and the *Framework for Success in Postsecondary Writing* (Writing Framework; CWPA, 2011) (see in particular the outcomes "Critical Thinking," p. 7, and "Writing Processes," p. 8). It comes as no surprise that a reading of the professional statements of writing faculty and librarians reveals some common ground.[1]

Yet careful reading of the statements also reveals telling differences that reflect divergent professional assumptions. This kind of reading is known as "symptomatic" reading in the traditions of English studies. Symptomatic reading may be especially familiar to writing faculty through the work of Kathleen McCormick, who promotes this reading practice among others within the undergraduate writing classroom. She encourages students to read symptomatically in order to "look beyond the literal message of any kind of text" and to explore the "tensions of a culture" (2003, p. 40). Similarly, symptomatic reading is employed here to better understand the possible disciplinary presuppositions of writing faculty in particular—that is, what convictions regarding research that writing faculty tend to adhere to in their professional identities and what blind spots they potentially suffer. The more aware writing faculty are of the ways their discipline may shape their understanding of research and research instruction, the more conscientious and reflective they can be as teachers and as collaborators.

In particular, professional self-awareness of difference can make evident the need for collaboration with librarians, both in terms of what writing faculty have to offer as well as what they have to learn. Of course, in most universities collaboration at some level is already typical; writing faculty regularly share their assignments with librarians, schedule research instruction for their courses, and so forth. What we propose here, however, is "deep collaboration" among writing faculty and librarians, the kind of collaboration in which professional ideological disjuncts might surface and be meaningfully discussed. Deep collaboration is unlikely to happen when communication is superficial (e.g., scheduling) or unidirectional (e.g., sharing an assignment without asking for feedback). Opportunities for deep collaboration can be time- and planning-intensive, yet they are vital if we are to meaningfully instruct students as researchers and writers without crossing purposes with one another.

One opportunity for deep collaboration occurs when writing faculty and librarians research and write with one another, something for which librarians have been calling for some time now (see, e.g., Rabinowitz, 2000). This chapter describes what we learned from one such ongoing research and writing collaboration. By reading and coding first-year student writing together, we "address the symptoms" by meaningfully interrogating the kinds of professional differences evident in our professional statements. Our work is deeply collaborative; it has provided us with opportunities to reconsider our professional assumptions and, on this basis, to change the ways we teach research in FYW.

DIVULGING THE DIFFERENCES: A SYMPTOMATIC READING OF THE *WRITING FRAMEWORK* AND *OUTCOMES*

What becomes clear in a symptomatic reading of the professional statements of writing faculty is that they highly value the activities of reading and writing in the research process. In the *Outcomes* (CWPA, 2014), for example, sense-making with respect to information is enacted in reading and writing; the outcome "critical thinking" occurs when students analyze, synthesize, interpret, and evaluate *as they read and compose*. The *Writing Framework* (CWPA, 2011) is even more specific in highlighting the ways in which a variety of reading and writing experiences can prepare students for college-level critical thinking: reading texts sympathetically and critically; writing in order to summarize, analyze, interpret, critique, respond, and synthesize; and writing so as to "put the writer's ideas in conversation with a text's" (p. 7). Underlying these statements are the professional convictions that information is materially, textually situated and that students think about and make meaning of information by working with texts.

However, another "symptom" is less a conviction than an oversight. Even while describing the activities of reading and writing with some nuance, the disciplinary statements of writing studies do not seem to acknowledge other complexities of the research process beyond the finding and evaluating of sources. The *Outcomes* (CWPA, 2014) do recognize that "composing processes" (pp. 146–147) involve many steps (including research) and are often nonlinear and require flexibility. Yet the term "research" seems to be employed in the sense of finding possible sources rather than the several ways librarians understand researchers as working conceptually with information (described above). "Research" first appears as part of the "critical thinking" outcome; it modifies the kind of material the student is to "[l]ocate and evaluate," categorized as "primary and secondary research materials" (p. 146). Examples are provided, including both kinds of sources ("journal articles and essays, books . . . and internet sources") as well as resources for finding sources ("scholarly and professionally established and maintained databases or archives, and informal electronic networks") (p. 146). "Research" next appears as a verb, as part of "composing processes." Yet here again, "research" is narrowly employed, this time not as a kind of material to be found but as an act of finding potentially recurring at different times: "a writer may research a topic before drafting, then conduct additional research while revising or after consulting a colleague" (p. 146). In both instances when "research" is discussed as part of FYW, it is associated with just two activities—finding and evaluating.

It is strange, too, how the *Outcomes* (CWPA, 2014) speak to the process of evaluating research materials, as decontextualized from otherwise rhetorically rich processes of reading and writing. The description of evaluation occurs as a heuristic chain of familiar means of assessment, bookended (to highlight? as a kind of afterthought?) by parentheses: "evaluate (for credibility, sufficiency, accuracy, timeliness, bias and so on)" (p. 146). The presentation represents the list as a kind of checklist for making an objective determination of the quality of a source in and of itself, albeit an open-ended one. There is no expressed concern for the source's context—its author's purposes, its audience, what is trying to be achieved—nor for the rhetorical situation of the student writer. Does the author's research project involve an overview of an issue for a general audience to be published as a blog? Dispute a definition used by scholars as part of an academic research paper? Analyze a trend in the rhetoric or representation of an issue? The contextual attributes of the source and of the writer's research project surely have implications for what criteria for source evaluation like "credibility," "sufficiency," or "bias" mean, yet context is nowhere acknowledged here. The decontextualization of evaluative criteria is particularly unexpected given the *Outcomes'* earlier emphases on the rhetorical with respect to practices of reading and writing.

These assumptions or symptoms—prioritizing texts and textual practices, reducing research to locating and evaluating research materials, and decontextualizing source evaluation—are highlighted not merely in order to celebrate or critique the orientation of writing studies with respect to research and its instruction. These assumptions inform our understanding and our instructional practices as writing faculty. They also make the "one-shot" library session make sense to writing faculty who otherwise protest that writing proficiency is not acquired from the "one-shot" experience of FYW. To share these understandings or to challenge them in order to enrich our mutual research instruction involves the kind of conceptual work characteristic of deep collaboration.

RECONSIDERING PROFESSIONAL ASSUMPTIONS, CHANGING TEACHING

Complexifying Processes of Writing and Research

Any writing faculty will be familiar with the processes of writing—for example, brainstorming and prewriting, drafting, peer review, revision, editing and polishing. And in our professional and personal lives, we engage regularly with the processes of research. Yet we may not be as aware of those research processes, or as readily able to articulate those processes to ourselves and our students. There exists longstanding scholarship in our field conceptualizing and examining students' processes of research and writing—for example, certain read-to-write studies (see, e.g., Nelson, 1992) and more recently a focus on "writing information literacy" (D'Angelo, Jamieson, Maid, & Walker, 2016; Norgaard, 2003). Even so, as demonstrated in the reading of the *Outcomes* (CWPA, 2014) above, there can be a tendency on the part of writing faculty to reduce the complexities of the research process to finding and evaluating sources, at least as far as their teaching.

This potentially reductive portrayal of research has implications for how we understand the teaching of research with respect to our first-year students as well the role of librarians with respect to instruction. If research is construed as finding and evaluating sources, then these activities are what we focus on in our classrooms and convey to students to be central to their research processes. We often outsource these activities to librarians, understanding them to be experts in these regards. We give librarians a single session to cover research—often referred to in the literature as the "one shot"—perhaps with a physical tour of the library and, more frequently these days, a virtual tour of the catalogue, databases, and other search tools. In other words, our pedagogies risk depicting research processes as an Easter egg hunt: special, occasional, and all about the finding. Students undoubtedly come to understand themselves and their task as researchers as finding the right sources, that is, research as a high-stakes exercise.

At least two challenges impede a different conceptualization of the research process, a better working relationship with librarians, and more effective research teaching. First, instructional librarians traditionally have seen and represented themselves primarily as experts in information retrieval and evaluation (Fister, 1993). It can be difficult as a result for writing faculty to imagine librarians' roles differently in order to better coordinate research instruction. Fortunately, the *IL Framework* (ACRL, 2015) is challenging some of those identity assumptions. Second, as with any discipline, librarians share a professional vocabulary with one another that may not be familiar to others with whom they work (like writing faculty) (Rabinowitz, 2000, p. 344). Despite the richly complex ways that librarians think of research processes, it can be difficult to articulate these complexities and to coordinate with writing faculty in teaching them.

Curious to understand the complexities of the research process and the ways first-year students perceive it in relation to their writing, we collaborated as part of a research team of two campus instructional librarians and four writing faculty. Several hundred students enrolled in FYW in fall 2012 agreed to participate. We asked these students to respond to a "process narrative" prompt, requiring them to imagine how they would go about writing a 1,500-word argument paper including at least three outside sources. Students were given 20 minutes in class to respond to the prompt at the beginning and end of the semester. A simple random sample of participating students yielded dozens of process narratives from the beginning and end of the term. Together as writing faculty and librarians, we collaboratively coded these process narratives, labeling each segment of a narrative that described a distinct activity and eventually developing a common list of codes. This "Code Log" included the everyday practices identified by students in which both writing and research were potentially involved, what we termed "writing-research" activities.

The coding of the process narratives and the creation of the Code Log was deeply collaborative work because it provided an opportunity to reconsider our assumptions regarding student research (and our teaching of it) as predominantly an activity of finding and evaluating. We certainly recognized these activities as we coded students' process narratives (as "gather sources" and "evaluate source quality"). However, they were just two among the 15 research-related activities we identified (see Box 22.1), spanning from "understanding an assignment and its tasks" to "integrating sources textually" (Scheidt et al., 2016). This list of activities provided us with a much more expansive view of students' research processes as well as our responsibilities in teaching and facilitating it. As a negotiated list of common terms, it literally put us as writing faculty and librarians on the same page, providing us with a shared vocabulary for conceptualization and action.

Our research work together also was deeply collaborative in that it prompted us to rethink our teaching and instructional practices. In the following sections we outline changes in our practice.

BOX 22.1
LEVEL 1 CODES

Determining Task, Purposes, and Beliefs

- understand **assignment** and its tasks
- find **topic** of interest
- **brainstorm** prior knowledge or beliefs

Exploring Research Contexts

- **gather** sources
- process/**engage** sources
- **learn** more about chosen topic
- determine what is **available**

Navigating and Locating Oneself With Respect to Specific Sources

- take a **position**
- locate **support** for claims
- acknowledge **different** views or opinions
- evaluate source **quality**
- determine **relevance** of sources to topic or purpose

Planning and Writing

- **organize**/arrange/outline
- **use** sources
- **integrate** sources textually

From the "One-Shot" to Shared Responsibility

In revealing the complexities of students' writing-research processes, the Code Log makes evident the improbability of one-person or one-shot coverage. It highlights the need to effectively scaffold and coordinate research instruction. What writing-research activities should be taught when? As acknowledged in the *Outcomes* (CWPA, 2014), writing (and research) processes are necessarily nonlinear and flexible. The Code Log activities can be grouped, however, into suggestive sequences of activities such as the one indicated above. These groupings might serve as a guide to organizing multiple classroom sessions with librarians, moving from a single "Find/Evaluate" session to a differentiated sequence: "Determine Task—Explore Context—Navigate/Locate Oneself—Plan/Write." Because the research process is as recursive as the writing process, the order may be determined by the course.

On our own campus, the Code Log informed how librarians involved with the study revised the research guide for FYW, opting to highlight connections between writing and research and contextualizing these activities within writing-research processes as a whole. For example, the librarians redesigned the research guide from a focus on finding sources (with tabs like Find Books, Find Articles) to highlighting four key steps in the research and writing process: Brainstorm, Learn, Evaluate, and Integrate. These terms are employed in ways suggested by the students in our study. Students who "brainstorm" are described as considering their purposes for writing as they read around in order to generate a topic. "Learning" involves students deepening their understanding of their chosen topic in order to create contexts for themselves and their readers in their writing. "Evaluate" concerns the credibility of potential sources but also whether they are appropriate for the student's assignment and purposes. Students "integrate" effectively when they consider how best to employ their research in light of their goals and their writing project (beyond just dropping a quote). These four steps are also described as nonlinear, as with the larger processes of writing and research of which they are part. Each page includes links to search tools, but it also includes information and guidance related to that particular research and writing activity. When librarians introduce students to the research guide for FYW, they ensure that students understand that they may navigate back and forth among the tabs as they conduct their research and writing.

Replacing the "Find Articles" and "Find Books" tabs acknowledges the illogic of the one-shot library session and raises a fundamental question: Who should teach what writing-research activities? Respective professional expertise may lend itself to particular activities: Writing faculty may be somewhat better equipped to instruct in writing planning (organizing/arranging/outlining) and librarians in gathering sources and determining what is available. With many writing-research activities, however, responsibility should probably be shared and coordinated, lest it be overlooked altogether. As just one example, librarians can be terrific partners in teaching students strategies for finding and narrowing their topics (or research questions). (It is after all Carol Kulthau [2004], a library and information sciences researcher, who has most carefully documented the anxious step of focusing a topic and its implications for young researchers.) In this way, the Code Log helps us to reimagine our identities and roles with respect to one another as writing faculty and librarians in the teaching of research.

Relevance and Rhetorical Use

In addition to changing the way both faculty and librarians talked about the processes of writing, the practice of collaborative coding also revealed that both groups valued context when determining the relevance of a particular source. This shared value, however, was belied by the type of instruction that librarians are typically called on to provide. In teaching students to distinguish between scholarly and popular sources, for example, these source types are often pitted against one another, with scholarly sources occupying the high ground of credibility and reliability. However, in our conversations both librarians and FYW faculty agreed that getting students to conflate scholarly sources with credibility should not be the aim of these sessions. Rather, it was more important that students choose sources that were appropriate for the given assignment and the questions they were seeking to address.

Students in our study readily acknowledged that locating sources was an important part of research and could easily enough locate scholarly articles. What they largely overlooked, however, was the importance of determining the relevance of those sources and how to integrate them into their writing. Furthermore, many FYW faculty were structuring their courses around current events and issues for which scholarly articles were not always available or necessarily appropriate. Thus, conversations about evaluating sources shifted from just talking about "scholarly versus popular sources" to a larger discussion around how to determine a source's value in the given context and for a particular rhetorical purpose.

This shift led to some important changes in vocabulary. Librarians had been teaching the ABCs acronym for source evaluation (Authority, Bias, Currency) and using the term "bias" to discuss how to evaluate the author's or publication's viewpoint. FYW faculty considered the term problematic, because first-year students tend to narrowly understand it in relation to media or political bias and then overgeneralize. If an instructor wants to teach that every writer has a perspective and every text positions a reader, "bias" is too blunt an instrument. In the librarians' redesign of the research guide for FYW, this discovery (as well as the others from this research project) prompted the librarians to design a method for source evaluation called PARTS (Position, Accuracy/Authority, Relevance, Time, Source Type). This new acronym addresses several of the issues discovered during the course of our study. First, by moving from "bias" to the more neutral "position," it eliminates the negative associations and political bent associated with the former. Second, adding "source type" encourages students to consider genre. Many of the sources students look at are simply words on a screen. By asking them to determine the genre of a source, students must look more deeply at the source and evaluate its characteristics, whom it speaks to and how, as well as its appropriateness in the given context.

That "bias" is delineated in the WPA *Outcomes* as one criterion for evaluating sources (see above) points again to the ways in which the professional statement articulates research as arhetorical in ways that reading and writing are not. To further integrate source evaluation as a situated and rhetorical activity, both writing faculty and librarians adopted Joseph Bizup's (2008) BEAM taxonomy for rhetorical use (Background, Exhibit, Argument, or Method). In a shift from intrinsically evaluating or categorizing primary and secondary sources, Bizup argues for an attention to the ways sophisticated writers put sources to rhetorical use: writers rely on background, analyze exhibits, engage arguments, and apply methods. In order to determine relevance, a writer has to evaluate the appropriateness of a source for its rhetorical function. Librarians added an illustration of the BEAM model to the research guide under the "Integrate" tab. When librarians work with students on evaluating sources, students are encouraged to use BEAM to consider a source's value, not just in and of itself, but for their purposes as writers and the context in which they are writing. For example, librarians sometimes ask students to question how the inclusion (or removal) of a particular quote/paraphrase/summary affects the structural integrity of the entire paper. Many writing faculty have also adopted BEAM as a method for teaching critical reading, research, and writing.

CONCLUSION

Librarians and FYW faculty share a common goal: to enable students to develop as researchers and writers and to apply their abilities across their academic lives and beyond. This goal is, however, frequently undermined by undertheorized mutual conceptualizations of research and shallow collaboration between the two groups. As our symptomatic reading of the disciplinary presuppositions of writing faculty and instructional librarians reveals, the two groups often bring to the partnership different conceptions of the intellectual habits and activities that are fundamental to effective research and writing. As a result, students can encounter unacknowledged gaps and contradictions in their learning about how to navigate and employ the vast amount of information available to them. Given that these gaps and contradictions so frequently materialize in students' first years of college and sometimes as their only direct instruction in research risks equipping these students with habits and ideas that limit, rather than expand, their research and writing.

The differences in conceptualization are, as librarian Celia Rabinowitz suggests, "differences in culture and language" (2000, 343). Our argument here is that such differences can and should be mitigated by deep collaboration, by work that is undertaken in the spirit of mutual respect, shared interests, and innovation. Deep collaboration between FYW faculty and librarians can, as our study has shown, unearth the complexities of students' research processes and our teaching of them. At the same time, it can fundamentally alter and deepen working relationships that can inspire further inquiry and improve our teaching efforts. On our campus, deep collaboration has led to greater student-librarian interactions in class, as well as to conscientiously scaffolded and coordinated learning activities between librarians and faculty. Our hope is that these changes in our conceptualization and teaching of research and writing impact our students' understanding of these as complex yet navigable and engaging activities of inquiry and sharing.

NOTE

1. See, for example, Part I of this volume.

REFERENCES

Association of College and Research Libraries. (2015). *Framework for information literacy for higher education.* Retrieved from http://www.ala.org/acrl/standards/ilframework

Bizup, J. (2008). BEAM: A rhetorical vocabulary for teaching research-based writing. *Rhetoric Review, 27*, 72–86.

Council of Writing Program Administrators. (2014). *WPA outcomes statement for first-year composition* (revisions adopted July 17, 2014). *Writing Program Administration, 38*(1), 129–143.

Council of Writing Program Administrators, National Council of Teachers of English, and National Writing Project. (2011). *Framework for success in postsecondary writing.* Retrieved from http://wpacouncil.org/framework

D'Angelo, B. J., Jamieson, S., Maid, B., & Walker, J. R. (Eds.). (2016). *Information literacy: Research and collaboration across disciplines.* Perspectives on Writing. Fort Collins, CO: WAC Clearinghouse and University of Colorado Press.

Fister, B. (1993). Teaching the rhetorical dimensions of research. *Research Strategies, 11*, 211–219.

Kuhlthau, C. (2004). *Seeking meaning: A process approach to library and information services* (2nd ed.). Westport, CT: Libraries Unlimited.

McCormick, K. (2003). Closer than close reading: Historical analysis, cultural analysis, and symptomatic reading in the undergraduate classroom. In M. Helmers (Ed.), *Intertexts: Reading pedagogy in college writing classrooms.* Mahwah, NJ: Lawrence Erlbaum Associates.

Nelson, J. (1992). *Constructing a research paper: A study of students' goals and approaches* (Technical Report No. 59). Retrieved from National Writing Project website: http://www.nwp.org/cs/public/print/resource/680

Norgaard, R. (2003). Writing information literacy: Contributions to a concept. *Reference & User Services Quarterly, 43*, 124–129.

Rabinowitz, C. (2000). Working in a vacuum: A study of the literature of student research and writing. *Research Strategies, 17*, 337–346.

Scheidt, D., Carpenter, W., Fitzgerald, R., Kozma, C., Middleton, H., & Shields, K. (2016). Writing information literacy in first-year composition: A collaboration among faculty and librarians. In B. J. D'Angelo, S. Jamieson, B. Maid, & J. R. Walker (Eds.), *Information literacy: Research and collaboration across disciplines.* Perspectives on Writing. Fort Collins, CO: WAC Clearinghouse and University of Colorado Press.

CONTRIBUTORS

Kathy Christie Anders is an assistant professor and graduate studies librarian at Texas A&M University. Her research examines the intersections of rhetoric and information literacy, as well as graduate student scholarly communications. She received her doctorate in English from the University of Nevada, Las Vegas; her master's in English from Duquesne University; and her master's in Library and Information Science from the University of Pittsburgh.

Jennifer Anderson is the Marketing and User Engagement Librarian at the Mary and Jeff Bell Library, Texas A&M University–Corpus Christi. She has an MA in Communication and serves as the library liaison to Communication, Psychology, and Sociology. While her main focus is creating and maintaining events and calendars, she enjoys teachable moments and getting people to cross thresholds (the conceptual and the literal).

Margaret Artman is an assistant professor of English at Daemen College. She teaches composition, journalism, public relations, and professional writing. In addition to information literacy, her research interests include business communication, student media, and advising.

Nicholas N. Behm is Associate Professor of English at Elmhurst College in Elmhurst, Illinois. He studies composition pedagogy and theory, writing assessment, and critical race theory. With Greg Glau, Deborah Holdstein, Duane Roen, and Ed White, he is co-editor of *The WPA Outcomes Statement—A Decade Later*, which won the 2013 "Best Book Award" from the Council of Writing Program Administrators. With Duane Roen and Sherry Rankins-Robertson, he is co-editor of the forthcoming collection *The Framework for Success in Postsecondary Writing: Scholarship and Applications.*

Glenn Blalock is the Coordinator of the First-Year Writing Program at Texas A&M University–Corpus Christi and an Associate Professor of Writing Studies/English. He is the co-founder of CompPile (comppile.org) and technical editor of REx (researchexchange.colostate.edu). His research interests include writing program administration, writing across the curriculum/writing in the disciplines, and teaching for transfer.

Jeanne Law Bohannon is an associate professor of English and an early-career distinguished faculty member at Kennesaw State University, teaching undergraduate and graduate courses in rhetorical grammar, research methods, and digital rhetorics. Research interests include: performing linguistic recoveries of underrepresented populations; conducting empirical studies in information literacies; and cultivating democratic-engagement learning in college writing. She has published in *Bellaterra Journal*, *Peitho*, *Writing Networks for Social Justice*, and the WAC Clearinghouse *Research Exchange Index*. She also blogs for Andrea Lunsford's *Multimodal Mondays* series. She believes in cultivating collaborative, democratic learning spaces where students become empowered stakeholders in their own rhetorical growth through engagement in diverse communities. Twitter: @drbohannon_ksu.

Elizabeth Brewer, PhD, is an Assistant Professor of English and the Director of Composition at Central Connecticut State University. Her research focuses on disability studies, writing program administration, and accessible composition pedagogy. She has co-authored the *Arts and Humanities* volume of *The SAGE Reference Series on Disability* and has published in *Composition Studies*, *Disability Studies Quarterly*, *Kairos*, and the *Writing Program Administration* journal.

Delores Carlito is the Information Literacy Coordinator and Liaison to English at the University of Alabama at Birmingham's Mervyn H. Sterne Library. As the English liaison, she teaches over 1,600 students a year. Delores works closely with faculty to set standards and create templates and in-class exercises for instruction. Delores has taught the UAB for-credit courses University 101, a course in critical thinking skills, and Freshman Composition. She holds an MLIS in Information Studies from the University of Alabama and an MA in English and MAEd in Secondary English Education from the University of Alabama at Birmingham.

William J. Carpenter is Professor of English and Director of the Honors Scholar Program at High Point University.

David Cook is the Undergraduate Research Coordinator at the University of Alabama in Huntsville. He also fills this role for UAH's Honors College. He is a member of the Council on Undergraduate Research, and has presented on the impacts and benefits of undergraduate research abroad programs at national and international symposia.

Margaret Cook is a Reference and Instruction Librarian at Elmhurst College in Elmhurst, Illinois. She developed the information literacy curriculum for first-year students and is responsible for library assessment efforts. She works with academic units to integrate information literacy instruction into many aspects of the college's curriculum and has served on the college's general education and assessment committees.

Emily Crist serves as the Experience Design Librarian at Champlain College in Burlington, Vermont, where she adopts an evidence-based approach to design, implement, and assess impactful library user experiences and to deliver course-embedded information literacy instruction. Her current research focuses on Chinese international students' understanding of information literacy concepts in North American academia.

Melissa Dennihy is Assistant Professor of English at Queensborough Community College, CUNY. Her research focuses on the teaching of writing and literature, particularly in the community college setting. Dennihy's work has been published or is forthcoming in *Pedagogy, Teaching English in the Two-Year College, MELUS*, and *Southern Studies*, as well as numerous essay collections. She is also a frequent contributor to *Inside Higher Ed.*

Vandy Dubre is a Professional Librarian and Information Literacy Coordinator at the University of Texas at Tyler. She focuses on music, art, literature, and children's literature librarianship as well as implementation and management of information literacy across the university. She bonded with Emily Standridge over European television and movies and all things Harry Potter.

Katherine Field-Rothschild, MFA, is an Associate Professor of English Composition at St. Mary's College in Moraga, California, and a PhD candidate at Indiana University of Pennsylvania. She is currently working on several projects on information literacy and multimedia in the first-year composition classroom. More about her publications and projects can found online at @Kath_Rothschild and by visiting Kathrothschild.com.

William T. FitzGerald is Associate Professor of English at Rutgers University Camden. As director of the Writing Program as well as the Teaching Matters and Assessment Center, he works on pedagogy, and especially writing pedagogy, through the vertical curriculum. He is the author of *Spiritual Modalities: Prayer as Rhetoric and Performance* (Penn State Press, 2012) and co-author of *The Craft of Research*, 4th ed. (University of Chicago Press, 2016).

Erica Frisicaro-Pawlowski is associate professor of English and writing coordinator at Daemen College, where she teaches courses in rhetoric, research writing, and English language history. Her research interests include disciplinary history, information literacy, and writing program administration.

Alanna Frost is an Associate Professor in the English Department at the University of Alabama Huntsville. Her work is invested in the intersections of students' communicative realities, English-education practice, and English language policy.

Crystal Goldman serves as the Instruction Coordinator for the University of California, San Diego Library. She received her MLS from Indiana University in 2004 and is currently attending the University of San Diego as a doctoral student in Leadership Studies, emphasizing Higher Education Leadership. Crystal has presented and published on a variety of topics, including mentoring, digital repositories, collection development, reference, and instruction.

Robert Hallis is Fine Arts librarian at the University of Central Missouri. He provides face-to-face instruction, flipped instruction, and embeds instructional modules in BlackBoard. Most recently, he is teaching the newly developed credit course in managing information, "Truth, Lies, and Managing Information," and taught sections embedded in learning communities. He has presented at state and regional conferences on flipping library instruction, integrating library instruction in Blackboard, immersing students in hands-on activities during library instruction, and using critical thinking in leading students beyond the library databases.

Cassie Hemstrom is a lecturer in the University Writing Program at the University of California, Davis. She teaches a variety of lower and upper division composition courses including Expository Writing, Writing for Business, and Writing in the Health Sciences. She earned her doctorate in Literature at the University of Nevada, Reno. She also holds a master's in Literature from Boise State University and a bachelor's in Liberal Arts from St. John's College, Santa Fe. Her interdisciplinary research focuses on intersections of identity theory, information literacy, and composition pedagogy.

Gaines Hubbell is an assistant professor and director of composition in the English department at UAH. His research explores the procedures of rhetoric and rhetoric's procedural concerns by reclaiming theories and practices of invention from the recent history of rhetoric and applying them in modern composition, pedagogy, and new media criticism. Dr. Hubbell also works in the field of game studies, where he is an editor for the *Journal of Games Criticism* and researches the rhetorical situations of games.

Brittney Johnson is Head of Library Instruction at St. Edward's University's Munday Library. Brittney is combining her background in Education and Cognitive Science to develop and implement a vertical curriculum in information literacy centered around threshold concepts and integrated into the disciplines. Brittney earned her BA in English Literature and BS in Psychology from Texas State University, her MS in Cognitive Science from Rensselaer Polytechnic Institute, and her MAT in Elementary Education from the University of Alaska–Southeast.

Tina S. Kazan is Associate Professor of English and directs the writing program at Elmhurst College in Elmhurst, Illinois. She teaches courses in writing, rhetorical theory, film studies, creative nonfiction, and LGBTQ studies. Her research interests include writing program administration and feminist theory and pedagogy. Her work has appeared in *WPA: Writing Program Administration Journal, Pedagogy, Lore: An e-Journal for Teachers of Writing,* and the collection *Brave New Classrooms: Democratic Education and the Internet.* She is currently collaborating on an archival project that stems from an interest in the historical and contemporary place of advanced writing courses in the larger curriculum.

Martha Kruy, MLS, MFA, is a Reference, Instruction and Assessment Librarian at Central Connecticut State University (CCSU). She specializes in teaching information literacy in the online environment, as well as assessing the broad variety of instructional delivery methods used by librarians. She co-founded the Connecticut Information Literacy Conference with Dr. Carl Antonucci in 2011. She participated in the 2013 ACRL Immersion Program Track. She has co-chaired the CCSU Academic Assessment Committee from the fall 2015 to the spring 2017 academic semester and actively participates on the Elihu Burritt Library's Assessment Committee.

Jinrong Li is an Assistant Professor in the Department of Writing and Linguistics at Georgia Southern University. Before that, she taught at Iowa State University and Boston University. Her research interests include computer-mediated communication and second language learning, L2 writing instruction and assessment, and research methods in applied linguistics. She has presented at the Second Language Research Forum, AAAL, and the Technology for Second Language Learning Conference, and her work has been published in *Assessing Writing, Journal of Second Language Writing, CALICO Journal,* and *International Journal of Computer-Assisted Language Learning and Teaching (IJCALT).*

Amy Lee Locklear is a Distinguished Lecturer in the Composition Program of Auburn University–Montgomery, Department of English and Philosophy, where she teacher first-year and upper-division writing courses. She is also finishing her PhD in Rhetoric/Writing and Technology and Media Studies at Old Dominion University in Virginia. Her research interests include digital and research writing pedagogy, adult learner theories, and cognitive neuroscience research, particularly in the field of neuroeducation (or MBE).

Lisa Louis is the Head of Research and Instruction at the Mary and Jeff Bell Library, Texas A&M University–Corpus Christi. Her research interests include reference service models and evaluation, performance skills in library instruction, mentoring teacher-librarians, and help-seeking behaviors of college students.

Michael Manasco is the Instructional Coordinator Librarian at the University of Alabama in Huntsville. His primary research interests revolve around the study of emerging open access publishing models, alternative metric applications toward scholarly prestige, and exploring the role of metaliteracy in collaborative course design at academic institutions.

Lacy Marschalk is a lecturer in English at the University of Alabama in Huntsville, where she teaches composition, literature, and the first-year experience (FYE). She holds a PhD in English literature and an MA in creative writing, both from Auburn University. Her teaching and research interests include identity, narratology, and women's travel writing, and her work has appeared in *Eighteenth-Century Fiction* and *Tulsa Studies in Women's Literature*, among other places.

I. Moriah McCracken, PhD, is an Associate Professor of Writing and Rhetoric and Director of the First-Year Writing Program at St. Edward's University in Austin, Texas. Her research areas focus on Writing About Writing pedagogies, threshold concepts, and transfer. She also specializes in literacy studies and place-based education.

Briana McGuckin, MLS, is a Reference and Instruction Librarian at Central Connecticut State University. She teaches a one-credit information literacy course, in addition to working with faculty to provide single-session and embedded information literacy instruction. She writes for *The Information Advisor's Guide to Internet Research* and has presented at the Connecticut Information Literacy Conference.

Samantha McNeilly is the Teaching & Outreach Librarian as well as the Archives & Special Collections Librarian at the Auburn University at Montgomery Library. McNeilly holds a BA and an MLA in History from Auburn University at Montgomery and an MLIS from the University of Alabama. She has worked at the AUM library since 2005, first as a staff member and more recently in her current positions as a faculty member. She is the co-author of a book chapter titled "Cross-Departmental Collaboration: The Key to Increasing Academic Library Relevancy" in the forthcoming book *Expanding Library Relevancy: Innovation to Meet Changing Needs.*

Holly Middleton is an Associate Professor of English and WPA at High Point University. She is a founding co-editor of *Literacy in Composition Studies* and collaborating on a CCCC Research Initiative–funded longitudinal study of undergraduates as writer-researchers. Her research interests include writing pedagogy, class, and the politics of style.

Libby Miles, Associate Professor of English, serves as the Director of Foundational Writing and Information Literacy at the University of Vermont. Her published work focuses on institutional change through a variety of mechanisms, such as administrative issues in higher education, curricular design in Writing and Rhetoric majors, programmatic assessment, and innovative classroom practices. She has published in *College Composition and Communication, Writing Program Administrator*, and *Journal of College Science Teaching*, among others. A co-author of *The Practice of Problem-Based Learning* (Amador, Miles, & Peters, 2006), she was part of the development team for ACRL's "Assessment in Action" curriculum.

Lilian W. Mina is an Assistant Professor of Rhetoric and Composition in the Department of English and Philosophy at Auburn University at Montgomery. She researches digital rhetoric with a focus on multimodal composing, the integration of social media platforms in teaching writing, and identity construction in online writing spaces. Her research on multilingual composition is centered around empowering multilingual writers through the use of digital technologies, incorporating translingual practices, and examining students' prior (digital) writing experiences. She is also interested in professional development of writing teachers, professionalization of graduate students, empirical research methods, information literacy and writing studies, and undergraduate research.

Neera Mohess is an Assistant Professor in the Library Department at Queensborough Community College (CUNY). She holds a master's in Library Science from Queens College (CUNY) and a master of science in Industrial/Organizational Psychology from Baruch College (CUNY). She can be reached at nmohess@qcc.cuny.edu

Susan Wolff Murphy is Associate Dean of the College of Liberal Arts and Associate Professor of English at Texas A&M University–Corpus Christi. Her research interests include developmental and first-year writing, writing centers, transfer of learning in writing, civic engagement, and learning communities. She is a CompPile.org editor. She co-edited *Teaching Writing with Latino/a Students: Lessons Learned at Hispanic Serving Institutions* and has published articles in *Writing Center Journal, Journal of Border Educational Research*, and other publications.

Tom Pace is Associate Professor of English and Director of Core Writing at John Carroll University, where he teaches writing and literature courses. He also directs the English Department's Professional Writing Track. His areas of interest include style, the history of writing instruction, and popular culture. He has published articles on style and audience and is the co-editor of *Refiguring Prose Style: Possibilities for Writing Pedagogy*. More recently, he has published on the influence of Jesuit education on Paulo Freire and on the rhetoric of Generation X in *Mad Men* and HBO's *Girls* and the construction of masculinity in the romantic comedies of Judd Apatow.

Marcia Rapchak is the Director of Research and Information Skills and the Instruction Librarian for Gumberg Library at Duquesne University. She received a master's in English from Ohio State University, and a master's in Library Science from the University of Kentucky. She coordinates, assesses, and teaches credit information literacy courses face-to-face and online. Her previous publications address IL assessment, the intersection of composition studies and information literacy, and instructional design. She is finishing her dissertation on social metacognition in online and face-to-face information literacy courses, and will receive a doctorate in Instructional Technology and Leadership.

Tamara Rhodes is the Subject Librarian for Psychology, Cognitive Science, Human Development, and Linguistics at the University of California, San Diego Library. She received her MLS from North Carolina Central University in 2013 and is a 2012 Spectrum Scholar. Tamara has presented and published on topics such as user experience, living archives, and Spanish-speaking populations' e-health information seeking in public libraries.

Valerie Ross is the founding director of the Critical Writing Program, University of Pennsylvania. She currently serves as Co-Chair of PWPA, the Philadelphia regional writing association, and an editor of the *Journal of Writing Analytics*. Her recent research focuses upon writing analytics, knowledge transfer, peer review, and writing assessment, concepts Ross is examining as part of a cross-institutional NSF grant exploring the role of peer review in advancing cognitive, interpersonal, and intrapersonal skills. She is also engaged in the study of university administration, including a recent publication on the challenges of leading and managing change in academic organizations.

Dagmar Stuehrk Scharold is an Assistant Professor at the University of Houston–Downtown. Dagmar is currently the director of the First-Year Composition Program and was the Writing and Reading Center Director from 2001 to 2016.

Donna Scheidt is an Assistant Professor of English at High Point University, specializing in rhetoric and writing studies. A former practicing attorney, her research interests include how writers (such as undergraduates and judges) conceive of research and engage with sources in educational and legal contexts. With funding from the CCCC Research Initiative, she and a research team of fellow writing faculty and librarians currently are collaborating on a longitudinal study of undergraduates as writer-researchers.

Kathy Shields is the Research and Instruction Librarian for History and Social Science at Wake Forest University. Prior to this position, she served as the Head of Research and Instructional Services at High Point University, where she worked closely with the Department of English and the Writing Center to integrate research and writing in first-year writing programs.

Lindsey Simard is a librarian and software developer in Berkeley, California, who has worked at academic libraries in the San Francisco Bay Area and Houston. She volunteers with San Francisco Zine Fest and Rad Med.

Susan Slaga-Metivier, MLIS, is Head of Reference and Instruction at Central Connecticut State University. She has presented at regional and national conferences. She has also taught a one-credit information literacy course and co-chaired the Connecticut Information Literacy Conference.

Emily Standridge, PhD is an Assistant Professor of English and Writing Center Director at the University of Texas at Tyler. Her research focuses on the teaching and learning of writing, particularly in the one-on-one tutorial setting. Favorite pastimes include British television and movies and Harry Potter.

Jerry Stinnett is Assistant Professor of Writing and Rhetoric at Duquesne University where he also serves as the Director of the First-Year Writing Program. His scholarship, which commonly focuses on the use of collaborative approaches to improve the teaching of writing as a rhetorical practice, has appeared in the journals *Compendium 2* and *College English.* His recent projects have focused on supporting student learning transfer in first-year composition classrooms by teaching students to define composing as the act of using texts to coordinate writer and reader exigence.

Grace Veach is an eight-time *Jeopardy!* champion. At work, she is Professor of English and Library Science, Dean of the Library, and Interim Director of Writing at Southeastern University in Lakeland, Florida. She has published on Kenneth Burke, St. Augustine, Charles Williams, and information literacy.

Dana M. Walker, who holds a PhD in Information Science from the University of Michigan, has been a lecturer with the University of Pennsylvania's Critical Writing Program since 2011. At Penn she teaches undergraduate writing in the discipline seminars in digital communication and food behavior. She also has extensive experience working with a range of students from high school to graduate studies on their writing. Dr. Walker has published work in digital ethnography and online deliberation and has worked with the Kettering Foundation and the American Library Association's Center for Public Life.

Zara T. Wilkinson is a Reference and Instruction Librarian at Rutgers University–Camden in Camden, New Jersey. As the Instruction and Outreach Coordinator at Rutgers–Camden's Paul Robeson Library, she oversees library instruction to the Writing Program. In addition, she serves as liaison librarian to the Rutgers–Camden departments of English, art, philosophy and religion, and digital studies. Her research interests include early career librarianship and outreach in academic libraries.

INDEX